Methodology of Educational Measurement and Assessment

Series Editors
Bernard Veldkamp, Research Center for Examinations and Certification (RCEC), University of Twente, Enschede, The Netherlands
Matthias von Davier, National Board of Medical Examiners (NBME), Philadelphia, USA

Editorial Board Members
Claus H. Carstensen, University of Bamberg, Bamberg, Germany
Hua-Hua Chang, Purdue University, West Lafayette, USA
Hong Jiao, University of Maryland, College Park, USA
David Kaplan, University of Wisconsin-Madison, Madison, USA
Jonathan Templin, The University of Iowa, Iowa City, USA
Andries van der Ark, Res Inst of Child Devt & Education, University of Amsterdam, Amsterdam, The Netherlands

This book series collates key contributions to a fast-developing field of education research. It is an international forum for theoretical and empirical studies exploring new and existing methods of collecting, analyzing, and reporting data from educational measurements and assessments. Covering a high-profile topic from multiple viewpoints, it aims to foster a broader understanding of fresh developments as innovative software tools and new concepts such as competency models and skills diagnosis continue to gain traction in educational institutions around the world. Methodology of Educational Measurement and Assessment offers readers reliable critical evaluations, reviews and comparisons of existing methodologies alongside authoritative analysis and commentary on new and emerging approaches. It will showcase empirical research on applications, examine issues such as reliability, validity, and comparability, and help keep readers up to speed on developments in statistical modeling approaches. The fully peer-reviewed publications in the series cover measurement and assessment at all levels of education and feature work by academics and education professionals from around the world. Providing an authoritative central clearing-house for research in a core sector in education, the series forms a major contribution to the international literature.

More information about this series at http://www.springer.com/series/13206

Débora B. Maehler • Beatrice Rammstedt
Editors

Large-Scale Cognitive Assessment

Analyzing PIAAC Data

Editors
Débora B. Maehler
Survey Design and Methodology
GESIS – Leibniz Institute for the Social Sciences
Mannheim, Germany

Beatrice Rammstedt
Survey Design and Methodology
GESIS – Leibniz Institute for the Social Sciences
Mannheim, Germany

ISSN 2367-170X ISSN 2367-1718 (electronic)
Methodology of Educational Measurement and Assessment
ISBN 978-3-030-47517-8 ISBN 978-3-030-47515-4 (eBook)
https://doi.org/10.1007/978-3-030-47515-4

© The Editor(s) (if applicable) and The Author(s) 2020. This book is an open access publication.
Open Access This book is licensed under the terms of the Creative Commons Attribution 4.0 International License (http://creativecommons.org/licenses/by/4.0/), which permits use, sharing, adaptation, distribution and reproduction in any medium or format, as long as you give appropriate credit to the original author(s) and the source, provide a link to the Creative Commons license and indicate if changes were made.
The images or other third party material in this book are included in the book's Creative Commons license, unless indicated otherwise in a credit line to the material. If material is not included in the book's Creative Commons license and your intended use is not permitted by statutory regulation or exceeds the permitted use, you will need to obtain permission directly from the copyright holder.
The use of general descriptive names, registered names, trademarks, service marks, etc. in this publication does not imply, even in the absence of a specific statement, that such names are exempt from the relevant protective laws and regulations and therefore free for general use.
The publisher, the authors, and the editors are safe to assume that the advice and information in this book are believed to be true and accurate at the date of publication. Neither the publisher nor the authors or the editors give a warranty, expressed or implied, with respect to the material contained herein or for any errors or omissions that may have been made. The publisher remains neutral with regard to jurisdictional claims in published maps and institutional affiliations.

This Springer imprint is published by the registered company Springer Nature Switzerland AG.
The registered company address is: Gewerbestrasse 11, 6330 Cham, Switzerland

Contents

1 **Large-Scale Assessment in Education: Analysing PIAAC Data** 1
 Débora B. Maehler and Beatrice Rammstedt

2 **Design and Key Features of the PIAAC Survey of Adults** 7
 Irwin Kirsch, Kentaro Yamamoto, and Lale Khorramdel

3 **Plausible Values: Principles of Item Response Theory and Multiple Imputations** 27
 Lale Khorramdel, Matthias von Davier, Eugenio Gonzalez, and Kentaro Yamamoto

4 **Adult Cognitive and Non-cognitive Skills: An Overview of Existing PIAAC Data** 49
 Débora B. Maehler and Ingo Konradt

5 **Analysing PIAAC Data with the International Data Explorer (IDE)** 93
 Emily Pawlowski and Jaleh Soroui

6 **Analysing PIAAC Data with the IDB Analyzer (SPSS and SAS)** 117
 Andres Sandoval-Hernandez and Diego Carrasco

7 **Analysing PIAAC Data with Stata** 149
 François Keslair

8 **Analysing PIAAC Data with Structural Equation Modelling in Mplus** 165
 Ronny Scherer

9 **Using EdSurvey to Analyse PIAAC Data** 209
 Paul Bailey, Michael Lee, Trang Nguyen, and Ting Zhang

10	**Analysing Log File Data from PIAAC**	239
	Frank Goldhammer, Carolin Hahnel, and Ulf Kroehne	
11	**Linking PIAAC Data to Individual Administrative Data:** **Insights from a German Pilot Project**	271
	Jessica Daikeler, Britta Gauly, and Matthias Rosenthal	

Reviewers

Alexander Robizsch (Leibniz Institute for Science and Mathematics Education/IPN, Germany)
Anna-Lena Keute (Statistics Norway, Norway)
Anouk Zabal (GESIS – Leibniz Institute for the Social Sciences, Germany)
Britta Gauly (GESIS – Leibniz Institute for the Social Sciences, Germany)
Débora B. Maehler (GESIS – Leibniz Institute for the Social Sciences, Germany)
Eugenio Gonzales (Educational Testing Service/ ETS, US)
Isabelle Thony (Statistics Canada, Canada)
Jamis He Jia (Leibniz Institute for Research and Information in Education/DIPF, Germany)
Jan Heisig (Berlin Social Science Center/WBZ, Germany)
Jan-Phillip Kolb (GESIS – Leibniz Institute for the Social Sciences, Germany)
Jens Bender (GESIS – Leibniz Institute for the Social Sciences, Germany)
Julia Gorges (Marburg University, Germany)
Lotta Larsson (Statistics Sweden, Sweden)
Manuel Reif (Statistic Austria, Austria)
Natascha Massing (GESIS – Leibniz Institute for the Social Sciences, Germany)
Paul Satherley (Ministry of Education, New Zealand)
Ralph Carstensen (International Association for the Evaluation of Educational Achievement/IEA, Germany)
Saida Mamedova (American Institutes for Research/AIR, US)
Sanja Kapidzic (GESIS – Leibniz Institute for the Social Sciences, Germany)
Silke Martin (GESIS – Leibniz Institute for the Social Sciences, Germany)
Silke Schneider (GESIS – Leibniz Institute for the Social Sciences, Germany)
Simon Wiederhold (Catholic University of Eichstätt-Ingolstadt, Germany)
Tobias Koch (Psychologische Hochschule Berlin, Germany)
Valentina Gualtieri (Istituto Nazionale per l'Analisi delle Politiche Pubbliche/INAPP, Italy)

Chapter 1
Large-Scale Assessment in Education: Analysing PIAAC Data

Débora B. Maehler and Beatrice Rammstedt

Abstract This methodological book aims to summarise existing techniques for analysing data resulting from the Programme for the International Assessment of Adult Competencies (PIAAC). The present chapter provides an overview of the programme, outlining its goal, the participating countries, the survey cycles, and the research questions that can be addressed with the available data. In addition, the structure of the textbook is described.

1.1 Large-Scale Assessment in Education: Analysing PIAAC Data

To actively participate in modern society, skills such as literacy and numeracy are of utmost importance. Essential information is usually provided in written format—for example, in manuals, memos, and medication package inserts. To adequately process and react to such information, individuals require sufficient skills.

In 2008, the Organisation for Economic Co-operation and Development (OECD) initiated the Programme for the International Assessment of Adult Competencies (PIAAC). PIAAC aims to assess in an internationally comparable way basic adult skills such as literacy, numeracy, and problem solving. These skills are considered to be essential for successful participation in modern society and to be a foundation for developing numerous other, more specific, skills and competencies (OECD 2013).

PIAAC provides information about the skill levels of the adult population in the participating countries and the extent to which countries differ in terms of these skills. Moreover, and in particular, PIAAC provides information on factors associated with the acquisition, maintenance, and outcomes of these skills. Thus,

---

D. B. Maehler (✉) · B. Rammstedt
GESIS – Leibniz Institute for the Social Sciences, Mannheim, Germany
e-mail: debora.maehler@gesis.org

© The Author(s) 2020
D. B. Maehler, B. Rammstedt (eds.), *Large-Scale Cognitive Assessment*, Methodology of Educational Measurement and Assessment,
https://doi.org/10.1007/978-3-030-47515-4_1

it sheds light on effects of these basic skills on social and, in particular, economic participation.

Like the OECD Programme for International Student Assessment (PISA), PIAAC is designed as a cross-sectional study to be repeated at regular intervals. The first cycle of PIAAC started in 2008 and comprised three rounds, in which a total of 38 countries participated. The second cycle of PIAAC was launched in 2018 and will likely cover 33 countries (see Table 1.1).

The OECD consistently pursues an open science strategy regarding the data resulting from PIAAC. To date, more than 60 PIAAC datasets have been published worldwide (see Chap. 4 in this volume); the first data were released in 2013 (OECD 2013). These datasets have been widely accessed and used by an interdisciplinary research community (for an overview, see Maehler et al. 2020). Furthermore, there are a large and increasing number of PIAAC-based publications.[1]

As in the case of other international large-scale assessments (Rutkowski et al. 2014), analyses with the PIAAC data are very challenging for users due to the complex data structure (e.g. plausible values computed by imputation, complex sampling). To ensure the quality and significance of the data analyses, users require instruction in the correct handling of the data. This methodological textbook therefore aims to summarise existing techniques for analysing PIAAC data. It provides a standardised approach to successfully implement these data analyses. The present volume provides examples and tools for the analysis of PIAAC data using different statistical approaches and software and also offers perspectives from various disciplines. The textbook is designed for use by researchers and students from diverse fields (e.g. educational research, economics, sociology, and psychology) who are interested in working with large-scale educational assessment data.

This methodological textbook covers the following topics: (1) background information on PIAAC that is required for the analyses—for example, the design of PIAAC and the available datasets; (2) the (web) tools available for the analysis of PIAAC data, particularly the public use files; and (3) the analysis of cross-sectional PIAAC data with multidisciplinary methods (e.g. Stata or R) using public use files or scientific use files.

The next three chapters provide background information that serves as a basis for working with PIAAC data. Chapter 2 summarises the core features of the PIAAC survey design and briefly addresses sampling and data collection. In addition, it provides an overview of the background questionnaire and the competence domains assessed in PIAAC. The chapter concludes with a discussion of potential improvements to future PIAAC cycles.

Chapter 3 introduces item response theory and the principles of multiple imputations. It describes plausible values and explains how they can be used to

---

[1] The relevant literature can be found via the bibliographic search on the homepage of the PIAAC Research Data Center (PIAAC RDC; see also Maehler, et al. 2020) at GESIS.

1 Large-Scale Assessment in Education: Analysing PIAAC Data

Table 1.1 Data assessment of participating countries in the first and second cycles of PIAAC

Country	First cycle	Second cycle
Australia	2011–2012	2021–2022
Austria	2011–2012	2021–2022
Belgium[a]	2011–2012	2021–2022
Canada	2011–2012	2021–2022
Chile	2014–2015	2021–2022
Croatia		2021–2022
Cyprus	2011–2012	
Czech Republic	2011–2012	2021–2022
Denmark	2011–2012	2021–2022
Ecuador	2017	
Estonia	2011–2012	2021–2022
Finland	2011–2012	2021–2022
France	2011–2012	2021–2022
Germany	2011–2012	2021–2022
Greece	2014–2015	
Hungary	2017	2021–2022
Indonesia	2014–2015	
Ireland	2011–2012	2021–2022
Israel	2014–2015	2021–2022
Italy	2011–2012	2021–2022
Japan	2011–2012	2021–2022
Kazakhstan	2017	
Korea	2011–2012	2021–2022
Latvia		2021–2022
Lithuania	2014–2015	2021–2022
Mexico	2017	
Netherlands	2011–2012	2021–2022
New Zealand	2014–2015	2021–2022
Norway	2011–2012	2021–2022
Peru	2017	
Poland	2011–2012	2021–2022
Portugal		2021–2022
Russian Federation	2011–2012	2021–2022
Singapore	2014–2015	2021–2022
Slovak Republic	2011–2012	2021–2022
Slovenia	2014–2015	
Spain	2011–2012	2021–2022
Sweden	2011–2012	2021–2022
Switzerland		2021–2022
Turkey	2014–2015	
United Kingdom[b,c]	2011–2012	2021–2022
United States	2011–2012; 2017	2021–2022

Notes. [a]Only Flanders
[b]In the first cycle, the survey was conducted in England and Northern Ireland
[c]In the second cycle, the survey was conducted only in England

address concerns regarding the introduction of bias when point estimates of latent indicators are used to estimate certain population parameters.

Chapter 4 provides an overview of the PIAAC datasets that are available for research purposes and outlines their structure, accessibility, and use. For example, public use files are accessible for public purposes and are thus highly anonymised, whereas scientific use files are available only for scientific research purposes and provide access to more detailed variables. Regarding the study design, most available datasets are cross-sectional, although some longitudinal data already exist. In addition to describing these longitudinal datasets, Chap. 4 presents PIAAC datasets that focus on specific population groups—for example, the population in Germany aged 65 years and over (Friebe et al. 2017) and the incarcerated adult population in the United States (Hogan et al. 2016).

The two subsequent chapters are devoted to the tools that are available for the analysis of PIAAC data. Chapter 5 presents PIAAC analyses using the web tool International Data Explorer (IDE), which is provided by the international PIAAC consortium. The IDE can be used to create tables and graphs that give an overview of the skills of adults aged 16 to 65 years in the areas of literacy, numeracy, and problem solving in technology-rich environments. It can also be used to calculate standard errors with complex designs, and it allows variables to be combined and indices to be created and validated. The data can be analysed both by country and by sociodemographic characteristics, such as education or employment status. The use of the tool to extract percentages, averages, benchmarks (proficiency levels), and percentiles is demonstrated, and limitations are outlined.

Chapter 6 introduces readers to the performance of both simple and complex analyses with PIAAC data using the International Database (IDB) Analyzer, a Windows-based tool that generates SPSS syntax. Using this syntax, corresponding analyses can be conducted in SPSS. The chapter presents the data-merging module and the analysis module. Potential analyses with the IDB Analyzer are demonstrated—for example, the calculation of percentages and percentiles, averages, benchmarks (proficiency levels), correlations, and regressions (linear only).

The final five chapters in this volume focus on the analysis of cross-sectional PIAAC data using multidisciplinary methods embedded in different disciplinary approaches. Chapter 7 is devoted to the analysis of PIAAC data using the statistical package Stata. Following an introduction to working with PIAAC data using Stata, it focuses on two features of the PIAAC data that present challenges to researchers: the availability of multiple plausible values for individual competence scores and the computation of statistics taking into account imputation and sampling errors. The chapter also presents *repest*, an OECD Stata module for running estimations with weighted replicate samples and plausible values.

Structural equation modelling (SEM) has become one of the most commonly applied statistical approaches to disentangling the relationships among latent variables across groups, over time, and at different analytical levels. Chapter 8 therefore provides an introduction to the principles and procedures of basic and more advanced SEM in Mplus using PIAAC data. Furthermore, it presents model specification and estimation by means of confirmatory factor analysis, showing approaches to testing measurement invariance across a few or many groups. Finally, the chapter introduces classes of structural models, such as path models, structural equation models, and multi-group versions thereof. The corresponding syntax files are provided for the reader.

Chapter 9 focuses on the analysis of PIAAC data using an R package that includes functions for importing data, performing data analysis, and visualising results. It describes the underlying methodology and provides examples based on PIAAC data. The data analysis functions presented take into account the complex sample design (with replicate weights) and plausible values in the calculation of point estimates and standard errors of means, standard deviations, regression coefficients, correlation coefficients, and frequency tables.

PIAAC Cycle 1 was the first fully computer-based large-scale assessment in education. The use of computers allowed not only for innovative item formats and an adaptive test design but also for the collection of a stream of user events (e.g. mouse clicks, text input) stored by the assessment system in log files. These data are interesting not only from a measurement point of view (e.g. to assess the quality of the response data) but also from the point of view of addressing substantive research questions (e.g. investigating the cognitive solution process). Chapter 10 introduces the accessibility, structure, and content of PIAAC log file data. It describes, in particular, the PIAAC LogDataAnalyzer, which allows log data to be extracted from PIAAC xml log files. The chapter includes a sample analysis in order to demonstrate how exported log data can be further processed using standard statistical software such as the R environment or Weka, a data mining software.

Finally, Chap. 11 addresses the linking of PIAAC data to administrative data, which are available, for instance, in the Nordic countries, such as Sweden (see Chap. 4 in this volume). The chapter presents the research procedure and exemplary analyses based on the linking of data from the German PIAAC-Longitudinal (PIAAC-L) study to administrative data provided by the German Institute for Employment Research (IAB) within the framework of a pilot project.

Although PIAAC itself is designed as a cross-sectional study, longitudinal data for PIAAC are available for some countries (e.g. Canada and Germany; see Chap. 4 in this volume). Unfortunately, in the present volume, we are unable to provide any chapters with exemplary longitudinal data analyses. However, we aim to cover this topic in the next edition.

References

Friebe, J., Gebrande, J., Gnahs, D., Knauber, C., Schmidt-Hertha, B., Setzer, B., Tippelt, R., & Weiß, C. (2017). *Competencies in Later Life (CiLL) – Programme for the International Assessment of Adult Competencies (PIAAC), Germany* (Data file version 1.1.0) [ZA5969]. Cologne: GESIS Data Archive. https://doi.org/10.4232/1.12814.

Hogan, J., Thornton, N., Diaz-Hoffmann, L., Mohadjer, L., Krenzke, T., Li, J., & Van De Kerckhove, W. (2016). *Program for the International Assessment of Adult Competencies*

(PIAAC) 2014: U.S. National Supplement Restricted Use Data Files-Prison. Washington, DC: National Center for Education Statistics.

Maehler, D. B., Jakowatz, S., & Konradt, I. (2020). *PIAAC bibliographie 2008 – 2019.* GESIS Papers, Nr. 04/2020. Cologne: GESIS – Leibniz Institute for the Social Sciences. https://doi.org/10.21241/ssoar.67732

Organisation for Economic Co-operation and Development (OECD). (2013). *Organisation for Economic Co-operation and Development (OECD) skills outlook 2013: First results from the Survey of Adult Skills.* Paris: OECD Publishing. http://www.oecd-ilibrary.org/education/oecd-skills-outlook-2013_9789264204256-en. Accessed 27 Mar 2019.

Rutkowski, L., von Davier, M., & Rutkowski, D. (Eds.). (2014). *Handbook of international large-scale assessment. Background, technical issues, and methods of data analyses.* Boca Raton: CRC Press.

Open Access This chapter is licensed under the terms of the Creative Commons Attribution 4.0 International License (http://creativecommons.org/licenses/by/4.0/), which permits use, sharing, adaptation, distribution and reproduction in any medium or format, as long as you give appropriate credit to the original author(s) and the source, provide a link to the Creative Commons license and indicate if changes were made.

The images or other third party material in this chapter are included in the chapter's Creative Commons license, unless indicated otherwise in a credit line to the material. If material is not included in the chapter's Creative Commons license and your intended use is not permitted by statutory regulation or exceeds the permitted use, you will need to obtain permission directly from the copyright holder.

Chapter 2
Design and Key Features of the PIAAC Survey of Adults

Irwin Kirsch, Kentaro Yamamoto, and Lale Khorramdel

Abstract This chapter gives an overview of the most important features of the Programme for the International Assessment of Adult Competencies (PIAAC) survey as it pertains to two main goals. First, only a well-designed survey will lead to accurate and comparable test scores across different countries and languages both within and across assessment cycles. Second, only an understanding of its complex survey design will lead to proper use of the PIAAC data in secondary analyses and meaningful interpretation of results by psychometricians, data analysts, scientists, and policymakers. The chapter begins with a brief introduction to the PIAAC survey followed by an overview of the background questionnaire and the cognitive measures. The cognitive measures are then compared to what was assessed in previous international adult surveys. Key features of the assessment design are discussed followed by a section describing what could be done to improve future PIAAC cycles.

2.1 Introduction

In today's world, what people know, and what they can do with this knowledge, matters more than ever—affecting both personal life outcomes and the well-being of societies. The demands of technologically infused economies, the rapid pace of change, and global competition have interacted to change the way we work and live. More and more, everyday tasks require the ability to navigate, critically analyse, and problem-solve in data-intensive, complex digital environments. Similarly, global forces have altered the workplace and increased the demand for more broadly skilled employees. Employers seek workers who can keep pace with rapidly changing

---

I. Kirsch (✉) · K. Yamamoto
Educational Testing Service, Princeton, NJ, USA
e-mail: ikirsch@ets.org

L. Khorramdel
National Board of Medical Examiners, Princeton, NJ, USA

© The Author(s) 2020
D. B. Maehler, B. Rammstedt (eds.), *Large-Scale Cognitive Assessment*, Methodology of Educational Measurement and Assessment,
https://doi.org/10.1007/978-3-030-47515-4_2

technologies. As a result, they are looking for individuals who have skills that enable them to benefit from ongoing training programmes and, perhaps most importantly, have the ability and initiative to learn on their own and continuously upgrade what they know and can do. Claudia Goldin and Lawrence Katz (2008: 352) described the consequences of this new reality in their book *The Race between Education and Technology*:

> As technological change races forward, demands for skills—some new and some old—are altered. If the workforce can rapidly make the adjustment, then economic growth is enhanced without greatly exacerbating inequality of economic outcomes. If, on the other hand, the skills that are currently demanded are produced slowly and if the workforce is less flexible in its skill set, then growth is slowed *and* inequality widens. Those who can make the adjustments as well as those who gain the new skills are rewarded. Others are left behind.

Recognising the ongoing changes that technology and globalisation are having on how we live and work, policymakers have become increasingly concerned not only about the levels of traditional literacy skills in their populations but also because of the growing importance of human capital and the broadening of the skills that will be needed to sustain productivity and social cohesion. The increased importance of human capital, and the learning associated with it, have led to a critical need for information about the distribution of knowledge, skills, and characteristics necessary for full participation in modern societies.

The Organisation for Economic Co-operation and Development (OECD) Programme for the International Assessment of Adult Competencies (PIAAC) took a significant step forwards in the assessment of adult skills by building on the pioneering work of two previous surveys implemented since the mid-1990s: the International Adult Literacy Survey (IALS, 1994–1998) and the Adult Literacy and Lifeskills Survey (ALL, 2003–2006).[1] As with the two earlier surveys, PIAAC was designed to provide internationally comparable data to help policymakers and other stakeholders better understand:

- The types and levels of adult skills that exist in each of the participating countries that are thought to underlie both personal and societal success
- The relationship between these skills and broader social and economic outcomes
- Factors that contribute to the development, maintenance, and loss of skills over the life cycle
- And help clarify some of the policy levers that could contribute to enhancing competencies

PIAAC has been planned by the OECD as an ongoing programme of work. The development and administration of the first cycle of PIAAC resulted in the largest

---

[1]The **International Adult Literacy Survey (IALS)** was conducted between 1994 and 1998 as the first large-scale international comparative assessment designed to measure literacy skills of adults (ages 16–65 years old) in 22 countries and regions. Trend items from IALS were included in the Adult Literacy and Lifeskills Survey (ALL), conducted in 2003, and the Programme for the International Assessment of Adult Competencies (PIAAC), allowing data from IALS to be linked to trend data from participating countries in ALL and PIAAC.

and most innovative international survey of adults ever conducted. Administered in three rounds from 2012 through 2018 (i.e. at three different time points, with different countries being assessed at each time point), the first cycle of PIAAC was unprecedented in scope, assessing close to 200,000 adults across 38 countries. Twenty four countries completed and reported results in the first round, nine in the second, and five in the third.

As the first computer-based survey of its kind, PIAAC expanded what could be measured and changed how a large-scale assessment could be designed and implemented. These advances were the result of a number of key innovations, which included:

- Developing an integrated platform that handled computer-based instruments as well as paper-based instruments to allow the assessment of those adults who were unable or unwilling to take a computer-based test
- Designing and delivering items that mirrored the kinds of technology-based tasks increasingly required both in the workplace and everyday life
- Conducting a mode study that enabled continuity with, and links to, IALS and ALL
- Incorporating multistage computer-adaptive algorithms into a large-scale assessment to provide more reliable information about participants' skills and support a more complex assessment design
- Implementing automatically scored items across some 50 language versions of the cognitive instruments to improve scoring reliability and reduce the burden on participating countries
- Using process data, in particular timing information, to both enhance the interpretation of performance and evaluate the quality of the assessment data

2.2 What PIAAC Measures

As the first computer-based, large-scale adult literacy assessment, PIAAC reflects the changing nature of information, its role in society, and its impact on people's lives. While linked by design to IALS and ALL, including sets of questions from these previous surveys, PIAAC has refined and expanded the existing assessment domains and introduced two new domains as well. The main instruments in PIAAC included a background questionnaire and cognitive assessments focused on literacy, numeracy, reading components, and problem solving in technology-rich environments.[2]

---

[2]Reading components and problem solving were optional domains in Round 1. Of the countries that reported results in Round 1, most implemented the reading components assessment, with the exceptions being Finland, France, and Japan. Most implemented problem solving, with the exceptions being France, Italy, and Spain. In Rounds 2 and 3, no components were optional, with these two domains treated as core components.

2.2.1 Background Questionnaire

The PIAAC background questionnaire (BQ) was a significant component of the survey, taking up to one-third of the total survey time. The scope of the questionnaire reflects an important goal of adult surveys: to relate skills to a variety of demographic characteristics and explanatory variables. The information collected via the BQ adds to the interpretability of the assessment, enhancing the reporting of results to policymakers and other stakeholders. These data make it possible to investigate how the distribution of skills is associated with variables including educational attainment, gender, employment, and the immigration status of groups. A better understanding of how performance is related to social and educational outcomes enhances insight into factors related to the observed distribution of skills across populations as well as factors that mediate the acquisition or decline of those skills.

The BQ was the most detailed of its kind to date for a large-scale assessment of adults. Questions went well beyond age, gender, and job title. The questionnaire addressed issues such as skills used at work and home, focusing specifically on literacy, numeracy, and the use of digital technologies. Furthermore, it addressed learning strategies, civic engagement, and whether respondents had trust in government or other individuals. It also included a short section on a person's health and subjective well-being. The reader is referred to the following for more information about the comprehensiveness of the PIAAC BQ including a collection of publications using the PIAAC data (Maehler et al. 2020; OECD 2016a, b).

The questionnaire provided not only breadth but also depth in terms of its questions. Rather than simply asking a person's job title, it delved into the work involved. If, for example, a person worked in sales, questions were posed on whether he or she made presentations and how often. The questionnaire also asked whether he or she advised colleagues and had to work cooperatively.

Furthermore, it looked deeply into the kinds of literacy and numeracy skills used at home. Rather than simply asking how often a person used writing skills, for example, it asked whether the individual wrote letters, memos, or emails. It also asked about the individual's reading habits—whether the person read newspapers, magazines, or newsletters; whether he or she looked at professional journals; and so on. It also asked about use of a calculator for complex problems. Significantly, as PIAAC was the first large-scale assessment for adults developed as a computer-based assessment, the questionnaire also probed into information and communication technologies (ICT) skills used at work and at home, specifically asking questions about how often individuals used a computer, or the types of things they did with it, ranging from the types of programmes they used to whether their focus was on learning or socialising.

The questionnaire also included a Jobs Requirement Approach (JRA) section. The objective was to collect information on skills used at work in contrast to the demographic characteristics and other personal background information collected in the BQ (OECD 2013). This section was included because case studies have shown that skills beyond literacy—communication, teamwork, multitasking, and the ability to work independently—are being rewarded in the labour market (Dickerson and Green 2004). The JRA was designed to assess the relevance of these skills.

One important new strategy with the questionnaire paid off with improved data on personal income. Income is chronically underreported in surveys (Pleis and Dahlhamer 2004), with rates of 20–50% of income having not been reported in the past (Moore et al. 2000). In PIAAC, categories were used that made respondents feel more comfortable to answer. The survey asked individuals to list income amounts they felt most comfortable sharing information about— annually, monthly, hourly, or by piece. Those unwilling to list a specific amount were asked whether they would provide amounts within specific ranges. With imputation techniques, it could be determined with some accuracy what those amounts were based on other variables such as occupation, industry, and age. PIAAC wound up with a total of 94.1% of respondents willing to report total earnings.

2.2.2 Cognitive Domains

The cognitive measures in PIAAC included literacy and numeracy, as well as the new domains of reading components and problem solving in technology-rich environments. The literacy and numeracy domains incorporated both new items developed for PIAAC and trend items from IALS and ALL. In order to maintain trend measurement, the PIAAC design required that 60% of literacy and numeracy items be taken from previous surveys, with the remaining 40% newly developed. In the case of literacy, items were included from both IALS and ALL. As numeracy was not a domain in IALS, all of the numeracy linking items came from ALL.

Like IALS and ALL, PIAAC included intact stimulus materials taken from a range of adult contexts, including the workplace, home, and community. As a computer-delivered assessment, PIAAC was able to include stimuli with interactive environments, such as webpages with hyperlinks, websites with multiple pages of information, and simulated email and spreadsheet applications.

To better reflect adult contexts as opposed to school-based environments, open-ended items have been included in international large-scale adult assessments since IALS. The innovation introduced in the first cycle of PIAAC was automatic scoring of these items, which contributed to improved scoring reliability within and across countries.

Literacy Literacy was defined in the first cycle of PIAAC as 'understanding, evaluating, using and engaging with written texts to participate in society, to achieve one's goals, and to develop one's knowledge and potential' (OECD, 2012: 20). 'Literacy' in PIAAC does not include the ability to write or produce text—skills commonly falling within the definition of literacy. While literacy had been a focus of both the IALS and ALL surveys, PIAAC was the first to address literacy in digital environments. As a computer-based assessment, PIAAC included literacy tasks that required respondents to use electronic texts, including webpages, emails, and discussion boards. These interactive stimulus materials included hypertext and multiple screens of information and simulated real-life literacy demands presented by digital media.

Reading Components The new domain of reading components was included in PIAAC to provide more detailed information about adults with limited literacy skills. Reading components represent the basic set of decoding skills that provide necessary preconditions for gaining meaning from written text. These include knowledge of vocabulary, ability to process meaning at the sentence level, as well as reading of short passages of text in terms of both speed and accuracy.

Adding this domain to PIAAC provided more information about the skills of individuals with low literacy proficiency than had been available from previous international assessments. This was an important cohort to assess, as it was known from previous assessments that there are varying percentages of adults across participating countries who demonstrate little, if any, literacy skills. Studies in the United States and Canada show that many of these adults have weak component skills, which are essential to the development of literacy and numeracy skills (Strucker et al. 2007; Grenier et al. 2008).

Numeracy The domain of numeracy remained largely unchanged between ALL and PIAAC. However, to better represent this broad, multifaceted construct, the definition of numeracy was coupled with a more detailed definition of numerate behaviour for PIAAC. Numerate behaviour involves managing a situation or solving a problem in a real context by responding to mathematical content, information, or ideas, represented in multiple ways (OECD 2012). Each aspect of numerate behaviour was further specified as follows:

- Real contexts including everyday life, work, society, and further learning.
- Responding to mathematical content, information, or ideas may require any of the following: identify, locate or access, act upon and use (to order, count, estimate, compute, measure, or model), interpret, evaluate or analyse, and communicate.
- Mathematical content, information, and ideas including quantity and number, dimension and shape, pattern, relationships and change, and data and chance.
- Representations possibly including objects and pictures, numbers and mathematical symbols, formulae, diagrams, maps, graphs and tables, texts, and technology-based displays.

Problem Solving in Technology-Rich Environments (PS-TRE) PS-TRE was a new domain introduced in PIAAC and represented the first attempt to assess it on a large scale and as a single dimension. While it has some relationship to problem solving as conceived in ALL, the emphasis in PIAAC was on assessing the skills required to solve information problems within the context of ICT rather than on analytic problems per se. PS-TRE was defined as 'using digital technology, communication tools and networks to acquire and evaluate information, communicate with others and perform practical tasks. The first PIAAC problem-solving survey focuses on

Table 2.1 Domains assessed in PIAAC, ALL, and IALS

PIAAC	ALL (2003–2006)	IALS (1994–1998)
Literacy (combined prose and document)	Literacy (combined prose and document[a])	Literacy (combined prose and document[a])
	Prose literacy	Prose literacy
	Document literacy	Document literacy
Reading components		
Numeracy	Numeracy	
		Quantitative literacy
Problem solving in technology-rich environments		
	Problem solving	

Note. [a]Rescaled to form a single literacy scale combining the former separate prose and document literacy scales

the abilities to solve problems for personal, work and civic purposes by setting up appropriate goals and plans and accessing and making use of information through computers and computer networks' (OECD 2012: 47).

The PS-TRE computer-based measures reflect a broadened view of literacy that includes skills and knowledge related to information and communication technologies—skills that are seen as increasingly essential components of human capital in the twenty-first century.

2.2.3 Relationship of PIAAC Domains to Previous Adult Surveys

As noted earlier, PIAAC was designed in a way that allowed for linking a subset of the domains assessed in the two earlier international surveys of adults—IALS and ALL. Table 2.1 shows the skill domains assessed in the three surveys. Shading indicates where the domains have been linked across the surveys.

IALS assessed three domains of literacy—prose, document, and quantitative. Prose literacy was defined as the knowledge and skills needed to understand and use *continuous* texts—information organised in sentence and paragraph formats. Document literacy represented the knowledge and skills needed to process documents or information organised in matrix structures (i.e. in rows and columns). The types of documents covered by this domain included tables, signs, indexes, lists, coupons, schedules, charts, graphs, maps, and forms. Quantitative literacy covered the skills needed to undertake arithmetic operations, such as addition, subtraction, multiplication, or division either singly or in combination using numbers or quantities embedded in printed material.

The major change between IALS and ALL was the replacement of the assessment of quantitative literacy with that of numeracy and the introduction of the assessment of problem solving. Numeracy represented a broader domain than that of quantitative literacy, covering a wider range of quantitative skills and knowledge (not just computational operations) as well as a broader range of situations in which actors had to deal with mathematical information of different types, and not just situations involving numbers embedded in printed materials (Gal et al. 2005: 151). Problem solving was defined as 'goal-directed thinking and action in situations for which no routine solution procedure is available' (Statistics Canada and OECD 2005: 16).

In literacy, PIAAC differs from IALS and ALL in two main ways. First, literacy is reported on a single scale rather than on two separate (prose and document literacy) ones. For the purposes of comparison, the results of IALS and ALL were rescaled on the PIAAC literacy scale. Second, while the measurement framework for literacy in PIAAC draws heavily on those used in IALS and ALL, it expands the kinds of texts covered to include electronic and combined texts in addition to the continuous (prose) and noncontinuous (document) texts of the IALS and ALL frameworks. In addition, the assessment of literacy was extended to include a measure of reading component skills that was not included in previous assessments.

The domain of numeracy remains largely unchanged between ALL and PIAAC. PS-TRE constitutes a new domain. While it has some relationship to problem solving as conceived in ALL, the emphasis is on the skills necessary to solve 'information problems' and the solution of problems in digital environments rather than on analytic problem skills per se presented in paper-and-pencil format.

2.3 Assessment Design: Key Features

To provide accurate, valid, and stable measures of the domains and constructs described above, PIAAC is based on a complex survey or test design. There are two main features of this design. First, it is a matrix sampling design where a large item pool is administered to test-takers in a way that reduces the testing time for individuals while providing a broad construct coverage at the group and country level. More precisely, each test-taker responds only to a subset of items, but these subsets are linked throughout the design to enable the construction of a single joint scale for each domain. Second, the design is administered as a multistage adaptive test design (MST), which matches the administration of test items with regard to their difficulty to the proficiency level of test-takers. The first adaptive level directs a test-taker either to the paper- or the computer-based assessment branch based on his/her computer experience and skills. The second adaptive level directs test-takers to either more or less difficult items based on their responses to prior administered items. To enable the success of this complex design in the large variety of countries,

PIAAC implemented a field test prior to the main study to evaluate the developed instruments, the efficiency and implementation of the design, the data collection processes, and the computer-based testing platform.

In the following section, we will describe in more detail the different but related goals of the PIAAC field test and main study, give an overview of the advantages of implementing adaptive testing in PIAAC, and illustrate the core features of the final MST study design for the main study.

2.3.1 Field Test Versus Main Study

As stated previously, PIAAC is a cyclical cross-country survey that consists of a field test and a main study.

The *goal of the main study* was to provide policymakers, stakeholders, and researchers with data and test scores that are accurate and comparable across different countries and over time to enable fair and meaningful comparisons as well as a stable measure of trends. To achieve this goal, PIAAC implemented an MST design that allows for higher test efficiency and more accurate measurements within the specified testing time, especially at the extreme ends of the proficiency scale. Moreover, the design needed to provide a successful link across the different cognitive domains within the PIAAC assessment cycle and between PIAAC and prior adult surveys (IALS and ALL). The main study design will be illustrated in more detail in Sect. 2.3.2. To ensure that all goals were met, a field test was implemented.

The *goal of the field test* was to prepare for the main study instrument, the MST design, computer delivery platform, data collection, and analysis. With regard to the MST design, the field test was used to examine the role of test-takers' computer familiarity, evaluate the equivalence of item parameters between the paper-based assessment (PBA) and computer-based assessment (CBA), and establish initial item parameters based on item response theory (IRT) models. The item parameters were used to select items for the final PIAAC instruments and construct the adaptive testing algorithm for branching test-takers in the final MST design. More details about the PIAAC field test design and analysis in preparation of the final PIAAC MST design can be found in the PIAAC Technical Report (OECD 2013; Kirsch and Yamamoto 2013).

2.3.1.1 Advantages and Efficiency of Multistage Testing in PIAAC

PIAAC was one of the first international large-scale assessments to introduce an adaptive test design in the form of MST. Using an MST design allowed PIAAC to assess a broader range of proficiency levels more accurately within and across countries. This is important given that more and more countries are participating in this international large-scale survey.

MST increases the efficiency, validity, and accuracy of the measured constructs by matching the administration of test items to the proficiency level of test-takers. This leads to an improvement of proficiency estimation and a reduction in measurement error across the entire proficiency distribution (Lord 1980; Wainer 1990) and particularly with regard to the ends of the proficiency scale (Hambleton and Swaminathan 1985; Lord 1980; Weiss 1974). A reduction of the linking error (Wu 2010) and a potential increase of test-taker engagement (Arvey et al. 1990; Asseburg and Frey 2013), especially for low-performing respondents (Betz and Weiss 1976), are additional advantages.

MST is an extension of item-level adaptive testing that allows the choice of the next item set as opposed to the selection of single items. Since international large-scale assessments make use of item sets in the test design, the implementation of MST for introducing adaptive testing is a reasonable choice. In item sets (or units), several items share the same stimulus. In PIAAC, item sets are used as intact entities (i.e. are not split), which provides the ability to control the presentation of items across different test forms for better construct coverage and balancing item position to prevent bias on parameter estimation. Moreover, MST accumulates more information after each adaptive step compared to approaches that use single items for each adaptive decision or path. This can lead to greater accuracy in the decision of the next adaptive path and reduce the likely dependency of the adaptive selection on item-by-country interactions (Kirsch and Thorn 2013). More details about benefits of MST for international large-scale assessments can be found in Yamamoto et al. (2018). In summary, the MST approach in PIAAC allows for matching item difficulty with the abilities of test-takers while meeting other design requirements (item parameter estimation, broad construct coverage, balancing item content, item type, and the position of items, linking) at the same time.

The PIAAC MST design was able to achieve its main goal—improvement in measurement precision—especially for higher and lower proficiency levels. Based on the international common item parameters of PIAAC, the MST design was 10–30% more efficient for literacy and 4–31% more efficient for numeracy compared to the nonadaptive average linear tests of equal length. In other words, it is possible to obtain the same amount of test information as one might expect from a test that is 10–30% longer with regard to literacy and 4–31% longer with regard to numeracy. There was no proficiency range where MST was less informative, with more gains for extreme scale scores.

2.3.2 Main Study Design

PIAAC used a variant of matrix sampling where each test-taker was administered a subset of items from the total item pool. Hence, different groups of test-takers answered different sets of items, leading to missing data by design. PIAAC consisted of a BQ administered at the beginning of the survey (30–40 min) followed by a cognitive *assessment* (60 min) measuring the four domains literacy, numeracy,

Table 2.2 Terminologies for describing the PIAAC main study design

PBA (nonadaptive)	CBA (adaptive)
Item: Refers to a task to which an examinee is directed to provide a response. The response is coded based on a coding guide; in PIAAC, all items are machine coded	*Item:* Same as PBA
Unit: Refers to a short, mutually exclusive set of items in the PIAAC adaptive test design	*Unit:* Same as PBA
Cluster: Refers to a mutually exclusive set of items in the PBA; one cluster takes 30-min testing time on average	*Block:* A set of units in the PIAAC adaptive test design; each respondent receives two blocks: one in adaptive Stage 1 and one in adaptive Stage 2
Booklet: Each respondent in the nonadaptive PBA receives one booklet; a booklet consists of two 30-min clusters (60 min on average)	*Module:* Refers to a domain-specific set of two blocks across the adaptive stages in the PIAAC adaptive test design (one Stage 1 block and one Stage 2 block); one module takes 30-min testing time on average; each examinee receives two cognitive domains, i.e. two modules (60 min on average)

Notes. PBA paper-based assessment, *CBA* computer-based assessment

reading components (RC), and problem solving (PS-TRE). Furthermore, a *link to prior adult surveys* (IALS and ALL) was established through 60% of literacy and numeracy linking items that are common across the different surveys. The different item types in PIAAC in the CBA (highlighting, clicking, single choice, multiple choice, and numeric entry) were scored automatically and instantaneously by the computer-based platform based on international and national scoring rules. This was done to enable adaptive testing in the CBA. In the following, we describe the PIAAC main study design in detail using the terminologies described in Table 2.2.

2.3.2.1 Levels of Adaptiveness

The PIAAC MST design as displayed in Fig. 2.1 was *adaptive on different levels*. The *first level* of adaptiveness accounted for test-takers' computer familiarity. Test-takers were either routed to the PBA or the CBA based on their responses to questions from the BQ and a core set of questions focusing on ICT skills. Test-takers who reported no familiarity with computers were routed to the PBA, as were those who refused to take the test on the computer. Test-takers who reported familiarity with computers in the main study were routed to the CBA. The *second level* of adaptation was within the CBA cognitive assessment. PIAAC used a probability-based multistage adaptive algorithm, where the cognitive items for literacy and

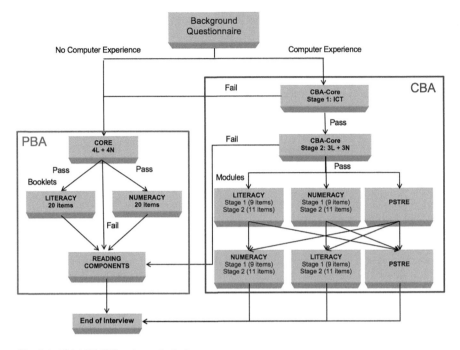

Fig. 2.1 PIAAC MST main study design

numeracy were administered to test-takers in an adaptive way. In other words, more able test-takers received a more difficult set of items than less able respondents did. Note that PS-TRE was not administered adaptively.

2.3.2.2 PBA and CBA Branches

The *PBA branch* started with a 10-min core assessment of literacy and numeracy. Test-takers who performed at or above a minimum standard were randomly assigned to a 30-minute cluster of literacy or numeracy items, followed by a 20-min assessment of reading components. The small proportion of test-takers who performed poorly on the PBA core items did not receive literacy and numeracy items and were routed directly to the reading component items.

The *CBA branch* started with the CBA core section, which was composed of two stages taking approximately 5 min each. Poor performance on either stage of the CBA core sections resulted in switching over to the appropriate sections of the PBA instruments. Test-takers who failed CBA Core Stage 1 (which contained ICT-related items) were redirected to the PBA. Those who passed CBA Core Stage 1 but failed CBA Core Stage 2 (which contained six cognitive items) were administered only the reading component items. Those who performed well on both CBA core

Table 2.3 Design of the main study CBA instruments for literacy and numeracy in the integrated design

Stage 1 (18 unique items—9 items per block. Each respondent takes 1 block)							
	Unit A1 4 items	*Unit B1* 5 items	*Unit C1* 4 items	*Unit D1* 5 items			
Block 1-1	X	X					
Block 1-2		X	X				
Block 1-3			X	X			
Stage 2 (31 unique items—11 items per block. Each respondent takes 1 block)							
	Unit A2 6 items	*Unit B2* 5 items	*Block C2* 3 items	*Unit D2* 3 items	*Unit E2* 3 items	*Unit F2* 5 items	*Unit G2* 6 items
Block 2-1	X	X					
Block 2-2		X	X	X			
Block 2-3				X	X	X	
Block 2-4						X	X

Note. One block consists of two or three item units; one module within a stage consists of two blocks

sections were routed to one of three possible CBA module combinations (each taking approximately 50 min):

1. A combination of literacy and numeracy modules
2. A PS-TRE module combined with either a literacy or a numeracy module
3. Only PS-TRE modules

The *literacy* and *numeracy modules* each consisted of two adaptive stages. Each stage contained a number of blocks varying in difficulty, with each block consisting of several item units (a unit is a mutually exclusive set of items). In each stage, only one block was delivered to a test-taker. The blocks within one stage were linked through a common item unit (see Table 2.3) to provide stable item parameter estimates in the main study. Within each of these modules, a test-taker took 20 items (9 in Stage 1; 11 in Stage 2). Hence, test-takers receiving literacy in Module 1 and numeracy in Module 2 (or vice versa) answered 40 items. Each module was designed to take an average of 30 min. The *PS-TRE modules* were not adaptive and comprised seven items in Module 1 and seven items in Module 2. The PS-TRE modules were also designed to take an average of 30 min. Table 2.3 provides an overview of the design of the MST Stages 1 and 2.

2.3.2.3 Controlled Item Exposure Rates and Module Selection

The diversity of countries, languages, and educational backgrounds would likely have resulted in certain subpopulations being exposed to only a small percentage of items when using a deterministic assignment of stages. This could have reduced the content coverage for single cognitive domains per country and the comparability of the PIAAC survey across countries. For achieving comparable data and test scores, a

Table 2.4 Number of cognitive items per assessment mode and domain in PIAAC

Domain	Assessment mode	Number of items
Literacy	CBA	52
	PBA	24
Numeracy	CBA	52
	PBA	24
PS-TRE	CBA	14
Reading components	PBA	100

Note. 18 literacy and 17 numeracy items were linking items between the PBA and CBA assessment mode, meaning they were identical. Thus, PIAAC contained a total of 131 unique items (excluding reading components)

set of *conditional probability tables* was used to control the *item exposure rates* for specified subpopulations (Chen et al. 2014). For more information on the module selection based on conditional probabilities, and for practical examples, see the PIAAC Technical Report (OECD 2013) as well as Yamamoto et al. (2018).

2.3.2.4 Items and Comparability

The PIAAC MST design was based on 76 literacy and 76 numeracy items that were scored dichotomously and 14 PS-TRE items that were scored dichotomously or polytomously. Table 2.4 provides an overview of the number of items per assessment mode (PBA and CBA).

Item position effects at the cross-country level as well as the *comparability of item parameters* across countries (item-by-country interactions) were examined in the field test and main study (OECD 2013; Yamamoto et al. 2018). There was the possibility that results would show a slight cluster position effect for literacy modules (2.9%) and numeracy modules (1.2%) on the per cent of correct responses. However, the IRT scaling provided comparable item parameters achieving high comparability and measurement invariance (92% and 94% for literacy and 93% and 97% for numeracy in the PIAAC Round 1 and Round 2 assessments, respectively). Overall, item parameters were shown to be stable and comparable across the different countries and languages.

2.4 Sampling Requirements

The target population for PIAAC included adults between the age of 16 and 65 years, excluding adults in institutions (e.g. prisons). The sampling unit for PIAAC was individuals or, in the case of countries not having register-based sampling frames, the household. In the latter case, each sampled household was administered a screener to determine the eligibility of household members. Within households, each selected adult was administered the BQ and cognitive assessment.

Countries also had national options to include oversamples of key subpopulations or to include additional subpopulations in their PIAAC target population (e.g. adults aged 66 to 74 years). Therefore, the sampling plan included guidelines for the national options chosen by countries as well as specifications for any necessary augmentation of the sample size to accommodate the analysis requirements for these additional subsamples.

The core sample design was a stratified multistage clustered area sample. However, deviations from the core design were expected due to geographically small countries that have less clustering and fewer stages of sampling. Some countries had lists of households or persons already available from population registries. The general approach was to allow for flexibility in the sample design, conduct a thorough assessment of the quality of sampling frames, and prepare to adapt to each country's best sampling scenario.

The minimum sample size required to produce reliable estimates of skills at the national level in a country was between $N = 4000$ and $N = 5000$. As stated above, all countries had the option of boosting sample size and oversampling to obtain estimates for subpopulations of special interest or to increase sample size to get reliable estimates at the subnational level (e.g. states, regions, or provinces or language groups). As the field test had distinct purposes that differed from those of the main study, their sampling requirements also differed. Since the field test was not used for any reporting, and was designed solely to test operational issues along with instrument quality, fewer respondents were needed. For example, only 1500 completed cases were required in PIAAC. The reader is referred to the PIAAC Technical Report for more detailed information on sampling requirements (OECD 2013).

2.5 Future Cycles of PIAAC: Potential Improvements

While many of the innovations from the first cycle of PIAAC are being carried forward to the second cycle, ongoing technological developments are expected to enable the implementation of new innovations that will be explored to further improve the accuracy and comparability of the data and the measurement of trend. They include:

- *New constructs:* New types of interactive stimulus materials and item formats can be incorporated to extend what is measured. In addition to measuring reading component skills, the component skills will be extended to the numeracy domain. Moreover, a new domain—adaptive problem solving—will replace PS-TRE.
- *Existing constructs and linking:* The current number of items for literacy and numeracy will be increased to provide better overall construct coverage and measurement along each scale. Furthermore, the number of core items will

be doubled to provide better measurement of low-performing adults in each participating country while not requiring that they take the full assessment. The measures of literacy and numeracy will be linked between PIAAC Cycle 1 and Cycle 2 as well as to previous adult surveys (IALS, ALL).

- *Process data and adaptive algorithm:* The use of process information from computer-based tests, such as timing data, will be explored to refine the adaptive algorithms for multistage adaptive testing to increase both the validity and efficiency of adaptive testing.
- *Delivery mode and hardware:* The use of tablet devices will be explored for possibly replacing the paper-based assessment. The tablet devices will need to be of high quality to ensure that the touch sensitivity is sufficiently responsive to user input. The tablet will be connected to a keyboard for the interviewer (for administering the BQ) and to a stylus for the test-taker (for completing the cognitive assessment). Another possibility would be to allow respondents to complete the BQ on a tablet rather than having it administered by the interviewer. The stylus should allow the tablet to function much like a paper-and-pencil instrument in terms of not requiring much ICT skill without compromising the overall functionality and item types that are feasible on a technology platform. Increasing the number of test-takers for the CBA by using tablets would reduce the need for scoring paper-based responses (which improves scoring reliability), more participants would be able to benefit from the MST design, and more would be able to take the newly developed innovative items that are administered only in the CBA. However, different test designs will be available, especially for countries that are not able to switch to tablet devices and for test-takers who could not or chose not to use the tablet or laptop. For any of these options, studies would need to be conducted to learn more about the feasibility and impact of using alternative devices before they can be incorporated into the Cycle 2 main study. Device effects are an important consideration for trend items from literacy and numeracy with regard to the comparability of Cycle 1 and Cycle 2 and to test-takers with limited technology skills.
- *New software for data capture:* The use of new technologies for capturing oral proficiencies of test-takers with limited literacy skills could be explored. Albeit, this would require a good deal more research and development. Work is being done around spoken language tests that are automatically delivered and scored (see, e.g. Bernstein et al. 2010), and it could be explored whether comparable measures could be developed across languages for PIAAC.
- *Accessibility:* XML and web-based technologies will be used to develop data products and analysis systems that can accommodate a constantly expanding set of analysis, visualisation, and reporting tools to make the PIAAC data more accessible and powerful for a range of users (e.g. test-takers with certain disabilities).

The second cycle of PIAAC will need to balance innovation with the ongoing constraints of this survey. These include the importance of maintaining trend measurement and a recognition that the testing population includes individuals who range broadly in terms of both age and familiarity with technology, as well as educational backgrounds and proficiencies. All possible improvements and innovations introduced in a second cycle of PIAAC could have considerable impact on the test design and will need to be considered when analysing the future PIAAC data.

2.6 Summary and Outlook

PIAAC needs to meet the goals and standards of international large-scale surveys while, at the same time, dealing with certain constraints and challenges. The major goal of PIAAC is to provide comparable, accurate, and fair measures of literacy, numeracy, problem solving, and reading component skills across participating countries, groups within countries, and different PIAAC cycles and prior adult surveys (i.e. across time points) to provide a stable measurement of trends. One important challenge PIAAC faces is the variability of proficiencies across and even within countries, as test-takers with a broad range in age (16–65 years) and educational levels are tested in multiple languages often associated with diverse cultural backgrounds. The PIAAC test design was developed to account for these constraints. The heart of the design is MST, which better matches the administration of test items to the proficiency level of test-takers. This provides an overall increase in test efficiency and accuracy within and across countries. The design also helps reduce the possible impact of item position and mode effects as well as item-by-country (and item-by-language) interactions. The improved measurement also allows for establishing a stable link over time and across assessment modes and different countries and languages.[3]

The PIAAC MST design uses information from both the BQ and cognitive assessment and was based on two levels of adaptation: (1) based on test-takers' computer skills and experience, they were routed to either PBA or CBA and (2) within the CBA, test-takers' proficiency levels with regard to responses to prior cognitive items as well as information about their educational level and native language were used to assign the different adaptive stages. A probability-based multistage adaptive algorithm was used to control the item exposure rate to enable a broad construct coverage and minimise item-by-country interactions.

---

[3]Please see the PIAAC Technical Report (OECD 2013) for more details around the development, implementation and analysis of the survey.

2.6.1 What to Keep in Mind When Using PIAAC Data for Analysis

The use of the data resulting from this complex test design for secondary analysis requires a good understanding of the design features. In the following, we summarise some of the most important points which should be considered when analysing the data.

- *Plausible values:* For secondary analysis (i.e. analysis based on the final test scores provided in the public use data file), plausible values should be used instead of raw responses, as they account for uncertainty in the measurement and reduce measurement error. Moreover, plausible values are placed on a common scale that allows for comparing different subgroups and countries in a fair and meaningful way. For details about the use of plausible values in analysis, see Chap. 3 in this volume.
- *Missing values:* PIAAC is based on an incomplete balanced block design. This means that every test-taker responded to just a subset of items, and the data include missing values. However, all items are linked together and can be placed on a common scale. In addition to these missing values by design, there are other types of missing data such as omitted responses (an item was presented, but the test-taker chose not to respond) and not-reached items. More information on different types of missing values can be found in the PIAAC Technical Report (OECD 2013). It is strongly recommended to use the plausible values for secondary analysis. However, if analysing the raw responses is needed, researchers and analysts have to consider how to treat these different types of missing values; again, the PIAAC Technical Report provides guidance in this regard.
- *Different administration modes due to adaptive testing:* PIAAC is based on an MST design. This means that some test-takers took PIAAC on paper, while the majority took it on computer.
- *Different domains due to administration mode and adaptive testing:* Not all test-takers received all cognitive domains. All test-takers responded to literacy and numeracy items, but not all received reading component or problem-solving (PS-TRE) items. All test-takers who received the PBA responded to reading component items (but not to PS-TRE items). Test-takers who received the CBA responded to problem-solving items; only a subset of test-takers from the CBA received reading component items.

PIAAC is the largest and most innovative assessment of adults in the world. It is both linked to and builds on two earlier adult surveys that allows for the measurement of changes in the distributions of adult skills among countries that have participated in all surveys. It also builds on the work of these two earlier surveys by assessing the use of digital texts and skills that better reflect the ways in which adults now access, use, and communicate information.

As reflected in the wide range of publications and papers that have been developed, when used properly and in a thoughtful way, the PIAAC dataset can provide policymakers, stakeholders, and researchers with a rich and accurate source of information to better understand the distributions of human capital in their country and the connections between these skills and important social, educational, and labour market outcomes. The next chapter will cover the statistical background of the PIAAC dataset. More precisely, Chap. 3 will illustrate the computation and correct use of plausible values, which are multiple imputations of group-level test scores for calculating group-level statistics in secondary analysis.

References

Arvey, R. D., Strickland, W., Drauden, G., & Martin, C. (1990). Motivational components of test taking. *Personnel Psychology, 43*, 695–716. https://doi.org/10.1111/j.1744-6570.1990.tb00679.x.

Asseburg, R., & Frey, A. (2013). Too hard, too easy, or just right? The relationship between effort or boredom and ability-difficulty fit. *Psychological Test and Assessment Modeling, 55*, 92–104.

Bernstein, J., Van Moere, A., & Cheng, J. (2010). Validating automated speaking tests. *Language Testing, 27*(3), 355–377.

Betz, N. E., & Weiss, D. J. (1976). *Psychological effects of immediate knowledge of results and adaptive ability testing* (Research Report No. 76-4). Minneapolis: University of Minnesota, Psychometric Methods Program.

Chen, H., Yamamoto, K., & von Davier, M. (2014). Controlling MST exposure rates in international large-scale assessments. In D. Yan, A. A. von Davier, & C. Lewis (Eds.), *Computerized multistage testing: Theory and applications* (pp. 391–409). Boca Raton: Chapman and Hall/CRC.

Dickerson, A., & Green, F. (2004). The growth and valuation of computing and other generic skills. *Oxford Economic Papers-New Series, 56*, 371–406.

Gal, I., van Groenestijn, M., Manly, M., Schmitt, M. J., & Tout, D. (2005). Adult numeracy and its assessment in the ALL Survey: A conceptual framework and pilot results. In S. Murray, Y. Clermont, & M. Binkley (Eds.), *Measuring adult literacy and life skills: New frameworks for assessment* (Catalogue 89-552-MIE, No. 13). Ottawa: Statistics Canada.

Goldin, C., & Katz, L. F. (2008). *The race between education and technology*. Cambridge, MA: The Belknap Press of Harvard University Press.

Grenier, S., Jones, S., Strucker, J., Murray, T. S., Gervais, G., & Brink, S. (2008). *International adult literacy survey: Learning literacy in Canada: Evidence from the international survey of Reading skills*. Ottawa: Statistics Canada.

Hambleton, R. K., & Swaminathan, H. (1985). *Item response theory: Principles and applications*. Boston: Kluwer-Nijhoff.

Kirsch, I., & Thorn, W. (2013). The Programme for International Assessment of Adult Competencies–An Overview. In Organisation for Economic Co-operation and Development (2013), *Technical report of the Survey of Adult Skills (PIAAC)*, foreword (pp. 5–24), PIAAC, OECD Publishing. Retrieved from http://www.oecd.org/site/piaac/All%20PIACC%20Technical%20Report%20final.pdf

Kirsch, I., & Yamamoto, K. (2013). PIAAC assessment design. In Organisation for Economic Co-operation and Development (2013), *Technical report of the Survey of Adult Skills (PIAAC)*, (pp. 27–43). Paris: OECD Publishing. Retrieved from http://www.oecd.org/site/piaac/All%20PIACC%20Technical%20Report%20final.pdf

Lord, F. M. (1980). *Applications of item response theory to practical testing problems*. Hillsdale: Lawrence Erlbaum Associates.

Maehler, D. B., Jakowatz, S., & Konradt, I. (2020). *PIAAC bibliographie 2008 – 2019*. GESIS Papers, Nr. 04/2020. Cologne: GESIS – Leibniz Institute for the Social Sciences. https://doi.org/10.21241/ssoar.67732.

Moore, J., Stinson, L. L., & Welniak, E. J., Jr. (2000). Income measurement error in surveys. *Journal of Official Statistics, 16*(4), 331–361.

Organisation for Economic Co-operation and Development (OECD). (2012). *Literacy, numeracy and problem solving in technology-rich environments: Framework for the OECD Survey of Adult Skills*.https://doi.org/10.1787/9789264128859-en

Organisation for Economic Co-operation and Development (OECD). (2013). *Technical report of the Survey of Adult Skills (PIAAC)*, (pp. 406–438). Retrieved from http://www.oecd.org/site/piaac/Technical%20Report_17OCT13.pdf

Organisation for Economic Co-operation and Development (OECD). (2016a). *Skills matter: Further results from the Survey of Adult Skills studies*. Paris: OECD Publishing.

Organisation for Economic Co-operation and Development (OECD). (2016b). *The Survey of Adult Skills: Reader's companion* (2nd ed.). Paris: OECD Publishing.

Pleis, J. R., & Dahlhamer, J. M. (2004). Family income response patterns for varying levels of income detail: An analysis of the National Health Interview Survey (NHIS). In *Proceedings of the American Statistical Association, Section on survey research methods* (CD-ROM) (pp. 4200–4207). Alexandria: American Statistical Association.

Statistics Canada and Organisation for Economic Co-operation and Development (OECD). (2005). *Learning a living: First results of the adult literacy and life skills survey*. Ottawa/Paris: Authors.

Strucker, J., Yamamoto, K., & Kirsch, I. (2007). *The relationship of the component skills of reading to IALS performance: Tipping points and five classes of adult literacy learners*. Cambridge, MA: Harvard Graduate School of Education, National Center for the Study of Adult Learning and Literacy.

Wainer, H. (1990). *Computerized adaptive testing: A primer*. Hillsdale: Lawrence Erlbaum Associates.

Weiss, D. J. (1974). *Strategies of adaptive ability measurement* (Research Report No. 74-5). Minneapolis: University of Minnesota, Psychometric Methods Program.

Wu, M. (2010). Measurement, sampling, and equating errors in large-scale assessments. *Educational Measurement: Issues and Practice, 29*, 15–27. https://doi.org/10.1111/j.1745-3992.2010.00190.x.

Yamamoto, K., Khorramdel, L., & Shin, H. J. (2018). Multistage adaptive testing design in PIAAC. *Psychological Test and Assessment Modeling, 60*, 347–368.

Open Access This chapter is licensed under the terms of the Creative Commons Attribution 4.0 International License (http://creativecommons.org/licenses/by/4.0/), which permits use, sharing, adaptation, distribution and reproduction in any medium or format, as long as you give appropriate credit to the original author(s) and the source, provide a link to the Creative Commons license and indicate if changes were made.

The images or other third party material in this chapter are included in the chapter's Creative Commons license, unless indicated otherwise in a credit line to the material. If material is not included in the chapter's Creative Commons license and your intended use is not permitted by statutory regulation or exceeds the permitted use, you will need to obtain permission directly from the copyright holder.

Chapter 3
Plausible Values: Principles of Item Response Theory and Multiple Imputations

Lale Khorramdel, Matthias von Davier, Eugenio Gonzalez, and Kentaro Yamamoto

Abstract This chapter introduces the principles of item response theory (IRT) and the latent regression model, also called population or conditioning model, which is central for generating plausible values (multiple imputations) in PIAAC. Moreover, it is illustrated how plausible values can reduce bias in secondary analyses compared to the use of customary point estimates of latent variables by taking explanatory variables into account. An overview of standard techniques for utilizing plausible values (PVs) in the analyses of large-scale assessment data will be provided, and it will be discussed how to calculate the different variance components for statistics based on PVs, which play an important role in the interpretation of subgroup and country differences.

The Programme for the International Assessment of Adult Competencies (PIAAC) provides a rich international database that can be used by policymakers, stakeholders, and educational researchers for examining differences in educational systems and outcomes across countries, groups of test-takers within countries, and over time for the measurement of trend. The PIAAC database includes measures of cognitive domains, such as literacy, numeracy, and problem solving in technology-rich environments (PS-TRE), as well as background information and non-cognitive measures obtained from a background questionnaire (BQ). For each cognitive domain and background variable, test-takers' raw responses are available in addition to proficiency estimates in the form of plausible values (PVs) for the cognitive domains and item response theory (IRT)-based estimates for some of the non-cognitive measures. For the computer-based assessment, two types of process data

L. Khorramdel (✉) · M. von Davier
National Board of Medical Examiners, Princeton, NJ, USA
e-mail: lale.khorramdelameri@gmail.com

E. Gonzalez · K. Yamamoto
Educational Testing Service, Princeton, NJ, USA

are included in the database as well—the number of actions (e.g. number of mouse clicks when interacting with an item on the computer) and the total response time—as well as the time to first action for each item. As we will see later in this chapter, utilising a latent regression model is necessary to reduce bias in the estimation of means and variances of the subgroups of interest. The source of this bias is the fact that, while the domains measured are broad, we have a limited amount of assessment time during which we can assess the respondent's skills, and therefore we need to resort to statistical techniques that will borrow information to correct for the unreliability of measurements.

In order to facilitate broad domain coverage while limiting individual testing time, which is aimed at reducing test-takers' burden, the PIAAC data are based on a variant of matrix sampling where different groups of respondents answered different sets of items (see Chap. 2 in this volume). Therefore, it is not appropriate to directly compare the group performance using conventional statistics such as the total score. This would only be feasible if one made very strong assumptions—for instance, that the different test forms are perfectly parallel and that there is hardly any measurement error. Since this is almost never the case, conventional scoring methods show several limitations, such as ignoring the variability and dissimilarities of proficiencies of subgroups. These limitations can be overcome in part by using IRT scaling where respondents as well as items can be characterised on a common scale, even if not all respondents take identical sets of items (e.g. in adaptive testing). This makes it possible to describe performance distributions in a population or subpopulation and to estimate the relationships between proficiencies and background variables.

As stated above, to improve the statistical properties of the group-level proficiency estimates, PIAAC uses PVs, which are multiple imputations. These imputations are drawn from a posterior distribution that is the result of combining information from the cognitive assessment and the BQ. To compute PVs, a latent regression model, also called population or conditioning model, is estimated that combines an IRT model with an explanatory model regressing proficiency on background data. In this model, which is tailored for use in large-scale assessments, IRT item parameter estimates are fixed to values from previous item calibrations, and the background variables are used as predictors.

The remainder of this chapter is organised as follows: First, we describe the IRT model and the scaling of item parameters. This is followed by a description of the latent regression model used for generating the PVs in PIAAC. It will be illustrated how the use of PVs can reduce bias (by accounting for measurement error) in secondary analyses and lead to more accurate results. It will also be described how PVs can be used appropriately in statistical analyses to avoid errors and biases when analysing the PIAAC data. Moreover, we will give an outlook on how the predictive power of the population model can be improved by including information from process data obtained from computer-based assessments.

3.1 IRT Scaling

3.1.1 IRT Models and Calibration of Item Parameters

The proficiency values θ for the PIAAC cognitive domains literacy, numeracy, and PS-TRE cannot be directly observed, as each respondent provides only a small number of answers, and respondents will only answer a subset of the domains. Hence, we do not have a very accurate picture on the individual level, but we have a large number of responses on the level of the 5000, or so, respondents per country (see the national sample requirements based on the PIAAC test design in Chap. 2 in this volume). Even if a person takes a long test, a case can be made that we never directly observe variables such as reading ability, general intelligence, or neuroticism, but that we rather observe only behavioural indicators that we believe are related to underlying individual differences.

In addition, tasks such as literacy items differ with respect to how well they measure aspects of literacy and in terms of how difficult they are on average. IRT is a model that takes into account interindividual differences as well as differences between items, and can be used to derive estimates that represent proficiencies on the one hand, and parameters representing features of the tasks, such as item difficulty, as well as discrimination, which can be described as the ability of an item to differentiate between high- and low-proficient respondents.

Latent variable or IRT models can disentangle differences between items from differences between test-takers and therefore have a number of advantages when it comes to statistical analyses of data from assessments such as PIAAC. Interested readers are referred to van der Linden and Hambleton (2016) for an overview of IRT, and to Rutkowski et al. (2014) for a handbook that describes in great detail the methods used in PIAAC, but also in student assessments such as the Programme for International Student Assessment (PISA), the Trends in International Mathematics and Science Study (TIMSS), and the Progress in International Reading Literacy Study (PIRLS). IRT is used to estimate the proficiency values as well as the item parameters in PIAAC using the two-parameter logistic model (2PLM; Birnbaum 1968) for items with two response categories and the generalised partial credit model (GPCM; Muraki 1992) for items with more than two response categories.

The *2PLM* is a mathematical model for the probability that an individual will respond correctly to a particular item depending only on the following parameters: the individual's ability or proficiency (the person parameter) and the difficulty and discrimination of the particular item (the item parameters). This probability is given as a function of the person parameter and the two item parameters and can be written as follows:

$$P(X = x | \theta, \beta_i, \alpha_i) = \frac{\exp(D\alpha_i (\theta - \beta_i))}{1 + \exp(D\alpha_i (\theta - \beta_i))} \quad (3.1)$$

with $X \in \{0, 1\}$ and $X = 1$ indicating a correct response to a binary coded item. The θ, β_i are real-valued parameters, commonly referred to as ability and difficulty parameters, respectively, and α_i is the discrimination or slope parameter (similar to a factor loading). $D > 0$ is a positive constant of arbitrary size, often either 1.0 or 1.7, depending on the parameterisation used in the software implementation; in PIAAC, D took on the value of 1.7. Note that for $\alpha_i > 0$ (a commonly made, but not necessary, assumption in IRT), this is a monotone increasing function with respect to θ; that is, the conditional probability of a correct response increases as θ increases.

For polytomous items, the *GPCM* is used. This is a generalisation of the 2PLM for responses to items with two or more ordered response categories and reduces to the 2PLM when applied to dichotomous responses. For an item i with $m_i + 1$ ordered categories, $x \in \{0, \ldots, m_i\}$, the GPCM can be written as

$$P\left(X = x | \theta, \boldsymbol{\beta}_i, \alpha_i\right) = \frac{\exp\left\{\sum_{r=1}^{x} D\alpha_i \ (\theta - \beta_{ir})\right\}}{\sum_{u=0}^{m_i} \exp\left\{\sum_{r=1}^{u} D\alpha_i \ (\theta - \beta_{ir})\right\}} \qquad (3.2)$$

where $\boldsymbol{\beta}_i = (\beta_{i1}, \ldots, \beta_{im})$ are the category threshold parameters. For only two categories, there is only a single threshold parameter that is equivalent to the item difficulty in the 2PLM.

A central assumption of the 2PLM and the GPCM, and most IRT models, is conditional independence (sometimes referred to as local independence). Under this assumption, item response probabilities depend only on θ and the specified item parameters. There is no dependence on any demographic characteristics of the respondents, on responses to any other items presented on the test, or on the survey administration conditions. Moreover, the 2PLM assumes unidimensionality—that is, a single latent variable (θ) accounts for the performance on the full set of items. This enables the formulation of the following joint probability of a particular response pattern $\boldsymbol{x} = (x_1, \ldots, x_n)$ across a set of n items:

$$P\left(\boldsymbol{x} | \theta, \boldsymbol{\beta}, \boldsymbol{\alpha}\right) = \prod_{i=1}^{n} P\left(X = x_i | \theta, \boldsymbol{\beta}_i, \alpha_i\right) \qquad (3.3)$$

where $\boldsymbol{\beta} = (\boldsymbol{\beta}_1, \ldots, \boldsymbol{\beta}_n)$ and $\boldsymbol{\alpha} = (\alpha_1, \ldots, \alpha_n)$. When replacing the hypothetical response pattern with the scored observed data, the above function can be viewed as a likelihood function that is to be maximised with respect to the item parameters. To do this, it is assumed that respondents provide their answers independently of one another and that the student's proficiencies are sampled from a distribution, $f(\theta)$. The (marginal) likelihood function for i.i.d. respondents $j = 1, \ldots, J$ and locally independent responses $\boldsymbol{x}_j = (x_{1j}, \ldots, x_{nj})$ can be written as

$$P\left(\boldsymbol{X} | \boldsymbol{\beta}, \boldsymbol{\alpha}\right) = \prod_{j=1}^{J} \int \left(\prod_{i=1}^{n} P\left(X = x_{ij} | \theta, \boldsymbol{\beta}_i, \alpha_i\right)\right) f(\theta) \, d\theta. \qquad (3.4)$$

Typically, the marginal log likelihood function, $L = \log P(X|\boldsymbol{\beta},\boldsymbol{\alpha})$, is maximised using customary approaches such as the EM algorithm (Dempster et al. 1997). The item parameter estimates obtained by maximising this function are used as fixed constants in the subsequent estimation of the latent regression model. This is a convenient choice that enables using fixed parameter linking across groups, as the item parameters are typically found by maximising the likelihood for a sample of respondents drawn from all countries. While PISA used only 500 students per country up until the 2012 cycle, PIAAC, as well as previous international adult assessments, such as the International Adult Literacy Survey (IALS) and the Adult Literacy and Lifeskills Survey (ALL), and PISA since 2015, use all available data in this item calibration, and the resulting item parameters represent the evidence on item difficulties and item discrimination parameters aggregated across all participating countries.

To ensure that the IRT model provides adequate fit to the observed data, different types of model checks are applied. One of these checks is the evaluation of the fit of the estimated item parameters to the observed empirical data. To assess differences in item fit across countries, or relative to previously calibrated parameters, the country-specific mean deviation (MD) and the root mean square deviation (RMSD) were computed for each item in each group of interest (i.e. the different country and language groups in PIAAC). For simplicity, the MD and RMSD are presented here for dichotomous variables only:

$$\text{MD} = \int (P_0(\theta) - P_e(\theta)) f(\theta) d\theta \tag{3.5}$$

$$\text{RMSD} = \sqrt{\int (P_0(\theta) - P_e(\theta))^2 f(\theta) d\theta} \tag{3.6}$$

$P_0(\theta) - P_e(\theta))$ describes the deviation of the pseudo-counts-based ('observed') item characteristic curve from its model-based expected counterpart for a given ability level θ, and $f(\theta)$ is the density of ability distribution at this ability level. More details can be found in Yamamoto et al. (2013). *MD* and *RMSD* both quantify the magnitude and direction of deviations in the observed data from the estimated item characteristic curves. The *MD* is more sensitive to deviations of observed item difficulties than the *RMSD*. The *RMSD* is more sensitive to the deviations of both the item difficulties and discriminations (Yamamoto et al. 2013). In PIAAC, *MD* values between −0.1 and 0.1 and *RMSD* values smaller than 0.1 indicated acceptable item fit.

3.1.2 Treatment of Missing Values

Because of the matrix sampling and the multistage testing (MST) design in PIAAC, the treatment of different types of missing values in the IRT scaling had to be considered.

1. *Missing by design:* Items that were not presented to each respondent due to the matrix sampling design (structural missing data) do not contribute information to respondents' cognitive skills and were excluded from the likelihood function of the IRT model.
2. *Not reached items:* Missing responses at the end of an item block or cluster (see Chap. 2 in this volume) were treated as if they were not presented due to the difficulty of determining if the respondent was unable to finish these items or simply abandoned them. Hence, these missing responses were also excluded from the likelihood function of the IRT model.
3. *Omitted responses:* Any missing response to an item that was administered to a particular respondent and that was followed by a valid response (whether correct or incorrect) was defined as an omitted response. Omitted responses in the paper-based assessment (PBA) were treated as incorrect responses and added information to the estimation. In the case of the computer-based assessment (CBA), where response times and the number of actions per item were available, nonresponses due to little or no interaction were treated differently from nonresponses after some interaction with the item took place. More specifically:

    (a) If a respondent spent less than five seconds on an item (a threshold defined in the literature on response latencies; see Setzer and Allspach 2007; Wise and DeMars 2005; Wise and Kong 2005) and showed only 0–2 actions, the nonresponse was considered not attempted and therefore excluded from estimation (similar to missing by design and not reached items).
    (b) In all other cases, omitted responses were treated as incorrect and included in the estimation. More precisely, if a respondent spent less than five seconds on an item but showed more than 0–2 actions, or if a respondent spent more than five seconds on an item (independent of the number of actions), these not observed responses were treated as incorrect responses.

Nonresponse in cases of refusal to participate or an inability to provide a written response due to a physical disability was considered as not related to the cognitive proficiencies and was therefore not included in the estimation.

3.1.3 Scaling, Linking, and Measurement Invariance

The IRT scaling in PIAAC had to provide a valid, reliable, and comparable scale for each cognitive domain to allow for meaningful group comparisons and stable trend measures. More precisely, the scaling needed to achieve the following goals:

- Linking across different sets of items and delivery modes (paper- and computer-based assessments) to provide a common scale for each cognitive domain for the *international comparison* of the average proficiencies of countries within the PIAAC cycle.
- Linking PIAAC to previous educational adult surveys (IALS and ALL) to provide a common scale for the *measurement of trends*.
- Examining and establishing the extent to which comparability or invariance of the item parameters across countries, languages, and surveys can be assumed. Only if the majority of item parameters are common (i.e. have the same characteristics) across different groups can it be assumed that the same construct is measured and groups can be compared with regard to that construct.
- Examining and establishing stable item parameters and sufficient model–data fit to achieve sufficient *reliability of the measures* to allow for accurate group comparisons. This can only be achieved by treating differential item functioning (DIF) and other sources of systematic error (such as translation deviations or technical issues) through the estimation of group-specific or unique item parameters or the exclusion of particular items.

3.1.3.1 Scaling and Linking Through Common Item Parameters

To create a common scale across countries, languages, and administration modes (paper- and computer-based modes) within one assessment cycle and across surveys over time, common sets of items must be used and linked together in the test design. More precisely, certain items were administered in both the paper-based and the computer-based branch in PIAAC (note that this pertains to literacy and numeracy items, as problem solving was available only for the CBA) as well as in different booklets/modules. Moreover, 60 items of the literacy and numeracy items administered in PIAAC came from IALS and ALL (note that numeracy was first introduced in ALL).

The initial IRT scaling was based on a large joint dataset including the data from prior large-scale adult skill surveys (IALS and ALL) and the data from PIAAC Round 1 (22 countries). A mixed 2PLM and GPCM IRT model was applied in the form of a multiple group model for a concurrent calibration of the PIAAC (and IALS and ALL) items across countries. More precisely, the IRT scaling accounted for country-by-language-by-cycle groups and estimated common (or international) item parameters across all groups. The same item difficulty and slope parameters were assumed for all groups in a first step using equality constraints in the IRT modelling.

By retaining as many common, international item parameters as possible, a high level of comparability of the IRT scales was maintained across countries, administration modes, and surveys. However, the appropriateness of the fit of these common item parameters to the empirical data had to be examined for each country and language in a subsequent step of the scaling as described in the next section.

3.1.3.2 Balancing Measurement Invariance and Model Fit Through Common and Unique Item Parameters

To ensure validity and accuracy of the measurement, the fit of the estimated common item parameters to the empirical data was examined through item fit statistics (RMSD and MD) as described above. Item-by-country interactions in the form of misfitting item parameters were examined and either treated by assigning unique (or country- and language-specific) item parameters—by relaxing the equality constraints in the scaling model—or excluded from the scaling, depending on the source of misfit (see procedures outlined in Glas and Jehangir 2014; Glas and Verhelst 1995; Oliveri and von Davier 2011, 2014; Yamamoto, 1997).

If the misfit was due to errors in the administration that were unable to be fixed, such as translation errors, items were excluded from the scaling in the affected groups. In case of group-level differential item functioning (DIF), unique item parameters were estimated for a particular country and language or a group of countries that showed DIF in the same direction. In the latter case, the unique item parameter was different from the international one, but common for the group of countries that showed similar patterns of DIF (those item parameters could be referred to as partially common). This approach was favoured over dropping the group-specific item responses for these items from the analysis in order to retain information from these responses. While the items with group-specific DIF treated with unique item parameters no longer contribute to the international set of comparable item parameters, they continue to contribute to the reduction of measurement uncertainty for the specific country and language group(s).

For countries participating in PIAAC Rounds 2 and 3 (i.e. at different time points but using the same instruments), the common item parameters obtained from the joint calibration of PIAAC Round 1, IALS, and ALL data were fixed, and their fit was evaluated as described above. Through this approach, the different countries participating in PIAAC at different time points were linked through a common scale for each domain, and their results were made comparable.

While establishing a high level of comparability (in terms of a high percentage of invariant parameters across countries) of the PIAAC scale was one of the main goals of PIAAC, achieving good model–data fit for sufficient measurement accuracy for each of the participating countries and language groups was important as well. An increasing number of unique item parameters will increase the model–data fit but decrease the measurement invariance across the relevant comparison groups. Hence, a balance between these two goals had to be achieved. In PIAAC, the majority of items received international item parameters common to all or almost all countries, while unique item parameters had to be estimated for a subset of items providing a comparable and reliable scale for group-level comparisons (more details can be found in Yamamoto et al. 2013, Chap. 17).

3.1.3.3 Software

The software used for the IRT scaling, *mdltm* (von Davier 2005), provides marginal maximum likelihood estimates (MML) obtained using customary expectation–maximisation methods (EM), with optional acceleration. Furthermore, it implements an algorithm that monitored DIF measures and that automatically generated a suggested list of group-specific item treatments for the estimation of unique parameters for an individual country-by-language group or multiple country-by-language groups that showed the same level and direction of DIF. The international and national calibrations were conducted simultaneously for all countries—that is, all estimated item parameters (common and unique) are on a common scale. During the item calibration, sample weights standardised to represent each country equally were used.

3.2 Latent Regression Model

In the latent regression model, the posterior distribution of the proficiency variable (θ) is assumed to depend on the cognitive item responses (X) as well as on a number of predictors (Y) obtained from the BQ (such as gender, education, occupation, employment status, etc.). Both the item parameters from the IRT scaling stage and the estimates from the latent regression analysis are needed to generate plausible values.

3.2.1 The Latent Regression Model

The regression uses the BQ variables to predict the proficiency variable θ. It is assumed that

$$\theta \sim N(\mathbf{y}\Gamma, \Sigma) \qquad (3.7)$$

The latent regression parameters Γ and Σ are estimated conditional on the previously determined item parameter estimates. Γ is the matrix of regression coefficients, and Σ is a common residual variance–covariance matrix.

The latent regression model of Θ on Y with $\Gamma = (\gamma_{sj}, s = 1, \ldots, S; l = 0, \ldots, L)$, $Y = (1, y_1, \ldots, y_L)^t$, and $\Theta = (\theta_1, \ldots, \theta_S)^t$ can be written as follows:

$$\theta_i = \gamma_{s0} + \gamma_{s1} y_1 + \cdots + \gamma_{sL} y_L + \varepsilon_s \qquad (3.8)$$

where ε_s is an error term.

The residual variance–covariance matrix is given by the following equation:

$$\Sigma = \Theta\Theta^t - \Gamma\left(YY^t\right)\Gamma t \tag{3.9}$$

The conditional distribution from which plausible values for each respondent j are drawn can be written as follows:

$$P\left(\theta_j | x_j, y_j, \Gamma, \Sigma\right) \tag{3.10}$$

Using standard rules of probability, this posterior probability of proficiency can be represented as follows:

$$\begin{aligned} P\left(\theta_j | x_j, y_j, \Gamma, \Sigma\right) &\propto P\left(x_j | \theta_j, y_j, \Gamma, \Sigma\right) P\left(\theta_j | y_j, \Gamma, \Sigma\right) \\ &= P\left(x_j | \theta_j\right) P\left(\theta_j | y_j, \Gamma, \Sigma\right) \end{aligned} \tag{3.11}$$

where θ_j is a vector of scale values (these values correspond to the performance on each of the three cognitive domains literacy, numeracy, and PS-TRE), $P(x_j|\theta_j)$ is the product over the scales of the independent likelihoods induced by responses to items within each scale, and $P(\theta_j|y_j, \Gamma, \Sigma)$ is the multivariate joint density of proficiencies of the scales, conditional on the observed value y_j of BQ responses and item parameters Γ and Σ. As described above, the item parameters are assumed to be fixed constant in the estimation.

An expectation–maximisation (EM) algorithm is used for estimating Γ and Σ; the basic method for the single scale case is described in Mislevy (1985). The EM algorithm requires the computation of the mean and variance of the posterior distribution in the equation above.

3.2.2 Generating Plausible Values

After the estimation of the regression parameters (Γ and Σ) is complete, plausible values are randomly drawn in a three-step process from the joint distribution of the values of Γ for all sampled respondents:

1. First, a value of Γ is drawn from a normal approximation to $P(\Gamma, \Sigma | x_j, y_j)$ that fixes Σ at the value $\hat{\Sigma}$ (Thomas 1993).
2. Second, conditional on the generated value of Γ (and the fixed value of $\Sigma = \hat{\Sigma}$), the mean m_j^p, and variance Σ_j^p of the posterior distribution of θ are computed using the same methods applied in the EM algorithm.
3. In the third step, the θ are drawn independently from a multivariate normal distribution with mean m_j^p and variance Σ_j^p.

These three steps were repeated ten times, producing ten independent PVs of θ for each sampled respondent in each administered cognitive domain. Each set of PVs is equally well designed to estimate population parameters; however, multiple PVs are required to appropriately represent the uncertainty in the domain measures (von Davier et al. 2009).

Because the presence of extensive background information related to respondents' cognitive skills is necessary to implement any method for the imputation of proficiency scores, cases where respondents did not answer a sufficient number of background questions (< 5 BQ items) were considered as incomplete cases and not used in the latent regression model. These cases did not receive plausible values.

Respondents who provided sufficient background information but did not respond to a minimum of five items per domain (<2% of cases in PIAAC) were not included in a first run of the latent regression to obtain unbiased regression parameters (Γ and Σ). In a second run of analysis, the regression parameters were treated as fixed to obtain plausible values for all cases, including those with fewer than five responses to cognitive items. This procedure aimed at reducing the uncertainty of the measurement.

3.2.3 Overview of the Analytic Steps in the Latent Regression Model

The latent regression modelling in PIAAC involves multiple steps. Some involve a comprehensive analysis across all participating countries to establish international scales of literacy proficiency variables, ensuring internationally comparable results, and some involve utilising country-specific models in order to reduce bias and support country-level analyses of explanatory variables:

1. *IRT scaling:* Estimation of IRT-based common and unique item parameters (slopes and difficulties) for dichotomous and polytomous items using the 2PLM and GPCM as described in the section above.
2. *Contrast coding* of the BQ items, by contrasting each level as well as a code for missing (omitted) and routed (skipped by design) responses for each variable, creating a very large number of contrast-coded variables.
3. *Principal component analyses* of the contrast-coded variables to reduce the number of variables needed in the model and to remove collinearity. Principal components were extracted, explaining 80% of the variance represented by the background questions to avoid overparameterisation. The use of principal components also served to incorporate information from examinees with missing responses to one or more background variables. Note that the principal component analysis was conducted separately for each country based on international variables (collected by every participating country) as well as national background variables (country-specific variables in addition to the international variables).
4. *Latent regression analysis* with IRT item parameter estimates (X) treated as fixed values and the principal components of the BQ variables as predictors (Y) for estimating the latent regression parameters Γ (regression coefficients)

and $\sum$ (residual variance–covariance matrix). Note that latent regression models are estimated separately for each country to take into account the differences in associations between the background variables and the cognitive skills. The regression model for each country consisted of two steps:

(a) First, the model was estimated on a dataset that excluded cases with fewer than five responses to cognitive items to estimate the regression parameters (Γ and $\sum$).
(b) Second, the model was applied to the full dataset, including cases with fewer than five responses to cognitive items but with the regression parameters (Γ and $\sum$) fixed to the values obtained in the first step.

This ensured that the population model was calculated based on cases that included a reasonable amount of information in the domain of interest, avoiding the potential bias from poorly measured cases, while at the same time being able to then calculate scores for all respondents, regardless of the amount of cognitive information collected.

5. *Plausible values* (PVs) are randomly drawn from the resulting posterior distribution for all sampled respondents in a three-step process described below. A total of ten plausible values are independently drawn for each respondent per cognitive domain. Note that paper-based respondents have PVs only for the literacy and numeracy domains that were administered to them (i.e. paper-based respondent did not receive any PS-TRE items and hence did not receive PVs for PS-TRE). Also note that respondents with an insufficient amount of background information (i.e. less than five BQ items) did not receive PVs. The PVs that were made available in the public use file (PUF) can be used in secondary analyses of the PIAAC data.

3.2.3.1 Software

The software DGROUP (Rogers et al. 2006) was used to estimate the latent regression model and generate plausible values. In PIAAC, a multidimensional variant of the latent regression model was used that is based on Laplace approximation (Thomas 1993).

3.3 Analyses with Plausible Values

As outlined above, PVs are based on a latent regression model that was specifically designed to estimate population characteristics. They should never be used to draw inferences at the individual level, as they are not a substitute for test scores for individuals. When the underlying population model is correctly specified, PVs will provide consistent estimates of population characteristics, even though they are not generally unbiased estimates of the proficiencies of individuals (von Davier et al.

2009). Moreover, if PVs are correctly used in statistical analyses, the accuracy of derived test statistics enables fair and meaningful group-level inferences. In the following, we explain how PVs are used properly.

First, it is important to remember that the proficiency values θ for the cognitive domains cannot be directly observed and that latent variable (IRT) models had to be used to make inferences about these latent variables. Hence, we follow the approach taken by Rubin (1987) and treat the latent variable θ as missing information. Any statistic $t(\theta,y)$, for example, a scale or composite subpopulation sample mean, is approximated by its expectation given the observed data (x,y):

$$t^*\left(\overline{x},\overline{y}\right) = E\left[t\left(\overline{\theta},\overline{y}\right)|\overline{x},\overline{y}\right] = \int t\left(\overline{\theta},\overline{y}\right) p\left(\overline{\theta}|\overline{x},\overline{y}\right) d\theta \qquad (3.12)$$

It is possible to approximate t^* using PVs instead of the unobserved θ values. For any respondent, the value of θ used in the computation of t is replaced by a PV.

Second, Rubin (1987) argued that this process should be repeated several times so that the uncertainty associated with the imputation can be quantified. For example, the average of multiple estimates of t, each computed from a different set of PVs, is a numerical approximation of t^* in the above equation; the variance among them reflects uncertainty due to not observing θ. It should be noted that this variance does not include any variability due to sampling from the population. This sampling variance is another important component of the total error variance of any statistic calculated in surveys.

To obtain a variance estimate for the proficiency means of each country and other statistics of interest, a replication approach (see, e.g. Johnson 1989; Johnson and Rust 1992) was used to estimate the sampling variability as well as the imputation variance associated with the plausible values. Variance estimates are crucial in the comparison of proficiencies across groups. In surveys such as PIAAC, several variance components are integrated into the estimate of variances, for example, the variance of the mean of literacy in a country.

The correct use of PVs to compute any statistics for an arbitrary function T and the computation of the different variance components are described in the following:

1. Calculate the statistic of interest using the first PV (i.e. the vector of the first PV across respondents). Call this T_1.
2. Calculate the sampling variance of T_1. Call this $SVar(T_1)$.
3. Repeat steps 1 and 2 for each of the remaining PVs obtaining T_2 through T_{10}, and $SVar(T_2)$ through $SVar(T_{10})$, thus obtaining T_u and $SVar_u$ for $u = 1, \ldots, 10$.
4. The statistic of interest, or T, would be the average of T_1 to T_{10}:

$$T = \frac{\sum_{u=1}^{10} T_u}{10} \qquad (3.13)$$

5. The sampling variance of T is the average of $SVar(T_1)$ to $SVar(T_{10})$:

$$SVar(T) = \frac{\sum_{u=1}^{10} SVar_u}{10} \qquad (3.14)$$

This sampling variance reflects uncertainty due to sampling from the population (i.e. the selection of a subset of respondents from the total population). This is potentially the largest contributor to the uncertainty of the estimated statistic.

6. The imputation variance is $Var(T_1$ to $T_{10}) * (11/10)$:

$$Var(T) = \frac{\sum_{u=1}^{10}(T_u - T)^2}{10-1}\left(\frac{11}{10}\right) \qquad (3.15)$$

This imputation variance is related to the lack of precision of the measurement instrument and reflects uncertainty because the respondents' proficiencies θ are only indirectly observed through x and y. This variance component is captured (approximately) by the variability of the PVs.

7. The overall error variance of T is sampling variance + imputation variance. An example of partitioning the error variance in the two error components (i.e. sampling and measurement error) is provided in the PIAAC Technical Report (Yamamoto et al. 2013, Chap. 17). The standard errors, or the square root of the overall error variance of the statistic T, can be used to evaluate the magnitude of the statistic. This error variance plays an important role in interpreting subpopulation results and in comparing the performances of two or more subpopulations or countries.

3.3.1 Software Tools

Different software tools based on STATA, R, SPSS, or SAS are available for utilising PVs in analysis using the procedures described above. They will be introduced and illustrated on practical examples in other chapters in this volume.

3.4 Why Plausible Values Should Be Used for Secondary Data Analyses

Plausible values (PVs) are multiple imputed proficiency values obtained from a latent regression or population model. PVs are used to obtain more accurate estimates of group-level proficiency than would be obtained through an aggregation of point estimates (Mislevy 1991; Mislevy and Sheehan 1987; Thomas 2002; von Davier et al. 2006, 2009). The aim is to reduce uncertainty and measurement error for quantities used in the analyses of large-scale surveys aiming at valid group-level comparisons rather than optimal point estimates for individual test-takers. In contrast to tests that are concerned with the measurement of skills of individuals (e.g. for the purposes of diagnosis or selection and placement), PIAAC aims to provide group-level test scores to describe populations and subpopulations. Usually, the amount of measurement error can be reduced by increasing the number of items for each individual. However, PIAAC uses matrix sampling as well as MST for the test design, resulting in the test-taker responding to a subset of items only. The reasons for this design are described in more detail in Chap. 2 of this volume. Thus, the survey solicits relatively few responses from each respondent while maintaining a wide range of representation of the constructs when responses are aggregated. In other words, the PIAAC test design facilitates the estimation of population characteristics more efficiently, while the individual measurement accuracy is reduced.

The IRT scaling in PIAAC solves the problem of the comparability of groups responding to different set of items by placing both the items and the proficiencies on the same scale. Point estimates of the proficiencies obtained from the IRT scaling could lead to seriously biased estimates of population characteristics due to the uncertainty in the measurement (Wingersky et al. 1987). Therefore, PIAAC provides PVs obtained from the latent regression model, thereby ensuring that the group-level effects are properly controlled for in the regression, thus eliminating this bias in group-level comparisons while reducing measurement error.

3.4.1 An Example Using Plausible Values and Background Data

We will use a simulated dataset to exemplify the limitations encountered when aggregating individual 'scores' for reporting group-level results and the advantages of using an approach as described in this chapter where IRT is implemented in combination with population modelling to obtain PVs. We will also illustrate some of the risks incurred when not using the PVs properly.

The advantage of using a simulated dataset is that we know the exact values (the 'truth') on which we based our simulation, and therefore we can test whether our proposed methods give us the right results.

For our example, we generated data from nine different hypothetical proficiency groups, each responding to different sets and combinations of a total of 56 items. We chose 56 items, as this is the number of items in the PIAAC numeracy domain. The 56 items were grouped into seven blocks or subsets of eight items each. Each item is included in one, and only one, of the subsets. We chose the seven subsets with eight items each, as this would allow us to experiment with the amount of items that each individual would be asked to respond to, similar to the design implemented in PIAAC, even if not exactly the same.

Table 3.1 above shows descriptive statistics for the item discrimination and difficulty of the simulated item pool. The statistics are presented overall and block

Table 3.1 Descriptive statistics of item parameters used in the simulation

	Discrimination			Difficulty		
Block	Average	Minimum	Maximum	Average	Minimum	Maximum
A	1.19	0.57	1.50	−0.13	−1.72	1.51
B	0.94	0.50	1.47	−0.63	−1.72	0.22
C	1.09	0.76	1.39	0.22	−1.51	1.94
D	0.90	0.55	1.38	0.05	−1.71	1.45
E	1.00	0.68	1.44	0.12	−1.98	1.72
F	0.70	0.56	0.91	−0.69	−1.79	1.86
G	1.05	0.53	1.43	0.56	−0.68	1.74
Overall	0.98	0.50	1.50	−0.07	−1.98	1.94

Table 3.2 Descriptive statistics of the simulated samples

Group	Mean	Standard deviation	Number of blocks							
			0	1	2	3	4	5	6	7
1	1.02	0.76	760	2036	2103	1977	2049	2095	1946	2034
2	0.75	0.76	724	2080	2042	2067	1942	2023	2065	2057
3	0.50	0.75	745	2022	2015	2058	2029	2031	2029	2071
4	0.26	0.75	737	2036	2055	2024	2030	2035	2085	1998
5	0.01	0.76	716	2122	2026	2055	1957	2032	2028	2064
6	−0.26	0.76	797	2069	1987	2077	1970	1930	2148	2022
7	−0.51	0.75	678	2041	2053	2030	2038	2016	2052	2092
8	−0.76	0.76	752	1988	2052	2080	2037	2007	2011	2073
9	−1.01	0.75	725	2035	2042	2019	2052	2097	2007	2023

by block. While these are not exactly the item parameters of the numeracy item pool, they resemble them closely enough for the purposes of this simulation.

The nine simulated proficiency groups ranged in average 'true' ability between −1.01 and 1.02, each with a standard deviation of 0.75–0.76. They go from a high average proficiency group (Group 1) to a low average proficiency group (Group 9), with Groups 4, 5, and 6 being of about average proficiency.

In total, we generated 15,000 respondents for each one of these proficiency groups, and each of these respondents was simulated to respond to all items, or a subset of 6, 5, 4, 3, 2, or 1 block of eight items each. To further test the strength of the statistical model described in this chapter, we deleted the responses for about 5% of the cases in the simulated sample. This was done to test what would happen if we used these models to estimate the ability of groups of respondents who did not respond to any of the items in the assessment, and all we knew was their group membership.

Table 3.2 above shows descriptive statistics (mean and standard deviation) for each of the subgroups and the number of cases that responded to a particular number of blocks from the simulated assessments.

We then calculated item parameters using the combined simulated sample of 135,000 cases. The items were calibrated using Parscale Version 4.1 (Muraki and

Bock 1997), and these item parameters were used to assign scores to each of the respondents using the following methods:

(a) Expected a posteriori (EAP)
(b) Maximum likelihood estimates (MLE)
(c) Warm's maximum likelihood estimates (WML)
(d) Plausible values taking into account group membership (PV1)
(e) Taking the average of ten plausible values (PVA)

Please note that PVA scores are not (!) recommended, and they are shown in this simulation to illustrate their deficiency as a group-level score. The EAP, MLE, and WML scores were computed using Parscale Version 4.1. The PVs were computed using Dgroup (Rogers et al. 2006). The syntax for Dgroup was generated using the windows interface DESI (Gladkova et al. 2006). Notice also that for the purpose of this example, we will use only the first plausible value, although the proper way to work with these is to compute the statistics with each of these and report the average of these statistics, and the variance associated with them, as is explained later in this chapter.

The results of the simulation by proficiency group are presented in Table 3.3. In particular, notice in the panel where means are presented. While we are able to reproduce relatively well the group means using the MLE, WML, PV1, and PVA scores, the mean of the EAP scores show a consistent regression towards the overall mean. Notice also in the panel where the standard deviations are shown for the different groups that the PV1 consistently reproduces the standard deviation of the generating scores, whereas the EAP and PVA consistently underestimates them, and the MLE and WML consistently overestimated them.

The results from the simulation by number of blocks taken (each block consisting of eight items) are presented in Table 3.4. Notice in the means panel that we are not able to estimate the means using the EAP, MLE, or WML scores for those who did not take any items. However, the average overall score is reproduced with the PV1 and consequently the PVA scores. Then, looking at standard deviation panel, we see that the EAP and PVA underestimate the standard deviation as we use fewer

Table 3.3 Summary statistics of estimated means and standard deviations by proficiency group

	Means						Standard deviation					
Group	Theta	EAP	MLE	WML	PV1	PVA	Theta	EAP	MLE	WML	PV1	PVA
1	1.02	0.89	1.00	1.01	1.02	1.02	0.76	0.72	0.85	0.85	0.75	0.66
2	0.75	0.65	0.73	0.73	0.74	0.74	0.76	0.73	0.85	0.85	0.76	0.67
3	0.50	0.44	0.49	0.49	0.50	0.50	0.75	0.74	0.85	0.85	0.76	0.67
4	0.26	0.24	0.26	0.26	0.26	0.26	0.75	0.74	0.83	0.83	0.76	0.67
5	0.01	0.01	0.01	0.00	0.00	0.00	0.76	0.75	0.85	0.84	0.76	0.68
6	−0.26	−0.22	−0.24	−0.24	−0.25	−0.25	0.76	0.74	0.84	0.84	0.75	0.67
7	−0.51	−0.45	−0.50	−0.51	−0.51	−0.51	0.75	0.74	0.84	0.84	0.75	0.67
8	−0.76	−0.68	−0.74	−0.76	−0.77	−0.76	0.76	0.75	0.85	0.85	0.76	0.67
9	−1.01	−0.89	−0.98	−1.00	−1.02	−1.01	0.75	0.73	0.83	0.83	0.75	0.67

Table 3.4 Summary statistics of estimated means and standard deviations by number of blocks

Number of blocks	Means						Standard deviation					
	Theta	EAP	MLE	WML	PV1	PVA	Theta	EAP	MLE	WML	PV1	PVA
0	0.00				−0.01	0.00	0.99				1.00	0.69
1	0.00	0.00	0.00	0.00	0.00	0.00	1.00	0.83	1.05	1.13	1.00	0.87
2	−0.01	0.00	0.00	−0.01	0.00	0.00	1.01	0.91	1.08	1.09	1.01	0.93
3	0.00	0.00	0.00	0.00	0.00	0.00	1.00	0.93	1.06	1.05	0.99	0.94
4	0.00	0.00	0.01	0.00	0.00	0.00	1.01	0.97	1.07	1.06	1.01	0.97
5	−0.01	−0.01	−0.01	−0.01	−0.01	−0.01	1.01	0.97	1.06	1.05	1.01	0.97
6	0.00	0.01	0.01	0.01	0.01	0.01	0.99	0.96	1.04	1.02	0.99	0.96
7	0.00	0.00	0.00	0.00	0.00	0.00	0.99	0.97	1.04	1.02	0.99	0.97

items, and even if all 56 items are used, the standard deviation is underestimated. On the other hand, the MLE and WML scores consistently overestimate the standard deviation. The only score type that estimates the means and standard deviations consistently, regardless of the number of items used in the estimation, is the PV1 score.

As can be seen from the tables presented above, we are able to reliably reproduce the mean and standard deviation for groups of different abilities, regardless of the proficiency level with respect to the average item difficulty, and also regardless of the number of items that are administered, to the extreme of being able to estimate the mean and standard deviation of the proficiency even in the case when no items are administered, and all we know is the group membership of the respondent.

3.5 Summary and Outlook

PIAAC uses a latent regression model to estimate plausible values (PVs) by incorporating item responses and background data. These can be used by researchers, policymakers, and stakeholders to conduct research in the area of adult competencies (including literacy, numeracy, and problem solving in technology-rich environments) and their relation to economy and society. The latent regression model uses item parameters of test items obtained from IRT scaling as fixed values and background variables obtained using a principal component analysis of contrast-coded background questionnaire items as predictors.

PVs are multiple imputations that are randomly drawn from the posterior proficiency distribution resulting from this modelling approach and are designed to facilitate comparisons at the group level to describe population and group-level characteristics. They should never be used to draw inferences at the individual level. PIAAC provides ten plausible values for each cognitive domain for all respondents with sufficient background information (i.e. responses to five or more BQ items). PVs provide less biased and more accurate measures than point estimates can for group-level comparisons and allow consistent estimates of population characteristics. If used correctly in statistical analyses as described above, they provide fair and meaningful results and subgroup comparisons and allow variance estimation accounting for measurement and sampling error.

In the first cycle of PIAAC, the latent regression model is based on item parameters and background variables only. However, the modelling approach can be improved in future cycles by including process or logfile data, such as response times and the number and sequence of actions (mouse clicks and interactions of the respondent with the test item), which are available in the computer-based assessment branch (e.g. Shin et al. 2018). Especially, since future PIAAC cycles will likely move the current paper-based assessment branch to a tablet administration mode (at least for the majority of test-takers), process data will be available for even more respondents. Moreover, more simulation-based tasks might be developed to better assess life-relevant skills and new aspects of the PIAAC framework (such as adaptive problem solving in the second cycle of PIAAC). Including additional process data information into the latent regression model may further decrease the bias related to measurement error and increase the accuracy of PVs (von Davier et al. 2019), especially at the extreme ends of the proficiency scale and for lower-performing countries and subgroups (Shin et al. 2018). However, the option of including additional variables in the already extensive latent regression model is challenged by the problem of overparameterisation and requires careful considerations and additional research before being considered for operational procedures (von Davier et al. 2019).

References

Birnbaum, A. (1968). Some latent trait models and their use in inferring an examinee's ability. In F. M. Lord & M. R. Novick (Eds.), *Statistical theories of mental test scores*. Reading: Addison-Wesley.

Dempster, A. P., Laird, N. M., & Rubin, D. B. (1997). Maximum likelihood from incomplete data via the EM algorithm. *Journal of the Royal Statistical Society: Series B (Methodological), 39*, 1–38.

Gladkova, L., Moran, R., & Blew, T. (2006). *Direct Estimation Software Interactive (DESI) – Manual*. Princeton: Educational Testing Service.

Glas, C. A. W., & Jehangir, K. (2014). Modeling country specific differential item functioning. In L. Rutkowski, M. von Davier, & D. Rutkowski (Eds.), *Handbook of international large-scale assessment*. Boca Raton: CRC Press.

Glas, C. A. W., & Verhelst, N. D. (1995). Testing the Rasch model. In G. H. Fischer & I. W. Molenaar (Eds.), *Rasch models: Foundations, recent developments, and applications* (pp. 69–95). New York: Springer.

Johnson, E. G. (1989). Considerations and techniques for the analysis of NAEP data. *Journal of Educational Statistics, 14*(4), 303–334. https://doi.org/10.3102/10769986014004303

Johnson, E. G., & Rust, K. F. (1992). Population inferences and variance estimation for NAEP data. *Journal of Educational Statistics, 17*, 175–190. https://doi.org/10.2307/1165168

Mislevy, R. J. (1985). Estimation of latent group effects. *Journal of the American Statistical Association, 80*(392), 993–997.

Mislevy, R. J. (1991). Randomization-based inference about latent variables from complex samples. *Psychometrika, 56*(2), 177–196. https://doi.org/10.1007/BF02294457

Mislevy, R. J., & Sheehan, K. M. (1987). Marginal estimation procedures. In A. E. Beaton (Ed.), *Implementing the new design: The NAEP 1983-84 technical report* (Report No. 15-TR-20). Princeton: Educational Testing Service.

Muraki, E. (1992). A generalized partial credit model: Application of an EM algorithm. *Applied Psychological Measurement, 16*(2), 159–177. https://doi.org/10.1177/014662169201600206

Muraki, E., & Bock, R. D. (1997). *PARSCALE: IRT item analysis and test scoring for rating-scale data [Computer software]*. Chicago: Scientific Software.

Oliveri, M. E., & von Davier, M. (2011). Investigation of model fit and score scale comparability in international assessments. *Psychological Test and Assessment Modeling, 53*(3), 315–333. Retrieved from http://www.psychologie-aktuell.com/fileadmin/download/ptam/3-2011_20110927/04_Oliveri.pdf

Oliveri, M. E., & von Davier, M. (2014). Toward increasing fairness in score scale calibrations employed in international large-scale assessments. *International Journal of Testing, 14*(1), 1–21. https://doi.org/10.1080/15305058.2013.825265

Rogers, A., Tang, C., Lin, M.-J., & Kandathil, M. (2006). *DGROUP (computer software)*. Princeton: Educational Testing Service.

Rubin, D. B. (1987). *Multiple imputation for nonresponse in surveys*. New York: Wiley.

Rutkowski, L., von Davier, M., & Rutkowski, D. (Eds.). (2014). *Handbook of international large-scale assessment: Background, technical issues, and methods of data analysis*. Boca Raton: CRC Press.

Setzer, J. C., & Allspach, J. R. (2007, October). *Studying the effect of rapid guessing on a low-stakes test: An application of the effort-moderated IRT model*. Paper presented at the annual meeting of the Northeastern Educational Research Association, Rocky Hill. http://www.psyc.jmu.edu/assessment/research/pdfs/SetzerAllspach_NERA07.pdf

Shin, H. J., Khorramdel, L., von Davier, M., Robin, F., Yamamoto, K. (2018). *Incorporating response time into population modeling for large-scale assessments*. Paper presented at the conference of the International Test Commission (ITC), Montreal, 2.–5. July 2018.

Thomas, N. (1993). Asymptotic corrections for multivariate posterior moments with factored likelihood functions. *Journal of Computational and Graphical Statistics, 2*, 309–322. https://doi.org/10.1080/10618600.1993.10474614

Thomas, N. (2002). The role of secondary covariates when estimating latent trait population distributions. *Psychometrika, 67*(1), 33–48. https://doi.org/10.1007/BF02294708

Van der Linden, W. J., & Hambleton, R. K. (2016). *Handbook of modern item response theory* (2nd ed.). New York: Springer.

Von Davier, M. (2005). *A general diagnostic model applied to language testing data* (Research Report No. RR-05-16). Princeton: Educational Testing Service.

Von Davier, M., Gonzalez, E., & Mislevy, R. (2009). What are plausible values and why are they useful? In *IERI monograph series: Issues and methodologies in large scale assessments, Vol. 2*. Retrieved from IERI website: http://www.ierinstitute.org/IERI_Monograph_Volume_02_Chapter_01.pdf

Von Davier, M., Khorramdel, L., He, Q., Shin, H., & Chen, H. (2019). Developments in psychometric population models for technology-based large-scale assessments: An overview of challenges and opportunities. *Journal of Educational and Behavioral Statistics, 44*(6), 671–705. https://doi.org/10.3102/1076998619881789

Von Davier, M., Sinharay, S., Oranje, A., & Beaton, A. (2006). Statistical procedures used in the National Assessment of Educational Progress (NAEP): Recent developments and future directions. In C. R. Rao & S. Sinharay (Eds.), *Handbook of statistics (Vol. 26): Psychometrics* (pp. 1039–1056). Amsterdam: Elsevier.

Wingersky, M., Kaplan, B., & Beaton, A. E. (1987). Joint estimation procedures. In A. E. Beaton (Ed.), *Implementing the new design: The NAEP 1983–84 technical report* (pp. 285–292). Princeton: ETS.

Wise, S. L., & DeMars, C. E. (2005). Low examinee effort in low-stakes assessment: Problems and potential solutions. *Educational Assessment, 10*(1), 1–17. https://doi.org/10.1207/s15326977ea1001_1

Wise, S. L., & Kong, X. (2005). Response time effort: A new measure of examinee motivation in computer-based tests. *Applied Measurement in Education, 18*, 163–183. https://doi.org/10.1207/s15324818ame1802_2

Yamamoto, K. (1997). A chapter: Scaling and scale linking. In *International Adult Literacy Survey technical report*. Ottawa: Statistics Canada.

Yamamoto, K., Khorramdel, L., & von Davier, M. (2013). Scaling PIAAC cognitive data. In OECD (Ed.), *Technical report of the survey of adult skills (PIAAC)* (pp. 406–438). Paris: OECD Publishing.

Open Access This chapter is licensed under the terms of the Creative Commons Attribution 4.0 International License (http://creativecommons.org/licenses/by/4.0/), which permits use, sharing, adaptation, distribution and reproduction in any medium or format, as long as you give appropriate credit to the original author(s) and the source, provide a link to the Creative Commons license and indicate if changes were made.

The images or other third party material in this chapter are included in the chapter's Creative Commons license, unless indicated otherwise in a credit line to the material. If material is not included in the chapter's Creative Commons license and your intended use is not permitted by statutory regulation or exceeds the permitted use, you will need to obtain permission directly from the copyright holder.

Chapter 4
Adult Cognitive and Non-cognitive Skills: An Overview of Existing PIAAC Data

Débora B. Maehler and Ingo Konradt

Abstract As of summer 2019, more than 60 PIAAC datasets from participating countries worldwide were available for research purposes. These datasets can be differentiated, for example, in terms of their accessibility, the extent of the information provided, the population group in focus, and the design of the underlying study. PIAAC Public Use Files, for instance, are freely available and are therefore highly anonymised, whereas PIAAC Scientific Use Files are available only for scientific research purposes and provide access to more detailed variables. The majority of the PIAAC data are available as public use files, but some participating countries (e.g. Germany and the United States) have also made several scientific use files or other extended file versions available to the research community. Some of the available PIAAC datasets focus on specific population groups—for example, the incarcerated adult population in the United States. Regarding the design of the underlying studies, most available datasets are cross-sectional, but some longitudinal data already exist (e.g. PIAAC-L in Germany). The present chapter provides an overview of the structure, accessibility, and use of the PIAAC datasets available worldwide.

4.1 Overview of PIAAC Data Available for Secondary Analysis

Based on the PIAAC data, diverse interdisciplinary questions—such as social inequality, competency and ageing issues, and the role of digitalisation—can be investigated in an internationally comparable way, thereby addressing genuine political demands. PIAAC data contain information about basic skills (literacy, numeracy, and problem solving in technology-rich environments) that are considered to be prerequisites for understanding specific domains of knowledge in a broad

---

D. B. Maehler (✉) · I. Konradt
GESIS – Leibniz Institute for the Social Sciences, Mannheim, Germany
e-mail: debora.maehler@gesis.org

© The Author(s) 2020
D. B. Maehler, B. Rammstedt (eds.), *Large-Scale Cognitive Assessment*,
Methodology of Educational Measurement and Assessment,
https://doi.org/10.1007/978-3-030-47515-4_4

range of contexts, from education through work to everyday life. Furthermore, the PIAAC data include a wide range of information on variables, such as social background, and engagement with literacy, numeracy, and information and communication technologies (ICTs) that influence the development and maintenance of skills. The data also include information on respondents' current activity, employment status and income, and generic skill use in the workplace (e.g. social skills, manual skills). In addition, PIAAC includes questions on health status, volunteering, political efficacy, and social trust (OECD 2014).

The number of publications that refer to PIAAC has increased strongly in recent years (for an overview, see Maehler et al. 2020). Questions addressed by these publications include, for example:

- To what extent does the educational attainment acquired through formal education predict literacy skills needed in daily life?
- What is the relationship between skills and labour market outcomes in terms of wages and employment chances?
- Who participates in further education, and why?
- How should the (forced) migrant population be covered in future surveys?
- How is test taking (dis)engagement related to cognitive ability or item difficulty?
- To what extent are non-cognitive skills (e.g. the Big Five) related to cognitive skills such as literacy?

The present chapter provides an overview of the PIAAC datasets available worldwide (see Table 4.1).[1] It differentiates the available datasets in terms of their accessibility, the extent of the information provided, the population group in focus, and the design of the underlying study. For example, PIAAC Public Use Files are accessible mainly for public purposes and are therefore highly anonymised, whereas PIAAC Scientific Use Files and Restricted Use Files provide access to more detailed variables and are available only for scientific research purposes after signing a data use agreement, as they may contain individually identifiable information that is confidential and protected by law. By contrast, public use files are freely available and integrated in data analysis web tools (see Chaps. 5 and 6 in this volume), which take the complex study design into account and allow international comparisons to be made without advanced knowledge of statistical programmes. Scientific use files are provided mainly by the statistics centres or research data centres of the respective countries. For data protection reasons, access to scientific use files is subject to the conclusion of a data use agreement, and sophisticated statistical knowledge is required for their evaluation (see, e.g. Chaps. 7, 8, 9, and 10 in this volume). The present chapter also presents PIAAC datasets that focus on specific population groups—for example, the population of 66- to 80-year-olds in Germany (Friebe

---

[1] In March 2019, we wrote to all current and former PIAAC national project managers inquiring whether PIAAC datasets other than public use files were available to the scientific community. Hence, although we do not claim that the information provided here is exhaustive, we did make every effort to ensure that it is comprehensive.

et al. 2017) and the incarcerated adult population in the United States (Hogan et al. 2016a). Regarding the design of the underlying studies, although some longitudinal data exist, most available datasets are cross-sectional. All datasets reported in this chapter are listed in the reference list.

The most datasets presented in what follows can be merged using the respondent ID in order to perform cross-national analyses. When merging the datasets for the various countries, the variables SEQID and CNTRYID_E should be used as identifiers. Although SEQID is a unique identification key within each country dataset, it is not unique across countries. Thus, an identifier combining both variables must be created. Variable labels are identical throughout all PIAAC Public Use Files. Labels in the PIAAC Scientific Use Files (e.g. the German Scientific Use File) may differ in the case of variables that include country-specific information when categories are collapsed for data protection reasons (e.g. CNT_CITSHIP). Therefore, in order to avoid loss of information, care must be taken when merging datasets. The International Database (IDB) Analyzer can also be used to merge PIAAC datasets (see also Chap. 6 in this volume).

The datasets are presented in this chapter in the order in which they appear in the columns in Table 4.1, beginning with the public use files and ending with the description of the PIAAC datasets on non-cognitive skills. The datasets of the countries within the different dataset groups are presented in alphabetical order.

4.2 PIAAC Public Use Files

File Description The PIAAC Public Use Files contain information on the respondents' background and on their cognitive assessment (in literacy, numeracy, and problem solving in technology-rich environments).

Mode of Data Collection Face-to-face interview (computer-assisted personal interview, CAPI) to collect the background information; computer-based or paper-based assessment of skills in literacy, numeracy, and problem solving in technology-rich environments.

Sample Description and Size In each participating country, the sample comprised approximately 5000 adults aged 16–65 years.[2]

Format and Access The PIAAC Public Use Files (see OECD 2016d to OECD 2016gg; OECD 2019b to OECD 2019g)[3] containing individual unit record data are freely available and accessible for downloading in SAS, SPSS, and CSV format (https://www.oecd.org/skills/piaac/data/) for each of the countries that participated

---

[2] Some countries have fewer participants, and some countries (e.g. Canada, with 27,285 participants) have an oversample.

[3] Data for Indonesia are not available; however, results for that country are presented in the international report for the second round of PIAAC (OECD 2016a).

Table 4.1 PIAAC datasets by country and year of assessment

Country	Year of assessment (first cycle)	Public use files (PUF)	PIAAC Log Files	Extended PIAAC data file versions (e.g. SUF or RUF)	PIAAC data files for specific population groups	Linking PIAAC data files to administrative data	Longitudinal PIAAC data files	Linking PIAAC data files to other large-scale assessments	PIAAC data files on non-cognitive skills
Australia	2011–2012	x							
Austria	2011–2012	x	x	x					
Belgium[a]	2011–2012	x	x						
Canada	2011–2012	x		x		x[d]	(x)[c,d]		
Chile	2014–2015	x							
Cyprus	2011–2012	x							
Czech Republic	2011–2012	x							
Denmark	2011–2012	x	x			x[d,e]			
Ecuador	2017	x							
Estonia	2011–2012	x	x			x[e]			
Finland	2011–2012	x	x			x[e]			
France	2011–2012	x	x						x
Germany	2011–2012	x	x	x	x	x[f]	x		x
Greece	2014–2015	x							
Hungary	2017	x							
Indonesia	2014–2015	x							
Ireland	2011–2012	x	x						
Israel	2014–2015	x							
Italy	2011–2012	x	x	x			x[c]		
Japan	2011–2012	x							x

4 Adult Cognitive and Non-cognitive Skills: An Overview of Existing PIAAC Data

Kazakhstan	2017	x			
Korea	2011–2012	x	x		
Lithuania	2014–2015	x			
Mexico	2017	x			
Netherlands	2011–2012	x	x		
New Zealand	2014–2015	x			
Norway	2011–2012	x	x	$x^{d,e}$	
Peru	2017	x			x
Poland	2011–2012	x		$x^{c,d}$	
Russian Federation	2011–2012	x			
Singapore	2014–2015	x			
Slovak Republic	2011–2012	x			
Slovenia	2014–2015	x			
Spain	2011–2012	x			x
Sweden	2011–2012	x	$(x)^g$	$x^{d,e,g}$	
Turkey	2014–2015	x			
United Kingdom[b]	2011–2012	x			x
United States	2011–2014; 2017	x	x^d	x	x

Notes. Bracket: respective data will be described in Sect. 4.6
SUF Scientific Use File, *RUF* Restricted Use File
[a] Only Flanders
[b] Only England and Northern Ireland
[c] Without a repeated measurement of skills
[d] Data provided only for researchers within the country
[e] Data provided only for researchers within the Nordic Network
[f] Data provided so far only for researchers within the pilot project described in Chap. 11
[g] Data provided for researchers within the country, the Nordic Network and the EU/EEA

in the Survey of Adult Skills in 2011–2012 (Round 1 of the first cycle: 24 countries), 2014–2015 (Round 2 of the first cycle: nine countries), and 2017 (Round 3 of the first cycle: six countries). A do-file to import CSV into Stata is also available.

The Australian PIAAC Public Use File is not available on the OECD website. However, researchers can apply to the Australian Bureau of Statistics for data access[4],[5] or use the International Data Explorer to analyse the Australian data (see Chap. 5 in this volume).

The Cypriot PIAAC Public Use File (Michaelidou-Evripidou et al. 2016) is available for downloading in SPSS and Stata format at the GESIS Data Archive.[6] The US PIAAC Public Use File (Holtzman et al. 2014a) is also downloadable in SPSS, SAS, and ASCII format at the National Center for Education Statistics.[7] The Canadian PIAAC Public Use File (Canadian Public Use Microdata File/PUMF)[8] is also provided by Statistics Canada.[9]

For cross-national analyses, the public use files can be merged using the respondent ID. The International Database (IDB) Analyzer can also be used to merge the PIAAC datasets (see Chap. 6 in this volume).

Documentation Information on the methodology, design, and implementation of PIAAC can be found in the technical reports on the study (OECD 2014, 2016a; see also Chap. 2 in this volume) and in the results reports (OECD 2013, 2016b, c). An international master questionnaire is available for downloading at the OECD PIAAC Data and Tools webpage.[10] The questionnaires in the country-specific languages are also available on that webpage, as are an international codebook and a derived variables codebook.

4.3 PIAAC Log Files

File Description The log files from the PIAAC study provide information on how participants processed their answers (OECD 2019a). During the PIAAC assessment 2011–2012 (Round 1 of the first cycle), user interactions with the computer were logged automatically. This means that respondents' actions (e.g. starting a unit, opening a webpage, entering an answer) within the assessment tool were recorded and stored with time stamps in separate log files. These log files contain paradata

---

[4]Current email address: microdata.access[at]abs[dot]gov[dot]au
[5]See also: https://www.abs.gov.au/websitedbs/D3310114.nsf/home/How+to+Apply+for+Microdata
[6]See https://doi.org/10.4232/1.12632
[7]https://nces.ed.gov/pubsearch/pubsinfo.asp?pubid=2014045REV
[8]See also http://www.piaac.ca/597/PUBLIC_USE_FILES.html
[9]Contact: STATCAN.infostats-infostats.STATCAN@canada.ca
[10]http://www.oecd.org/skills/piaac/data/

for each participant in the domains of literacy, numeracy, and/or problem solving in technology-rich environments. More information on the log files and their analysis is available in Chap. 10 of this volume.

Sample Description and Size PIAAC log file data are available for 17 countries that participated in Round 1 of the PIAAC study (see Table 4.1). The sample in each participating country comprised approximately 5000 adults aged 16–65 years.

Format and Access The log data from the PIAAC cognitive assessments are available as public use files (see OECD 2017a to OECD 2017q) and can be downloaded free of charge from the GESIS Data Archive[11] after registering on the corresponding webpage. The PIAAC log files are provided in their raw XML format. The files usually contain the complete log data for individual respondents. However, information that could potentially identify an individual respondent has been removed. The data can be matched with corresponding background and cognitive response data available in the PIAAC Public Use Files using the SEQID variable.

To help researchers to analyse log data, a customised analysis tool—the PIAAC LogDataAnalyzer—is available (access currently here: http://piaac-logdata.tba-hosting.de/download/). The tool includes functions such as data extraction, data cleaning, and the visualisation of the log data files. The tool can be used for some data analysis tasks as well as for the export of selected data to data files that can be used by other tools. Users can select variables for export. When doing so, predefined variables can be generated, for example: 'Number of using cancel button'; 'Time on task'; and 'Number of page visits'.

Documentation Information on the methodology, design, and implementation of PIAAC can be found in the technical reports on the study (OECD 2014, 2016a; see also Chap. 2 in this volume) and in the results reports (OECD 2013, 2016b, c). An overview of process data recorded in log files in the PIAAC study and how to use them can be found in OECD (2019a), in Chap. 10 of the present volume, and on the PIAAC Log Data Documentation webpage[12]. The aforementioned webpage provides, inter alia, information on released items, an overview of the interactions that are possible with the items, the corresponding log events, and the booklet order of the domains of cognitive assessment.

The documentation regarding released items is available for all users. Depending on the research question, the full documentation with information about non-released items may be required. As the full documentation contains information regarding non-released items, individuals who wish to obtain access must apply to the OECD and sign a confidentiality agreement.[13] The completed application form and the signed confidentiality agreement must be sent to the contact officer at the

---

[11] https://doi.org/10.4232/1.12955

[12] https://piaac-logdata.tba-hosting.de/

[13] https://www.oecd.org/skills/piaac/data/piaaclogfiles

OECD[14]. If the application is approved, the user will be provided with a username and password that will grant access to the full documentation online.

4.4 Extended PIAAC Data File Versions

This section describes extended national datasets that are available for Austria, Canada, Germany, Italy, New Zealand, and the United States. They contain additional information (e.g. some of the national adaptations) and/or more detailed information (e.g. age or income).

Extended data files are also available for Norway (see Norwegian Center for Research Data)[15] and Sweden (see Statistics Sweden).[16] However, rules of use in these countries are more restrictive (permitted only for researchers within the country), and information is available only in the language of the respective country. As the Norwegian and Swedish PIAAC data can be linked to administrative information, the datasets will be presented in Sect. 4.6 on the linking of PIAAC data to administrative data.

4.4.1 Austria

4.4.1.1 Extended PIAAC Public Use File for Austria

File Description The Austrian PIAAC Public Use File (OECD 2016d) contains information on the respondents' background and on their cognitive assessment (in literacy, numeracy, and problem solving in technology-rich environments). The Extended PIAAC Public Use File for Austria contains additional national education variables.

Mode of Data Collection Face-to-face interview (computer-assisted personal interview, CAPI) to collect the background information; computer-based or paper-based assessment of skills in literacy, numeracy, and problem solving in technology-rich environments.

Sample Description and Size The sample comprised 5130 adults aged 16–65 years.

Format and Access The dataset (Statistics Austria 2015) is available for downloading free of charge (in SPSS and Excel format) at Statistics Austria's website.[17] The Extended PIAAC Public Use File for Austria can be merged with the PIAAC

---

[14]edu[dot]piaac[at]oecd[dot]org
[15]https://nsd.no/nsd/english/index.html
[16]https://www.scb.se/en/
[17]http://www.statistik.at/web_en/statistics/

datasets of other participating countries in order to perform cross-national analyses. The International Database (IDB) Analyzer can be used to merge the PIAAC datasets (see Chap. 6 in this volume).

Documentation Information on the methodology, design, and implementation of PIAAC can be found in the technical reports on the study (OECD 2014, 2016a; see also Chap. 2 in the present volume) and in the results reports (OECD 2013, 2016b, c). The international master questionnaire, the international codebook, and a derived variables codebook are available on the OECD PIAAC Data and Tools webpage. A German version of the background questionnaire is available for downloading at Statistics Austria's website.[18]

4.4.1.2 Scientific Use File PIAAC 2011/2012 for Austria

File Description The Austrian PIAAC Public Use File (OECD 2016d) contains information on the respondents' background and on their cognitive assessment (in literacy, numeracy, and problem solving in technology-rich environments). It excludes certain background variables (e.g. some of the national adaptations), and some variables were not released in all the available detail. The majority of the variables were suppressed or coarsened to comply with national data protection legislation. The Austrian PIAAC Scientific Use File includes many of the suppressed background variables. Furthermore, other variables (e.g. age and income) have been released in full detail.

Mode of Data Collection Face-to-face interview (computer-assisted personal interview, CAPI) to collect the background information; computer-based or paper-based assessment of skills in literacy, numeracy, and problem solving in technology-rich environments.

Sample Description and Size The sample comprised 5130 adults aged 16–65 years.

Format and Access The dataset (Statistics Austria 2014) is available in SPSS format and is accessible for academic research only. Researchers must sign an individual data distribution contract (in English or German) provided at Statistics Austria's website[19]. The data distribution contract must be signed by the project leader; key information (e.g. title, description, and duration of project) about the project and the user(s) must be provided. The data are delivered free of charge. Users are expected to make publications resulting from the research available to the data provider. The Scientific Use File PIAAC 2011/2012 for Austria can be merged with the PIAAC datasets of other participating countries in order to perform cross-national analyses.

---

[18] http://www.statistik.at/web_de/statistiken/menschen_und_gesellschaft/bildung/piaac/piaac_2011_12_datensaetze_und_fragebogen/index.html

[19] http://www.statistik.at/web_en/statistics/

The International Database (IDB) Analyzer can also be used to merge the PIAAC datasets (see Chap. 6 in this volume).

Documentation Information on the methodology, design, and implementation of PIAAC can be found in the technical reports on the study (OECD 2014, 2016a; see also Chap. 2 in this volume) and in the results reports (OECD 2013, 2016b, c). The international master questionnaire, the international codebook, and a derived variables codebook are available on the OECD PIAAC Data and Tools webpage. A German version of the background questionnaire is available for downloading at Statistics Austria's website.[20]

4.4.2 Canada

4.4.2.1 Canadian Public Use Microdata File (PUMF)

File Description While the Canadian PIAAC Public Use File (OECD 2016f) contains information on the respondents' background and on their cognitive assessment (in literacy, numeracy, and problem solving in technology-rich environments), the Canadian PIAAC Public Use Microdata File (PUMF; Statistics Canada 2013) contains additional national variables (e.g. education).

Mode of Data Collection Face-to-face interview (computer-assisted personal interview, CAPI) to collect the background information; computer-based or paper-based assessment of skills in literacy, numeracy, and problem solving in technology-rich environments.

Sample Description and Size The sample comprised 26,683 adults aged 16–65 years.

Format and Access The dataset (Statistics Canada 2013)[21] can be ordered free of charge (in SPSS and Excel format) at Statistics Canada's website.[22] The PUMF can be merged with the PIAAC datasets of other participating countries in order to perform cross-national analyses. The International Database (IDB) Analyzer can be used to merge the PIAAC datasets (see Chap. 6 in this volume).

Documentation English-language and French-language information on the methodology, design, and implementation of PIAAC can be found on the Canadian PIAAC website (http://www.piaac.ca). Furthermore, general information on the methodology, design, and implementation of PIAAC can be found in the technical

---

[20]http://www.statistik.at/web_de/statistiken/menschen_und_gesellschaft/bildung/piaac/piaac_2011_12_datensaetze_und_fragebogen/index.html

[21]See also http://www.piaac.ca/597/PUBLIC_USE_FILES.html.

[22]https://www150.statcan.gc.ca/n1/en/catalogue/89-555-X2013002

reports on the study (OECD 2014, 2016a; see also Chap. 2 in this volume) and in the results reports (OECD 2013, 2016b, c). The PIAAC questionnaires (in English and French) can be downloaded at Statistics Canada's website.[23] The international master questionnaire, the international codebook, and a derived variables codebook are available on the OECD PIAAC Data and Tools webpage. Furthermore, a Canadian Data Dictionary is available at the Canadian PIAAC website.

4.4.3 Germany

4.4.3.1 PIAAC Germany Scientific Use File (SUF)

File Description The German PIAAC Public Use File (OECD 2016h) contains information on the respondents' background and on their cognitive assessment (in literacy, numeracy, and problem solving in technology-rich environments). It suppresses certain background variables (e.g. some of the national adaptations), and some of the included variables have not been released in all available detail. Background variables were suppressed or coarsened to comply with national data protection legislation. The German PIAAC Scientific Use File includes many of these suppressed variables and releases other variables in full detail (e.g. age and income).

Mode of Data Collection Face-to-face interview (computer-assisted personal interview, CAPI) to collect the background information; computer-based or paper-based assessment of skills in literacy, numeracy, and problem solving in technology-rich environments.

Sample Description and Size The sample comprised 5465 adults aged 16–65 years.

Format and Access The dataset (Rammstedt et al. 2016a) is available in SPSS and Stata format for academic research only, after signing a data distribution contract (in English or German).[24] The data distribution contract requires the provision of key information about the project (e.g. title, description, and duration) and the users. The data can be used only during the time period specified by the contract. Users are charged a processing fee. The PIAAC Germany Scientific Use File can be merged with the PIAAC datasets of other participating countries in order to perform cross-national analyses (the procedure is described by Perry et al. 2017). The International Database (IDB) Analyzer can also be used to merge the PIAAC datasets (see Chap. 6 in this volume).

Documentation Information on the methodology, design, and implementation of PIAAC in Germany can be found in the technical report on the study (Zabal et al.

---

[23] http://www23.statcan.gc.ca/imdb-bmdi/instrument/4406_Q1_V4_B.pdf

[24] https://www.gesis.org/en/piaac/rdc/data/national-scientific-use-files

2014) and in the results reports (OECD 2013; Rammstedt et al. 2013). The German background questionnaire is available in PDF format[25] and in HTML format.[26] A codebook in Excel format and a study description are available at the GESIS Data Archive.[27] Further documentation is also available on the PIAAC Research Data Center website.[28] Moreover, a User Guide (Perry et al. 2017) provides information necessary for conducting basic analyses using the corresponding PIAAC data.

4.4.3.2 PIAAC Germany Scientific Use File (SUF): Regional Data

File Description This dataset provides detailed regional information that was excluded from the regular German PIAAC Scientific Use File due to national data protection legislation. Additionally available indicators include, for example, municipality code, classified size of the political municipality, and number of the sample point.

Mode of Data Collection For the sample selection of the PIAAC study in Germany, the regional information was extracted from the official statistics of the Federal Statistical Office as of December 30, 2009 (Zabal et al. 2014).

Sample Description and Size The sample comprised 5465 adults aged 16–65 years.

Format and Access The dataset (Rammstedt et al. 2016b) is available in SPSS and Stata format and accessible for academic research only. For analyses, the data must be merged with the German PIAAC Scientific Use File (Rammstedt et al. 2016a) using the respondent ID. Use of these regional data is subject to special contractual provisions. Due to the sensitive nature of the data, special restrictions apply, and the data can be analysed only on-site at a guest workstation in the Safe Room at GESIS (contact: PIAAC Research Data Center).[29]

Documentation Information on the methodology, design, and implementation of PIAAC in Germany can be found in the technical report on the study (Zabal et al. 2014) and in the results reports (OECD 2013; Rammstedt et al. 2013). The German background questionnaire is available in PDF format[30] and in HTML format.[31] A codebook in Excel format and a study description are available at the GESIS Data

---

[25] https://dbk.gesis.org/dbksearch/download.asp?id=52598
[26] https://www.oecd.org/skills/piaac/data/Translated_HTML_de-DE.htm
[27] https://search.gesis.org/research_data/ZA5845
[28] https://www.gesis.org/en/piaac/rdc/data/national-scientific-use-files
[29] fdz-piaac(at)gesis(dot)org
[30] https://dbk.gesis.org/dbksearch/download.asp?id=52598
[31] https://www.oecd.org/skills/piaac/data/Translated_HTML_de-DE.htm

Archive.[32] Further documentation is also available on the PIAAC Research Data Center website.[33]

4.4.3.3 PIAAC Germany Scientific Use File (SUF): Microm Data

File Description The dataset contains contextual information that describes either the household or the neighbourhood of the respondents. This information was not included in the regular PIAAC Scientific Use File due to national data protection legislation. These spatial data are provided by microm Micromarketing-Systeme und Consult GmbH in Neuss, Germany.[34] The microm data available include more than 100 variables from the domains of sociodemographics and socio-economics, consumer behaviour, area and site planning, and strategic segmentation models. For example, variables contain information about the type of residential area, the number of private households and businesses, sociodemographic and socio-economic characteristics (e.g. unemployment, religious denominations, ethnic composition), mobility (e.g. population fluctuation), affinity towards fundraising, communications and print media, Sinus-Milieus®, and purchasing power at the level of street sections.

Mode of Data Collection The microm data are compiled from several cooperation partners, with a focus on market research (e.g. public opinion), financial data (e.g. credit institutions), or institutions working with digital or IT data (e.g. telephone companies). The PIAAC survey collects the background information by means of a face-to-face interview (computer-assisted personal interview, CAPI); the assessment of skills in literacy, numeracy, and problem solving in technology-rich environments is computer-based or paper-based.

Sample Description and Size The sample comprised 5465 adults aged 16–65 years.

Format and Access The dataset (Rammstedt et al. 2017a, b) is available in SPSS and Stata format and accessible for academic research only. For analyses, the data must be merged with the German PIAAC Scientific Use File (Rammstedt et al. 2016a) using the respondent ID. Use of this dataset is subject to special contractual provisions. Due to the sensitive nature of the data, special restrictions apply, and the data can be analysed only on-site at a guest workstation in the Safe Room at GESIS (contact: PIAAC Research Data Center).[35]

Documentation Information on the methodology, design, and implementation of PIAAC in Germany can be found in the technical report on the study (Zabal et al. 2014) and in the results reports (OECD 2013; Rammstedt et al. 2013). The German

---

[32] https://search.gesis.org/research_data/ZA5963
[33] https://www.gesis.org/en/piaac/rdc/data/national-scientific-use-files
[34] https://www.microm.de/
[35] fdz-piaac(at)gesis(dot)org

background questionnaire is available in PDF format[36] and in HTML format.[37] A codebook in Excel format and a study description are available at the GESIS Data Archive[38]. Further documentation is also available on the PIAAC Research Data Center website.[39]

4.4.4 Italy

4.4.4.1 PIAAC Italian Extended File

File Description For Italy, an Extended PIAAC Public Use File contains additional national variables on respondent's background—for example, regional information (macro region: North East, North West, Centre, South, Islands) and information on parents' occupation (e.g. according to ISCO-08).

Mode of Data Collection Face-to-face interview (computer-assisted personal interview, CAPI) to collect the background information; computer-based or paper-based assessment of skills in literacy, numeracy, and problem solving in technology-rich environments.

Sample Description and Size The sample comprised 4621 adults aged 16–65 years.

Format and Access The Italian PIAAC Public Use File – Extended (INAPP 2018) is usually provided in SPSS format. However, on specific request, the dataset can also be provided in SAS or Stata format. Researchers or other interested persons must sign an individual data distribution contract (in English or Italian) provided by the Istituto Nazionale per l'Analisi delle Politiche Pubbliche INAPP[40]. The agreement does not specify a data usage period. The data are provided free of charge. The Italian PIAAC Public Use File – Extended can be merged with the public use files of other participating countries in order to perform cross-national analyses. The International Database (IDB) Analyzer can be used to merge the PIAAC datasets (see Chap. 6 in this volume).

Documentation Information on the methodology, design, and implementation of PIAAC can be found in the technical reports on the study (OECD 2014, 2016a; see also Chap. 2 in this volume) and in the results reports (OECD 2013, 2016b, c). An Italian-language version of the background questionnaire is available for downloading at the INAPP website[41]. The questionnaire is also available on the

---

[36] https://dbk.gesis.org/dbksearch/download.asp?id=52598

[37] https://www.oecd.org/skills/piaac/data/Translated_HTML_de-DE.htm

[38] https://search.gesis.org/research_data/ZA5963

[39] https://www.gesis.org/en/piaac/rdc/data/national-scientific-use-files

[40] Current email address: serviziost(at)istico(dot)inapp(dot)org

[41] https://inapp.org/it/dati/piaac

OECD PIAAC Data and Tools webpage, as are an international codebook and a derived variables codebook.

4.4.5 New Zealand

4.4.5.1 PIAAC New Zealand Extended File

File Description The New Zealand PIAAC Public Use File (OECD 2016w) contains information on respondents' background and on their cognitive assessment (in literacy, numeracy, and problem solving in technology-rich environments). For New Zealand, an extended public use file is available with country-specific variables (e.g. education) and international variables (e.g. a continuous age variable) that were confidentialised or suppressed for the public use file version.

Mode of Data Collection Face-to-face interview (computer-assisted personal interview, CAPI) to collect the background information; computer-based or paper-based assessment of skills in literacy, numeracy, and problem solving in technology-rich environments.

Sample Description and Size The sample comprised 6177 adults aged 16–65 years. The sample design included screening for two subpopulations, 16- to 25-year-olds and persons of Māori ethnicity. This supports more in-depth analysis by providing additional samples for these subpopulations. The total achieved sample sizes for the subpopulations were 16- to 25-year-olds, $N = 1422$, and Māori, $N = 1146$.

Format and Access The extended New Zealand PIAAC Public Use File (Ministry of Education of New Zealand 2016) is provided in a range of formats (SPSS, Stata, and SAS) by the Government of New Zealand. The Ministry of Education makes this dataset available to researchers under a memorandum of understanding (MOU). The following webpage provides information on New Zealand's participation in PIAAC: https://www.educationcounts.govt.nz/data-services/data-collections/international/piaac.[42] A data usage period is not specified by the contract. The MOU continues to apply while the researcher is using or retains the dataset. The data are provided free of charge.

The PIAAC New Zealand Extended File can be merged with the public or extended use files of other participating countries in order to perform cross-national analyses. The International Database (IDB) Analyzer can be used to merge the PIAAC datasets (see Chap. 6 in this volume).

Documentation Information on the methodology, design, and implementation of PIAAC can be found in the technical reports on the study (OECD 2014, 2016a;

---

[42]The email address for enquiries about this is currently: tertiary[dot]information[at]education[dot]govt[dot]nz.

see also Chap. 2 in this volume) and in the results reports (OECD 2013, 2016b, c). The international master questionnaire, the international codebook, and a derived variables codebook are available on the OECD PIAAC Data and Tools webpage. Furthermore, a data dictionary is available for the New Zealand national variables.

4.4.6 United States

4.4.6.1 US PIAAC 2012 Restricted Use File (RUF)

File Description The US PIAAC Restricted Use File (RUF) contains information on respondents' background and on their cognitive assessment (in literacy, numeracy, and problem solving in technology-rich environments) from the US PIAAC main study, for which data collection was completed in 2012. In addition to the variables in the US PIAAC Public Use File (NCES 2014-045REV; OECD 2016gg), the US PIAAC Restricted Use File contains detailed versions of variables (e.g. continuous age and earnings variables) and additional data (e.g. on race and ethnicity) collected through US-specific questionnaire routing. The data contain sensitive information, which is confidential and protected by US federal law.

Mode of Data Collection Face-to-face interview (computer-assisted personal interview, CAPI) to collect the background information; computer-based or paper-based assessment of skills in literacy, numeracy, and problem solving in technology-rich environments.

Sample Description and Size The sample comprised 5010 adults aged 16–65 years.

Format and Access The US PIAAC Restricted Use File (Holtzman et al. 2014b) is available in SPSS and SAS formats and accessible only for scientific research purposes and only in the United States. Individual researchers must apply through an organisation in the United States (e.g. a university or a research institution). The organisation must apply for and sign a contract prior to obtaining access to the restricted-use data. Depending on the type of organisation, this contract takes the form of a restricted-use data licence or a memorandum of understanding (MOU).[43] The application must be submitted via an online application system[44]. Key information must be provided about the project (e.g. title, description, and duration) and the user. The data can be used only during the time period specified by the contract. Users are charged a processing fee and are expected to make publications resulting from the research available to the data provider.

Documentation Information on the methodology, design, and implementation of PIAAC can be found in the technical reports on the study (OECD 2014, 2016a;

---

[43] For details see https://nces.ed.gov/statprog/instruct_gettingstarted.asp
[44] Currently available at https://nces.ed.gov/statprog/instruct.asp

see also Chap. 2 in this volume) and in the results reports (OECD 2013, 2016b, c). In addition, specific information on the methodology, design, and implementation of PIAAC in the United States can be found in the technical report on the study (Hogan et al. 2013) and in the results reports (Goodman et al. 2013; OECD 2013). An English-language and a Spanish-language background questionnaire (HTML format) are available for downloading at the National Center for Education Statistics website.[45] The US codebook and background compendium are provided together with the data.

4.4.6.2 PIAAC 2012/202014: US National Supplement Public Use Data File (PUF) – Household

File Description The PIAAC 2012/2014 US National Supplement Public Use Data Files – Household (Holtzman et al. 2016a; NCES 2016667REV) contain information on respondents' background and on their cognitive assessment (in literacy, numeracy, and problem solving in technology-rich environments) from the first and second US PIAAC data collections completed in 2012 and 2014, respectively. The 2014 sampling design supported oversampling (younger adults, aged 16–35, and unemployed adults) and the addition of a population group (older adults, aged 66–74), but the data cannot be analysed separately from the 2012 data on a national level. The expanded national sample of the combined data collections supports more accurate and reliable national estimates for these subgroups and, in the case of older adults, estimates for new groups not represented in the first round of PIAAC.

Mode of Data Collection Face-to-face interview (computer-assisted personal interview, CAPI) to collect the background information; computer-based or paper-based assessment of skills in literacy, numeracy, and problem solving in technology-rich environments.

Sample Description and Size The US PIAAC main study (2012) sample comprised 5010 adults aged 16–65 years. The US PIAAC National Supplement (2014) household sample comprised 3660 adults aged 16–74 years. Hence, the dataset contains a total of 8670 surveyed respondents.

Format and Access The US PIAAC 2012/2014 National Supplement Public Use File (Holtzman et al. 2016a) is available for downloading in SPSS, SAS, and raw format at the National Center for Education Statistics website.[46] A version of the Public Use File is provided on the OECD website [47], thus enabling researchers

---

[45] https://nces.ed.gov/surveys/piaac/

[46] https://nces.ed.gov/pubsearch/pubsinfo.asp?pubid=2016667REV

[47] http://www.oecd.org/skills/piaac/publicdataandanalysis/

to conduct cross-country analyses using the 2012/2014 combined household US sample.

Documentation Information on the methodology, design, and implementation of PIAAC can be found in the technical reports on the study (OECD 2014, 2016a; see also Chap. 2 in this volume) and in the results reports (OECD 2013, 2016b, c). In addition, specific information on the methodology, design, and implementation of PIAAC in the United States can be found in the technical report on the study (Hogan et al. 2016a) and in the results report (Rampey et al. 2016). An English-language and a Spanish-language background questionnaire (HTML format) and a codebook and background compendium are available for downloading at the National Center for Education Statistics website.[48]

4.4.6.3 PIAAC 2012/2014: US National Supplement Restricted Use Data File (RUF) – Household

File Description The US PIAAC 2012/2014 National Supplement Restricted Use Data Files – Household (Holtzman et al. 2016b; NCES 2016668REV) contain information on respondents' background and on their cognitive assessment (in literacy, numeracy, and problem solving in technology-rich environments) from the first and second US PIAAC data collections, completed in 2012 and 2014, respectively. The 2014 sampling design supported oversampling (younger adults, aged 16–35, and unemployed adults) and the addition of a population group (older adults, aged 66–74), but the data cannot be analysed separately from the 2012 data on a national level. The expanded national sample of the combined data collections supports more accurate and reliable national estimates for these subgroups and, in the case of older adults, estimates for new groups not represented in the first round of PIAAC. The Restricted Use Files contain detailed versions of variables and additional data collected through US-specific questionnaire routing (e.g. continuous age and earnings variables, language spoken). A detailed variable-level comparison of the PUF and RUF versions is available in the technical report (Table E-5; Hogan et al. 2016).

Mode of Data Collection Face-to-face interview (computer-assisted personal interview, CAPI) to collect the background information; computer-based or paper-based assessment of skills in literacy, numeracy, and problem solving in technology-rich environments.

Sample Description and Size The US PIAAC main study (2012) sample comprised 5010 adults aged 16–65 years. The US PIAAC National Supplement (2014) household sample comprised 3660 adults aged 16–74 years. Hence, the dataset contains a total of 8670 surveyed respondents.

---

[48] https://nces.ed.gov/surveys/piaac/

Format and Access The PIAAC 2012/2014 US National Supplement Restricted Use File (Holtzman et al. 2016b) is available in SPSS and SAS format and accessible only for scientific research purposes and only in the United States. Individual researchers must apply through an organisation in the United States (e.g. a university or a research institution). The organisation must apply for and sign a contract prior to obtaining access to the restricted-use data. Depending on the type of organisation, this contract takes the form of a restricted-use data licence or a memorandum of understanding (MOU). The application must be submitted via an online application system[49]. Key information must be provided about the project (e.g. title, description, and duration) and the user. The data can be used only during the time period specified by the contract. Users are charged a processing fee and are expected to make publications resulting from the research available to the data provider.

A synthetic version of the Restricted Use File (S-RUF) is provided on the OECD website[50] in order to enable researchers outside the United States to prepare computer code for the analysis of PIAAC data on the US Restricted Use File (RUF). The generated code (in SAS, SPSS, or Stata) must then be submitted to the American Institutes for Research[51], where the requested analyses will be run on the real US RUF. The output undergoes a confidentiality review and is returned to the researcher after approval. The synthetic version does not include variables with open-ended/verbatim responses or variables with a high degree of detail (e.g. occupation).

Documentation Information on the methodology, design, and implementation of PIAAC can be found in the technical reports on the study (OECD 2014, 2016a; see also Chap. 2 in this volume) and in the results reports (OECD 2013, 2016b, c). In addition, specific information on the methodology, design, and implementation of PIAAC in the United States can be found in the technical report on the study (Hogan et al. 2016a) and in the results report (Rampey et al. 2016). An English-language and a Spanish-language background questionnaire (HTML format) are available for downloading at the National Center for Education Statistics website.[52] The codebook and background compendium are provided together with the data. For the synthetic version of the RUF (and researchers outside the United States), a codebook and a User Guide are available on the OECD PIAAC Data and Tools webpage.

---

[49]Currently available at https://nces.ed.gov/statprog/instruct.asp
[50]http://www.oecd.org/skills/piaac/publicdataandanalysis/
[51]piaac[at]air[dot]org
[52]https://nces.ed.gov/surveys/piaac/

4.5 PIAAC Data Files with a Focus on Specific Population Groups

4.5.1 Germany

4.5.1.1 German PIAAC National Supplement (SUF): Prime Age

File Description The German PIAAC Prime Age dataset comprises a national oversample of adults in former East Germany aged 26–55 years from Round 1 of the PIAAC data collection in Germany, which was completed in 2012. This is considered to be an age group whose members are in the active employment phase and have usually completed vocational training. Respondents were surveyed using the same procedures, instruments, and assessments that were used for the PIAAC main study. The dataset contains background information and information on the cognitive assessment (in literacy, numeracy, and problem solving in technology-rich environments).

Mode of Data Collection Face-to-face interview (computer-assisted personal interview, CAPI) to collect the background information; computer-based or paper-based assessment of skills in literacy, numeracy, and problem solving in technology-rich environments.

Sample Description and Size The oversample comprised 560 adults aged 26–55 years. In total (i.e. together with the participants of the German PIAAC main study in the corresponding age group), the sample contains 4000 adults aged 26–55 years.

Format and Access The dataset (Solga and Heisig 2015) is available in SPSS and Stata format for academic research only, after signing a data distribution contract (in English or German).[53] In addition, key information about the project (e.g. title, description, and duration) and the user must be provided. The data can be used only during the time period specified by the contract. Users are charged a processing fee and are expected to make publications resulting from the research available to the data provider.

Documentation Information on the methodology, design, and implementation of PIAAC in Germany can be found in the technical report on the study (Zabal et al. 2014) and in the results reports (OECD 2013; Rammstedt et al. 2013). The German background questionnaire is available in PDF format[54] and in HTML format.[55] The

---

[53] Available at https://www.gesis.org/en/piaac/rdc/data/german-piaac-national-supplement
[54] https://dbk.gesis.org/dbksearch/download.asp?id=56322
[55] https://www.oecd.org/skills/piaac/data/Translated_HTML_de-DE.htm

codebook (in Excel format) is available at the GESIS Data Archive [56], and further documentation is also available on the PIAAC Research Data Center website.[57]

4.5.1.2 German PIAAC National Supplement (SUF): Competencies in Later Life (CiLL)

File Description The German PIAAC CiLL study (Friebe et al. 2014) comprises a national oversample of adults aged 66–80 years from Round 1 of the PIAAC data collection in Germany, which was completed in 2012. Respondents were surveyed using the same procedures, instruments, and assessments that were used for the PIAAC main study. The dataset contains background information and information on the cognitive assessment (in literacy, numeracy, and problem solving in technology-rich environments).

Mode of Data Collection Face-to-face interview (computer-assisted personal interview, CAPI) to collect the background information; computer-based or paper-based assessment of skills in literacy, numeracy, and problem solving in technology-rich environments.

Sample Description and Size The sample comprised 1392 adults aged 66–80 years.

Format and Access The dataset (Friebe et al. 2017) is available in SPSS and Stata format for academic research only, after signing a data distribution contract (in English or German).[58] In addition, key information about the project (e.g. title, description, and duration) and the user must be provided. The data can be used only during the time period specified by the contract. Users are charged a processing fee and are expected to make publications resulting from the research available to the data provider.

Documentation Information on the methodology, design, and implementation of PIAAC in Germany can be found in the technical report on the study (Zabal et al. 2014) and in the results reports (OECD 2013; Rammstedt et al. 2013). The German background questionnaire is available in PDF format[59] and in HTML format.[60] The codebook in Excel format and a study description are available at the GESIS Data Archive[61]. Further documentation is also available on the PIAAC Research Data Center website.[62]

---

[56] https://search.gesis.org/research_data/ZA5951

[57] https://www.gesis.org/en/piaac/rdc/data/german-piaac-national-supplement

[58] Available at https://www.gesis.org/en/piaac/rdc/data/german-piaac-national-supplement

[59] https://dbk.gesis.org/dbksearch/download.asp?id=58939

[60] https://www.oecd.org/skills/piaac/data/Translated_HTML_de-DE.htm

[61] https://search.gesis.org/research_data/ZA5969

[62] https://www.gesis.org/en/piaac/rdc/data/german-piaac-national-supplement

4.5.2 United States

4.5.2.1 PIAAC 2014: US National Supplement Public Use Data Files (PUF)-Prison

File Description The PIAAC 2014 US National Supplement Public Use Data Files-Prison (Hogan et al. 2016a; NCES 2016337REV) contain information on the background and the cognitive assessment (in literacy, numeracy, and problem solving in technology-rich environments) of incarcerated adults surveyed in the US PIAAC National Supplement Prison Study, data collection for which was conducted in 2014. The direct assessments of literacy, numeracy, and problem solving in technology-rich environments administered to adult inmates were the same as those administered to the US PIAAC household participants. However, the household background questionnaire was modified and tailored specifically to address the experiences and needs of this subgroup.

Mode of Data Collection Face-to-face interview (computer-assisted personal interview, CAPI) to collect the background information; computer-based or paper-based assessment of skills in literacy, numeracy, and problem solving in technology-rich environments.

Sample Description and Size The sample comprised 1319 adults aged 16–74 years incarcerated in prisons in the United States.

Format and Access The PIAAC 2014 US National Supplement Public Use Data Files-Prison (Hogan et al. 2016a) are available for downloading in SPSS, SAS, and raw format at the National Center for Education Statistics website [63].

Documentation Information on the methodology, design, and implementation of US PIAAC can be found in the technical report on the study (Hogan et al. 2016a) and in the results report (Rampey et al. 2016). An English-language and a Spanish-language background questionnaire (HTML format) and a codebook and background compendium are available for downloading at the National Center for Education Statistics website[64].

4.5.2.2 PIAAC 2014: US National Supplement Restricted Use Data Files (RUF)-Prison

File Description The PIAAC 2014 US National Supplement Restricted Use Data Files-Prison (Hogan et al. 2016b; NCES 2016058REV) contain information on the background and the cognitive assessment (in literacy, numeracy, and problem solving in technology-rich environments) of incarcerated adults who were surveyed

---

[63]https://nces.ed.gov/pubsearch/pubsinfo.asp?pubid=2016337REV
[64]https://nces.ed.gov/surveys/piaac/

in the US PIAAC National Supplement Prison Study, data collection for which was conducted in 2014. The direct assessments of literacy, numeracy, and problem solving in technology-rich environments administered to adult inmates were the same as those administered to the US PIAAC household participants. However, the household background questionnaire was modified and tailored specifically to address the experiences and needs of this subgroup. The Restricted Use File contains detailed versions of variables and additional data collected through US-specific questionnaire routing (e.g. continuous age and earnings variables, language spoken). A detailed variable-level comparison of the PUF and RUF version is available in the technical report (Table E-6; Hogan et al. 2016b).

Mode of Data Collection Face-to-face interview (computer-assisted personal interview, CAPI); computer-based or paper-based measurement of basic skills in literacy, numeracy, and problem solving in technology-rich environments.

Sample Description and Size The sample comprised 1319 adults aged 16–74 years incarcerated in prisons in the United States.

Format and Access The PIAAC 2014 US National Supplement Restricted Use Files-Prison (Hogan et al. 2016b) are available in SPSS and SAS format and accessible only for academic research and only in the United States. Individual researchers must apply for access through an organisation in the United States (e.g. a university or a research institution). The organisation must apply for and sign a contract prior to obtaining access to the restricted-use data. Depending on the type of organisation, this contract takes the form of a restricted-use data licence or a memorandum of understanding (MOU).[65] The application must be submitted via an online application system[66]. Key information must be provided about the project (e.g. title, description, and duration) and the user. The data can be used only during the time period specified by the contract. Users are charged a processing fee and are expected to make publications resulting from the research available to the data provider.

Documentation Information on the methodology, design, and implementation of US PIAAC can be found in the technical report on the study (Hogan et al. 2016a) and in the results report (Rampey et al. 2016). An English-language and a Spanish-language background questionnaire (HTML format) are available for downloading at the National Center for Education Statistics website[67]. The codebook and background compendium are provided together with the data.

---

[65] For details see https://nces.ed.gov/statprog/instruct_gettingstarted.asp

[66] Currently available at https://nces.ed.gov/statprog/instruct.asp

[67] https://nces.ed.gov/surveys/piaac/

4.6 Linking PIAAC Data Files to Administrative Data

To date, datasets linking PIAAC data to administrative data are in the pilot phase and are partially available in Canada (Longitudinal and International Study of Adults, LISA), the Nordic countries (Denmark, Estonia, Finland, Norway, and Sweden), and Germany.

In Canada, the LISA data, which include the PIAAC data in the first wave of measurement, are available for in-country research. The LISA data can be linked to historical administrative data since 1982 (e.g. Pension Plan in Canada, PPIC, or the Immigration Database). The linkage to administrative data is available for 8600 LISA respondents who underwent PIAAC assessments (at Wave 1).

Norway and Sweden already offer researchers the possibility of analysing the respective country data on PIAAC by linking them to administrative data. In Norway, however, this possibility is available only to researchers within the country. Therefore, NordMAN (Nordic Microdata Access Network; http://nordman.network/) has been established; it will integrate PIAAC survey data linked to administrative data for five European countries (Denmark, Estonia, Finland, Norway and Sweden) on a common platform, thereby extending the user radius for researchers within the Network. An extension of the use for researchers outside this network is currently being discussed; it is bound up, for example, with legal issues. These data will be described in Sect. 4.6.4.

By means of a pilot project, the German PIAAC-Longitudinal (PIAAC-L) data have been individually linked to the employment biography data provided by the German Institute for Employment Research (IAB). The resulting dataset is known as PIAAC-L-ADIAB. The linked administrative data are available for 2086 PIAAC-L respondents (at Wave 1). The data was tested and analysed by researchers in a pilot project. An exemplary description of the work with these data can be found in Chap. 11 in this volume.

4.6.1 Canada

4.6.1.1 Longitudinal and International Study of Adults (LISA)

File Description The Longitudinal and International Study of Adults (LISA) examines changes in Canadian society over time. There have been four waves of LISA data collection to date: Wave 1 in 2012, Wave 2 in 2014, Wave 3 in 2016, and Wave 4 in 2018 (not yet released). Data collection for Wave 5 will begin in January 2020. In Wave 1 (2011–2012), to improve operational efficiency and enhance analytical value, LISA and PIAAC shared a portion of their samples. LISA collects a wide range of information about education, training and learning, families, housing, health, labour, income, pensions, spending, and wealth. Variables are obtained through the administration of the survey component and subsequent integration with various administrative files. The Canadian PIAAC data contain information on respondents' background and on their cognitive assessment (in literacy, numeracy, and problem solving in technology-rich environments). The target populations of LISA and PIAAC (2011–2012) differed. The LISA target population covered individuals aged 15 years and over, whereas the PIAAC target population covered only 16- to 65-year-olds. The common sample for both PIAAC and LISA allows the analysis of various variables and administrative data with which proficiency scores can be analysed.

Mode of Data Collection Face-to-face interview (computer-assisted personal interview, CAPI) to collect the background information; computer-based or paper-based assessment of skills in literacy, numeracy, and problem solving in technology-rich environments.

Sample Description and Size LISA uses household interviews to collect information from approximately 34,000 Canadians aged 15 years and over from more than 11,000 households (23,900 responding persons in 2012). Data from the PIAAC assessment are available for 8600 respondents and are available only in the LISA 2012 (Wave 1) microdata files.

Format and Access It should be noted that the LISA data are currently available only in Canada, via Canadian Research Data Centres (RDCs). Researchers must submit proposals to the RDC Program requesting LISA data and must specify whether they require access to the LISA survey data or the LISA data integrated with administrative data. The application process and guidelines depend on the affiliation of the principal investigator (e.g. researcher who works for an academic institution that is or is not a member of the Canadian Research Data Centre Network) and the type of research to be conducted. Detailed information on the data access process can be found on the Statistics Canada website.[68] Users are expected to make publications resulting from the research available to the data provider.

Documentation English-language and French-language information on the methodology, design, and implementation of LISA and PIAAC can be found on the Statistics Canada website[69] and on the Canadian PIAAC website[70]. Furthermore, general information on the methodology, design, and implementation of PIAAC can be found in the technical reports on the study (OECD 2014, 2016a; see also Chap. 2 in this volume) and in the results reports (OECD 2013, 2016b, c). The questionnaires (in English and French) of all waves of LISA can be downloaded at Statistics Canada's website.[71] The international master questionnaire, the international

---

[68] Current application site: https://www.statcan.gc.ca/eng/rdc/process
[69] http://www23.statcan.gc.ca/imdb/p2SV.pl?Function=getSurvey&Id=248501
[70] http://www.piaac.ca
[71] http://www23.statcan.gc.ca/imdb/p3Instr.pl?Function=getInstrumentList&Item_Id=424373&UL=AV

codebook, and a derived variables codebook are available on the OECD PIAAC Data and Tools webpage.

4.6.2 Norway

4.6.2.1 Linking PIAAC Norway Data to Administrative Data

File Description The Norwegian PIAAC data contain information on respondents' background and on their cognitive assessment (in literacy, numeracy, and problem solving in technology-rich environments). The PIAAC data provided by the Norwegian Centre for Research Data (NSD)[72] contain more detailed information—for example, on earnings, country of birth, and occupation (detailed, four-digit, ISCO-08 codes)—than that available in the Norwegian PIAAC Public Use File (OECD 2016v).

Furthermore, the Norwegian PIAAC data can be extended with administrative (register) data, such as demographic data (e.g. citizenship and marital status), data on educational attainment and current education, employment, occupation and industry, and information about the workplace of the respondents and about social security for the years 2010–2020. These linked data are provided by Statistics Norway.

Mode of Data Collection PIAAC data: face-to-face interview (computer-assisted personal interview, CAPI) to collect the background information; computer-based or paper-based assessment of skills in literacy, numeracy, and problem solving in technology-rich environments. The administrative data are derived from administrative registers (e.g. the population register).

Sample Description and Size The sample comprised 5128 adults aged 16–65 years.

Format and Access The Norwegian PIAAC data (Statistics Norway 2015) are provided in SPSS, Stata, and SAS format by the Norwegian Centre for Research Data (NSD) to researchers, teachers, and students located in Norway. Data can be ordered via NSD's order form (currently at https://nsd.no/nsd/english/orderform.html).[73] Users must sign an access letter and a confidentiality agreement that stipulates conditions for use. The data distribution contract must be signed by each member of a project who wishes to use the data. In addition, key information about the project and the user must be provided. The data contract can be concluded for a term of 2 years.

The Norwegian PIAAC dataset can also be extended with variables from administrative registers. Anonymous datasets are created by Statistics Norway for

---

[72]In Norway, PIAAC data are available via NSD, Statistics Norway, and the Nordic PIAAC database (see Sect. 4.6.3 in this volume).

[73]Or: bestilledata[at]nsd[dot]uib[dot]no

specific research projects. In other words, when researchers apply for access, a dataset with the specific variables ordered is created for the research project in question.[74]

Documentation Information on the methodology, design, and implementation of PIAAC can be found in the technical reports on the study (OECD 2014, 2016a; see also Chap. 2 in this volume) and in the results reports (Fridberg et al. 2015; OECD 2013, 2016b, c). There is also a national documentation report (Gravem and Lagerstrøm 2013). Further documentation for administrative data is made available when the data/variables are ordered. A Norwegian-language version of the background questionnaire is available for downloading at the OECD PIAAC Data and Tools webpage, as are an international codebook and a derived variables codebook.

4.6.3 Sweden

4.6.3.1 Linking PIAAC Sweden Data to Administrative Data

File Description The Swedish PIAAC data contain information on respondents' background and on their cognitive assessment (in literacy, numeracy, and problem solving in technology-rich environments). The PIAAC data at Statistics Sweden contain more detailed information—for example, on earnings, country of birth, and occupation (detailed, four-digit, ISCO-08)—than that available in the Swedish PIAAC Public Use File (OECD 2016dd). Furthermore, the Swedish PIAAC data were extended with administrative (register) data, such as demographic data (e.g. citizenship and marital status), data on educational attainment and current education, employment, occupation and industry, and information about the workplace of the respondents and about social security. This information is available for the years 2008 and 2011 for each respondent of PIAAC 2012. It is also possible to combine the PIAAC data with register data about the region in which the respondent lives (e.g. NUTS 2).

Mode of Data Collection PIAAC data: face-to-face interview (computer-assisted personal interview, CAPI) to collect the background information; computer-based or paper-based assessment of skills in literacy, numeracy, and problem solving in technology-rich environments. The administrative data are derived from administrative registers (e.g. the population register).

Sample Description and Size The sample comprised 4469 adults aged 16–65 years.

---

[74]More information on access to microdata from Statistics Norway can be found here: https://www.ssb.no/en/omssb/tjenester-og-verktoy/data-til-forskning.

Format and Access The Swedish PIAAC data are provided in SPSS, Stata, SAS, and R format for research purposes within the EU/EEA through the remote access system MONA (Microdata Online Access) at Statistics Sweden[75]. MONA is a tool for delivering microdata at Statistics Sweden. Users of MONA work in a Windows environment via remote connection. Microdata are visible on the computer screen and can be processed using statistical software available in MONA. Results can be retrieved via email, but processed microdata are stored in MONA and may not be downloaded.

There is not one standard dataset. Rather, datasets with register variables have to be created for a specific research project. When researchers apply for access, a dataset with the specific variables ordered is created for the research project in question. Research projects must apply to Statistics Sweden for access to the data; a research plan, also containing a description of variables, should be included in the application. Statistics Sweden conducts a confidentiality review based on the research plan. If the application is approved and confidentiality agreements between Statistics Sweden and the research project are signed, the project obtains access to the data through MONA.

Documentation Information on the methodology, design, and implementation of PIAAC can be found in the technical reports on the study (OECD 2014, 2016a; see also Chap. 2 in this volume) and in the results reports (Fridberg et al. 2015; OECD 2013, 2016b, c). Further documentation for administrative data is made available when the data/variables are ordered. A Swedish-language version of the background questionnaire is available for downloading at the OECD PIAAC Data and Tools webpage, as are an international codebook and a derived variables codebook.

4.6.4 The Nordic PIAAC Database

File Description The Nordic PIAAC database contains microdata from the survey, as well as data from registers of five Nordic European countries: Denmark, Estonia, Finland, Norway, and Sweden. It contains information on respondents' background and on their cognitive assessment (in literacy, numeracy, and problem solving in technology-rich environments) from the PIAAC data collection completed in 2012. Furthermore, data from national registers in Denmark, Estonia, Finland, and Sweden for the reference years 2008 and 2011 and in Norway for 2011 are available for each respondent. Diverse types of register data are available, such as demographic data (e.g. citizenship and marital status), data on educational attainment and current education, employment, occupation and industry, and information about the workplace of the respondents and about social security.

---

[75]https://www.scb.se/en/.

Mode of Data Collection PIAAC data: face-to-face interview (computer-assisted personal interview, CAPI) to collect the background information; computer-based or paper-based assessment of skills in literacy, numeracy, and problem solving in technology-rich environments. The administrative data are derived from the administrative registers of the respective countries (e.g. the population register).

Sample Description and Size The sample comprised 7328 adults aged 16–74 years in Denmark, 7632 adults aged 16–74 years in Estonia, 5464 adults aged 16–74 years in Finland, 5128 adults aged 16–74 years in Norway, and 4469 adults aged 16–74 years in Sweden (Fridberg et al. 2015).

Format and Access The Nordic PIAAC database is stored in safe domains of the Nordic National Statistical Institutions (Nordic NSIs). It is currently provided only for research purposes within the Network countries and can be accessed via NordMAN (Nordic Microdata Access Network)[76]. NordMAN describes the processes for obtaining access to Nordic PIAAC data combined with register data (application forms and procedures, confidentiality review and agreements, etc.). The data can be accessed via remote access systems at the statistical offices in Sweden, Finland, and Denmark.

There is not one standard dataset. Rather, datasets with register variables have to be created for specific research projects. When researchers apply for access, a dataset with the specific variables ordered is created for the research project in question. The application must be submitted to a committee comprising representatives from each country. In Sweden, for instance, the application must be approved by Statistics Sweden. If the application is approved, the researcher signs the necessary contracts and confidentiality agreements and is then allowed to analyse the Nordic microdata in SPSS, Stata, SAS, or R format via NordMAN. Prior to data delivery, all outputs are subject to output control by the data-hosting NSI. Fees are charged for the data preparation procedure and the use of the system.

Documentation Information on the methodology, design, and implementation of PIAAC can be found in the technical reports on the study (OECD 2014, 2016a; see also Chap. 2 in this volume) and in the results reports (Fridberg et al. 2015; OECD 2013, 2016b, c). A Danish-language, Estonian-language (and Russian-language), Finnish-language, Norwegian-language (and English-language), and Swedish-language version of the background questionnaire are available for downloading at the OECD PIAAC Data and Tools webpage, as are an international codebook and a derived variables codebook.

---

[76] http://nordman.network/

4.7 PIAAC Longitudinal Data Files

Four countries that participated in the first cycle of PIAAC (2011–2012)—Canada, Germany, Italy, and Poland—have carried out follow-up studies with different strategies and focus. Thereby, only the German PIAAC Longitudinal study included a reassessment of basic skills using PIAAC instruments (see Rammstedt et al. 2017a, b).

In *Canada*, a subset of the respondents of the Canadian social survey Longitudinal and International Study of Adults (LISA; $N = 27{,}285$) participated in PIAAC. These respondents are being reinterviewed biennially as part of LISA (see Situ 2015). The LISA study is described in more detail in Sect. 4.6 on linking PIAAC data to administrative data.

In *Germany*, respondents who had participated in the 2011/2012 PIAAC survey were reapproached for the panel study PIAAC-Longitudinal (PIAAC-L). PIAAC-L ($N = 3758$) consisted of three follow-up waves to the initial PIAAC 2012 survey, which were conducted in 2014, 2015, and 2016. Extensive background information and information on non-cognitive skills, household composition, and living conditions was collected, and a reassessment of literacy and numeracy was carried out in 2015.

A follow-up to PIAAC in *Italy* (2014/2015) collected longitudinal information on Italian PIAAC respondents ($N = 2003$) and focused on non-cognitive skills. A *Polish* follow-up to PIAAC (postPIAAC) also focused on non-cognitive skills. Conducted in 2014/2015 ($N = 5224$), it collected additional background information on the PIAAC respondents as well as information on their non-cognitive skills (e.g. the Big Five personality traits, grit). Basic cognitive skills tests (e.g. working memory test or coding speed test) and a basic ICT skills test were applied (e.g. Palczyńska and Świst 2016). As the data from the Italian[77] and Polish (to access the data, contact the Polish Educational Research Institute [IBE])[78] follow-up studies have not yet been published and made available to external researchers, they are not presented in detail here. As only the German PIAAC-L study included a reassessment of basic skills, it will therefore be described in the following section.

4.7.1 Germany

4.7.1.1 PIAAC-Longitudinal Scientific Use File

File Description The German PIAAC-Longitudinal (PIAAC-L) study was a collaborative effort undertaken by GESIS – Leibniz Institute for the Social Sciences

---

[77]Istituto Nazionale per l'Analisi delle Politiche Pubbliche (INAPP); current email address: serviziost[at]istico[dot]inapp[dot]org.

[78]Current email: ibe[at]ibe[dot]edu[dot]pl.

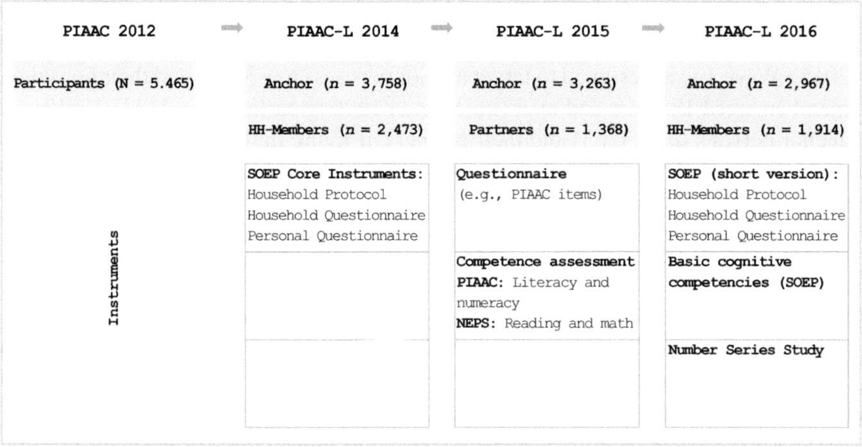

4 Adult Cognitive and Non-cognitive Skills: An Overview of Existing PIAAC Data 79

	PIAAC 2012 ⇒	PIAAC-L 2014 ⇒	PIAAC-L 2015 ⇒	PIAAC-L 2016
Participants	(N = 5.465)	Anchor (n = 3,758)	Anchor (n = 3,263)	Anchor (n = 2,967)
		HH-Members (n = 2,473)	Partners (n = 1,368)	HH-Members (n = 1,914)
Instruments		SOEP Core Instruments: Household Protocol Household Questionnaire Personal Questionnaire	Questionnaire (e.g., PIAAC items)	SOEP (short version): Household Protocol Household Questionnaire Personal Questionnaire
			Competence assessment PIAAC: Literacy and numeracy NEPS: Reading and math	Basic cognitive competencies (SOEP)
				Number Series Study

Note: SOEP=German Socio-Economic Panel; HH-Members = Additional household members

Fig. 4.1 German PIAAC-Longitudinal (PIAAC-L) study

(lead), the German Institute for Economic Research (DIW), and the Leibniz Institute for Educational Trajectories (LIfBi). PIAAC-L was designed as a three-wave follow-up survey to PIAAC (2012), with data collections in 2014, 2015, and 2016 (for a overview see Fig. 4.1). The PIAAC-L questionnaires were based on core instruments from the German Socio-Economic Panel (SOEP) and also included various additional questions and modules on the respondents' background. In addition, assessment instruments from PIAAC and the National Educational Panel Study (NEPS) measuring key competencies were implemented.

The person questionnaire included questions on the following topics: background information, family, and childhood; biographical calendar; formal education (general and vocational education) and continuing professional education; work status, situation, and history; income and benefits; health, attitudes, personality, opinions, and satisfaction; and time use and leisure activities. The household questionnaire assessed living situation, conditions, and costs; household income and benefits and wealth; and children and other household members.

The objective of the PIAAC-L project was to significantly expand the German PIAAC database by adding a longitudinal dimension and enhancing the depth and breadth of information available on the German PIAAC respondents (for an overview of the rationale and design of the study, see Rammstedt et al. 2017a, b).

Mode of Data Collection Face-to-face interview (CAPI) and computer-based or paper-based cognitive assessment.

Sample Description and Size The sample comprised German PIAAC 2012 respondents aged 18–65 years who agreed to participate in PIAAC-L and other members of their household aged 18 years and over (total initial sample at the first wave: $N = 6231$). Whereas the focus and the groups of addressed persons varied somewhat across waves, German PIAAC 2012 respondents ($N = 5465$)—the so-called anchor persons—were consistently the central response units in PIAAC-L (Zabal et al. 2016). Wave 1 was designed to target anchor persons ($n = 3758$) and their household members aged 18 years and over (i.e. born in 1996 or earlier; $n = 2473$). In Wave 2, anchor persons ($n = 3263$) and their partners, if living in the same household, were addressed ($n = 1368$). The design of the third wave was similar to that of the first wave: anchor persons ($n = 2967$) and all household members aged 18 years and over (i.e. born in 1998 or earlier) were to be interviewed ($n = 1914$).

Format and Access The German PIAAC-L data (GESIS et al. 2017) are available as a scientific use file (SPSS and Stata format) for academic research only, after signing a data distribution contract (in English or German).[79] In addition, key information about the project (e.g. title, description, and duration) and the user must be provided. The data can be used only during the time period specified by the contract. Users are charged a processing fee and are expected to make publications resulting from the research available to the data provider. The data of the anchor persons from all three PIAAC-L waves can be matched to data from the German PIAAC Scientific Use File (see Sect. 4.4.3).

Documentation Information on the methodology, design, and implementation of PIAAC-L can be found in the German-language fieldwork report (Steinacker and Wolfert 2017) and the English-language technical reports on the study (Bartsch et al. 2017; Martin et al. 2018; Zabal et al. 2016). The person and household questionnaires (in German, as administered in the field, but with English labels) can be downloaded at the PIAAC Research Data Center website[80] English-language codebooks for data on persons, households, and weights are available (in Excel and PDF format) on the respective websites.

4.8 Linking PIAAC Data to Other Surveys

Three PIAAC participating countries—Denmark, Singapore, and the United States—have surveyed persons who had been surveyed before in another large-scale assessment, namely, the Programme for International Student Assessment (PISA).

In *Denmark* 1881 participants aged 15–16 years at PISA 2000 were retested and interviewed again in PIAAC 2011–2012. The Danish Center for Social Science Research (VIVE) is responsible for PIAAC; for more information on the corresponding data and the availability for the scientific research, please contact

---

[79] Available at https://www.gesis.org/en/piaac/rdc/data/piaac-longitudinal

[80] https://www.gesis.org/en/piaac/rdc/data/piaac-longitudinal/

4 Adult Cognitive and Non-cognitive Skills: An Overview of Existing PIAAC Data

VIVE.[81] As no updated information on this dataset is currently available, it cannot be described in this volume.

Singapore surveyed persons who participated in PISA 2009. However, these data are not available for research purposes (OECD 2016a). Finally, in the *United States*, PISA 2012 participants were issued with PIAAC questionnaires. These datasets can be used for research purposes and will be described below.

4.8.1 US Program for International Student Assessment Young Adult Follow-Up Study (PISA YAFS) Data

File Description The Program for International Student Assessment Young Adult Follow-Up Study (PISA YAFS) is a new study that examines a key transition period for US young adults in terms of their characteristics, academic skills, and other life outcomes. It was conducted in the United States with a sample of students who participated in PISA 2012, when they were 15 years old. These students were assessed again 4 years later in 2016, at about age 19, with the OECD's Education and Skills Online (ESO) literacy, numeracy, and problem solving in technology-rich environments assessments, which were based on the Programme for the International Assessment of Adult Competencies (PIAAC). They were also given a background questionnaire about their education and employment status, attitudes, and interests.

Thus, in addition to providing information on skills performance at age 19, PISA YAFS can also examine the relationship between that performance and young adults' performance on PISA 2012 at age 15. Moreover, it can examine the relationship between their earlier PISA 2012 performance and other aspects of their lives at age 19, such as their engagement in postsecondary education, their participation in the workforce, their attitudes towards their lives, their ability to make their own choices, and their vocational interests.

Mode of Data Collection Online data collection, using a platform developed for PISA YAFS in combination with the OECD-provided platform Education and Skills Online (ESO). The specially developed PISA YAFS platform gathered information on (i) current education study status (participation, level of degree, area of study); (ii) formal education activities; and (iii) nonformal learning activities in the 12 months preceding the study. The ESO non-cognitive modules collected information on respondents' (i) basic demographics, (ii) career interests and intentionality (CII), (iii) behavioural performance competencies (BPC), and (iv) subjective well-being and health (SWBH). The ESO platform also assessed participants' skills in literacy, numeracy, and problem solving in technology-rich environments.

---

[81] https://www.vive.dk/da/velkommen/

Sample Description and Size The PISA YAFS sample comprised around 2320 young adults who were about 19 years old in 2016, who participated in PISA 2012 at the age of 15, and who provided contact information for follow-up.

Format and Access The PISA YAFS data are scheduled to be available in 2020. The data will be in the form of the public use files, provided in SPSS and SAS formats on the National Center for Education Statistics website.[82]

Documentation Information on the methodology, design, and implementation of PISA YAFS are planned to be available in 2020 and will be found in the technical and in the results reports on the study (https://nces.ed.gov/surveys/pisa/followup.asp). General information on the methodology, design, and implementation of PIAAC can be found in the technical reports on the study (OECD 2014, 2016a; see also Chap. 2 in this volume) and in the results reports (OECD 2013, 2016b, c). Information, questionnaires, and codebooks on PISA are available on the OECD website.[83]

4.9 PIAAC Data Files on Non-Cognitive Skills

The PIAAC Pilot Studies on Non-Cognitive Skills were designed to test the measurement properties of nine personality scales: the Big Five, Traditionalism, Self-Control, Self-Efficacy, Honesty/Integrity, Socio-Emotional Skills, Intellectual Curiosity, Job Orientation Preferences, and Vocational Interests (Kankaraš 2017). The first study—the English Pilot Study on Non-Cognitive Skills—was realised with a complex design in the United States and the United Kingdom. The second study—the International Pilot Study on Non-Cognitive Skills—was realised in five countries (Germany, Spain, France, Japan, and Poland); the questionnaire focused on the properties of selected personality scales.

4.9.1 PIAAC English Pilot Study on Non-Cognitive Skills (SUF)

File Description This online survey (see also Kankaraš 2017) was designed to test the measurement properties of nine personality scales: the Big Five, Traditionalism, Self-Control, Self-Efficacy, Honesty/Integrity, Socio-Emotional Skills, Intellectual Curiosity, Job Orientation Preferences, and Vocational Interests. Eight of these nine scales were existing scales (or combinations of existing scales) available for use in the public domain. The study (data collection period: June–July 2016)

---

[82] https://nces.ed.gov/surveys/pisa/followup.asp
[83] http://www.oecd.org/pisa/data/database-pisa2000.htm

was conducted in two phases, each with a somewhat different study design. The objectives of the online survey were to test (a) the measurement characteristics of the selected scales; (b) the relationships of the selected scales with background and other characteristics of respondents; (c) different item formulations—original vs. simplified; (d) different response options—with or without a neutral/middle category; (e) scales with different item formats—multiple choice vs. forced choice (Vocational Interests Scale); and (f) the new balanced scales (compared to the original unbalanced scales).

Mode of Data Collection The entire survey was conducted online. It was implemented using the SurveyMonkey platform.

Sample Description and Size The sample comprised 5910 adults aged 16–65 years from the United States and the United Kingdom in the first phase and 1606 in the second phase (only United States).

Format and Access The English Pilot Study on Non-Cognitive Skills (OECD 2018a) is available as a scientific use file (in SPSS and Stata format) for academic research only, after signing a data distribution contract.[84] The scientific use file contains data from the first and second phases. In addition, key information about the project (e.g. title, description, and duration) and the user(s) must be provided. The data can be used only during the time period specified by the contract. Users are charged a processing fee.

Documentation Information on the methodology, design, and implementation of the PIAAC English Pilot Study on Non-Cognitive Skills can be found on the PIAAC Research Data Center website[85] and the GESIS Data Archive.[86] A questionnaire item bank (Excel format), a codebook (Excel format), and further information are also available on the aforementioned webpage.

4.9.2 International Pilot Study on Non-Cognitive Skills (SUF)

File Description This study was designed with the following objectives: first, to test the measurement characteristics of selected scales, and second, to test the cross-national comparability of selected scales. The measurement properties of nine personality scales—the Big Five, Traditionalism, Self-Control, Self-Efficacy, Honesty/Integrity, Socio-Emotional Skills, Intellectual Curiosity, Job Orientation Preferences, and Vocational Interests—were tested (data collection period: January–March 2017).

---

[84] Available at https://www.gesis.org/en/piaac/rdc/data/piaac-pilot-studies-on-non-cognitive-skills
[85] https://www.gesis.org/en/piaac/rdc/data/piaac-pilot-studies-on-non-cognitive-skills/
[86] https://search.gesis.org/research_data/ZA6940

Mode of Data Collection The entire survey was conducted online. It was implemented using the SurveyMonkey platform.

Sample Description and Size The sample comprised 6924 adults aged 16–65 years from Germany, Spain, France, Japan, and Poland.

Format and Access The International Pilot Study on Non-Cognitive Skills (OECD 2018b) is available as a scientific use file (in SPSS and Stata format) for academic research only, after signing a data distribution contract.[87] In addition, key information about the project (e.g. title, description, and duration) and the user(s) must be provided. The data can be used only during the time period specified by the contract. Users are charged a processing fee.

Documentation Information on the methodology, design, and implementation of the PIAAC International Pilot Study on Non-Cognitive Skills can be found on the PIAAC Research Data Center website[88] and at the GESIS Data Archive.[89] The questionnaires in the respective country languages (PDF format), item translations in the respective country languages (Excel format), an English-language codebook (Excel format), and further information are also available on the aforementioned webpage.

References

Bartsch, S., Poschmann, K., & Burkhardt, L. (2017). *Weighting in PIAAC-L 2014* (GESIS Papers No. 2017|06). Cologne: GESIS – Leibniz-Institute for the Social Sciences. http://www.ssoar.info/ssoar/handle/document/50569. Accessed 12 December 2017.

Fridberg, T., Rosdahl, A., Halapuu, V., Valk, A., Malin, A., Hämäläinen, R., Andressen, A., Bjoerkeng, B., Stoerset, H., Soennesyn, J., Larsoson, A.-C., Lind, P., & Mellander, E. (2015). *Adult skills in the Nordic region. Key information-processing skills among adults in the Nordic region*. Denmark: Nordic Council of Ministers. https://doi.org/10.6027/TN2015-535.

Friebe, J., Schmidt-Hertha, B., & Tippelt, R. (Eds.). (2014). *Kompetenzen im höheren Lebensalter. Ergebnisse der Studie "Competencies in Later Life" (CiLL)*. Bielefeld: Bertelsmann.

Friebe, J., Gebrande, J., Gnahs, D., Knauber, C., Schmidt-Hertha, B., Setzer, B., Tippelt, R., & Weiß, C. (2017). *Competencies in Later Life (CiLL) – Programme for the International Assessment of Adult Competencies (PIAAC), Germany* ((Data file version 1.1.0) [ZA5969]). Cologne: GESIS Data Archive. https://doi.org/10.4232/1.12814.

GESIS – Leibniz Institute for the Social Sciences, German Socio-Economic Panel (SOEP) at DIW Berlin, LIfBi – Leibniz Institute for Educational Trajectories. (2017). *PIAAC-Longitudinal (PIAAC-L), Germany* ((Data file version 3.0.0) [ZA5989]). Cologne: GESIS Data Archive. https://doi.org/10.4232/1.12925.

Goodman, M., Finnegan, R., Mohadjer, L., Krenzke, T., & Hogan, J. (2013). *Literacy, numeracy, and problem solving in technology-rich environments among U.S. adults: Results from the Program for the International Assessment of Adult Competencies 2012: First look (NCES*

---

[87] Available at https://www.gesis.org/en/piaac/rdc/data/piaac-pilot-studies-on-non-cognitive-skills

[88] https://www.gesis.org/en/piaac/rdc/data/piaac-pilot-studies-on-non-cognitive-skills/

[89] https://search.gesis.org/research_data/ZA6941

2014-008) (U.S. Department of Education). Washington, DC: National Center for Education Statistics. http://nces.ed.gov/pubsearch. Accessed 19 July 2019.

Gravem, D. F., & Lagerstrøm, B. O. (2013). *Den internasjonale undersøkelsen om lese- og tallforståelse – PIAAC* (Dokumentasjonsrapport). Oslo: Statistics Norway. https://www.ssb.no/utdanning/artikler-og-publikasjoner/_attachment/148094?_ts=142477b72f0. Accessed 19 July 2019.

Hogan, J., Montalvan, P., Diaz-Hoffmann, L., Dohrmann, S., Krenzke, T., Lemay, M., Mohadjer, L., & Thornton, N. (2013). *Program for the International Assessment of Adult Competencies 2012: U.S. Main Study Technical Report (NCES2014-047)* (U.S. Department of Education). Washington, DC: National Center for Education Statistics. http://nces.ed.gov/pubsearch. Accessed 19 July 2019.

Hogan, J., Thornton, N., Diaz-Hoffmann, L., Mohadjer, L., Krenzke, T., Li, J., Van De Kerckhove, W., Yamamoto, K., & Khorramdel, L. (2016a). *U.S. Program for the International Assessment of Adult Competencies (PIAAC) 2012/2014: Main Study and National Supplement Technical Report (NCES2016-036REV)* (U.S. Department of Education). Washington, DC: National Center for Education Statistics. http://nces.ed.gov/pubsearch. Accessed 19 July 2019.

Hogan, J., Thornton, N., Diaz-Hoffmann, L., Mohadjer, L., Krenzke, T., Li, J., & Van De Kerckhove, W. (2016b). *Program for the International Assessment of Adult Competencies (PIAAC) 2014: U.S. National Supplement Public Use Data Files-Prison (NCES 2016337REV)*. Washington, DC: National Center for Education Statistics. https://nces.ed.gov/pubsearch/pubsinfo.asp?pubid=2016337REV. Accessed 19 July 2019.

Holtzman, S., Barone, J., Li, L., Krenzke, T., Hogan, J., Mohadjer, L., Carstens, R., & Daniel, T. (2014a). *Program for the International Assessment of Adult Competencies (PIAAC) 2012 U.S. Public Use File (NCES 2014045REV)*. Washington, DC: National Center for Education Statistics. https://nces.ed.gov/pubsearch/pubsinfo.asp?pubid=2014045REV. Accessed 19 July 2019.

Holtzman, S., Barone, J., Li, L., Krenzke, T., Hogan, J., Mohadjer, L., Carstens, R., & Daniel, T. (2014b). *Program for the International Assessment of Adult Competencies (PIAAC) 2012 U.S. Restricted Use File (NCES 2014046REV)*. Washington, DC: National Center for Education Statistics.

Holtzman, S., Kandathil, M., Kapur, L., Kline, D., Barone, J., Li, L., Krenzke, T., Hogan, J., Mohadjer, L., Carstens, R., Koehler, H., & Daniel, T. (2016a). *Program for the International Assessment of Adult Competencies (PIAAC) 2012/2014: U.S. National Supplement Public Use Data Files-Household (NCES 2016667REV)*. Washington, DC: National Center for Education Statistics.

Holtzman, S., Kandathil, M., Kapur, L., Kline, D., Barone, J., Li, L., Krenzke, T., Hogan, J., Mohadjer, L., Carstens, R., Koehler, H., & Daniel, T. (2016b). *Program for the International Assessment of Adult Competencies (PIAAC) 2012/2014: U.S. National Supplement Restricted Use Data Files–Household (NCES 2016668REV)*. Washington, DC: National Center for Education Statistics.

Istituto Nazionale per l'Analisi delle Politiche Pubbliche (INAPP). (2018). *Program for the International Assessment of Adult Competencies (PIAAC) 2012 Italy*. Rome: Istituto Nazionale per l'Analisi delle Politiche Pubbliche.

Kankaraš, M. (2017). *Personality matters* (OECD Education Working Papers No. 157). Paris: OECD Publishing.

Maehler, D. B., Jakowatz, S., & Konradt, I. (2020). *PIAAC Bibliographie – 2008–2019* (GESIS Papers, Nr. 04/2020). Cologne: GESIS – Leibniz Institute for the Social Sciences. https://doi.org/10.21241/ssoar.67732.

Martin, S., Zabal, A., & Rammstedt, B. (2018). *PIAAC-L data collection 2016: Technical report* (GESIS Papers No. 2018|05). Cologne: GESIS – Leibniz-Institute for the Social Sciences. https://nbn-resolving.org/urn:nbn:de:0168. Accessed 5 May 2019.

Michaelidou-Evripidou, A., Modestou, M., Karagiorgi, Y., Polydorou, A., Nicolaidou, M., Afantiti-Lamprianou, T., Kendeou, P., Tsouris, C., & Loukaides, C. (2016). *Programme for* the *International Assessment of Adult Competencies (PIAAC), Cyprus* (Data file version 1.1.0 [ZA5650]). Cologne: GESIS Data Archive. https://doi.org/10.4232/1.12632.

Ministry of Education of New Zealand. (2016). *Programme for the International Assessment of Adult Competencies (PIAAC), New Zealand Public Use File – Extended*. Wellington: Ministry of Education.

Organisation for Economic Co-operation and Development (OECD). (2013). *OECD skills outlook 2013: First results from the survey of adult skills*. Paris: OECD Publishing. https://doi.org/10.1787/9789264204256-en.

Organisation for Economic Co-operation and Development (OECD). (2014). *Technical report of the Survey of Adult Skills (PIAAC)*. Paris: OECD. http://www.oecd.org/skills/piaac/_Technical%20Report_17OCT13.pdf. Accessed 5 May, 2019.

Organisation for Economic Co-operation and Development (OECD). (2016a). *Survey of adult skills technical report* (2nd ed.). Paris: OECD. http://www.oecd.org/skills/piaac/PIAAC_Technical_Report_2nd_Edition_Full_Report.pdf. Accessed 5 May 2019.

Organisation for Economic Co-operation and Development (OECD). (2016b). *Skills matter: Further results from the survey of adult skills*. Paris: OECD Publishing. https://doi.org/10.1787/9789264258051-en.

Organisation for Economic Co-operation and Development (OECD). (2016c). *The survey of adult skills – Reader's companion* (2nd ed.). Paris: OECD Publishing. https://doi.org/10.1787/9789264258075-en.

Organisation for Economic Co-operation and Development (OECD). (2016d). *Programme for the International Assessment of Adult Competencies (PIAAC), Austria Public Use File* (Version: 17343010, prgautp1.sav). Paris: OECD Publishing. https://'webfs.oecd.org/piaac/puf-data/. Accessed 5 May 2019.

Organisation for Economic Co-operation and Development (OECD). (2016e). *Programme for the International Assessment of Adult Competencies (PIAAC), Belgium Public Use File* (Version: 18224205, prgbelp1.sav). Paris: OECD Publishing. https://webfs.oecd.org/piaac/puf-data/. Accessed 5 May 2019.

Organisation for Economic Co-operation and Development (OECD). (2016f). *Programme for the International Assessment of Adult Competencies (PIAAC), Canada Public Use File* (Version: 88830378, prgcanp1.sav). Paris: OECD Publishing. https://webfs.oecd.org/piaac/puf-data/. Accessed 5 May 2019.

Organisation for Economic Co-operation and Development (OECD). (2016g). *Programme for the International Assessment of Adult Competencies (PIAAC), Chile Public Use File* (Version: 17135698, prgchlp1.sav). Paris: OECD Publishing. https://webfs.oecd.org/piaac/puf-data/. Accessed 5 May 2019.

Organisation for Economic Co-operation and Development (OECD). (2016h). *Programme for the International Assessment of Adult Competencies (PIAAC), Czech Republic Public Use File* (Version: 20736629, prgczep1.sav). Paris: OECD Publishing. https://webfs.oecd.org/piaac/puf-data/. Accessed 5 May 2019.

Organisation for Economic Co-operation and Development (OECD). (2016i). *Programme for the International Assessment of Adult Competencies (PIAAC), Denmark Public Use File* (Version: 24972525, prgdnkp1.sav). Paris: OECD Publishing. https://webfs.oecd.org/piaac/puf-data/. Accessed 5 May 2019.

Organisation for Economic Co-operation and Development (OECD). (2016j). *Programme for the International Assessment of Adult Competencies (PIAAC), Estonia Public Use File* (Version: 25276973, prgestp1.sav). Paris: OECD Publishing. https://webfs.oecd.org/piaac/puf-data/. Accessed 5 May 2019.

Organisation for Economic Co-operation and Development (OECD). (2016k). *Programme for the International Assessment of Adult Competencies (PIAAC), France Public Use File* (Version: 23516989, prgfrap1.sav). Paris: OECD Publishing. https://webfs.oecd.org/piaac/puf-data/. Accessed 5 May 2019.

Organisation for Economic Co-operation and Development (OECD). (2016l). *Programme for the International Assessment of Adult Competencies (PIAAC), Finland Public Use File* (Version:

18842845, prgfinp1.sav). Paris: OECD Publishing. https://webfs.oecd.org/piaac/puf-data/. Accessed 5 May 2019.

Organisation for Economic Co-operation and Development (OECD). (2016m). *Programme for the International Assessment of Adult Competencies (PIAAC), Germany Public Use File* (Version: 30110173, prggbrp1.sav). Paris: OECD Publishing. https://webfs.oecd.org/piaac/puf-data/. Accessed 5 May, 2019.

Organisation for Economic Co-operation and Development (OECD). (2016n). *Programme for the International Assessment of Adult Competencies (PIAAC), Greece Public Use File* (Version: 15965250, prggrcp1.sav). Paris: OECD Publishing. https://webfs.oecd.org/piaac/puf-data/. Accessed 5 May 2019.

Organisation for Economic Co-operation and Development (OECD). (2016o). *Programme for the International Assessment of Adult Competencies (PIAAC), Ireland Public Use File* (Version: 19982813, prgirlp1.sav). Paris: OECD Publishing. https://webfs.oecd.org/piaac/puf-data/. Accessed 5 May 2019.

Organisation for Economic Co-operation and Development (OECD). (2016p). *Programme for the International Assessment of Adult Competencies (PIAAC), Israel Public Use File* (Version: 18069090, prgisrp1.sav). Paris: OECD Publishing. https://webfs.oecd.org/piaac/puf-data/. Accessed 5 May 2019.

Organisation for Economic Co-operation and Development (OECD). (2016q). *Programme for the International Assessment of Adult Competencies (PIAAC), Italy Public Use File* (Version: 15433181, prgitap1.sav). Paris: OECD Publishing. https://webfs.oecd.org/piaac/puf-data/. Accessed 5 May 2019.

Organisation for Economic Co-operation and Development (OECD). (2016r). *Programme for the International Assessment of Adult Competencies (PIAAC), Japan Public Use File* (Version: 17505957, prgjpnp1.sav). Paris: OECD Publishing. https://webfs.oecd.org/piaac/puf-data/. Accessed 5 May 2019.

Organisation for Economic Co-operation and Development (OECD). (2016s). *Programme for the International Assessment of Adult Competencies (PIAAC), Korea Public Use File* (Version: 22217045, prgkorp1.sav). Paris: OECD Publishing. https://webfs.oecd.org/piaac/puf-data/. Accessed 5 May 2019.

Organisation for Economic Co-operation and Development (OECD). (2016t). *Programme for the International Assessment of Adult Competencies (PIAAC), Lithuania Public Use File* (Version: 17305986, prgltup1.sav). Paris: OECD Publishing. https://webfs.oecd.org/piaac/puf-data/. Accessed 5 May 2019.

Organisation for Economic Co-operation and Development (OECD). (2016u). *Programme for the International Assessment of Adult Competencies (PIAAC), Netherlands Public Use File* (Version: 18028845, prgnldp1.sav). Paris: OECD Publishing. https://webfs.oecd.org/piaac/puf-data/. Accessed 5 May 2019.

Organisation for Economic Co-operation and Development (OECD). (2016v). *Programme for the International Assessment of Adult Competencies (PIAAC), Norway Public Use File* (Version: 17723269, prgnorp1.sav). Paris: OECD Publishing. https://webfs.oecd.org/piaac/puf-data/. Accessed 5 May 2019.

Organisation for Economic Co-operation and Development (OECD). (2016w). *Programme for the International Assessment of Adult Competencies (PIAAC), New Zealand Public Use File* (Version: 21235362, prgnzlp1.sav). Paris: OECD Publishing. https://webfs.oecd.org/piaac/puf-data/. Accessed 5 May, 2019.

Organisation for Economic Co-operation and Development (OECD). (2016x). *Programme for the International Assessment of Adult Competencies (PIAAC), Poland Public Use File* (Version: 30634733, prgpolp1.sav). Paris: OECD Publishing. https://webfs.oecd.org/piaac/puf-data/. Accessed 5 May 2019.

Organisation for Economic Co-operation and Development (OECD). (2016y). *Programme for the International Assessment of Adult Competencies (PIAAC), Russian Federation Public Use File* (Version: 13378965, prgrusp1.sav). Paris: OECD Publishing. https://webfs.oecd.org/piaac/puf-data/. Accessed 5 May 2019.

Organisation for Economic Co-operation and Development (OECD). (2016z). *Programme for the International Assessment of Adult Competencies (PIAAC), Singapore Public Use File* (Version: 18353722, prgsgpp1.sav). Paris: OECD Publishing. https://webfs.oecd.org/piaac/puf-data/. Accessed 5 May 2019.

Organisation for Economic Co-operation and Development (OECD). (2016aa). *Programme for the International Assessment of Adult Competencies (PIAAC), Slovak Republic Public Use File* (Version: 18921861, prgsvkp1.sav). Paris: OECD Publishing. https://webfs.oecd.org/piaac/puf-data/. Accessed 5 May, 2019.

Organisation for Economic Co-operation and Development (OECD). (2016bb). *Programme for the International Assessment of Adult Competencies (PIAAC), Slovenia Public Use File* (Version: 18125930, prgsvnp1.sav). Paris: OECD Publishing. https://webfs.oecd.org/piaac/puf-data/. Accessed 5 May 2019.

Organisation for Economic Co-operation and Development (OECD). (2016cc). *Programme for the International Assessment of Adult Competencies (PIAAC), Spain Public Use File* (Version: 20201797, prgespp1.sav). Paris: OECD Publishing. https://webfs.oecd.org/piaac/puf-data/. Accessed 5 May, 2019.

Organisation for Economic Co-operation and Development (OECD). (2016dd). *Programme for the International Assessment of Adult Competencies (PIAAC), Sweden Public Use File* (Version: 15716978, prgswep1.sav). Paris: OECD Publishing. https://webfs.oecd.org/piaac/puf-data/. Accessed 5 May 2019.

Organisation for Economic Co-operation and Development (OECD). (2016ee). *Programme for the International Assessment of Adult Competencies (PIAAC), Turkey Public Use File* (Version: 16765802, prgturp1.sav). Paris: OECD Publishing. https://webfs.oecd.org/piaac/puf-data/. Accessed 5 May 2019.

Organisation for Economic Co-operation and Development (OECD). (2016ff). *Programme for the International Assessment of Adult Competencies (PIAAC), United Kingdom Public Use File* (Version: 17016050, prgusap1.sav). Paris: OECD Publishing. https://webfs.oecd.org/piaac/puf-data/. Accessed 5 May 2019.

Organisation for Economic Co-operation and Development (OECD). (2016gg). *Programme for the International Assessment of Adult Competencies (PIAAC), United States Public Use File* (Version: 17016050, prgusap1.sav). Paris: OECD Publishing. https://webfs.oecd.org/piaac/puf-data/. Accessed 5 May 2019.

Organisation for Economic Co-operation and Development (OECD). (2017a). *Programme for the International Assessment of Adult Competencies (PIAAC), Austria log file*. Data file version 2.0.0 [ZA6712_AT.data.zip]. Cologne: GESIS Data Archive. https://doi.org/10.4232/1.12955

Organisation for Economic Co-operation and Development (OECD). (2017b). *Programme for the International Assessment of Adult Competencies (PIAAC), Belgium log file*. Data file version 2.0.0 [ZA6712_BE.data.zip]. Cologne: GESIS Data Archive. https://doi.org/10.4232/1.12955

Organisation for Economic Co-operation and Development (OECD). (2017c). *Programme for the International Assessment of Adult Competencies (PIAAC), Germany log file*. Data file version 2.0.0 [ZA6712_DE.data.zip]. Cologne: GESIS Data Archive. https://doi.org/10.4232/1.12955

Organisation for Economic Co-operation and Development (OECD). (2017d). *Programme for the International Assessment of Adult Competencies (PIAAC), Denmark log file*. Data file version 2.0.0 [ZA6712_DK.data.zip]. Cologne: GESIS Data Archive. https://doi.org/10.4232/1.12955

Organisation for Economic Co-operation and Development (OECD). (2017e). *Programme for the International Assessment of Adult Competencies (PIAAC), Estonia log file*. Data file version 2.0.0 [ZA6712_EE.data.zip]. Cologne: GESIS Data Archive. https://doi.org/10.4232/1.12955

Organisation for Economic Co-operation and Development (OECD). (2017f). *Programme for the International Assessment of Adult Competencies (PIAAC), Spain log file*. Data file version 2.0.0 [ZA6712_ES.data.zip]. Cologne: GESIS Data Archive. https://doi.org/10.4232/1.12955

Organisation for Economic Co-operation and Development (OECD). (2017g). *Programme for the International Assessment of Adult Competencies (PIAAC), Finland log file*. Data file version 2.0.0 [ZA6712_FI.data.zip]. Cologne: GESIS Data Archive. https://doi.org/10.4232/1.12955

Organisation for Economic Co-operation and Development (OECD). (2017h). *Programme for the International Assessment of Adult Competencies (PIAAC), France log file*. Data file version 2.0.0 [ZA6712_FR.data.zip]. Cologne: GESIS Data Archive. https://doi.org/10.4232/1.12955

Organisation for Economic Co-operation and Development (OECD). (2017i). *Programme for the International Assessment of Adult Competencies (PIAAC), United Kingdom log file*. Data file version 2.0.0 [ZA6712_GB.data.zip]. Cologne: GESIS Data Archive. https://doi.org/10.4232/1.12955

Organisation for Economic Co-operation and Development (OECD). (2017j). *Programme for the International Assessment of Adult Competencies (PIAAC), Ireland log file*. Data file version 2.0.0 [ZA6712_IE.data.zip]. Cologne: GESIS Data Archive. https://doi.org/10.4232/1.12955

Organisation for Economic Co-operation and Development (OECD). (2017k). *Programme for the International Assessment of Adult Competencies (PIAAC), Italy log file*. Data file version 2.0.0 [ZA6712_IT.data.zip]. Cologne: GESIS Data Archive. https://doi.org/10.4232/1.12955

Organisation for Economic Co-operation and Development (OECD). (2017l). *Programme for the International Assessment of Adult Competencies (PIAAC), South Korea log file*. Data file version 2.0.0 [ZA6712_KR.data.zip]. Cologne: GESIS Data Archive. https://doi.org/10.4232/1.12955

Organisation for Economic Co-operation and Development (OECD). (2017m). *Programme for the International Assessment of Adult Competencies (PIAAC), Netherlands log file*. Data file version 2.0.0 [ZA6712_NL.data.zip]. Cologne: GESIS Data Archive. https://doi.org/10.4232/1.12955

Organisation for Economic Co-operation and Development (OECD). (2017n). *Programme for the International Assessment of Adult Competencies (PIAAC), Norway log file*. Data file version 2.0.0 [ZA6712_NO.data.zip]. Cologne: GESIS Data Archive. https://doi.org/10.4232/1.12955

Organisation for Economic Co-operation and Development (OECD). (2017o). *Programme for the International Assessment of Adult Competencies (PIAAC), Poland log file*. Data file version 2.0.0 [ZA6712_PL.data.zip]. Cologne: GESIS Data Archive. https://doi.org/10.4232/1.12955

Organisation for Economic Co-operation and Development (OECD). (2017p). *Programme for the International Assessment of Adult Competencies (PIAAC), Slovakia log file*. Data file version 2.0.0 [ZA6712_SK.data.zip]. Cologne: GESIS Data Archive. https://doi.org/10.4232/1.12955

Organisation for Economic Co-operation and Development (OECD). (2017q). *Programme for the International Assessment of Adult Competencies (PIAAC), United States log file*. Data file version 2.0.0 [ZA6712_US.data.zip]. Cologne: GESIS Data Archive. https://doi.org/10.4232/1.12955

Organisation for Economic Co-operation and Development (OECD). (2018a). *Programme for the International Assessment of Adult Competencies (PIAAC), English Pilot Study on Non-Cognitive Skills*. Data file version 1.0.0 [ZA6940]. Cologne: GESIS Data Archive. https://doi.org/10.4232/1.13062

Organisation for Economic Co-operation and Development (OECD). (2018b). *Programme for the International Assessment of Adult Competencies (PIAAC), international pilot study on non-cognitive skills* (Data file version 1.0.0 [ZA6941]). Cologne: GESIS Data Archive. https://doi.org/10.4232/1.13063.

Organisation for Economic Co-operation and Development (OECD). (2019a). *Beyond proficiency. Using log files to understand respondent behaviour in the survey of adult skills*. Paris: OECD Publishing. https://doi.org/10.1787/23078731. Accessed 5 May 2019.

Organisation for Economic Co-operation and Development (OECD). (2019b). *Programme for the International Assessment of Adult Competencies (PIAAC), Ecuador Public Use File* (Version: 17688347, prgecup1.sav). Paris: OECD Publishing. https://webfs.oecd.org/piaac/puf-data/. Accessed 20 December 2019.

Organisation for Economic Co-operation and Development (OECD). (2019c). *Programme for the International Assessment of Adult Competencies (PIAAC), Hungary Public Use File* (Version: 20439451, prghunp1.sav). Paris: OECD Publishing. https://webfs.oecd.org/piaac/puf-data/. Accessed 20 December 2019.

Organisation for Economic Co-operation and Development (OECD). (2019d). *Programme for the International Assessment of Adult Competencies (PIAAC), Kazakhstan Public Use File* (Version: 20450859, prgkazp1.sav). Paris: OECD Publishing. https://webfs.oecd.org/piaac/puf-data/. Accessed 20 December 2019.

Organisation for Economic Co-operation and Development (OECD). (2019e). *Programme for the International Assessment of Adult Competencies (PIAAC), Mexico Public Use File* (Version: 19760643, prgmexp1.sav). Paris: OECD Publishing. https://webfs.oecd.org/piaac/puf-data/. Accessed 20 December 2019.

Organisation for Economic Co-operation and Development (OECD). (2019f). *Programme for the International Assessment of Adult Competencies (PIAAC), Peru Public Use File* (Version: 22883339, prgperp1.sav). Paris: OECD Publishing. https://webfs.oecd.org/piaac/puf-data/. Accessed 20 December 2019.

Organisation for Economic Co-operation and Development (OECD). (2019g). *Programme for the International Assessment of Adult Competencies (PIAAC), United States Public Use File* (Version: 19748455, prgusap1_2017.sav). Paris: OECD Publishing. https://webfs.oecd.org/piaac/puf-data/. Accessed 20 December 2019.

Palczyńska, M., & Świst, K. (2016). *Measurement properties of non-cognitive scales in the Polish follow-up study on PIAAC (POSTPIAAC)* (OECD Education Working Paper No. 149). Paris: OECD Publishing. https://doi.org/10.1787/19939019. Accessed 5 May 2019.

Perry, A., Helmschrott, S., Konradt, I., & Maehler, D. B. (2017). *User guide for the German PIAAC scientific use file* (GESIS Papers No 2017|23). Cologne: GESIS – Leibniz-Institute for the Social Sciences. http://nbn-resolving.de/urn:nbn:de:0168-ssoar-54438-3. Accessed 10 May 2019.

Rammstedt, B., Ackermann, D., Helmschrott, S., Klaukien, A., Maehler, D., Martin, S., Massing, N., Zabal, A. (Eds). (2013). Grundlegende Kompetenzen Erwachsener im internationalen Vergleich: Ergebnissevon PIAAC 2012. Münster: Waxmann. https://nbn-resolving.org/urn:nbn:de:0168-ssoar-360687

Rammstedt, B., Martin, S., Zabal, A., Konradt, I., Maehler, D., Perry, A., et al. (2016a). *Programme for the International Assessment of Adult Competencies (PIAAC), Germany – Reduced version* ((Data file version 2.2.0) [ZA5845]). Cologne: GESIS Data Archive. https://doi.org/10.4232/1.12660.

Rammstedt, B., Martin, S., Zabal, A., Konradt, I., Maehler, D., Perry, A., et al. (2016b). *Programme for the International Assessment of Adult Competencies (PIAAC), Germany – Extended version – Regional data* ((Data file version 1.0.0) [ZA5846]). Cologne: GESIS Data Archive. https://doi.org/10.4232/1.12560.

Rammstedt, B., Martin, S., Zabal, A., Helmschrott, S., Konradt, I., & Maehler, D. (2017a). *Programme for the International Assessment of Adult Competencies (PIAAC), Germany – Extended version – microm data* ((Data file version 1.0.0) [ZA5963]). Cologne: GESIS Data Archive. https://doi.org/10.4232/1.12926.

Rammstedt, B., Martin, S., Zabal, A., Carstensen, C., & Schupp, J. (2017b). The PIAAC longitudinal study in Germany: Rationale and design. *Large-scale Assessment in Education, 5*(4). https://doi.org/10.1186/s40536-017-0040-.

Rampey, B. D., Finnegan, R., Goodman, M., Mohadjer, L., Krenzke, T., Hogan, J., & Provasnik, S. (2016). *Skills of U.S. unemployed, young, and older adults in sharper focus: Results from the Program for the International Assessment of Adult Competencies (PIAAC) 2012/2014: First look (NCES 2016-039rev)* (U.S. Department of Education). Washington, DC: National Center for Education Statistics. http://nces.ed.gov/pubsearch. Accessed 19 July 2019.

Situ, J. (2015). *Using the program for international assessment of adult competencies direct measures of skills in the longitudinal and international study of adults* (Longitudinal and International Study of Adults Research Paper Series No. 89-648-X). Statistics Canada. https://www150.statcan.gc.ca/n1/pub/89-648-x/89-648-x2015001-eng.htm. Accessed 5 May 2019.

Solga, H., & Heisig, J. P. (2015). *Programme for the International Assessment of Adult Competencies (PIAAC), Germany – Prime Age (2012)* (Data file version 1.1.0 [ZA5951]). Cologne: GESIS Data Archive. https://doi.org/10.4232/1.12386.

Statistics Austria. (2014). *Programme for the International Assessment of Adult Competencies (PIAAC), Scientific Use File PIAAC 2011/12 for Austria*. Vienna: Statistics Austria.

Statistics Austria. (2015). *Programme for the International Assessment of Adult Competencies (PIAAC), public use file extended PIAAC 2011/12 for Austria*. Vienna: Statistics Austria.

Statistics Canada. (2013). *PUMF 2012 – Programme for the International Assessment of Adult Competencies (PIAAC)* (Catalogue number. 89-555-X2013002). Ottawa: Statistics Canada.

Statistics Norway. (2015). *Survey of adult skills (PIAAC) 2012* ([Dataset] (NSD2135)). Bergen: Norwegian Social Science Data Services. https://doi.org/10.18712/NSD-NSD2135-V1.

Steinacker, G., & Wolfert, S. (2017). *Durchführung der 2. Erhebungswelle von PIAAC-L (Kooperative längsschnittliche Weiterverfolgung der PIAAC-Studie in Deutschland): Feldbericht zur Erhebung 2015* (GESIS Papers No. 2017|04). Cologne: GESIS – Leibniz Institute for the Social Sciences. http://www.ssoar.info/ssoar/handle/document/50488. Accessed 12 December 2017.

Zabal, A., Martin, S., Massing, N., Ackermann, D., Helmschrott, S., Barkow, I., & Rammstedt, B. (2014). *PIAAC Germany 2012: Technical report*. Münster: Waxmann.

Zabal, A., Martin, S., & Rammstedt, B. (2016). *PIAAC-L data collection 2014: Technical report. Follow-up to PIAAC Germany 2012* (GESIS Papers No. 2016|17). Cologne: GESIS – Leibniz-Institute for the Social Sciences. http://www.ssoar.info/ssoar/handle/document/49665. Accessed 12 December 2017.

Open Access This chapter is licensed under the terms of the Creative Commons Attribution 4.0 International License (http://creativecommons.org/licenses/by/4.0/), which permits use, sharing, adaptation, distribution and reproduction in any medium or format, as long as you give appropriate credit to the original author(s) and the source, provide a link to the Creative Commons license and indicate if changes were made.

The images or other third party material in this chapter are included in the chapter's Creative Commons license, unless indicated otherwise in a credit line to the material. If material is not included in the chapter's Creative Commons license and your intended use is not permitted by statutory regulation or exceeds the permitted use, you will need to obtain permission directly from the copyright holder.

Chapter 5
Analysing PIAAC Data with the International Data Explorer (IDE)

Emily Pawlowski and Jaleh Soroui

Abstract This chapter introduces readers to the PIAAC International Data Explorer (IDE), an online tool for conducting analyses with the Programme for the International Assessment of Adult Competencies (PIAAC) data using a simple point-and-click interface without any special software or advanced statistical knowledge. It describes the data available in the IDE and provides an overview of how the data in the IDE is organised. It also covers the analysis types and statistical estimates available in the IDE, as well as its display and reporting options. These statistic and analysis options include averages, percentages (including proficiency level distributions), standard deviations, and percentiles, as well as significance testing, gap analysis, and regression analysis. The chapter also provides example research scenarios that illustrate how to answer questions using the IDE and how to interpret results from the IDE.

5.1 Introduction to the IDE

5.1.1 What Is the PIAAC IDE?

The PIAAC International Data Explorer (IDE) is a web-based tool for conducting analyses using a simple point-and-click interface without the need for special software on the user's desktop or related statistical knowledge. It was commissioned by the OECD but developed and licensed to the OECD by Educational Testing Service (ETS). The IDE can produce design-unbiased estimates and standard errors that reflect PIAAC's complex sampling and assessment design, accounting for its multi-matrix sampling of items and people, weights, and plausible values, to answer a variety of research questions. These questions can range in complexity from

---

E. Pawlowski (✉) · J. Soroui
American Institutes for Research, Washington, DC, USA
e-mail: epawlowski@air.org

© The Author(s) 2020
D. B. Maehler, B. Rammstedt (eds.), *Large-Scale Cognitive Assessment*,
Methodology of Educational Measurement and Assessment,
https://doi.org/10.1007/978-3-030-47515-4_5

simple descriptive results using one or multiple variables, such as average score by gender, to more complex ones that require using a combination of variables, such as a linear regression of literacy scores on age, gender, and education.

5.1.2 Differences Between the OECD IDE and the US IDE

There are two versions of the PIAAC IDE based on the same technology but containing somewhat different data and hosted by different organizations. The first, which we will refer to as the 'US IDE' (accessed at https://nces.ed.gov/surveys/piaac/ideuspiaac/), is supported by the National Center for Educational Statistics (NCES) in the United States; the second, the 'OECD IDE' (accessed at https://piaacdataexplorer.oecd.org/ide/idepiaac/), is supported by the OECD.

While both IDEs are similar, there are some differences between the two, primarily in terms of data availability and analytical functions (see Table 5.1), as a result of respective sharing agreements, quality considerations, and aspects related to organisational policies. Both IDEs include the countries and economies that participated in PIAAC Cycle 1, more specifically Rounds 1 and 2.[1] The US IDE includes data for Cyprus (Michaelidou-Evripidou et al. 2016), which is not in the OECD version. The OECD IDE includes data for Australia and the Russian Federation (OECD 2016a) that are not available in the US IDE. As a unique source, the US IDE contains the US combined 2012/2014 household data (Holtzman et al. 2016) as well as US prison data (Hogan et al. 2016a),[2] while the OECD IDE contains only the US 2012 data (OECD 2016b). Additionally, the US version contains variables specific to the US and the prison study (e.g. Hogan et al. 2016b) that are not available in the OECD version. There are also some differences in the structure and organization of variables between the two IDEs.

The US IDE has some additional analytical functions, such as gap analysis and regression analysis. It also groups subjects together so they can be displayed simultaneously and has proficiency levels/benchmarks as 'variables' instead of 'statistics options', which provide additional options for analysis.

Most of the details in this chapter will apply to both versions of the IDE, and differences will be noted or discussed as relevant throughout the chapter.

---

[1] The countries that participated in Round 3 of PIAAC Cycle 1 are likely to be added in November 2019 or some other date after publication of results.

[2] In addition to collecting data in 2012, the United States conducted a PIAAC National Supplement in 2013 to 2014, which included an oversample of unemployed adults aged 16–65 years and young adults aged 16–34 years; it further extended the sample to include older adults aged 66–74 years in the United States as well as the incarcerated population.

Table 5.1 Differences between US IDE and OECD IDE

	US IDE only	OECD IDE only
Data availability		
US data	2012/2014 household	2012 household
	2014 prison	
	US-specific and prison-specific variables	
International data	Cyprus	Australia
		Russian Federation
Additional functions		
	Gap analysis	
	Regression analysis	
	Grouping of subjects	
	Proficiency levels/benchmarks as 'variables'	

5.1.3 What Can and Cannot Be Done in the IDE?

The IDE can be used to compute various types of statistical estimates, including averages, percentages (including proficiency level distributions), standard deviations, and percentiles, along with their respective standard errors, while accounting for design (i.e. the use of estimation weights for correct population representation, replicate weights to account for sampling variance, and plausible values to account for measurement variance).

The IDE can also be used to apply basic recoding or collapsing of categories for a variable. Results can be displayed in a variety of formats, including tables, maps, and charts, such as bar charts, column charts, line charts, and percentiles charts. The IDE can also be used to run statistical significance testing, and, as mentioned previously, the US PIAAC IDE can be used to run regression and gap analysis.

Some advanced types of analyses cannot be done in the IDE, including more complex linear regressions and logistic regressions; correlation between variables or scale scores on multiple domains; or analyses that involve more complex recoding of variables, such as creating new variables from multiple existing ones. To conduct more advanced analyses, or those using variables available only on the US Restricted Use File, use of the microdata files and other analytical tools, such as the International Association for the Evaluation of Educational Achievement (IEA) International Database Analyzer (IDB Analyzer; see Chap. 6 in this volume) or the REPEST module for Stata developed by the OECD (see Chap. 7 in this volume), is required.

5.2 Content of the IDE

There are four categories of types of data available in the PIAAC IDE. They include:

- *Direct assessment data*—that is, data on the three cognitive domains of literacy, numeracy, and digital problem solving.
- *Background questionnaire (BQ) data.* Both the OECD and US IDE contain international variables that are common across all countries (OECD 2014), including some variables derived from original responses through recoding or categorisation of direct responses to the BQ. The US IDE contains specific variables administered only to the household and/or prison population in the United States.
- *Trend data* from the two prior international adult literacy assessments, including literacy data from the International Adult Literacy Survey (IALS; OECD and Statistics Canada 2000), conducted in 1994 to 1998, and literacy and numeracy data from the Adult Literacy and Life Skills Survey (ALL; Statistics Canada and OECD 2005), conducted in 2003–2008.
- *Jurisdiction* information, meaning data organised by OECD Entities, OECD member countries that participated in PIAAC at the national level, such as the United States; OECD Sub-National Entities, or OECD members that participated in PIAAC at the sub-national level; and Partners, or participating countries that are not OECD members. In addition, the US IDE contains data from the full 2012/14 US data for those aged 16–74 years, as well as from the incarcerated population.

5.3 Organisation of the IDE

In this section we will describe the IDE's user interface and how the data are organised and presented. The content and functions of the IDE are organised under four main tabs or pages (as seen in Fig. 5.1):

- *Select Criteria*
- *Select Variables*
- *Edit Reports*
- *Build Reports*

The content and functions of these tabs are outlined in Table 5.2, and we will introduce each in turn.

Additional details on the content and organisation of the IDE can be found in the PIAAC International Data Explorer (IDE) Training Video on the PIAAC Gateway website at http://piaacgateway.com/ide-training-video.

5 Analysing PIAAC Data with the International Data Explorer (IDE)

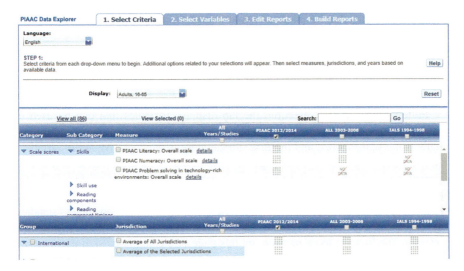

Fig. 5.1 Overview of IDE tab organisation

Table 5.2 Selection options and functions within each tab or page of the IDE

Tab or page	Options and functions
Select criteria	Select continuous, dependent measures (including skills scale scores)
	Select jurisdictions
	Select years/studies
Select variables	Select categorical variables
Edit reports	Select statistics (e.g. averages, percentages, standard deviations, percentiles, proficiency levels)
	Use format options (e.g. select display of missing values or decimals)
	Edit tables (e.g. recoding variables or changing table layout)
Build reports	Display data tables
	Produce charts
	Use additional statistical functions (e.g. significance testing, gap analysis, regression analysis)
	Export and save reports

5.3.1 Select Criteria Tab

In the OECD IDE, on the *Select Criteria* page, the user begins by selecting a *Subject* (literacy, numeracy, or problem solving) that will be the only cognitive domain available for analysis.

In the US IDE, the user begins by selecting a *Display*, or population of interest. These displays are Adults aged 16–65; Young adults aged 16–34; and US adults residing in households and prisons aged 16–74. The 16–65 display and 16–34 display allow for international comparison, while the last display is focused on US adults only. After this initial selection is made, selection of years, measures, and jurisdictions will become available on the Select Criteria tab.

In the OECD IDE and the US IDE, displays allowing for international comparison (Adults 16–65 or Young adults 16–34), there are column headers to select the years/studies for analysis, which can be used to analyse the data from ALL 2003–2008 or IALS 1994–1998.

Following the initial selection, the tab displays variables that can be used as dependent measures for the target analysis. The first category of variables in both IDEs is the scale scores, and the first sub-category is the cognitive skills variables. All variables included in this page are continuous variables. These continuous variables include the specific values of actual responses or derived measures and indices rather than the range or group in which they fit. So, for example, one would find the specific earnings variable on this tab. One can produce averages, standard deviations, and percentiles of the dependent measures on this page. Therefore, selecting the literacy score measure on this page or a continuous skill use measure would allow one to later conduct analyses such as producing averages or percentiles of these measures.

Note that in the OECD IDE, only the cognitive domain initially selected as the *Subject* is available for selection, while in the US version, all three cognitive domains are available.

Other variables available on this tab include:

- The 'skill use' indices (continuous measures derived from responses to several questions on frequency of use of specific reading, writing, numeracy, or ICT skills) and reading components variables
- The population category, which is used to look at percentages across the full sample without looking at any specific continuous measures
- Categories and variables from the International BQ, with various sub-categories from each section of the International BQ that was common across countries, such as Formal education, Current work, and Background
- Derived variables, including PIAAC-specific variables as well as comparable trend variables that are available from IALS, ALL, and PIAAC and can be used to do analysis over time
- Prison-specific variables on topics such as prison jobs, available when the US Adults, 16–74 years old (Household and Prison) display is selected in the US IDE

Data from the jurisdictions (or all participating countries and entities) are included in the lower portion of this tab, allowing for international comparison. In the OECD IDE, the International group includes the OECD Average, which provides the average of OECD national and sub-national entities in the OECD IDE, while the US IDE can provide the Average of All Jurisdictions, which also includes the Partners in the average. These averages always stay the same regardless of the specific jurisdictions selected. The other average listed in this group is the Average of the Selected Jurisdictions, which provides the average of all the specific jurisdictions selected in the analysis; it will vary depending on the selections. For example, if Canada, Japan, and the United States were selected in addition to the Average of the Selected Jurisdictions, this would provide the average of those three selected countries.

Note that when US Adults 16–74 is selected as the target population in the US IDE, then only the US Household (16–74 years old) and US Prison (16–74 years old) will be available in the jurisdiction section.

5.3.2 Select Variables Tab

This tab contains variables organised by category and sub-category, similar to the previous page. The variables here are not at a continuous measurement level. Rather, they are all categorical variables (ordered or nominal). For example, the tab includes variables categorising detailed income into deciles, which is related to but different from the continuous income variables available on the first tab. The variables here can be used differently in analysis than the variables on the first page. They can be used to produce percentage distributions or crosstabs and can also be used to cross or subset the results for the measures selected on the *Select Criteria* page.

Major reporting groups, the first category on this tab, provides easy access to commonly used variables. This category begins with the *All adults* option, which allows one to get results for the full population, without breaking it down by additional categories or variables. It also includes common demographic variables, such as gender, age, education level, and employment status.

In the US IDE, proficiency levels is another major subcategory; it allows access to the six proficiency levels for literacy and numeracy and four levels for digital problem solving.

Other variables available on this tab include:

- The International BQ variables, including current work, education, skill use, and background; see the Background Questionnaire – Conceptual Framework (OECD 2011),
- Derived variables as well as trend variables
- US prison variables available within the 16–74 (Household and Prison) display; see examples in the US PIAAC prison report (Rampey et al. 2016).

On this page, multiple variables can be selected, and the reports produced on the next two tabs will use them in separate or combined ways in the analyses as selected.

On both the *Select Criteria* and *Select Variables* pages, the search function is available to search for a measure or variable by keyword(s) or variable names, as an alternative to looking through the categories for a measure or variable.

5.4 IDE Functions, Analysis Types, and Statistic Options

In the following sections, most of the IDE's major functions, types of analysis, and statistic options will be covered.

These options are accessible in the *Edit Reports* and *Build Reports* tabs.

5.4.1 Edit Reports Tab: Statistic Options

The following statistics are available through the Statistics Option button on the Edit Reports tab.

5.4.1.1 Averages

The IDE computes the mean of the selected measure, such as estimating the average scores of the literacy, numeracy, or digital problem-solving domains for a given population or subgroup. Using the average statistic with the cognitive scale scores selected on the first tab can answer questions ranging from 'How do average numeracy scores compare across countries?' to 'What are the average problem solving in technology-rich environments scores of US young adults aged 16–34 by employment status?'

The averages statistic can also be used for other continuous, noncognitive variables, to answer questions like 'How do the average monthly earnings compare between males and females in the United States, Japan, and Canada?' or 'How does the number of hours of participation in non-formal education vary by education level?'

5.4.1.2 Percentages

The percentages statistic produces the percentage distribution of the column variable within each category for the row variable, meaning that the categories of the column variable will add up to 100% for each category of the row variable. So, for example, if gender is the row variable (i.e. gender categories are listed as the row labels), and analysis is done by level of educational attainment, the results would show the percentage in each educational attainment category for males and for females. This function is useful to answer questions such as 'What is the percentage distribution of males and females in different areas of study?' or 'What percentage of the US adult population are employed?'

The percentage distributions do not include missing data (i.e. data missing due to nonresponse, or valid skips due to survey design) unless additional selections are made in the *Format Options* section of the *Edit Reports* page (see below).

5.4.1.3 Standard Deviations

The standard deviation statistic is a measure of variation or dispersion of the values for a particular variable. This statistic option can be used to answer questions such as 'What is the standard deviation of the literacy scale across all countries?' or 'What is the standard deviation of income in each country?'

5.4.1.4 Percentiles

The percentiles option shows the threshold, or cut point, below which certain percentage of adults score at or below that cut point. For example, the 50th percentile literacy score shows the median value, of which half the adults performed above the threshold and half below, and the 75th percentile would show the cut point above which the top 25 percent of adults performed. The OECD IDE has selection options for the 5th, 10th, 25th, 50th, 75th, 90th, and 95th percentiles, while the US IDE has the 10th, 25th, 50th, 75th, and 90th percentiles available. The percentiles statistic can be used to answer questions such as 'What are the percentiles on the literacy scale, including the median, for each age group?' or 'How does the monthly income cut point for being in the top 10% of earners vary by education level?'

Note: The IDEs do not support the definition of user-defined cut points for percentiles.

5.4.1.5 Achievement Levels

Achievement levels (discrete and combined), commonly referred to as proficiency levels, are available as a statistic option only in the OECD IDE, while this type of analysis would be done using proficiency levels as variables in the US IDE, as described later. These proficiency levels are reported as the percentage of adults scoring at performance levels anchored by a specific set of concrete skills.

5.4.1.6 Discrete Achievement Levels (OECD IDE Only)

The discrete achievement levels option allows users to look at each individual level in the proficiency distribution, so Below Level 1 through Level 5 for literacy and numeracy and Below Level 1 through Level 3 for problem solving. Note that the literacy-related nonresponse category in literacy and the computer-related nonresponse categories in problem solving will display estimates from non-missing values only when *Percentage across full sample* is selected as the measure. Literacy-related nonresponse includes those adults unable to communicate in the language(s) of the BQ, or those with a learning or mental disability, while the computer-related nonresponse groups include those with no computer experience, those who failed the ICT core, and those who refused the computer-based assessment. The discrete performance levels statistic type can be used to answer questions such as 'What is the literacy proficiency distribution within each employment status category in Australia?' or 'What is the percentage of employed adults performing at the lowest literacy level in the United States and Australia?'

5.4.1.7 Combined Achievement Levels (OECD IDE Only)

The *Combined Achievement Levels* option allows users to analyse combined groupings of adjacent proficiency levels, enabling them to focus on those adults performing at higher or lower ranges of levels. For example, if Below Level 3 was selected within the *Combined Achievement Levels* selection, the percentage of adults at Below Level 1, Level 1, and Level 2 would be reported as a combined grouping. For literacy and numeracy, the grouping options available for the combined achievement levels are Below Level 2, Below Level 3, Low Levels (1 and 2), High Levels (4 and 5), and At or above Level 3. For problem solving, the grouping options are Below Level 2, Below Level 3, Low Levels (1 and 2), and High Levels (2 and 3). Questions that can be answered using combined achievement levels include 'What is the percentage of young adults performing at the low levels in numeracy within each level of educational attainment?' or 'Which age groups have the largest percentage of high performers in digital problem solving?'

5.4.1.8 Levels as Variables, Profile by Level, and Score by Level (US IDE Only)

Proficiency levels are available as variables in the US IDE, rather than as a statistic typed, so selection of proficiency levels for analysis occurs on the *Select Variables* page rather than the *Edit Reports* page. This analysis option is not available in the OECD IDE.

If proficiency levels are selected as a variable, then selecting *Percentages* as the statistic will provide the percentage distribution of proficiency levels. Having proficiency levels as variables allows for some additional flexibility in analysis. For example, the proficiency level categories can be collapsed as desired—for example, collapsing Levels 4 and 5 but leaving the other levels in the proficiency distribution as is—using the *Edit* action on the *Edit Reports* page (described in more detail later). Using the proficiency levels in this way can answer similar questions to those in the combined or discrete achievement levels in the OECD IDE.

Having the proficiency levels as variables also allows one to create profiles of those at different skill levels by looking at the percentage distribution of characteristics within each level. One can create profiles within levels by using the *Edit* action on the *Edit Reports* page (see below). This can be used to answer questions such as 'Among those at the lowest numeracy levels, what percentage have a tertiary education?' or 'What is the distribution of health status among US young adults within each numeracy proficiency level?'

One can also look at averages of the continuous measures available on the *Select Criteria* page, including cognitive scale scores, within each level if proficiency levels are selected as a variable and *Averages* is selected as the statistic. This can be used to answer questions such as 'What is the average literacy score at each numeracy proficiency level for older adults?' or 'How do average monthly earnings vary by problem-solving proficiency level?'

5.4.2 Build Reports Tab: Additional Statistical Functions

In addition to those statistic types, there are some other analytical functions available in the IDE on the next page, *Build Reports*. The following is available in both versions of the IDE.

5.4.2.1 Significance Test

Significance testing can be used to estimate if differences in results reflect a true difference in the population, or are likely to have been observed due to sampling variation or chance. On the B*uild Reports* page, there is a *Significance Test* selection above the table displaying results for the analysis. In the *Significance Test* window, users can select to conduct testing either *Between Jurisdictions* (comparing similar populations across countries, e.g. determining whether females perform higher in numeracy in Germany or Spain), *Within Variables* (comparing groups or categories of a variable within a jurisdiction, e.g. determining whether females or males perform differently in numeracy in Italy), or *Across Years* (comparing groups or a full population within a jurisdiction over time, e.g. determining whether the numeracy score of females in Canada was different across IALS, ALL, and PIAAC).

Depending on the variable and jurisdiction selections, some significance testing options that are not applicable will be greyed out and not available for selection. For example, if only PIAAC data were used in analysis, one will not be able to conduct testing across years (i.e. with IALS or ALL). Similarly, if only one jurisdiction was selected, one will not be able to conduct testing between jurisdictions. Other steps in this *Significance Testing* window allow users to name their significance tests, select whether they want their results displayed in a table format or map format (available only when *Between Jurisdictions Testing* is selected), or choose to display score details—that is, display the estimates and standard errors on the table. The last section is used to select which jurisdictions, variables, and/or categories, years, and statistics to compare.

A few additional analytical functions, gap analysis and regression analysis, are available only on the *Build Reports* page of the US IDE.

5.4.2.2 Gap Analysis (US IDE Only)

The *Gap Analysis* function can compare differences in gaps between countries and/or across different time points. For example, the most basic type of gap analysis for comparing average literacy scores by gender for two countries would be to compare the male–female gap (i.e. score difference between males and females) in one country to the male–female gap in another country. The *Gap Analysis* window is available from the *Build Reports* page. Selecting the basis for comparison on this page, either *Between Jurisdictions* or *Across Years*, users can also select the gap, or difference measure, to analyse either *Between Groups*, *Between Years*, *Between Groups and Years*, or *Between Percentiles* within the selected variable.

Similar to the significance testing, other steps in this window allow users to name their significance tests, select whether they want their results displayed in a table format or map format, or choose to display score details. The last section is used to select which jurisdictions, variables and/or categories, years, and statistics to compare. This function can be used to answer questions such as 'Is the gap in numeracy skills between young adults (16–24) and older adults (55–65) different in the United States than in Canada?' or 'Did the gender gap in numeracy skills change over time between ALL and PIAAC?'

5.4.2.3 Regression Analysis (US IDE Only)

Regression analysis functionality is available only in the US IDE and uses a linear regression approach. Although the function is more restrictive, and there are fewer options than when conducting the analysis using standard statistical packages, this function allows users to examine and test the level of association between one continuous dependent variable (predicted) and up to three independent variables (predictors). Dummy coding (i.e. a 0/1 flag) is used to code independent variables, where the first subgroup of the independent variable is the reference group and cannot be changed. This is useful for comparing each subgroup against a reference group. For example, if the subgroup *Excellent* is the reference group for the independent variable Health Status, the IDE creates a *Very Good* dummy variable (1 for respondents who answered *Very Good*, 0 otherwise), a *Good* dummy variable (1 for respondents who answered *Good*, 0 otherwise), a *Fair* dummy variable (1 for respondents who answered *Fair*, 0 otherwise), and a *Poor* dummy variable (1 for respondents who answered *Poor*, 0 otherwise). The reference group *Excellent* is excluded from the regression analysis. This way, each of the other health groups is compared to the *Excellent* group using a total of four dummy variables.

Regression analysis is accessible on the *Build Reports* page. In the *Regression Analysis* window, one can create a name for the regression analysis and select jurisdictions, year, and up to three independent variables for analysis. Regressions can be used to answer questions such as 'Do US males have higher monthly earnings than females, even when controlling for occupation and industry?' or 'Do employed US adults have higher numeracy skills than unemployed adults, even when controlling for educational attainment and age?'

Note that regression analysis can only be performed for 1 year and one jurisdiction at a time, unlike most other analysis types. The continuous measure selected on the *Select Criteria* page will become the dependent variable for regression, and the independent variables are from the categorical variables selected on the *Select Variables* page and cannot include continuous measures.

5.4.3 Display and Reporting Results Options

The following are different options to display and format results.

5.4.3.1 Format Options

The *Format Options* selection on the *Edit Reports* page allows users to select various options on how to display variable labels, whether to display missing values in percentage results, and year order. It also includes options on the number of decimal places displayed in the results, whether standard errors are included and whether parentheses/brackets are used. The selections will apply to all reports.

5.4.3.2 Edit Option

In addition, the *Edit* option, available for each individual report in the *Action* column on the *Edit Reports* page, allows users to change or select the measure, jurisdiction, year, and statistic or create new variables by collapsing or combining categories of a selected variable. It also allows users to edit the table layout by changing whether the variables are located in the rows and columns. Particularly for percentages analysis, changing the rows and columns of the table will impact the results and change how the distributions are analysed and reported (i.e. the categories of which variable(s) add up to 100%). For example, within proficiency levels analysis in the US IDE, moving the proficiency levels variable to the row section and one (or both) of the other selected variables to the column section produces results showing a profile by levels.

Other display format and options available on the *Build Reports* page include:

Data Tables
By default, the IDE will present statistical results in a data table format that is displayed on the *Build Reports* page. Note that up to two statistics and up to three variables can be selected for inclusion in each report table.

Chart

On the *Build Reports* page, the *Chart* selection allows another option to display results. Multiple years/studies or jurisdictions may be selected, but only a single statistic type can be selected for inclusion in the chart. In the *Chart Options* window, one can choose the chart type and how the data are displayed. Chart types available in both the OECD and US versions of the IDE include *Bar Chart*, *Column Chart*, *Line Chart*, and *Percentiles Chart*. Note that the *Percentiles Chart* is available only when the percentiles statistic is selected.

The OECD IDE also includes *Discrete Chart* and *Cumulative Chart* types, which are available when the *Discrete Achievement Levels* or *Combined Achievement Levels* statistic is selected, respectively. Below the chart type selection, one can choose what the bar/column/line values will display and what these values will be grouped by. The selections here will determine how the data are displayed and organised. After previewing the chart, use the drop-down menus above the chart to view other sub-sets of the data, depending on previous selections. Once the chart selections are complete, the Done button finalises the chart and allows it to later be saved or exported.

Export Reports

On the *Build Reports* page, the *Export Reports* button allows tables, charts, and significance tests produced in the IDE to be saved or printed. The reports checked off in the *Edit Reports* page, and any associated charts or significance tests, will be available for selection to export. The user also must select the format for export here. In both the OECD and US versions of the IDE, HTML, Excel, or Word formats are available. In the US IDE, a PDF format is also available for export.

The US IDE has one other option to save results on the *Build Reports* page. The *Link to this Page* button can be used to produce a link that can be copied and pasted into an email or browser. Note that only the main results table is produced through this link, and if the user had collapsed variables, conducted significance testing, or created charts for the analysis, they would not be directly available.

5.5 Example Research Scenarios

The following research scenarios will provide a basic idea of the kind of questions that can be answered using the IDE and how to interpret the IDE results. A more detailed step-by-step walk of additional research questions can be found in the PIAAC International Data Explorer (IDE) Training Video on the PIAAC Gateway website at http://piaacgateway.com/ide-training-video.

5.5.1 Scenario 1: Averages Analysis

For the first scenario, the IDE will be used to answer the following question: *What are the average problem solving in technology-rich environments scores in Australia, Canada, and England/Northern Ireland by employment status?*

This scenario covers a basic research question and the simplest way of reporting the results. The OECD IDE will be used here, but the process for answering this question in the US IDE would be similar. To answer this question, the *Subject* used is *Problem Solving*, and the continuous measure selected on the *Select Criteria* page is the skills scale score for problem solving (*PIAAC Problem Solving: Solving* located in the *Scale Scores Category* and *Skills Sub-Category*). The jurisdictions or countries of interest in the scenario are Australia and Canada from the *OECD National Entities Group* and England/Northern Ireland from the *OECD Sub-National Entities Group* on the *Select Criteria* page. The categorical variable for analysis selected on the *Select Variables* page is the derived employment status variable, the variable *Current status/work history – Employment status (DERIVED BY CAPI)* found in the *International Background Questionnaire Category* and *Current Sub-Category*. Finally, on the *Edit Reports* page, *Averages* is the *Statistic* to answer this type of question.

On the *Build Reports* page, a table like that in Fig. 5.2 is produced. In this output, read each row across to find results (averages with the related standard errors) for the relevant jurisdiction. For example, the average problem-solving score in Australia is 291 for employed adults, 282 for the unemployed, and 282 for those out of the labour force. The related standard errors appear in parentheses next to the main estimate and provide information about the uncertainty of the estimates. It appears that employed adults perform better in problem solving than those who are unemployed and out of the labour force, but a significance test would need to be conducted to determine whether this apparent difference is statistically significant.

5.5.2 Scenario 2: Proficiency Levels Analysis, Significance Testing, and Charts

This scenario uses the OECD IDE to introduce proficiency levels analysis, conduct significance testing, and create charts to answer the following question: *How does the percentage of non-native-born US adults performing at low levels on the numeracy proficiency scale compare to the percentage among their peers internationally?*

As described in the overview of the analysis types, the process for conducting analysis with proficiency levels is different in the US IDE (not illustrated here). For this scenario, the *Subject* is *Numeracy*, the measure chosen on the *Select Criteria* page can be the numeracy score (*PIAAC Numeric: Numeracy* located in the *Scale Scores Category* and *Skills Sub-Category*), and the jurisdictions are the *OECD*

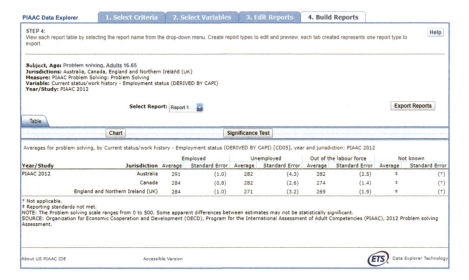

Fig. 5.2 Table output from Scenario 1
(Source: Organisation for Economic Co-operation and Development (OECD) PIAAC International Data Explorer)

Average (which is the average of the OECD National and Sub-National Entities and does not include Partners) in the *International Group* and the United States in the *OECD National Entities Group*. On the *Select Variables* page, the variable of interest is *Background – Born in country* in the *Major reporting groups Category* and *Sub-Category*. On the *Edit Reports* page, within the *Combined Achievement Levels Statistic Option*, the *Below Level 2* option can be used to focus on the group of low-skilled adults.

The results table displayed on the *Build Reports* page shows that, internationally, 36% of non-native born adults perform Below Level 2 in numeracy, while 49% in the United States do. The *Significance Test* function on this page can be used to see if the difference between these two numbers is statistically significant.

The *Between Jurisdictions* significance testing type is used to compare proficiency levels between the US and the OECD average rather than *Within Variables*, which compares proficiency levels within each jurisdiction for the native born and non-native born. The testing of interest would use *All Jurisdictions* in the *Jurisdiction* section and the *No* (not born in the country) category in the *Variable* section. The significance results shown in Fig. 5.3 are the *Table* output type. The title provides details and information that this significance test is for the statistic and group of interest (Below Level 2 and not born in the country). In the legend below the table, the less-than arrow (<) with lighter blue shading indicates 'significantly lower', the greater-than arrow (>) with darker blue shading indicates 'significantly higher', and the x with white shading indicates 'no significant difference'.

5 Analysing PIAAC Data with the International Data Explorer (IDE)

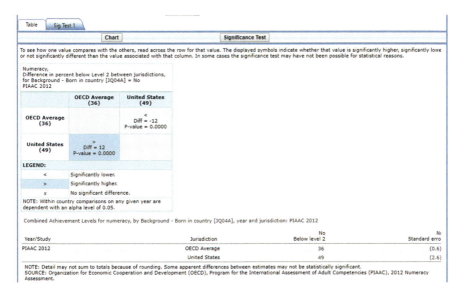

Fig. 5.3 Significance test output from Scenario 2
(Source: Organisation for Economic Co-operation and Development (OECD) PIAAC International Data Explorer)

To interpret the table, read across the row that shows, for example, that the OECD Average percentage at Below Level 2 is significantly lower than the percentage for the United States. The proficiency level percentage values being compared for each jurisdiction is in parentheses after each jurisdiction label (e.g. for the United States it was 49%). Within the table, the differences in percentage points between the two jurisdictions or groups being compared are found under the symbol indicating the results of the testing. In this example, the difference is 12 percentage points for the OECD average and the United States. The difference is estimated based on the values with full precision (i.e. unrounded values), so even though it may seem that the difference should be 13, the rounded difference based on estimates with full precision is 12. The value in parentheses is the standard error of this difference. The p-value for that testing is indicated under the difference. As indicated in the note, an alpha level of 0.05 is being used for these comparisons, so testing with a p-value lower than this indicates a significant difference.

The IDE also provides a *Chart* option on the *Build Reports* page as another way to display your results. To compare the results from the OECD Average and United States visually, select both in the *Jurisdiction* section within the *Data Options* selections. Use the *Bar Chart* type and use the *Jurisdiction* for the *Bar Values* and have the *Values Grouped by Combined Achievement levels* within the *Chart Options* selections in order to create a chart comparing the level of low-skilled adults across jurisdictions. The figure produced would display results from those who were not born in the country, as shown in Fig. 5.4.

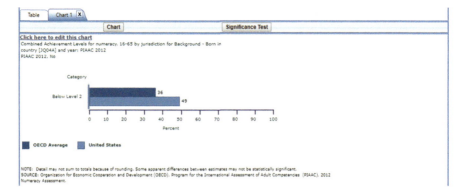

Fig. 5.4 Chart output from Scenario 2
(Source: Organisation for Economic Co-operation and Development (OECD) PIAAC International Data Explorer)

5.5.3 Scenario 3: Gap Analysis

The next scenario uses the US IDE to go over the *Gap Analysis* function and look at the question: *Is the gap in literacy skills between younger adults (16–24) and older adults (55–65) different in the United States than internationally?*

As mentioned previously, the gap analysis function is available only in the US IDE. The *Adults, 16–65 Display* is used to conduct this international comparison. On the *Select Criteria* page, the *PIAAC Literacy: Overall scale* is the *Measure*, and the jurisdictions include the *Average of All Jurisdictions* (which includes OECD National and Sub-National Entities as well as Partners) and the United States, found in the *International* and *OECD National Entities Groups*, respectively. *Age groups in 10-year intervals (derived)* within the *Major reporting groups Category* and *Sub-Category* is selected on the *Select Variables* page, as it can be used to look at the relevant categories of younger and older adults. The gap analysis will be comparing the differences between averages of the age groups, so the *Averages* statistic type is used on the *Edit Reports* page. After producing an output table displaying average literacy scores by age group in the United States and internationally on the *Build Reports* page, the *Gap Analysis* function on this page is used to see whether the score-point difference between younger adults and older adults is significantly different in the United States and internationally. In the *Gap Analysis* window, *Between Jurisdictions* is used as the basis for comparison, and the *Between Groups* gap should be analysed. *All Jurisdictions* is selected in the *Jurisdiction* section to include both the *Average of All Jurisdictions* and the United States, and in the *Variables* section, only the *24 or less* and *55 plus* variable categories need to be included.

In the *Gap Test* tab, a table similar to the tables for significance testing is produced (see Fig. 5.5). The title of the table indicates that this testing is focused on finding differences between jurisdictions for gaps in averages between age groups.

5 Analysing PIAAC Data with the International Data Explorer (IDE)

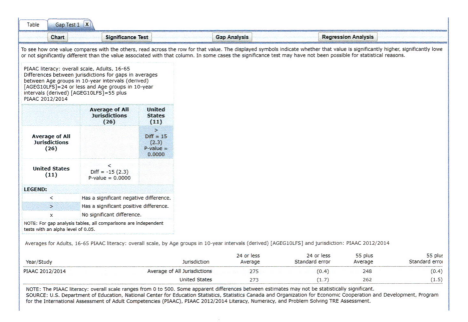

Fig. 5.5 Gap analysis output from Scenario 3
(Source: National Center for Education Statistics (NCES) PIAAC International Data Explorer)

Reading across the table shows that the gap for *Average of All Jurisdictions* has a significant positive difference compared to the United States, meaning that the gap in literacy skills between younger and older adults is larger internationally than in the United States. The size of the gap, or score-point difference, is shown in parentheses next to each jurisdiction, so the 11 next to United States is the difference between the literacy score of 273 for younger adults and the score of 262 for older adults listed in the table under the testing results. These gaps are what are being tested or compared here. Also, within the table, under the symbol indicating the direction of the difference, is the difference in the size of the gap and its standard error, so in this case the gap internationally is 15 points larger than the US gap. Under that, the p-value is listed.

5.5.4 Scenario 4: Regression Analysis

This last scenario demonstrates the regression analysis function in the IDE and focuses on the following question: *Do US adults (16–74) who are employed have higher numeracy skills than those who are unemployed, even when controlling for age and education level?*

This scenario will also use the US IDE, as the regression analysis is available only in this version. This question focuses on the full US 16–74 population,

Literacy, Numeracy, and Problem Solving TRE, U.S. Adults, 16-74 (Household and Prison) PIAAC 2012/2014
Dependent Variable: PIAAC Numeracy: Overall scale
Independent Variable(s): Age in 10 year bands extended to include ages over 65 (derived) [AGEG10LFSEXT] , Education - Highest qualification - Level (collapsed, 3 categories) [BQ01AC] , Current status/work history - Employment status (derived) [CD05]
Contrast Coding Reference Group: Age 24 or less; ISCED 2 and below; Employed
U.S. Household (16-74 years old)

Multiple Correlation	0.52
R Squared	0.27

	Degrees of Freedom	Mean square	F Ratio	P Value
Model	10	18283157757.97	185.04	0
Error	5028.19	98808081.56		

	Standardized Regression Coefficients	S.E. of Standardized Coefficients	Regression Coefficients	S.E. of Regression Coefficients	T Statistic	Probability	Significance
Intercept	0	0	227.066	2.4742	91.7727	0	>
Age in 10 year bands extended to include ages over 65 (derived)							
25-34	-0.0792	0.0174	-11.4168	2.5498	-4.4776	0	<
35-44	-0.1093	0.0188	-15.977	2.7752	-5.7571	0	<
45-54	-0.1562	0.0195	-22.0446	2.8908	-7.6259	0	<
55-65	-0.1463	0.0167	-21.1071	2.4608	-8.5772	0	<
66 plus	-0.1448	0.0155	-28.5235	3.0723	-9.2842	0	<
Education - Highest qualification - Level (collapsed, 3 categories)							
ISCED 3 and 4a-b	0.3452	0.0169	38.6406	1.9873	19.4442	0	>
ISCED 5a-b and 6	0.6856	0.0179	79.8923	2.5571	31.2433	0	>
Current status/work history - Employment status (derived)							
Unemployed	-0.073	0.0102	-16.6931	2.3156	-7.2089	0	<
Out of the labour force	-0.0984	0.0139	-12.9385	1.8297	-7.0715	0	<
Not known	0.0004	0.0078	1.3971	35.7291	0.0391	0.9689	x

NOTE: A 0-1 contrast coding has been used where the first subgroup of the (independent) variable is the reference group. Except for the reference group, each subgroup is contrasted (code 1) in a separate dummy variable against all the other subgroups of the variable (code 0). For more details about contrast coding with multiple variables see the help documentation.
SOURCE: U.S. Department of Education, National Center for Education Statistics, Statistics Canada and Organization for Economic Cooperation and Development, Program for the International Assessment of Adult Competencies (PIAAC), PIAAC 2012/2014 Literacy, Numeracy, and Problem Solving TRE Assessment.

Fig. 5.6 Regression analysis output from Scenario 4
(Source: National Center for Education Statistics (NCES) PIAAC International Data Explorer)

so US Adults 16–74 (Household and Prison) is the *Display* of interest. *PIAAC Numeracy: Overall scale* is the *Measure* and *US Household (16–74 years old)* the *Jurisdiction* selected on the *Select Criteria* page. So here, numeracy scores will be the measure or dependent variable for regression. In the *Select Variables* tab, the independent variables or control variables that will go into the regression are *Age in 10 year bands extended to include ages over 65 (derived)*, *Education – Highest qualification – Level (collapsed, 3 categories)*, and *Current status/work history – Employment status (derived)*. These variables are all located in the *Major reporting groups Category* and *Sub-Category*. When conducting regression analysis, the statistic should be set as *Averages* on the *Edit Reports* page. From the *Cross-Tabulated Report* that contains all the independent or control variables, one can use the *Regression Analysis* function on the *Build Reports* page. In the *Regression Analysis* selection page, all three variables—age, education level, and employment status—are included in the *Variable* section.

Regression analysis output, as seen in Fig. 5.6, is produced. The title for the regression results table includes the information of the predicted variable that is called the dependent variable, which here is numeracy; predictor or explanatory variables that are called the independent variables, which here are age, education level, and employment status; and the reference groups for the explanatory variables called the contrast coding reference groups, which are the categories for each variable to which all other categories of the variable are compared, which here are the *24 or less* age group, those with education *ISCED 2 and below*, and the *Employed*.

To review how much explanatory power the variables have on numeracy scores or our outcome variable, one should look under R Squared in the top portion of the results. The R-squared value here is 0.27, which means that 27 percent of the variation in the numeracy scores are accounted for by the independent variables in our model.

In the lower portion of the table, one can find the regression coefficients for the variables. This includes the standardised and unstandardised regression coefficients, along with their standard errors. The standardised regression coefficients are standardised against the independent variables' mean and standard deviation, which is done to allow comparison of the units across the variables. Using the standardised coefficient, one can answer the question of which of the categories have a stronger or weaker relationship with the outcome variable (or numeracy). For example, looking at *Unemployed*, which has a standardised regression coefficient of -0.07, and comparing that to the standardised coefficient for the age groups (ranging from -0.08 to -0.16), indicates that age has a stronger relationship with the dependent variable, or numeracy, than being unemployed. In order to interpret the results within each of the variables, look at the unstandardised regression coefficients, labelled here as just regression coefficients. So, for example, the unstandardised regression coefficient for *Unemployed* is -17, meaning that those who are unemployed scored 17 points lower in numeracy than those who were employed, holding other explanatory variables included here constant. Moving to the right of the table, the *t*-statistic is -7, and the probability is 0, which is less than the significance threshold of probability less than 0.05. This means that the independent variable, being employed, is significantly associated with changes in the dependent variable, numeracy score. This statistical significance is also marked in the significance column, with a less-than (<) symbol. So, controlling for the two other explanatory variables (age and education level) in our regression, numeracy scores for those who are unemployed are lower than for those who are employed.

5.6 Summary

PIAAC is a complex large-scale study with the major components of a direct assessment of three domains and an extensive background questionnaire. The IDE is a user-friendly online tool that allows users to conduct different types of analyses, from basic statistical analyses to some more advanced analyses, such as regression and gap analysis, using PIAAC data; it is available in two different versions through the OECD and NCES in the United States. The IDE contains data on the PIAAC direct assessment and background questionnaire from jurisdictions that participated in PIAAC, as well as trend data from previous large-scale assessments that were rescaled to PIAAC. It can be used to conduct analyses of averages, percentages (including proficiency level distributions), standard deviations, and percentiles,and to produce significance testing, gap analysis, and regression analysis (depending on the version). Analysis in the IDE follows the basic steps organised under the four main tabs: *1. Select Criteria*, *2. Select Variables*, *3. Edit Reports*, and *4. Build Reports*. The example research scenarios provide an overview of these basic steps and how to answer research questions using the IDE.

References

Hogan, J., Thornton, N., Diaz-Hoffmann, L., Mohadjer, L., Krenzke, T., Li, J., & Van De Kerckhove, W. (2016a). *Program for the International Assessment of Adult Competencies (PIAAC) 2014: U.S. national supplement public use data files-prison* (NCES 2016337REV). Washington, DC: National Center for Education Statistics. https://nces.ed.gov/pubsearch/pubsinfo.asp?pubid=2016337REV. Accessed 19 July 2019.

Hogan, J., Thornton, N., Diaz-Hoffmann, L., Mohadjer, L., Krenzke, T., Li, J., Van De Kerckhove, W., Yamamoto, K., & Khorramdel, L. (2016b). *U.S. Program for the International Assessment of Adult Competencies (PIAAC) 2012/2014: Main study and national supplement technical report* (NCES2016-036REV). Washington, DC: U.S. Department of Education, National Center for Education Statistics. http://nces.ed.gov/pubsearch. Accessed 19 July 2019.

Holtzman, S., Kandathil, M., Kapur, L., Kline, D., Barone, J., Li, L., Krenzke, T., Hogan, J., Mohadjer, L., Carstens, R., Koehler, H., & Daniel, T. (2016). *Program for the International Assessment of Adult Competencies (PIAAC) 2012/2014: U.S. national supplement public use data files-household* (NCES 2016667REV). Washington, DC: National Center for Education Statistics.

Michaelidou-Evripidou, A., Modestou, M., Karagiorgi, Y., Polydorou, A., Nicolaidou, M., Afantiti-Lamprianou, T., Kendeou, P., Tsouris, C., & Loukaides, C. (2016). *Programme for the International Assessment of Adult Competencies (PIAAC), Cyprus* (Data file version 1.1.0 [ZA5650]). Cologne: GESIS Data Archive. https://doi.org/10.4232/1.12632.

Organisation for Economic Co-operation and Development (OECD). (2011). *PIAAC conceptual framework of the background questionnaire main survey*. Paris: OECD Publishing.

Organisation for Economic Co-operation and Development (OECD). (2014). *Technical report of the Survey of Adult Skills (PIAAC)*. Paris: OECD. http://www.oecd.org/skills/piaac/_Technical%20Report_17OCT13.pdf. Accessed 5 May 2019.

Organisation for Economic Co-operation and Development (OECD). (2016a). *Programme for the International Assessment of Adult Competencies (PIAAC), Russian federation public use file* (Version: 13378965, prgrusp1.sav). Paris: OECD Publishing. https://webfs.oecd.org/piaac/puf-data/. Accessed 5 May 2019.

Organisation for Economic Co-operation and Development (OECD). (2016b). *Programme for the International Assessment of Adult Competencies (PIAAC), United states public use file* (Version: 17016050, prgusap1.sav). Paris: OECD Publishing. https://webfs.oecd.org/piaac/puf-data/. Accessed 5 May 2019.

Organisation for Economic Co-operation and Development (OECD), Statistics Canada. (2000). *Literacy in the information age: Final report of the International Adult Literacy Survey*. Paris: OECD.

Rampey, B., Keiper, S., Mohadjer, L., Krenzke, T., Li, J., Thornton, N., & Provasnik, S. (2016). *Highlights from the U.S. PIAAC survey of incarcerated adults: Their skills, work experience, education, and training*. Washington, DC: National Center for Education Statistics, US Department of Education.

Statistics Canada, Organisation for Economic Co-operation and Development (OECD). (2005). *Learning a living: First results of the adult literacy and life skills survey*. Paris: OECD.

Open Access This chapter is licensed under the terms of the Creative Commons Attribution 4.0 International License (http://creativecommons.org/licenses/by/4.0/), which permits use, sharing, adaptation, distribution and reproduction in any medium or format, as long as you give appropriate credit to the original author(s) and the source, provide a link to the Creative Commons license and indicate if changes were made.

The images or other third party material in this chapter are included in the chapter's Creative Commons license, unless indicated otherwise in a credit line to the material. If material is not included in the chapter's Creative Commons license and your intended use is not permitted by statutory regulation or exceeds the permitted use, you will need to obtain permission directly from the copyright holder.

Chapter 6
Analysing PIAAC Data with the IDB Analyzer (SPSS and SAS)

Andres Sandoval-Hernandez and Diego Carrasco

Abstract This chapter provides readers with a step-by-step guide to performing both simple and complex analyses with data from the Programme for the International Assessment of Adult Competencies (PIAAC) using the IEA International Database (IDB) Analyzer. The IDB Analyzer is a Windows-based tool that generates SPSS and SAS syntax. Using this syntax, corresponding analyses can be conducted in SPSS and SAS. The chapter presents the data-merging module and the analysis module. Potential analyses with the IDB Analyzer are demonstrated—for example, the calculation of percentages, averages, proficiency levels, linear regression, correlations, and percentiles.

This chapter describes the general use of the International Association for the Evaluation of Educational Achievement's (IEA) International Database Analyzer (IDB Analyzer) for analysing PIAAC data (IEA 2019). The IDB Analyzer provides a user-friendly interface to easily merge the data files of the different countries participating in PIAAC. Furthermore, it seamlessly takes into account the sampling information and the multiple imputed achievement scores to produce accurate statistical results (see Chap. 2 in this volume for details about PIAAC's complex sample and assessment design).

This chapter is subdivided into three main sections. In the first section, we will provide a brief overview of the software.[1] Sections 6.2 and 6.3 will be dedicated

---
[1]Most of the information for this section is adapted from the last version of the Help Manual for the IDB analyzer (IEA 2019).

A. Sandoval-Hernandez (✉)
University of Bath, Bath, UK
e-mail: A.Sandoval@bath.ac.uk

D. Carrasco
Centro de Medición MIDE UC – Pontificia Universidad Católica de Chile, Santiago, Chile

© The Author(s) 2020
D. B. Maehler, B. Rammstedt (eds.), *Large-Scale Cognitive Assessment*,
Methodology of Educational Measurement and Assessment,
https://doi.org/10.1007/978-3-030-47515-4_6

to the Merge and Analysis modules of the IDB Analyzer, respectively. For each of these two sections, we will provide a description of the functionalities of the respective modules and examples to illustrate some of the capabilities of the IDB Analyzer (Version 4.0) to merge files and to compute a variety of statistics, including the calculation of percentages, averages, benchmarks (proficiency levels), linear regression, logistic regression, correlations, and percentiles.

6.1 The IDB Analyzer

Developed by IEA Hamburg, the IDB Analyzer is an interface that creates syntax for SPSS (IBM 2013) and SAS (SAS 2012). The IDB Analyzer was originally designed to allow users to combine and analyse data from IEA's large-scale assessments, but it has been adapted to work with data from most major large-scale assessment surveys, including those conducted by the Organisation for Economic Co-operation and Development (OECD), such as the Programme for the International Assessment of Adult Competencies (PIAAC), the Programme for International Student Assessment (PISA), and the Teaching and Learning International Survey (TALIS).

The IDB Analyzer generates SPSS or SAS syntax files that take into account information from the complex sampling design of the study to produce population estimates. In addition, the generated syntax makes appropriate use of plausible values for calculating estimates of achievement scores, combining both sampling variance and imputation variance. Considering PIAAC's complex sample and complex assessment design, using either SPSS or SAS to analyse PIAAC data without the IDB Analyzer would require the user to have programming knowledge in order to create their own macros. The IDB Analyzer automatically generates these macros (syntax files) in a user-friendly environment that allows their customisation according to the purposes of the intended analysis.

The IDB Analyzer consists of two modules: the merge module and the analysis module. These two modules are integrated and executed in one common application. When working with PIAAC data, the merge module is used to create analysis datasets by combining data files from different countries and selecting subsets of variables for analysis. The analysis module provides procedures for computing various statistics and their standard errors.

Once the IDB Analyzer application is launched,[2] the main window will appear, as shown in Fig. 6.1. Users have then the option of choosing either SPSS or SAS as their statistical software of choice. For the examples in this chapter, we will use the SPSS software. The main window also has options to select the 'Merge Module', the 'Analysis Module', the 'Help Manual' or to exit the application.

---

[2]The latest version of the IDB Analyzer (Version 4.0) and instructions to install it are available from the IEA website: https://www.iea.nl/index.php/data-tools/tools.

6 Analysing PIAAC Data with the IDB Analyzer (SPSS and SAS)

Fig. 6.1 IDB Analyzer main window

There are at least two ways to access guidance on how to use the IDB Analyzer: video tutorials made by IEA and the main 'Help' manual that accompanies this software installation. An easy way to get you started with the IDB Analyzer is to watch IEA video tutorials. These have been made available at the following link: https://www.iea.nl/training#IDB_Analyzer_Video_Tutorials.

These videos have been shared via YouTube; they cover step-by-step examples of how to estimate correlations, percentiles, percentages and means, logistic regression, linear regression, and benchmarks.

A second way to get help and guidance is to consult the 'Help' manual via the main menu in the IDB Analyzer. This official manual can be accessed by clicking on the third button present in the main menu. Figure 6.1 shows what this main menu looks like.

The IDB Analyzer will work on most IBM-compatible computers using current Microsoft Windows[3] operating systems. The IDB Analyzer is licensed free of charge and may be used only in accordance with the terms of the licencing agreement. While the IDB Analyzer is free, the user must own a valid licence for at least one of the software packages used as statistical engine (i.e., SPSS Version 18 or later or SAS Version 9 or later). Additionally, the user should have a valid licence for Microsoft Excel 2003 or a later version (as outputs are also produced in this format). The IDB Analyzer licence expires at the end of each calendar year.

---

[3]Currently there is no stand-alone Mac version of the IDB Analyzer. However, the software can be used on Mac through a virtual machine and Windows installed on it. The current version was tested using Windows installed on Parallels Desktop for Mac (http://www.parallels.com/products/desktop/).

So, every year, users have to download and reinstall the most current version of the software and agree to the terms and conditions of the new licence.

6.2 Merging Files with the IDB Analyzer

PIAAC Public Use Files containing both responses to the background questionnaire and the cognitive assessment are available for downloading for each of the participant countries separately. The Merge Module of the IDB Analyzer allows users to combine datasets from more than one country into a single data file for cross-country analyses. For the purposes of this chapter, we will assume all data files have been copied within a folder named 'C:\Data\PIAAC\'. PIAAC data files are available in both SPSS and SAS from the PIAAC website.[4] Users should download the data files in the format of their preference.

The Merge Module recognises the data files for PIAAC by reading the file names in the selected directory and matching them to the file-naming convention prespecified in the IDB Analyzer configuration files. For this reason, in order to ensure that the IDB Analyzer will correctly identify the different files contained in the PIAAC datasets, as well as the user-generated files:

- Users should not change the name of the files once downloaded from the PIAAC website.
- Users should not save the merged file in the same directory where the source files are located.
- Users should keep files from different studies and years in separate directories.

The following steps will create an SPSS or SAS data file with data from multiple countries and/or multiple file types:

1. Open the IDB Analyzer.
2. Select the statistical software you want to work with (choose between SAS or SPSS).
3. Select the Merge Module of the IDB Analyzer.
4. Click the Merge Module button. The Merge Module interface is divided into two different tabs. In the first one, you can select the countries and edit country labels. In the second tab, you can select the variables you want to include in your analysis and specify the name of the merged file.
5. Under the 'Select Data Files and Participants' tab and in the 'Select Directory' field, browse to the folder where all data files are located. For example, in Fig. 6.2, all SPSS data files are located in the folder 'C:\Data\PIAAC\'. The program will automatically recognise and complete the 'Select Study' and 'Select Cycle'

---

[4]http://www.oecd.org/skills/piaac/

Fig. 6.2 IDB Analyzer merge module: select data files and participants

fields and list all countries available in this folder as possible candidates for merging.

6. Click the countries of interest from the 'Available Participants' list and click the right arrow button (▷) to move them to the 'Selected Participants' panel on the right. Individual countries can also be moved directly to the 'Selected Participants' panel by double-clicking on them. To select multiple countries, hold the CTRL-key of the keyboard when clicking on countries. Click the tab-right arrow button (▷) to move all countries to the 'Selected Participants' panel. For this example, we selected all the countries available.

7. Click the 'Next >' button to proceed to the next step. The software will open the 'Select File Types and Variables' tab of the merge module (see Fig. 6.3), to select the file types and the variables to be included in the merged data file.

8. Select the files for merging by checking the appropriate boxes to the left of the window. For example, in Fig. 6.3, the 'General Response File' has been selected.[5] Checking this box will automatically populate the 'Selected Variables' panel with the three scores available in PIAAC (i.e. Literacy Scale Score, Numeracy Scale Score, and Problem-Solving Scale Score), as well as with all the ID (e.g. Country ID) and sampling variables (e.g. sampling and replicate weights) needed for the corresponding analyses (Fig. 6.4).

9. Select the variables of interest from the 'Available Variables' list in the left panel. In SPSS, you can *right-click* on the variable names to open a menu with details about each of the available variables (i.e. variable name, label, measurement level, and value labels). Variables are selected by clicking on them

---

[5] With other studies such as PISA and TALIS, there are more options. In the case of PIAAC, there is only one option.

Fig. 6.3 IDB Analyzer merge module: selecting all countries

Fig. 6.4 IDB Analyzer merge module: select data files and participants

and then clicking the right arrow (▷) button. Clicking the tab-right arrow (▷) button selects all variables (Fig. 6.5).

10. When selecting the variables, you can search variables by variable name or by variable label using the filter boxes (blue space between column header and list of variables) in the 'Available Variables' list and 'Selected Variables' list.
11. Note that the IDB Analyzer assumes that files have the same structure and the variables have the same properties (e.g. variables, formats, labels) in each of these files. Any deviation from this can cause unexpected results. Should you want to modify the contents of a file for a country, or a set of countries, it is recommended to do this on the resulting merged file, after the merge is completed.

6 Analysing PIAAC Data with the IDB Analyzer (SPSS and SAS)

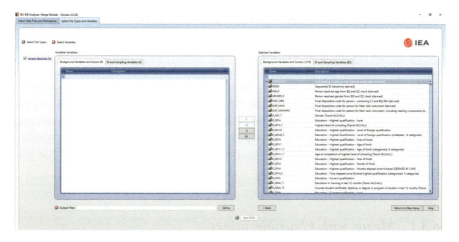

Fig. 6.5 IDB Analyzer merge module: selecting all variables

12. In the 'Output Files' field, click on the 'Define' button to specify the name for the merged data file and the folder where it will be saved. The IDB Analyzer will also create an SPSS syntax file ($_*$SPS) (or a SAS syntax file, $_*$.SAS, if you are using this software) of the same name and in the same folder with the code necessary to perform the merge. In the example shown in Fig. 6.3, the merged data file 'merge_piaac.sav' and the syntax file 'merge_piaac.sps' both will be created and stored in the folder titled 'C:\Data\'. The merged data file will contain all the variables listed in the 'Selected Variables' panel, and if all available variables were selected, the resulting merge file should be about 622 megabytes in size.
13. Click the 'Start SPSS' button to create the SPSS syntax file. An SPSS Syntax Editor window with the created syntax code will be automatically opened. The syntax file can be executed by opening the 'Run' menu of SPSS and selecting the 'All' menu option. Alternatively, you can also submit the code for processing with the keystrokes Ctrl+A (to select all), followed by Ctrl+R (to run the selection). In SAS, the syntax file can be executed by selecting the 'Submit' option from the 'Run' menu.

Once SPSS or SAS has completed its execution, it is important to check the SPSS output window or SAS log for possible warnings. If warnings appear, they should be examined carefully because they might indicate that the merge process was not performed properly and that the resulting merged data file might not include all the relevant variables or countries.

6.3 Example Analyses with the IDB Analyzer

In the following section, we will describe step-by-step instructions to produce means, percentiles, percentages, linear regressions, correlations, and benchmarks, using the latest PIAAC public-use data files. In each subsection, a sequence of steps will be included as a numbered list. These steps are reiterated for each analysis routine. In this way, each subsection is self-contained, and the reader does not need to consult any other part of the chapter to complete the steps she or he needs to follow to produce means, percentiles, percentages, linear regressions, correlations, or benchmarks.

6.3.1 Means with Plausible Values

In this section, we illustrate how to estimate the means of literacy scores by country. The first example contains a variable with plausible values. In PIAAC there are three variables with plausible values: the literacy scale scores, the numeracy scale score, and the problem-solving scale score. Each of these variables consists of ten different columns of values within the PIAAC dataset. For each test, plausible values are generated as random draws of the posterior distribution of the participant's proficiency (Wu 2005). To produce population estimates with these scores, the IDB Analyzer computes the results for each plausible value and combines these estimates using Rubin-Shaffer rules (Rutkowski et al. 2010). The following steps produce mean estimates of literacy proficiency by country, for females and males:

1. Open the IDB Analyzer.
2. Select the statistical software you want to work with (choose between SAS or SPSS).
3. Open the Analysis Module of the IDB Analyzer.
4. For this example, specify the data file 'merge_piaac.sav' as the Analysis File (see Sect. 6.2 in this chapter for details on how this file was created).
5. Select 'PIAAC (using final full sample weight)' as the Analysis Type.
6. Select 'Percentages and Means' as the Statistic Type.
7. Under the 'Plausible Values Options', select 'Use PVs'.
8. Click on the 'Separate Tables by' section at the right-hand side of the software window. This section will become active and highlighted in light yellow.
9. Go to the 'Select variables' section, and click on the 'GENDER_R' variable in the fourth row of the name list.
10. Drag the 'GENDER_R' variable to the 'Separate Tables by' section.
11. Click on the 'Plausible Values' section at the right-hand side of the software window. This section will become active and highlighted in light yellow.
12. Go to the 'Select variables' section and click on the 'PVLIT1–10' variable in the first row of the name list.
13. Drag the 'PVLIT1–10' variable to the 'Plausible Values' section.

14. The Weight Variable is automatically selected by the software. SPFTWT0 is selected by default; this variable contains the final sampling weight.
15. Specify the name and the folder of the output files in the 'Output Files' field by clicking the Define/Modify button. For this example, we use the term 'mean_with_pv'.

After all these steps, the reached setup should look similar to Fig. 6.6:

16. Then, click the 'Start SPSS' button. This will create an SPSS syntax file and open it in an SPSS editor window.
17. To start the computations, one needs to press the following keys combinations: CTRL+A first, to select the entire generated code present in the syntax window, and then CTRL+R to run these commands. The output of these analyses is depicted in Fig. 6.7.

In the generated output, the first column contains the list of countries. The second column presents the categorical values of the 'GENDER_R' variable: 'Male' and 'Female'. In the third column, the nominal sample size is presented for each group, within each country. In the fourth column, the sum of survey weights is included. These later numbers represent the survey population to which the estimates are projected (Heeringa et al. 2009). Additionally, the IDB Analyzer generates standard errors for the survey population size (sixth column). In the 'Percent' column, the estimate of the proportion of each group in the population is presented. These point estimates are accompanied by their standard errors in the 'Percent (s.e.)' column. In the column 'PVLIT (Mean)', we find the point estimates of the literacy scores. Each country has two values, one for males and one for females. These point estimates present uncertainty, due to measurement error and due to sampling error. This uncertainty is summarised in the 'PVLIT (s.e.)' column. Standard deviations of these means are included in the 'Std.Dev' column. Similarly to previous estimates, on its right, standard errors of the standard deviations are provided in the column 'Std.Dev. (s.e.)'. Finally, the last column, 'pctmiss', contains

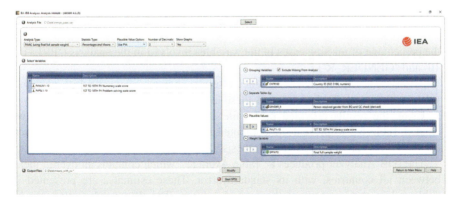

Fig. 6.6 Analysis of means by group setup

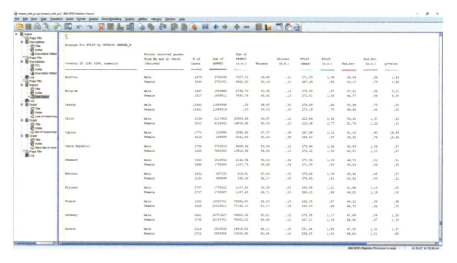

Fig. 6.7 Analysis of mean by group output

Table 6.1 Generated files by an analysis of means

Generated files	File type	Content
means_with_pv.sps	SPSS	Syntax to run the means computations
means_with_pv.spv	SPSS	Output of the means computations
means_with_pvGENDER_R.sav	SPSS	Contains the means estimates and their standard errors
means_with_pvGENDER_R.xlsx	Excel	
means_with_pv_PVLIT_by_GENDER_R_Sig.sav	SPSS	Contains a group within-country comparison for the estimated means and percentages, providing t-statistics for these comparisons
means_with_pv_PVLIT_by_GENDER_R_Sig.xlsx	Excel	

the percentage of missing cases in the variables involved in the analysis ('PVLIT1-10' and 'GENDER_R').

The IDB Analyzer creates six files after an analysis of means with plausible values is complete. Table 6.1 details these files and their content.

Using the results provided in the file 'means_with_pvGENDER_R.xlsx', we created Table 6.2 to present the computed results. Means are presented and their standard errors are included in parenthesis.

The IDB Analyzer produces a 'Table Average', which contains an overall mean between all countries, with its standard error. These estimates are presented in Table 6.2 in the last row, in the second column. The illustrated routine can be

Table 6.2 Means of literacy scores for female and males in each country

Country	Female	Male	Country	Female	Male
Austria	267.39 (0.93)	271.53 (1.04)	Korea, Republic of	269.43 (0.87)	275.72 (0.75)
Belgium	272.81 (1.08)	278.09 (0.97)	Lithuania	268.47 (1.20)	264.97 (1.32)
Canada	272.19 (0.78)	274.49 (0.86)	Netherlands	280.92 (0.94)	287.06 (1.08)
Chile	216.36 (2.77)	223.94 (2.48)	New Zealand	280.69 (1.06)	280.66 (1.20)
Cyprus	269.60 (0.97)	267.99 (1.18)	Norway	276.43 (0.91)	280.34 (0.97)
Czech Republic	272.32 (1.30)	275.68 (1.26)	Poland	270.08 (0.86)	263.66 (0.97)
Denmark	271.00 (0.80)	270.58 (1.03)	Russian Federation	277.37 (2.88)	272.90 (2.98)
Estonia	276.64 (0.81)	275.06 (1.09)	Singapore	253.89 (1.01)	261.42 (0.98)
Finland	289.15 (0.99)	285.96 (1.21)	Slovak Republic	274.22 (0.82)	273.47 (0.86)
France	262.23 (0.69)	262.05 (0.87)	Slovenia	257.67 (0.99)	255.17 (1.08)
Germany	267.21 (1.19)	272.35 (1.17)	Spain	249.45 (1.04)	254.11 (1.00)
Greece	256.25 (1.23)	251.44 (1.54)	Sweden	277.54 (1.10)	280.88 (1.08)
Ireland	265.43 (1.10)	267.71 (1.17)	Turkey	220.89 (1.35)	231.98 (1.56)
Israel	255.04 (0.96)	255.45 (1.14)	United Kingdom	271.03 (1.29)	273.90 (1.37)
Italy	250.61 (1.32)	250.36 (1.50)	United States	269.47 (1.33)	270.16 (1.21)
Japan	294.69 (1.01)	297.78 (0.88)	Table Average	266.34 (0.22)	267.96 (0.23)

replicated with the numeracy scale scores and with the problem-solving scores present in PIAAC study.

6.3.2 Means with Other Variables

In the following example, which is simpler than its previous counterpart, we compute the mean of total years of schooling in each country. In the PIAAC study, total years of schooling was derived using different responses of participants regarding their educational participation during their lifetime. These values can be found in the 'YRSQUAL_T' variable. Using the IDB Analyzer, we need to follow the next steps:

1. Open the IDB Analyzer.
2. Select the statistical software you want to work with (choose between SAS or SPSS).
3. Open the Analysis Module of the IDB Analyzer.
4. For this example, specify the data file 'merge_piaac.sav' as the Analysis File (see Sect. 6.2 in this chapter for the details of how this file was created).
5. Select 'PIAAC (using final full sample weight)' as the Analysis Type.
6. Select 'Percentages and Means' as the Statistic Type.
7. Under the 'Plausible Values Options', select 'None Used'.
8. Click on the 'Analysis Variables' section at the right-hand side of the software window. This section will become active and highlighted in light yellow.

9. Go to the 'Select variables' section, and under the 'Description' heading click on it, and type in 'total years'. This action would look for all the variables containing 'total' and 'year' in their description field.
10. Specify the variable YRSQUAL_T as the analysis variable by clicking the 'Analysis Variables' field to activate it. Select YRSQUAL_T from the list of available variables present in the 'Select Variables' section and move it to the 'Analysis variables' by clicking the right arrow button in this section.
11. The Weight Variable is automatically selected by the software. SPFTWT0 is selected by default; this variable contains the final sampling weight.
12. Specify the name and the folder of the output files in the 'Output Files' field by clicking the Define/Modify button. For this example, we use the term 'mean'.

After all these steps, the reached setup should look similar to Fig. 6.8:

13. Then, click the 'Start SPSS' button. This will create an SPSS syntax file and open it in an SPSS editor window.
14. To start the computations, one needs to press the following key combinations: CTRL+A first, to select the entire generated code present in the syntax window, and then CTRL+R to run these commands. The output of these analyses is depicted in Fig. 6.9.

Similar to the previous example, the generated output presents several columns. The first column is the list of countries. In the second column is the nominal sample size of each country. Notice that Austria and Germany do not have observations for this variable and present 100% of missing. The third column contains the sum of survey weights, which represents the survey population size (Heeringa et al. 2009), and in the fourth column, the IDB Analyzer includes the standards errors of the survey population size. In the 'Percent' column, the proportion of the survey population size is depicted. For example, the United States projects its number of cases (4286) to a survey population of more than 166 million people, and its resulting proportion in the table is of '24,13', whereas Canada has a larger

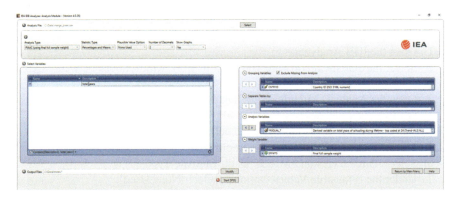

Fig. 6.8 Analysis of means setup

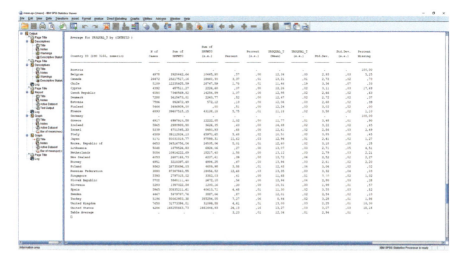

Fig. 6.9 Analysis of means output

Table 6.3 Generated files by an analysis of means

Generated files	File type	Content
mean.sps	SPSS	Syntax to run the means computations
mean.spv	SPSS	Output of the means computations
mean.sav	SPSS	Contains the means estimates and their standard errors
mean.xlsx	Excel	
mean_YRSQUAL_T_by_CNTRYID_Sig.sav	SPSS	Contains a country-by-country comparison for the estimated means, providing t-statistics
mean_YRSQUAL_T_by_CNTRYID_Sig.xlsx	Excel	

nominal sample of 26,472 cases, yet projected to a survey population of more than 23 million people, and hence its proportion in the table is of '3,37'. These percentages are accompanied by their standard errors included in the sixth column. In the seventh column, the estimates of interest are included: the mean of total years of schooling per country, under the heading 'YRSQUAL_T (Mean)'. Next to it, in the eighth column, we find the standard errors of these estimates, below the heading 'YRSQUAL_T (s.e.)'. The 'Std.Dev' column contains the standard deviations of the analysis variable, and the 'Std.Dev (s.e.)' contains the standard deviations standard errors. The last column of the table presents the percentage of missing values of the analysed variable.

When the analysis of means is complete, the IDB Analyzer generates six files. Table 6.3 details these files and their content.

Using the results provided in the file 'mean.xlsx', we created Table 6.4 to present the computed results.

Table 6.4 Means of lifetime years of schooling

Country	Mean	Standard Error	Country	Mean	Standard Error
Belgium	12.34	0.03	Lithuania	13.07	0.03
Canada	13.21	0.01	Netherlands	13.12	0.03
Chile	11.46	0.19	New Zealand	13.72	0.04
Cyprus	12.26	0.02	Norway	13.94	0.03
Czech Republic	12.95	0.02	Poland	12.48	0.04
Denmark	12.47	0.02	Russian Federation	13.35	0.03
Estonia	12.06	0.03	Singapore	11.68	0.01
Finland	12.24	0.03	Slovak Republic	12.94	0.04
France	11.18	0.02	Slovenia	10.31	0.00
Greece	11.77	0.01	Spain	11.30	0.02
Ireland	14.48	0.02	Sweden	12.01	0.02
Israel	12.61	0.02	Turkey	8.44	0.02
Italy	10.51	0.02	United Kingdom	13.00	0.03
Japan	12.94	0.01	United States	13.27	0.03
Korea, Republic of	12.60	0.02	Table Average	12.34	0.01

Considering that the population average might not be the most informative location parameter to describe the variable's distribution, in the next section we describe how to obtain percentiles of a continuous variable.

6.3.3 Percentiles

Means and percentiles are different location parameters in a distribution (Wilcox 2017). The arithmetic mean is the expected location of the value with the least difference to the rest of the values within a distribution. In contrast, percentiles are any location under which there is a certain proportion of cases. Means are informative for symmetric distributions, such as the normal distribution. However, when distributions depart from normality, medians (50th percentile) or other location parameters could be of interest. For the following example, we choose the 25th, 50th, and 75th percentile for the same variable. We will repeat Steps 1–3 from the previous routine, but we will change the statistic type.

1. Open the Analysis Module of the IDB Analyzer.
2. For this example, specify the data file 'merge_piaac.sav' as the Analysis File (see Sect. 6.2 in this chapter for the details of how this file was created).
3. Select 'PIAAC (using final full sample weight)' as the Analysis Type.
4. Select 'Percentiles' as the Statistic Type.
5. Under the 'Plausible Values Options', select 'None Used'.
6. Click on the 'Analysis Variables' section on the right-hand side of the software window. This section will become active and highlighted.

7. Go to the 'Select variables' section, and under the 'Description' heading, click on it, and type in 'years'. This action would look for all the variables containing 'years' in their description field.
8. Specify the variable YRSQUAL_T as the analysis variable by clicking the 'Analysis Variables' field to activate it. Select YRSQUAL_T from the list of available variables present in the 'Select Variables' section, and move it to the 'Analysis variables' by clicking the right arrow button in this section. In this step, it is also possible to select more than one variable in this routine. However, for the sake of simplicity, in this example, we are including only one variable.
9. In the 'Percentiles' section, type in '25 50 75', all separated by a space.
10. Specify the name and the folder of the output files in the 'Output Files' field by clicking the 'Define/Modify' button. For this example, we use the term 'percentile'.

The generated setup should be similar to the screenshot presented in Fig. 6.10.

11. Afterwards, click the 'Start SPSS' button, run the syntax, and wait for the results to appear in the output window. The output from this routine is presented in Fig. 6.11

The generated output presents nine columns. The first is the list of countries; the second is the nominal sample size for each country; and in the third column, we find the sum of survey weights, which represents survey population size (Heeringa et al. 2009). In the 'Percent' column, the IDB Analyzer includes the proportion that the survey population size represents within the output table. Then, for each requested percentile (p25, p50, p75), we can find the point estimates, and its standard error on its right (p25_se, p50_se, p75_se).

For the computation of percentiles, the IDB Analyzer generates four files. Table 6.5 details these files and their content.

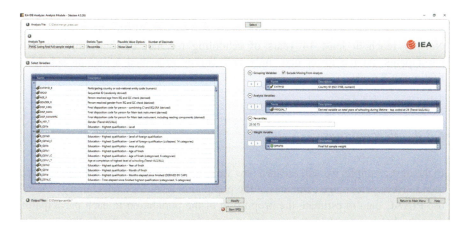

Fig. 6.10 Percentile setup

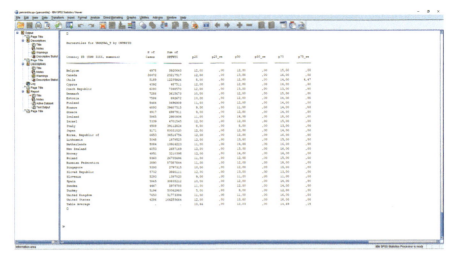

Fig. 6.11 Percentile output

Table 6.5 Generated files by an analysis of percentiles

Generated files	File type	Content
percentile.sps	SPSS	Syntax to run the means computations
percentile.spv	SPSS	Output of the means computations
percentile.sav	SPSS	Contains the means estimates and their standard errors
percentile.xlsx	Excel	

Using the results provided in the file 'percentile.xlsx', we created Table 6.6 to present the computed results. The estimated percentiles are included for each country, alongside their standard errors in parenthesis.

From the generated results, we notice that most of the participating countries have a median lifetime of schooling of 12 years. Ireland, the Netherlands, and Norway reach at least 14 years of schooling for half of their population of participants. At the lower end, Italy and Turkey presented a median schooling lifetime of 8 years.

6.3.4 Percentages

In the next example, we will create a new variable, not present in the merged files, to then retrieve percentage estimates at the population level for each country. We will use PIAAC data to estimate the proportion of the population in each participating country that has reached at least upper secondary education. To do this, we first need to recode a derived variable present in the public use file of the study. We will recode variable EDCAT8 into a dummy variable. EDCAT8 contains codes from the

Table 6.6 Percentiles (25th, 50th, and 75th) for total years of schooling by country

Country	P25	P50	P75
Belgium	12.00 (0.00)	12.00 (0.00)	15.00 (0.00)
Canada	12.00 (0.00)	13.00 (0.00)	16.00 (0.00)
Chile	8.00 (0.00)	12.00 (0.00)	14.00 (4.47)
Cyprus	12.00 (0.00)	12.00 (0.00)	14.00 (0.00)
Czech Republic	12.00 (0.00)	13.00 (0.00)	13.00 (0.00)
Denmark	10.00 (0.00)	12.00 (0.00)	15.00 (0.00)
Estonia	10.00 (0.00)	12.00 (0.00)	14.00 (0.00)
Finland	11.00 (0.00)	12.00 (0.00)	14.00 (0.00)
France	9.00 (0.00)	11.00 (0.00)	14.00 (0.00)
Greece	9.00 (0.00)	12.00 (0.00)	14.00 (0.00)
Ireland	11.00 (0.00)	14.00 (0.00)	18.00 (0.00)
Israel	12.00 (0.00)	12.00 (0.00)	15.00 (0.00)
Italy	8.00 (0.00)	8.00 (0.00)	13.00 (0.00)
Japan	12.00 (0.00)	12.00 (0.00)	14.00 (0.00)
Korea, Republic of	12.00 (0.00)	12.00 (0.00)	16.00 (0.00)
Lithuania	12.00 (0.00)	13.00 (0.00)	15.00 (0.00)
Netherlands	11.00 (0.00)	14.00 (0.00)	16.00 (0.00)
New Zealand	12.00 (0.00)	13.00 (0.00)	16.00 (0.00)
Norway	12.00 (0.00)	14.00 (0.00)	16.00 (0.00)
Poland	11.00 (0.00)	12.00 (0.00)	15.00 (0.00)
Russian Federation	11.00 (0.00)	12.00 (0.00)	18.00 (0.00)
Singapore	10.00 (0.00)	12.00 (0.00)	15.00 (0.00)
Slovak Republic	12.00 (0.00)	13.00 (0.00)	13.00 (0.00)
Slovenia	9.00 (0.00)	11.00 (0.00)	11.00 (0.00)
Spain	10.00 (0.00)	12.00 (0.00)	14.00 (0.00)
Sweden	11.00 (0.00)	12.00 (0.00)	14.00 (0.00)
Turkey	5.00 (0.00)	8.00 (0.00)	12.00 (0.00)
United Kingdom	11.00 (0.00)	11.00 (0.00)	16.00 (0.00)
United States	12.00 (0.00)	13.00 (0.00)	16.00 (0.00)
Table Average	10.66 (0.00)	12.03 (0.00)	14.69 (0.15)

International Standard Classification of Education (ISCED) to express the highest level of formal education of the participants (OECD 2015).

Using the following syntax code (see Table 6.4), we can create a dummy variable that differentiates between the participants who hold an upper secondary qualification (coded as one) and the participants who present lower educational qualifications, such as a primary school qualification or an incomplete secondary school qualification (coded as zero).

To include this new variable in the generated merged file, the user needs to open the merged file in SPSS. Then, open a new syntax window; type in the syntax code included in Code 6.1; press CTRL+A and CTRL+R to create this variable. Click

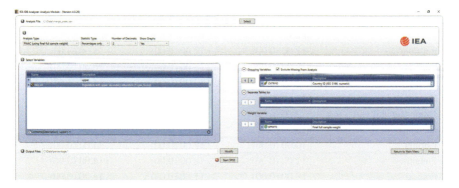

Fig. 6.12 Selecting a newly generated variable

on the window with the merged data, and press CTRL+S to save this variable in the merged file.

Code 6.1: Recoding Highest Educational Level to a Dummy Variable
```
if (EDCAT8 <= 2) edu_usl = 0 .
if (EDCAT8 >= 3) edu_usl = 1 .
execute .

VARIABLE LABELS edu_usl 'Population with upper secondary
education (1=yes, 0=no)'.

VALUE LABELS edu_usl
0 'No'
1 'Yes'.
```

With the merged file closed, one can open the IDB Analyzer and use this new variable for further analysis. In the next example, we will estimate what proportion of the population of the participant countries has at least upper secondary educational qualifications. Similarly to previous examples, we start by opening the IDB Analyzer:

1. Open the Analysis Module of the IDB Analyzer.
2. For this example, specify the data file 'merge_piaac.sav' as the Analysis File (see Sect. 6.2 in this chapter for the details on how this file was created).
3. Select 'PIAAC (using final full sample weight)' as the Analysis Type.
4. Select 'Percentages only' as the Statistic Type.
5. Click on the 'Grouping Variables' section.
6. Go to the 'Select variables' section, and under the 'Description' heading, click on it, and type in 'upper'. This action would look for all the variables containing 'upper' in their description field. This is presented in Fig. 6.12.
7. Drag the variable 'edu_usl' to the 'Grouping variable' section. By clicking the 'Analysis Variables' field to activate it, select 'edu_usl' from the list of available

Fig. 6.13 Percentage setup

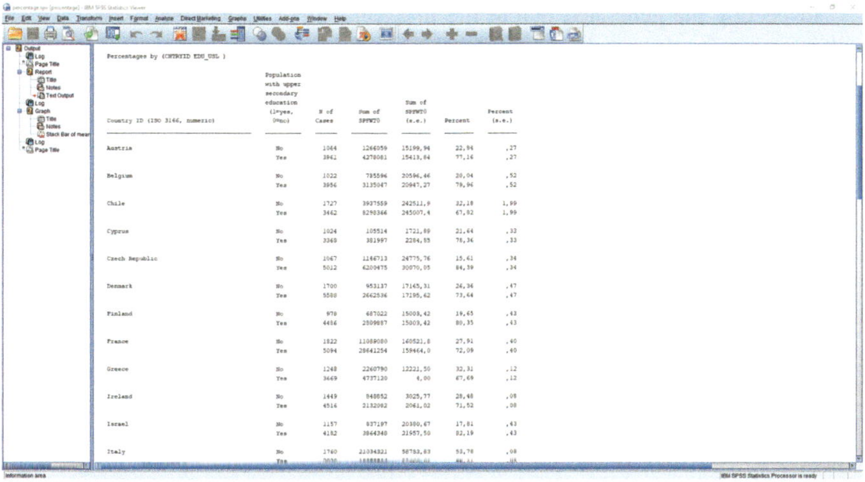

Fig. 6.14 Percentage output

variables present in the 'Select Variables' section, and move it to the 'Grouping Variables' field by clicking the right arrow button in this section.
8. Specify the name and the folder of the output files in the 'Output Files' field by clicking the 'Define/Modify' button. In this example, we will use the term 'percentage'. This setup is presented in Fig. 6.13.
9. Click the 'Start SPSS' button to create the SPSS syntax file and open it in an SPSS editor window.
10. After the user has executed the generated syntax, by pressing the sequence of keys CTRL+A and CTRL+R, the IDB Analyzer will start to run their macros to compute the requested percentages.

Once the calculations are finished, the SPSS output window would present the following results (see Fig. 6.14).

Table 6.7 Generated files by percentage analysis

Generated files	File type	Content
percentage.sps	SPSS	Syntax to run the percentage computations
percentage.spv	SPSS	Output of the percentage computations
percentage.sav	SPSS	Contains the percentage estimates and their standard errors
percentage.xlsx	Excel	
percentage_by_EDU_USL_Sig.sav	SPSS	Contains a country-by-country comparison for the estimated percentages
percentage_by_EDU_USL_Sig.xlsx	Excel	

Similarly to the procedure of means estimation, the procedure to estimate percentages produces six files as outputs. These files and their contents are described in Table 6.7.

Inspecting the generated output file in excel format, 'percentage.xlsx', we can filter and order the results to produce Table 6.8 and display the proportions of participants without upper secondary education for each participating country in PIAAC.

In the following section, we will use the dummy variable we have created, 'edu_usl', and estimate its relation to literacy scores in the population of each country.

6.3.5 Linear Regression

Apart from descriptive estimates such as means, percentiles, and percentages, the IDB Analyzer can also estimate regression models and logistic regression models (IEA 2019). In the following example, we will estimate the relationships between educational qualifications and literacy in each country. Specifically, we will estimate the gap in literacy scores between those who have at least an upper secondary education and the rest of the population. Although this gap can be obtained with a mean comparison, we want to retrieve more estimates than the mean differences between the two groups. We will use the linear regression routine for these purposes and get this difference as a standardised effect while also retrieving a measure of explained variance. These results can answer the question of 'how much difference in literacy skills is there between those with and without upper secondary education?'. To estimate a regression analysis, we need to follow the next steps in the IDB Analyzer:

1. Open the Analysis Module of the IDB Analyzer.
2. For this example, specify the data file 'merge_piaac.sav' as the Analysis File (see Sect. 6.2 in this chapter for the details of how this file was created).
3. Select 'PIAAC (using final full sample weight)' as the Analysis Type.
4. Select 'Regression' as the Statistic Type.
5. Under the 'Plausible Values Options', select 'Use PVs'.

Table 6.8 Proportion of participants without upper secondary education

Country	Estimate	Standard Error
Turkey	64.51	0.17
Italy	53.78	0.08
Spain	47.46	0.05
Greece	32.31	0.12
Chile	32.18	1.99
Netherlands	31.02	0.63
Ireland	28.48	0.08
France	27.91	0.40
Norway	27.43	0.53
Denmark	26.36	0.47
United Kingdom	24.09	0.59
Sweden	23.74	0.39
Slovenia	23.63	0.20
Austria	22.84	0.27
New Zealand	22.63	0.72
Korea, Republic of	21.66	0.49
Cyprus	21.64	0.33
Slovak Republic	20.61	0.62
Belgium	20.04	0.52
Finland	19.65	0.43
Singapore	18.92	0.17
Israel	17.81	0.43
Czech Republic	15.61	0.34
Poland	15.34	0.42
Japan	14.78	0.40
United States	14.74	0.28
Lithuania	11.93	0.47
Russian Federation	7.03	0.78
Table Average	25.29	0.11

6. On the right-hand side of the window, click on the area of 'Dependent variables'. This will become highlighted once it is clicked.
7. Then, select 'Plausible Values' in the right-hand side window.
8. Move the cursor to the left-hand side of the window and click on the 'PVLIT1–10' variable to select the literacy scores.
9. Go back to the right-hand side and click on the right arrow to move the 'PVLIT1–10' variables, to the 'Dependent Variables' section.
10. Move the cursor to the 'Independent Variables' section, and click on the 'Categorical Variables' to activate this section.
11. Move the cursor to 'Select Variables' section on the left. Just right before the variable list, in the first row under the description section, type in 'upper'. This will filter all present variables from the merged file.

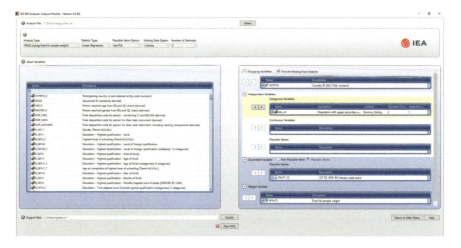

Fig. 6.15 Regression setup

12. Select the variable 'edu_usl', and move it to the right-hand side, by clicking on the right arrow, under 'Independent Variables', specifically using the right arrow from the 'Categorical Variables' subsection.
13. Specify the name and the folder of the output files in the 'Output Files' field by clicking the 'Define/Modify' button. In this example, we will name the syntax file as 'regression'.

Once all these steps have been completed, the regression setup should look like Fig. 6.15.

14. Click the 'Start SPSS' button. This action will open SPSS and create the syntax to run the regression model.
15. To execute the generated syntax, select all the written commands in the syntax editor, and run these commands using the 'Run Selection' button. Alternatively, press CTRL+A, to select all the commands, and then press CTRL+R to execute the syntax. This action would make SPSS run the regression analysis.

Because this analysis involves plausible values, it may take considerably longer in comparison with examples without plausible values in their calculations. This is because the regression analysis needs to be computed for each plausible value once, and then these results are synthetically presented using Rubin–Shaffer rules (Rutkowski et al. 2010). As such, this routine may take ten times longer than a regression analysis without the use of plausible values.

Once the regression analysis is done, SPSS will present the results in its output window. Figure 6.16 depicts how these results are displayed.

Once the analysis is concluded, the IDB Analyzer will generate eight files. These files include the syntax, the output, the model fit, the coefficients of the regression, and the descriptives of the included variables in the model. Table 6.9 lists the eight generated files and provides a description of their contents.

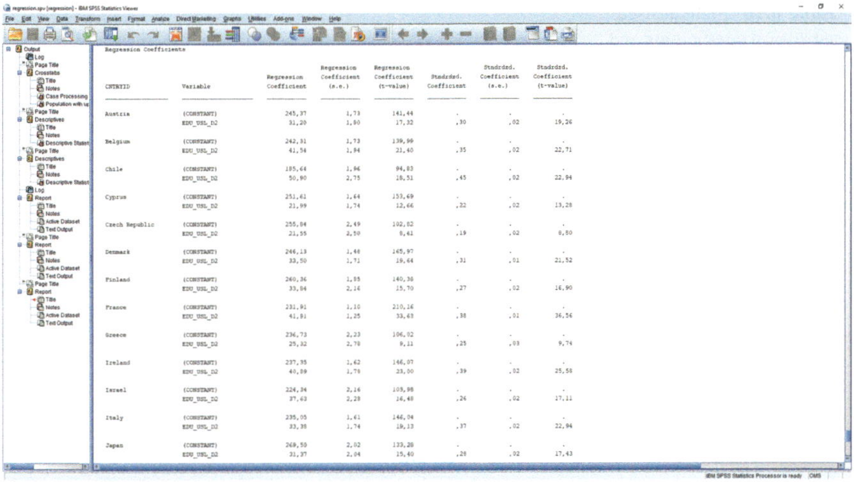

6 Analysing PIAAC Data with the IDB Analyzer (SPSS and SAS)

Fig. 6.16 Regression output

Table 6.9 Files generated by a regression analysis

Generated files	File type	Content
regression.sps	SPSS	Syntax to run the regression analysis
regression.spv	SPSS	Output of the regression analysis
regression_Model.sav	SPSS	Contains R-squared of the regression model and its adjusted R-squared
regression_Model.xlsx	Excel	
regression_Coef.sav	SPSS	Contains unstandardised and standardised regression coefficients and their standard errors
regression_Coef.xlsx	Excel	
regression_Desc.sav	SPSS	Contains descriptive statistics for all the variables included in the regression model. These include means, standard deviations, and variances
regression_Desc.xlsx	Excel	

Using the estimates present in 'regression_Coef.xlsx' and in 'regression_Model.xlsx', we created Table 6.10, to show at a glance the general results of the fitted model. These results are ranked in descending order using the R^2, a measure of explained variance (see, e.g. Field 2013, for more information about regression analysis).

Inspecting the regression coefficients present in 'regression_Coef.xlsx' and their t-values, we can conclude that all estimated differences are above the sampling error and all beta.t are larger than two. Thus, in all countries, those who have at least upper secondary education obtain higher literacy scores in the PIAAC test. The average difference of all participating countries is 0.32 standard deviations of literacy scores. The estimated gap varies between countries. For example, in Singapore, Spain, and Chile, it is larger than 0.45 standard deviations. In contrast, in Lithuania, the Russian Federation, and Poland, this difference is less than or equal to 0.16 standard deviations of literacy scores.

Table 6.10 Standardised regression coefficients and model fit

Countries	Standardised Estimate	Standard Error	R^2
Singapore	0.55	0.01	0.30
Spain	0.46	0.01	0.21
Chile	0.45	0.02	0.20
Netherlands	0.42	0.02	0.18
Ireland	0.39	0.02	0.15
United Kingdom	0.39	0.01	0.15
Turkey	0.39	0.02	0.15
France	0.38	0.01	0.15
Italy	0.37	0.02	0.14
New Zealand	0.37	0.02	0.13
Korea, Republic of	0.36	0.02	0.13
Belgium	0.35	0.02	0.12
Sweden	0.35	0.01	0.12
United States	0.33	0.01	0.11
Slovak Republic	0.33	0.02	0.11
Denmark	0.31	0.01	0.10
Austria	0.30	0.02	0.09
Norway	0.30	0.01	0.09
Slovenia	0.29	0.02	0.09
Japan	0.28	0.02	0.08
Finland	0.27	0.02	0.07
Israel	0.26	0.02	0.07
Greece	0.25	0.03	0.06
Cyprus	0.22	0.02	0.05
Czech Republic	0.19	0.02	0.04
Poland	0.16	0.02	0.03
Russian Federation	0.15	0.03	0.02
Lithuania	0.06	0.02	0.00
Table Average	0.32	0.00	0.11

6.3.6 *Correlations*

In the PIAACe study, literacy, numeracy, and problem solving in technology-rich environments were measured. How are these different skills related to each other? In other words, to what extent do these three variables fluctuate together? In the OECD (2016a) report, 'Skills Matter', these variables were reported to be highly and positively correlated, with correlations of 0.86 for literacy and numeracy for the OECD partners (see, e.g. Field 2013, for more information about correlation analysis). In the following example, we will estimate the correlation between proficiency in literacy, numeracy, and problem solving in technology-rich environments. To compute these correlations, we need to follow the next steps:

1. Open the Analysis Module of the IDB Analyzer.

2. For this example, specify the data file 'merge_piaac.sav' as the Analysis File (see Sect. 6.2 in this chapter for the details of how this file was created).
3. Select 'PIAAC (using final full sample weight)' as the Analysis Type.
4. Select 'Correlations' as the Statistic Type.
5. Under the 'Plausible Values Options', select 'Use PVs'.
6. Under the 'Missing Data' option, select 'Pairwise'.
7. Click on the 'Plausible Values' section on the right-hand side of the software window.
8. Go to the 'Select variables' section, and select the three plausible values variables.
9. Move all the selected variables, by clicking the right arrow in the right-hand side window under the 'Plausible Values' subsection.
10. Specify the name and the folder of the output files in the 'Output Files' field by clicking the 'Define/Modify' button. In this example, we define the syntax as 'correlation'.

The final setup should resemble the setup presented in Fig. 6.17.

11. Then, click the 'Start SPSS' button. This will create an SPSS syntax file and open it in an SPSS editor window.
12. To start the computations, one needs to press the following key combinations: CTRL+A first, to select the entire generated code present in the syntax window, and then CTRL+R to run these commands. The output of these analyses is depicted in Fig. 6.18.

Because these computations involve the plausible values of the three proficiency scores, its estimation will take longer compared with correlations between variables with no plausible values. When the computations are done, six files are generated. These files are described in Table 6.11.

The output of these computations is displayed in Fig. 6.18.

These results match those shown in Table A2.7 of the report 'Skills Matter: Further Results from the Survey of Adult Skills' (OECD 2016a). In Table 6.12, we include only the matching countries from the OECD report, and the countries

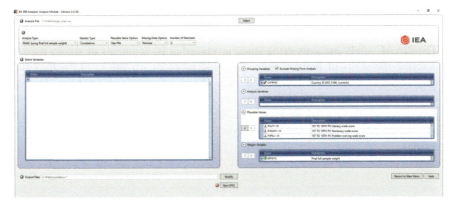

Fig. 6.17 Correlation setup

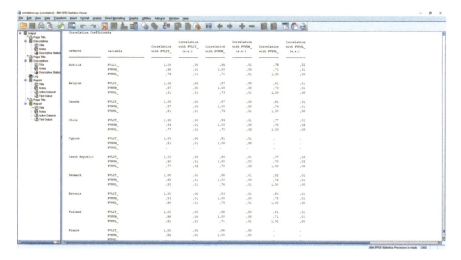

Fig. 6.18 Correlation output

Table 6.11 Files generated by a correlation analysis

Generated files	File type	Content
correlation.spv	SPSS	Syntax to run the correlation analysis
correlation.sps	SPSS	Output of the correlation analysis
correlation_Corr.sav	SPSS	Contains the correlation estimates and their standard errors
correlation_Corr.xlsx	Excel	
correlation_Desc.sav	SPSS	Contains descriptives for all the variables included in the correlation analysis. These include means, standard deviations, and variances
correlation_Desc.xlsx	Excel	

present in the current merged file. Thus, the correlations from Australia, Northern Ireland, and Jakarta (Indonesia) are excluded in the present table.

6.3.7 *Proficiency Levels*

The PIAAC study presents proficiency levels—that is, segments of scores used to describe the skills of literacy, numeracy, and problem solving in technology-rich environments at different levels of ability. These are ranges of scores to describe in qualitative terms what participants can do at different levels of proficiency. In general terms, those participants with higher scores in each domain are more likely to resolve more difficult tasks than their counterparts with lower scores (OECD 2016a).

Table 6.12 Correlations between literacy and numeracy scale scores

	OECD estimates	IDB estimates
Austria	0.86	0.86
Belgium	0.87	0.87
Canada	0.87	0.87
Chile	0.84	0.84
Cyprus	0.81	0.81
Czech Republic	0.80	0.80
Denmark	0.88	0.88
Estonia	0.83	0.83
Finland	0.86	0.86
France	0.86	0.86
Germany	0.87	0.87
Greece	0.81	0.81
Ireland	0.87	0.87
Israel	0.86	0.86
Italy	0.83	0.83
Japan	0.86	0.86
Korea, Republic of	0.88	0.88
Lithuania	0.84	0.84
Netherlands	0.89	0.89
New Zealand	0.87	0.87
Norway	0.89	0.89
Poland	0.85	0.85
Russian Federation	0.79	0.79
Singapore	0.93	0.93
Slovak Republic	0.85	0.85
Slovenia	0.88	0.88
Spain	0.89	0.89
Sweden	0.89	0.89
Turkey	0.85	0.85
United Kingdom	0.87	0.87
United States	0.89	0.89

Literacy scale scores have six proficiency levels. These proficiency levels are briefly described in Table 6.13; more details can be found in 'The Survey of Adults Skills: Reader's Companion' (OECD 2016b).

1. Open the Analysis Module of the IDB Analyzer.
2. For this example, specify the data file 'merge_piaac.sav' as the Analysis File (see Sect. 6.2 in this chapter for the details of how this file was created).
3. Select 'PIAAC (using final full sample weight)' as the Analysis Type.
4. Select 'Benchmarks' as the Statistic Type.
5. Under the 'Benchmarks Options' select 'Discrete'. This option will retrieve what proportion of the population falls within each proficiency level. Other options include 'Cumulative', which computes the proportion of people at

Table 6.13 Levels of proficiency

Level	Cut scores	Brief descriptions of more likely resolved tasks
Below level 1	Below 176	Basic reading comprehension with a basic vocabulary
Level 1	From 176 to below 226	Reading tasks resolved at this level include the integration of information, using identical or synonymous terms
Level 2	From 226 to below 276	Reading tasks from this level require the integration of information of similar meaning, via low inference or paraphrase, and discerning competing information
Level 3	From 276 to below 326	Reading tasks require the participant to read through larger pieces of text and construct meaning across paragraphs
Level 4	From 326 to below 376	Reading tasks from this level require complex inferences and application of background knowledge. The participants need to evaluate subtle evidence-claims or persuasive discourse relationships
Level 5	At or above 376	Tasks may require the respondent to search for information and integrate information of similar and contrasting ideas, points of view, or evaluate evidence-based arguments. Evaluating the reliability of evidentiary sources and selecting key information is frequently a requirement

or above the cut score, and 'Discrete with analysis variables', which permits the user to calculate the mean of an analysis variable for those within each proficiency level. For this example, we will use the 'Discrete' option.

6. Click on the 'Plausible Values' section on the right-hand side of the software window.
7. Move the cursor to the left-hand side of the window and click on the 'PVLIT1–10' variable to select the literacy scores.
8. Move the selected variable, by clicking on the right arrow in the right-hand side window, under the 'Plausible Values' subsection.
9. Under the 'Achievement Benchmarks' section, select the corresponding scores for the literacy scores; these are '176 226 276 326 376'.
10. Specify the name and the folder of the output files in the 'Output Files' field by clicking the 'Define/Modify' button. Here we define the syntax as 'benchmark'.

The setup of this analysis is depicted in Fig. 6.19.

11. Click the 'Start SPSS' button. This action will open SPSS and create the syntax to run the regression model.
12. To execute the generated syntax, press CTRL+A to select all the commands, and then press CTRL+R to execute the syntax. Now, SPSS will compute the proportion of cases at each benchmark.

Results are displayed in Fig. 6.20, as they appear in SPSS.

6 Analysing PIAAC Data with the IDB Analyzer (SPSS and SAS)

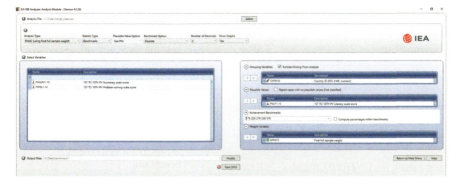

Fig. 6.19 Benchmark setup

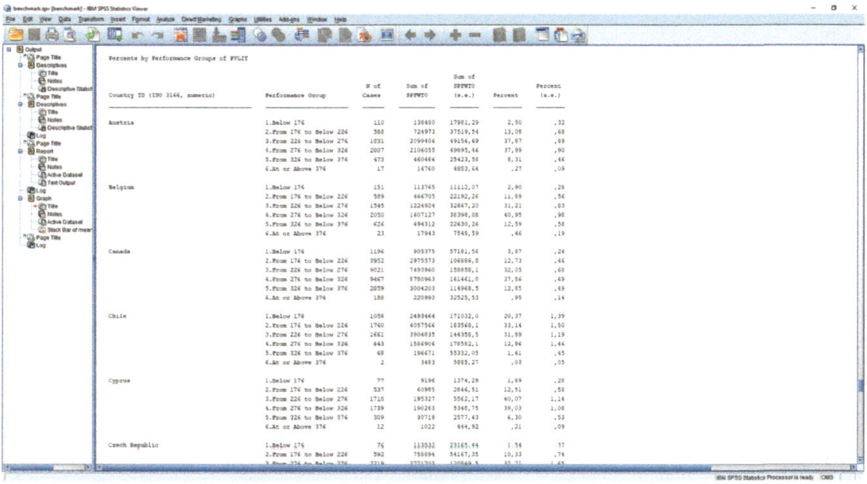

Fig. 6.20 Benchmark output

What do these results mean? We need to consider the procedure the benchmark routine is doing to explain this output. Each cut score is the lower bound value for each defined range (IEA 2019). We used the following cut scores: '176 226 276 326 376'. Thus, it computes all the cases below 176 points, all the cases between 176 and 226, between 226 and 276, between 276 and 326, between 326 and 376, and finally all the cases above 376. In the last two columns of the output, the estimates are the percentage of cases and their standard errors that fall into the specified ranges. This procedure generates the following files in the specified location (see Table 6.14).

Using the information contained in 'benchmark.xlsx', we created Table 6.15. This table displays the proportions of participants who performed below Level 1 in the literacy proficiency scale.

Table 6.14 Files generated by a correlation analysis

Generated files	File type	Content
benchmark.spv	SPSS	Syntax to run the benchmark computations
benchmark.sps	SPSS	Output of the benchmark computations
benchmark.sav	SPSS	Contains the benchmark estimates and their standard errors
benchmark.xlsx	Excel	
benchmark_by_CNTRYID_Sig.sav	SPSS	Contains a country-by-country comparison for the percentages at each benchmark
benchmark_by_CNTRYID_Sig.xlsx	Excel	

Table 6.15 Percentage of participants below Proficiency Level 1

Country	Estimate	Standard error	Country	Estimate	Standard error
Chile	20.37	1.39	United Kingdom	3.32	0.38
Turkey	12.92	0.85	Norway	3.05	0.3
Singapore	10.21	0.39	Belgium	2.9	0.28
Israel	8.25	0.41	Finland	2.66	0.23
Spain	7.27	0.47	Netherlands	2.62	0.27
Slovenia	6.01	0.41	New Zealand	2.57	0.28
Italy	5.56	0.57	Austria	2.5	0.32
France	5.37	0.31	Lithuania	2.26	0.38
Greece	4.95	0.53	Korea, Republic of	2.23	0.2
Ireland	4.3	0.43	Estonia	2.02	0.19
United States	4.09	0.47	Slovak Republic	1.89	0.24
Poland	3.94	0.32	Cyprus	1.89	0.28
Canada	3.87	0.24	Russian Federation	1.56	0.54
Denmark	3.83	0.29	Czech Republic	1.54	0.32
Sweden	3.68	0.33	Japan	0.57	0.15
Germany	3.33	0.39	Table Average	4.57	0.08

In Chile, 20% are below Level 1, whereas in Japan, Czech Republic, the Russian Federation, Cyprus, and the Slovak Republic, there are fewer than 2% below Level 1.

6.4 Concluding Remarks

In this chapter, we demonstrated how to perform both simple and complex analysis with PIAAC data using the IEA International Database (IDB) Analyzer. We showed examples of how to combine datasets from more than one country into a single data file for cross-country analyses. We also described and illustrated in a step-by-step fashion how to run descriptive statistical analyses, including means, percentiles, and percentages, as well as inferential analyses, such as correlations and regressions.

Although the examples included in this chapter used data from OECD's PIAAC study, it is important to mention that the IDB Analyzer can be used to analyse not only PIAAC data but many other international large-scale assessments, such as the OECD's PISA and TALIS studies, as well as, for example, IEA's Trends in International Mathematics and Science Study (TIMSS), Progress in International Reading Literacy Study (PIRLS), and International Civic and Citizenship Study (ICCS).

The IDB Analyzer is certainly not the only tool available to obtain correct estimates when analysing PIAAC data, but it is probably the most user-friendly one. As mentioned before, the IDB Analyzer is a Windows-based tool that creates SAS code or SPSS syntax to perform analyses with PIAAC data. The code or syntax generated by the IDB Analyzer automatically takes into account the complex sample (e.g. sampling weights, replicate weights) and complex assessment design (e.g. plausible values) of PIAAC to compute analyses with the correct standard errors. It enables researchers to test statistical hypotheses in the population without having to write any programming code.

References

Field, A. (2013). *Discovering statistics using IBM SPSS*. London: Sage Publications.
Heeringa, S. G., West, B., & Berglund, P. A. (2009). *Applied survey data analysis*. Boca Raton: Taylor & Francis Group.
IBM. (2013). *IBM SPSS statistics (Version 22.0)*. Somers: IBM corporation.
IEA. (2019). *Help manual for the IEA IDB analyzer (Version 4.0)*. Hamburg, Germany. Retrieved from www.iea.nl/data.htm
OECD. (2015). *Codebook for derived variables for PIAAC public database (with SAS code)*. Paris: OECD Publishing. Retrieved from http://www.oecd.org/skills/piaac/codebook for DVs 3_16 March 2015.docx.
OECD. (2016a). *Skills matter: Further results from the survey of adult skills*. Paris: OECD Publishing. https://doi.org/10.1787/9789264258051-en.
OECD. (2016b). *The survey of adult skills: Reader's companion*. Paris: OECD Publishing. https://doi.org/10.1787/9789264204256-en.
Rutkowski, L., Gonzalez, E., Joncas, M., & von Davier, M. (2010). International large-scale assessment data: Issues in secondary analysis and reporting. *Educational Researcher, 39*(2), 142–151. https://doi.org/10.3102/0013189X10363170.
SAS. (2012). *SAS system for windows (Version 9.4)*. Cary: SAS Institute.

Wilcox, R. R. (2017). *Understanding and applying basic statistical methods using R*. Hoboken: Wiley.

Wu, M. (2005). The role of plausible values in large-scale surveys. *Studies in Educational Evaluation, 31*(2–3), 114–128. https://doi.org/10.1016/j.stueduc.2005.05.005.

Open Access This chapter is licensed under the terms of the Creative Commons Attribution 4.0 International License (http://creativecommons.org/licenses/by/4.0/), which permits use, sharing, adaptation, distribution and reproduction in any medium or format, as long as you give appropriate credit to the original author(s) and the source, provide a link to the Creative Commons license and indicate if changes were made.

The images or other third party material in this chapter are included in the chapter's Creative Commons license, unless indicated otherwise in a credit line to the material. If material is not included in the chapter's Creative Commons license and your intended use is not permitted by statutory regulation or exceeds the permitted use, you will need to obtain permission directly from the copyright holder.

Chapter 7
Analysing PIAAC Data with Stata

François Keslair

Abstract This chapter explains the basics of analysing data from the Programme for the International Assessment of Adult Competencies (PIAAC) with Stata. It describes how to import the PIAAC datasets into Stata, gives an overview of the different categories of variables available in these datasets, and mentions a number of features of some types of variables about which users should be aware. The different types of missing values are explained. Routines frequently used with PIAAC datasets are presented using examples. Furthermore, the chapter is devoted to the use of plausible values variables and to the computation of imputation errors and sampling errors. In particular, it presents *repest*, a Stata ado file written to facilitate the analysis of international skills assessments, such as PIAAC.

Stata is an integrated statistical analysis package designed for research professionals. It is particularly well suited for analysing the Organisation for Economic Co-operation and Development's (OECD) Programme for the International Assessment of Adult Competencies (PIAAC) survey (OECD 2013, 2016b, c). Among existing statistical software packages, Stata stands out as it is designed to operate on one dataset at a time, using a dataset that has been previously loaded in memory. With a one-dataset survey such as PIAAC, it brings a simplicity of use and computation speeds difficult to find elsewhere. Moreover, Stata users can benefit from *repest*, a Stata *ado* file developed at the OECD and designed to facilitate the analysis of international skills assessments.

Stata works as a command-line-driven software. It also includes a graphic user interface. Commands can be run—one command at a time—from a prompt located below the results window. This makes the preliminary exploration of a dataset both simple and interactive, in particular, because another window is dedicated to displaying the list of all variables. Commands can be regrouped and saved in

---

F. Keslair (✉)
Organisation for Economic Co-operation and Development, OECD, Paris, France
e-mail: francois.keslair@oecd.org

a do-file in a separated window. Do-files include files that create new functions that can enrich the Stata library. These files are called ado files, and *repest*, which is described below, is one of them. All native Stata functions can be accessed through the graphic interface. Any action from the graphic interface is translated into the equivalent command inside the prompt. This latter feature is of great help in generating commands with a complex syntax, especially the commands used to generate charts.

It should be noted that, the brief description of the interface aside, this chapter is not intended as an introduction to Stata (therefore, see, e.g. Kohler and Kreuter 2012). Rather, it will focus on how to use Stata with PIAAC. It is assumed that readers have at least a basic knowledge of Stata and know how to perform simple procedures such as loading a dataset and creating new variables. Users unfamiliar with Stata can obtain a good introduction to the package from the Stata help files. The Stata help files deserve a word of praise. They are well written, comprehensive, and represent one of the main assets of the software.[1] They are accompanied by documentation in PDF format that offers detailed examples for each Stata function, as well as by YouTube tutorial videos. These resources are relevant for all Stata users—from beginners to experts—and make working with Stata a very pleasant experience.

This chapter is structured as follows: The first section will describe basic management of the PIAAC dataset using Stata, commonly used procedures, and some pitfalls to avoid. The second section will present *repest*, a Stata macro designed to help perform data analysis in international skills assessments. The third section will describe in detail all of *repest*'s features. Examples are provided to illustrate the commands described and to present Stata routines useful in analyses of PIAAC data.

7.1 Basic Manipulation of PIAAC Data Using Stata

7.1.1 Importing the Datasets

PIAAC data are accessible in public use files (PUFs; see Chap. 4 in this volume) that can be downloaded from the data section of the PIAAC website.[2] There is one single file for each participating country containing all publicly available variables. Unfortunately, PIAAC PUFs are not available in the Stata native *dta* format and have to be imported into STATA from the generic comma-separated-values (csv) versions. Because of the complexity of the datasets— most notably the encoding of missing values—this procedure is not straightforward without any loss

---

[1] New users can simply type *help resources* in the command prompt in order to have access to all available help resources.

[2] https://www.oecd.org/skills/piaac/data/

of information. In order to simplify the access to the datasets, a Stata do-file is also available in the data section of the PIAAC website. Once all CSV files have been downloaded into a directory, this do-file imports and appends all PUFs and then formats all variables into a unique *dta* dataset ready to be used. This do-file will also work if the target directory contains only one country dataset.[3]

7.1.2 Different Types of Variables

The PUFs contain more than 1300 variables divided into three broad categories. With a few exceptions, most of these variables are either numeric or categorical variables. Note that categorical variables in Stata are numeric variables that accept value labels. The *lookfor* command provides an easy way to search for variables; it displays all variables containing the desired keywords in its name or label. The reader can also consult questionnaires and codebooks available online (OECD 2014, 2016a).

7.1.2.1 Respondent and Interviewer Inputs

This category covers respondents' answers to the background questionnaire and the cognitive instruments. Variables relating to the background questionnaire are named according to the position of the question to which they relate. For instance, *b_q01b* refers to Question 1b in Section B of the background questionnaire. Most of these variables were collected for the purpose of building the derived variables introduced before. Background questions might be useful for more detailed analysis, but data users should consider using them only when derived variables cannot be used in their place (OECD 2011). Users should be careful when employing them—and should be particularly careful to handle missing values correctly. For each of the cognitive test items, the PUFs also include the respondents' answer status, supplemented with a set of variables on item timing for those respondents who were assessed on the computer. These variables are named after the item identifier (a six-digit number), with the last letter in the variable name standing for the type of variable. For instance, E644002S is the scored response for item 644002. The cognitive variables should not be used in analysis without a very good knowledge of the design of the cognitive assessment. In addition, the PUFs also include answers to the observation module that was filled in by the interviewer following completion of the interview.

---

[3]For the rest of the chapter, it will be assumed that the loaded dataset includes all participating countries.

7.1.2.2 Variables Derived from the Survey Instruments

These variables are designed to be used directly in analysis, and data users should focus principally on this set. Derived variables include proficiency scores, education levels, earning variables, indexes, or occupation variables. The process of derivation can take many forms: from the very simple creation of gender and age interval variables to the human coding of occupation descriptions into ISCO categories, or the computation of plausible values of individual proficiency scores through an IRT and population model (see Chap. 3 in this volume). Derived variables have generally meaningful names such as *gender_r* or *readytolearn*. However, some derived variables were created by the survey software and are named following the same convention as the background questionnaire variables. *c_d05* is thus a derived variable created in Section C of the questionnaire after its fifth question. All derived variables bear variable labels including the word 'derived'.

7.1.2.3 Auxiliary Variables

Auxiliary variables represent information about the survey workflow and the survey design, including the set of final weights and balanced repeated replicated (BRR) weights. Other than the replicate weights, auxiliary variables are not used in most analyses. Other auxiliary variables of interest include *pbroute*, which indicates whether the respondent took the paper-based or computer-based assessment, and the disposition codes, which indicate whether the observation is considered to be complete, or the reason why it is considered incomplete.

7.1.3 *The Correct Handling of Missing Values*

The handling of missing values is one of the main sources of mistakes in the analysis of PIAAC data. There are a number of different types of missing values that must be clearly distinguished. In Stata, missing values for numeric variables (including categorical variables) are coded with a letter preceded by a dot character. The function *missing(myvarname)* will yield 1 if and only if the observation has one of these missing value codes recorded in *myvarname*. The different types of missing values codes used in PIAAC are as follows:

- .d : the respondent *didn't know* how to answer.
- .r : the respondent *refused* to answer.
- .n: the answer cannot be interpreted and is considered as *non stated*.
- .u, .a, .z, .m : these codes are rarer and specific to some derived variables.
- .v : the respondent did not have to answer the question and a *valid skip* was recorded.
- . : the value is missing for other reasons.

All these codes except *valid skip* (and sometimes '.') refer to values that are missing due to nonresponse or errors. In contrast, missing values coded as *valid skip* do not represent forms of nonresponse or other response errors. These values are missing by design (see also Chap. 2 in this volume). Variables with *valid skip* must be interpreted in the context of the questionnaire and assessment. The background questionnaire is a complex set of questions, and in order to prevent nonsensical or redundant questions, many questions are administered only when some specific conditions are satisfied.

First, questions are administered only to the population for which the question has a meaning. For instance, the set of questions in Section D in the background questionnaire (OECD 2014) collects information on the respondent's current occupation, including income, and only respondents who are currently working are presented with the questions in this section. For all other respondents, the response to the variables in this section is imputed as *valid skip*. Thus, respondents who refused to answer the set of questions about their work income and respondents who are not working both have missing values in these questions. However, as they should not be confused with each other, they have missing values with different codes.

Second, questions are administered only if the information requested cannot be inferred from answers to previous questions. For instance, respondents are asked about their household composition only if they previously reported that there was more than one member in their household. Households with only one member are, by definition, single-person households. Respondents who live in single-person households are assigned *valid skips* for the question about household composition. In analysis, however, these *valid skips* must be assigned their true value—that is, the value code for single-person households.

In order to avoid problems with missing values, data users should, as a rule, check for the occurrence of missing values and should tabulate all categorical variables they use with the following command:

```
tabulate myvarname , missing
```

If *valid skips* are present, data users should consult the question section in the background questionnaires to determine whether observations with these missing codes result from the redundancy of the question or from it not being relevant to the particular respondent. In the former case, a new variable with the correct values should be created. It is important to note that derived variables can sometimes feature *valid skips*. In these cases, however, this coding is always due to the lack of relevance of the question and not from its redundancy.

The coding of missing values in the PIAAC dataset has nonetheless one exception. All ISCO and ISIC variables describing occupations and industry sectors, respectively, are coded as string variables. For these variables, all strings starting with *999* indicate codes for missing values.

7.1.4 Working with Plausible Values

PIAAC includes proficiency measures in three domains: literacy, numeracy, and problem solving in technology-rich environments. Proficiency scores in PIAAC proceed from a complex computation. One of the consequences of this model is the presence of imputation error, which requires the use of plausible values variables in order to account for it. Scores in each of the three assessment domains, *literacy*, *numeracy*, and *problem solving in technology-rich environments*, are described by ten different plausible values variables, numbered from 1 to 10. Any one of these variables will give an unbiased estimate of individual proficiency, but the full set is required in order to compute accurate standard errors of population estimates (for more details see Chap. 3 in this volume).

The PUFs include proficiency scores only in the form of point estimates. Other variables derived from proficiency scores must be created by data users. This is the case, for example, with the proficiency levels, which are often used to describe the distribution of proficiency scores. Categorical variables for the proficiency levels in literacy and numeracy have to be created using the following loop over the ten plausible values (the example relates to the creation of proficiency levels categorical variables for literacy):

```
forvalues i=1/10 {
        generate litlev`i'= (pvlit`i'>176) + (pvlit`i'>226)+///
        (pvlit`i'>276)+ (pvlit`i'>326) + (pvlit`i'>376) ///
        if missing(pvlit`i')==0
        }
```

This short string of code provides the opportunity to discuss a common mistake. The brackets are used to create a function that yields 1 if and only if the predicate inside the brackets is true and 0 for all other observations in the dataset. Importantly, the predicate remains defined for observations in which *pvlit* is missing. In this situation, missing values are considered by Stata to be larger than any number, and, as a result, each inequality is true for observations with missing literacy scores. In this example the value 0 would have been created for observations in which the literacy score is missing, were it not for the *if* statement at the end that causes these observations to have a missing value. The ten *litlev* variables will then be defined based on each *pvlit* variable and will cover the five different proficiency levels. Respondents with their i[th] plausible value scoring below the Level 1 threshold category (176) would have their i[th] plausible value level assigned to 0.

7.1.5 Computing Point Estimates in Stata

One of the main advantages of working with Stata is the simplicity of its syntax. Once the dataset has been properly imported, most statistics can be computed using a short command, with results being displayed in the Stata results window. While the computation of accurate standard errors requires using the *repest* macro, the computation of accurate point estimates requires only the name of the final weight *spfwt0* to be mentioned in the command.[4] Importantly, these computations are much faster than those required for accurate standard errors and are thus more convenient for preliminary work and for obtaining an overview of the PIAAC dataset. The following examples cover some frequent cases of data exploration:

```
(1) tabulate ageg10lfs if cntry_e=="ENG" [aw= spfwt0]
```

`tabulate` returns the frequencies of categorical or string variables. This command will give the age distribution of the English target population displayed in 10-year age bands. Importantly, in the absence of an *if* statement, the command would give the age distribution for all countries appearing in the dataset, with each country weighted according to the size of its target population.

```
(2) bysort cntry_e: summarize pvlit1 [aw= spfwt0]
```

`summarize` returns common statistics (average, standard deviation, minimum, and maximum) for a continuous variable. This command will describe the literacy distribution for the target population of each country in the dataset based on the first set of plausible values. The *bysort* prefix will loop the *summarize* command over all groups defined by the *cntry_e* variable. To obtain unbiased estimates, it is sufficient to use only *pvlit1*. However, for reasons of efficiency, the average statistics published by the OECD represent the averages of each of the ten statistics associated with the ten sets of plausible values.

```
(3) bysort cntry_e edlevel3: regress pvlit1 ib1.gender_r
[aw= spfwt0]
```

regress will give OLS regression coefficients of *pvlit1* on the *gender_r* variable, taking 1 as a reference. In plain language, it will estimate gender gaps in literacy proficiency. *bysort* accepts several variables, and in this case the regression will be computed for each country identified by *cntry_e* and, within each country, for each of the education levels identified by *edlevel3*.

---

[4]It should be kept in mind that *spfwt0* represents the number of persons that each observation represents in their country's target population. As a result, each country contributes to the statistics in proportion to its size. If the user works with pooled samples and wishes that all countries contribute equally, he or she will have to rescale all weights.

7.2 The *Repest* Command: Computing Correct Standard Errors

The main purpose of the *repest* ado file is the correct computation of standard errors of statistics in international skills surveys such as PIAAC.

Computing standard errors in PIAAC is not as straightforward as computing point estimates. Since the sampling structure in each PIAAC country is not purely random, but rather involves complex random draws from the sampling frame performed in several stages, it has to be taken into account in a particular way. To do so, PIAAC uses a replication method with 80 replicate weights to account for the resulting sampling error. These weights simulate alternative samples, and the comparison of all these alternative samples yields an estimation of sampling errors. All population statistics are affected by sampling error. In the case of proficiency scores, as mentioned above, imputation error also needs to be taken into account. The ten plausible values are all different imputations of the proficiency scores using the same model. Following the same principle underlying the BRR, the comparison of these ten plausible values with each other allows estimation of the magnitude of the imputation error.

The operating principle of BRR and plausible values is simple: an empirical distribution of a statistic is estimated by computing it as many times as there are BRR weights and plausible values and then drawing a standard error from this distribution. The core of *repest* is thus a loop going over all 80 BRR weights and the final weights (and the ten plausible values if applicable). This method is extremely flexible, as it can be applied to any statistics, but it is also slow: if there are no plausible values, 81 statistics must be computed, and when plausible values are present, 810 statistics must be computed.

7.2.1 Installing Repest

Repest can be installed from within Stata by using the following simple command:

```
ssc install repest, replace
```

The command will download the *repest* ado file, along with its help file, and install it into the user's ado directory.[5] Once the installation is completed, the *repest* command can be used in the same way as any other command. The help file covers all options in detail: it can be accessed via the following command:

---

[5]*Repest* can also be downloaded from the data section of the PIAAC website. However, in this case, the user will have to install it in Stata manually.

```
help repest
```

7.2.2 General Syntax

Repest general syntax is framed as a meta-command surrounding the respective Stata command for the desired statistics. This section will cover only the properties of its main syntax and of its mandatory components. The description of options, many of them aimed at facilitating its use, will be addressed in the next section.

When using PIAAC data, the *repest* syntax is as follows:

```
repest PIAAC [if] [in] , estimate([stata:]cmd) [repest_options]
```

The left-hand side includes only the PIAAC keyword, along with any *if* or *in* statements. For efficient computations, *if* and *in* statements must be mentioned here rather than in the estimate argument. The PIAAC keyword instructs the program to load parameters associated with PIAAC:

- Final weight: *spfwt0*
- Replicate weights: *spfwt1-spfwt80*
- Variance method: Jackknife 1 or 2, depending on variable *vemethodn*
- Number of replications: 80
- Number of plausible values: 10

It is important to note that *repest* will not work if any of these variables are missing or have been renamed.

The *estimate* main option is mandatory and will contain the full Stata command associated with the desired statistic and any specific option associated to this command. Any *eclass* Stata command will work. *eclass* commands are Stata estimation commands; they are characterised by the presence in the output of an estimation vector *e(b)* and an associated variance matrix *e(V)*.[6] By default, *repest* will compute the simulated empirical distribution of the *e(b)* vector. Importantly, as some usual Stata commands are not *eclass* and do not return a *e(b)* vector, *repest* includes built-in commands designed to replace them. As a result, the *estimate* argument can take two forms.

The first one is dedicated to built-in commands:

```
estimate(built_in_cmd [,cmd_options])
```

Available built-in commands are *means* for computing averages, *freq* for frequencies tables, *corr* for correlations, and *summarize* for describing univariate

---
[6]Which, incidentally, does not account for sampling or imputation error.

distributions. The syntax for these commands is kept simple, as shown in the examples below:

```
repest PIAAC, estimate(means pvlit@ ictwork)
 repest PIAAC if ageg10lfs==4, estimate(freq edlevels3)
 repest PIAAC, estimate(summarize pvlit@ pvnum@, stats(sd p50))
 repest PIAAC, estimate(corr pvlit@ pvnum@)
```

The commands *means*, *summarize*, and *corr* can take any number of variables, while *freq* will accept only one variable at a time. The *stats* option in *summarize* is mandatory and contains keywords for the desired univariate statistics: in this case, the median and the standard deviation. The full list of possible statistics is available in the help file. Please note that the *if* statement in the *freq* example, which constrained the frequencies to be computed for respondents aged between 45 and 54 years, is mentioned before the comma, as mentioned above. Weights do not have to be mentioned, as they are automatically added once the PIAAC keyword is specified.

The second form of the *estimate* argument is the general syntax dedicated to Stata *eclass* commands. It simply adds the prefix *stata:*

```
estimate(stata: e_cmd [,e_cmd_options])
```

Regression commands in Stata are all *eclass*, with regression coefficients stored in the *e(b)* vector. As a consequence, this syntax should be used for computing any regression—for instance, a regression of literacy scores on education levels and including country fixed effects:

```
repest PIAAC, estimate(stata: xi: areg pvlit@ i.edlevels3,
 absorb (cntry_e))
```

Without any further options, all statistics in the Stata command *e(b)* vector will be computed, using the full sample, potentially conditioned with an *if* statement. The program will return these statistics with their standard errors in the results window.

One important remark: any plausible values variables (native or user-built)—be it in the *if/in* statement, inside the *estimate* argument or inside one of the option arguments—must be included using an @ character in place of the plausible value number. For example, plausible values for literacy scores that appear in the database as `pvlit1, pvlit2, etc.` have to be indicated only once as `pvlit@`. The *repest* program recognises the @ character as indicating the presence of a variable with plausible values and will automatically include a loop over the right number of plausible values.

7.2.3 Repest Options

Available options are as follows:

- *by*: produces separate estimates by levels of the specified variable (e.g. countries)
- *over*: joint estimates across the different levels of a variable list
- *outfile*: creates a Stata dataset recording all results
- *display*: displays results in output window
- *results*: keep, add, and combine estimation results
- *svypar*: change survey parameters
- *store*: saves the estimation results stored in e()
- *fast*: when a plausible value variable is specified, computes sampling variance only for the first plausible value

7.2.3.1 By Option

This option allows the desired statistics to be computed separately for each group defined by *varname*. Without any *by* option, *repest* computes the desired statistics once, using the complete dataset. Akin to Stata *bysort*, the *by* option will instruct *repest* to compute the desired statistics for each value of *varname*. In contrast to the *over* option described below, *by* is not intended to split a sample into subsamples of interest, but rather to isolate samples from one another. In practice, *varname* will always be a country indicator. We recommend that the *cntry_e* variable be used to identify countries. The *cntry_e* variable contains ISO3 country codes and remains short, without space characters, and readable.

by accepts two different options. *average (list_of_countries)* will compute the simple average of statistics for countries appearing in its argument. It will also compute the standard error of this average, with the assumption that all samples are independent of each other. *levels(list_of_countries)* will restrain the computation over the countries. By default, *repest* will loop over all countries present in the dataset. Results tables will be displayed for each country, as they are computed, and the results for the average, if requested, will be displayed at the end. The following examples cover different uses of *by*:

```
repest PIAAC, estimate(means pvlit@ pvnum@) by(cntry_e)
```

The above command will compute literacy and numeracy averages in all countries present in the sample, as identified by the *cntry_e* variable.

```
repest PIAAC if ageg10lfs==5, estimate(freq c_d05) by(cntry_e,
average(USA FRA DEU))
```

The above command will compute the labour force status of the population aged between 55 and 65 years for each country in the dataset and then display the simple average of statistics for the United States, France, and Germany.

```
repest PIAAC if litlev@==4, estimate(freq gender_r) by
(cntry_e, levels(USA FRA))
```

This command will compute gender frequencies of the target population scoring at Level 4 in literacy, but only for the United States and France.

7.2.3.2 *Over* Option

Like *by*, *over* splits the sample into different groups in which the desired statistics will be computed. However, these groups are intended to be categories of interest (such as gender, age groups, or education levels) within a country rather than countries. This choice of two different options is justified by the possibility provided in *over* to compute differences of statistics across categories of interest. In contrast to the *by* option, the simulated distribution of the desired statistics is jointly computed for all categories, so that the simulated distribution of a difference can be generated as well. In contrast to *by*, which accepts both string and numeric variables, *over* accepts only numerical variables. *over* includes also a *test* option, which will compute the difference (and its standard error) between the statistics in the groups associated with the two extreme values and the smallest values, along with its standard error. *over* accepts several variables in its argument. In such a case, statistics will be computed in every possible combination of categories.

```
repest PIAAC, estimate(means pvlit@) over(gender, test) by
(cntry_e)
```

The above command will compute in each country average literacy for men and for women, and their difference.

```
repest PIAAC, estimate(freq c_d05) over(gender litlev@) by
(cntry_e)
```

This command will compute labour force status frequencies in each country, for every combination of gender and literacy levels.

7.2.3.3 *Outfile* Option

A large number of statistics can be produced by *repest* (particularly if they are computed by country), and a simple display of the results is not enough to obtain easy access to and reuse these numbers. For this purpose, *outfile* will export all statistics into a Stata dataset called *filename*, with one observation per country and point estimates and standard errors as variables. The file will be saved in the current Stata working directory. Statistics bear the same names as in the *e(b)* vector, with suffixes *_b* and *_se* identifying point estimates and standard errors. In the presence of an *over* variable, a prefix *_x_* will be added in order to identify statistics for category *x*.

outfile accepts two different options: (1) *pvalue* will add the p-value for every statistic on top of standard errors and point estimates, using the *_pv* suffix. These p-values are computed assuming that the point estimates follow a normal distribution. *long_over* is to be used only if *over* was specified. It will create one observation per country and per combination of *over* variables, in order to have a more readable output. (2) *long_over* is turned on automatically if there is more than one *over* variable. When *outfile* is specified, results are not displayed in the output window.

```
repest PIAAC, estimate(freq c_d05) over(gender) outfile(myfile)
```

7.2.3.4 *Display* Option

display causes *repest* to display the results in the output window when *outfile* is specified. In this case, results will be display both in a *dta* file and in the output window.

```
repest PIAAC, estimate(freq c_d05) display outfile(myfile)
```

7.2.3.5 *Results* Option

By default, *repest* output consists of the contents of the *e(b)* vector. The *results* option manipulates the vector of desired statistics. It requires one (or several) of the following suboptions:

keep will instruct *repest* to keep only statistics of the *e(b)* vector mentioned in its argument.
add will extend the output to scalar statistics stored in e() but not in the e(b) vector.
    For most *eclass* commands, the help file provides a list of stored results.
combine will take functions of the e(b) vector and create new statistics.

Importantly, *results* cannot manipulate the output across subsamples created by the *over* or the *by* options. When using *results*, knowing which exact names the statistics bear can be difficult. The set of examples below will cover potential difficulties.

```
repest PIAAC, estimate(stata: xi: reg pvlit@ ib2.edlevels3
readytolearn ) by(cntry_e) results(add(r2 N))
```

The above command will run the desired regression for each country and add the R-squared coefficient and the number of observations to the output. Note that only the 'r2' keyword is required rather than $e(r2)$. Standard errors will be computed for these two new outputs despite their difficult interpretation.

```
repest PIAAC, estimate(stata: xi: reg readytolearn ib2.
edlevel3 ib2.litlev@  ) by(cntry_e) results(keep(1_litlev@
2b_litlev@ 3_litlev@ 4_litlev@ 5_litlev@))
```

This command will run the desired regression for each country and retain in the output only coefficients associated with the literacy levels. The '@' indicating the presence of a plausible value variable is required. This example shows that the names of statistics to be mentioned in this option might differ from those written in the *outfile* dataset. The starting '_' appearing in the *outfile* dataset for dummy variables must be dropped, while the *b* character indicating the reference must be maintained.

```
repest PIAAC, estimate(summarize pvlit@, stats(p75 p25) ) by
(cntry_e) results(combine( pvlit@_iqr :  _b[pvlit@_p75]-
_b[pvlit@_p25] ))
```

While the *summarize* built-in command allows some selected percentiles to be produced, it lacks keywords for interquartile ranges. However they can be computed using the *combine* suboption. Each derivation starts with the name of the new statistics, including the @ character in case of the presence of plausible value, followed by '_iqr', a colon, and a formula definition. The name of each statistic in the formula must be enclosed in _b[...]. Additional new statistics can be added after a comma.

7.2.3.6 *Svypar* Option

The *svypar* option allows the survey parameters to be manipulated and directly specified. This option is designed to adapt *repest* to currently unfeatured surveys. As such, it is not directly useful to PIAAC users. However, as *svypar* allows the number of replicated weights used by the program to be manipulated, this option can help to considerably reduce computing time at the expense of incorrect standard errors. This can be useful in case of debugging, and it works as follows:

```
repest PIAAC, estimate(summarize pvlit@) by(cntry_e) svypar
(NREP(3))
```

7.2.3.7 *Store* Option

The *store* option provides another way of saving results using Stata's estimates store tool. If the option *store* is active, results for each country will be saved using *string* as a prefix and the country identifier as a suffix. Every estimates vector can then be recollected and potentially reused during the rest of the Stata session.

```
repest PIAAC, estimate(freq c_d05) store(freq_c_d05)
```

7.2.3.8 *Fast* Option

The computation of standard errors for statistics that use plausible values variables normally requires an empirical distribution with 810 points. However, the sampling error can be computed using one plausible value instead of all of them without introducing any bias. The *fast* option uses this in order to greatly decrease computation time by almost factor 10. Nonetheless, even though the standard error will be unbiased, it will not be numerically the same.

```
repest PIAAC, estimate(freq c_d05) fast
```

7.2.4 Conclusion

This chapter provided an overview of how to use and analyse PIAAC data with Stata. Other statistical software packages, such as SAS, SPSS, or R (see Chap. 9 in this volume), are also well suited for this task, and the user should first consider using the software with which he or she is more familiar. Nonetheless, the availability of the *repest* command is a great asset—all the more so because it is also designed to work with other international skills surveys created by the OECD, such as the Programme for International Student Assessment (PISA) or the Teaching and Learning International Survey (TALIS), or by other institutions (Trends in International Mathematics and Science Study, TIMMS).

References

Kohler, U., & Kreuter, F. (2012). *Data analysis using Stata*. College Station: Stata Press.

Organisation for Economic Co-operation and Development (OECD). (2011). *PIAAC conceptual framework of the background questionnaire main survey*. Paris: OECD Publishing.

Organisation for Economic Co-operation and Development (OECD). (2013). *OECD skills outlook 2013: First results from the Survey of Adult Skills*. Paris: OECD Publishing. https://doi.org/10.1787/9789264204256-en.

Organisation for Economic Co-operation and Development (OECD). (2014). *Technical report of the Survey of Adult Skills (PIAAC)*. Paris: OECD. http://www.oecd.org/skills/piaac/_Technical%20Report_17OCT13.pdf. Accessed 5 May, 2019.

Organisation for Economic Co-operation and Development (OECD). (2016a). *Survey of Adult Skills technical report (2nd ed.)*. Paris: OECD. http://www.oecd.org/skills/piaac/PIAAC_Technical_Report_2nd_Edition_Full_Report.pd. Accessed 5 May, 2019.

Organisation for Economic Co-operation and Development (OECD). (2016b). *Skills matter: Further results from the survey of adult skills*. Paris: OECD Publishing. https://doi.org/10.1787/9789264258051-en.

Organisation for Economic Co-operation and Development (OECD). (2016c). *The survey of adult skills – Reader's companion (2nd. ed.)*. Paris: OECD Publishing. https://doi.org/10.1787/9789264258075-en.

Open Access This chapter is licensed under the terms of the Creative Commons Attribution 4.0 International License (http://creativecommons.org/licenses/by/4.0/), which permits use, sharing, adaptation, distribution and reproduction in any medium or format, as long as you give appropriate credit to the original author(s) and the source, provide a link to the Creative Commons license and indicate if changes were made.

The images or other third party material in this chapter are included in the chapter's Creative Commons license, unless indicated otherwise in a credit line to the material. If material is not included in the chapter's Creative Commons license and your intended use is not permitted by statutory regulation or exceeds the permitted use, you will need to obtain permission directly from the copyright holder.

Chapter 8
Analysing PIAAC Data with Structural Equation Modelling in Mplus

Ronny Scherer

Abstract Structural equation modelling (SEM) has become one of the most prominent approaches to testing substantive theories about the relations among observed and/or unobserved variables. Applying this multivariate procedure, researchers are faced with several methodological decisions, including the treatment of indicator variables (e.g. categorical vs. continuous treatment), the handling of missing data, and the selection of an appropriate level of analysis. The PIAAC data pose additional issues, such as the clustering of individual-level data, the large number of participating countries, the representation of performance scores by a set of plausible values, and the differences in the selection probabilities. Therefore, a flexible software package is required to handle them. This chapter introduces readers to analysing PIAAC data with SEM in the software M*plus* by (a) presenting the key concepts behind SEM, (b) discussing the complexities of the PIAAC data and their possible handling, (c) illustrating the specification and evaluation of measurement and structural models, and (d) pointing to current developments in the areas of measurement invariance testing and multilevel SEM. Sample input and output files are provided.

Structural equation modelling (SEM) represents a broad range of multivariate approaches that allow researchers to test hypotheses related to the means, variances, and covariances of manifest and latent variables (Kaplan 2009). It includes approaches such as path analysis, confirmatory factor analysis, and structural models that are based on researchers' hypotheses and theories about the relations among variables. In his seminal book, Kline (2016) emphasised that SEM requires

Electronic Supplementary Material The online version of this chapter (https://doi.org/10.1007/978-3-030-47515-4_8) contains supplementary material.

R. Scherer (✉)
University of Oslo, Oslo, Norway
e-mail: ronny.scherer@cemo.uio.no

three inputs: first, a set of hypotheses about the relations among variables (based on theory or informed by the results of empirical studies); second, a set of specific questions about these relations (e.g. To what extent does an indirect effect of a variable X on a variable Y via a variable M exist?); and third, appropriate datasets to test these hypotheses and answer these questions. Ultimately, the process of SEM generates three outputs (Kline 2016): numeric estimates of model parameters, a set of logical implications of the model, and information about the extent to which the data support the model. Given the richness of outputs, SEM has become a prominent tool for researchers to test substantive theories and assumptions about the relations among variables. Moreover, SEM is considered a flexible modelling approach that allows for the inclusion of both manifest (observable) and latent (unobservable) variables in the measurement and structural models (Raykov and Marcoulides 2006). Due to this flexibility, researchers are faced with several methodological decisions, including the treatment of indicator variables (e.g. categorical vs. continuous treatment), the handling of missing data, and the selection of an appropriate level of analysis (e.g. individual vs. country level). Besides these decisions, international large-scale assessment data add further complexities, such as the weighting of samples and the use of plausible values as performance scores (Rutkowski and Zhou 2014).

In the light of these considerations, this chapter seeks to (1) draw attention to the data issues associated with the SEM of PIAAC data; (2) illustrate ways to address these issues in the software package M*plus* (Version 8.2); and (3) exemplify the application of typical classes of models within SEM using PIAAC data. All examples are supplemented by explanations of the M*plus* syntax and the interpretation of the outputs. Although this chapter provides a brief introduction to the classes of SEM approaches, it does not deliver a complete introduction to SEM. Readers are encouraged to refer to the seminal SEM literature to learn more about model specification, identification, estimation, and interpretation (e.g. Hancock and Mueller 2013; Hoyle 2012; Kaplan 2009; Kline 2016; Loehlin and Beaujean 2017; Raykov and Marcoulides 2006). Moreover, this chapter does not deliver an introduction to the software M*plus*. Readers are encouraged to review the material provided by Muthén et al. (2017) and Muthén and Muthén (1998–2017).

The first section of this chapter highlights the complexities associated with the PIAAC data and reviews the options M*plus* offers to handle them. The second section briefly reviews the application of SEM using PIAAC data and draws attention to the extent to which these data complexities have been addressed in the extant literature. The third section focuses on specifying and estimating measurement models by means of confirmatory factor analysis (CFA). This section also showcases approaches to the testing of measurement invariance across few or many groups. The fourth and final section introduces classes of structural models, including path models, structural equation models, and multi-group versions thereof. However, the examples and structural equation modelling approaches will focus mainly on measurement models. A short summary concludes this chapter. All syntax files are contained in the Supplementary Material.

8 Analysing PIAAC Data with Structural Equation Modelling in Mplus

8.1 Issues with the SEM of PIAAC Data

As noted in the previous chapters in this volume, the complexity of the PIAAC data is driven by several elements. These elements include, but are not limited to, the use of survey weights; the nested data structure with study participants nested in, for instance, countries; the use of a set of plausible values to represent participants' performance on the literacy, numeracy, and problem-solving assessments; and the occurrence of missing data in the background questionnaire data. The PIAAC Technical Report notes that 'inferences will not be valid unless the corresponding variance estimators appropriately reflect all of the complex features of the PIAAC sample design' (OECD 2013, p. 26). These issues are by no means unique to the PIAAC data—several international large-scale assessments, including the Programme for International Student Assessment (PISA), the Teaching and Learning International Survey (TALIS), the Trends in International Mathematics and Science Study (TIMSS), the International Computer and Information Literacy Study (ICILS), and the Progress in International Reading Literacy Study (PIRLS), follow similar study designs (Rutkowski et al. 2010; Rutkowski and Zhou 2014). In the following, I will briefly review these issues and describe ways to deal with them in M*plus*. Table 8.1 provides an overview of the relevant M*plus* commands.

- *Weighting.* The PIAAC data accommodate two types of weights, a final participants' weight (SPFWT0) and a set of replicate weights (SPFWT1-SPFWT80). The former were created by a base weight that included the selection probabilities of households and several adjustment factors (OECD 2013). The latter represent a set of weights that can be used for improving the variance estimation through jackknifing or other approaches. Several authors have suggested examining how informative sampling weights are before including them in the analysis of international large-scale assessment data for instance, by evaluating the effective sample sizes and design effects (Laukaityte and Wiberg 2018; Rutkowski and Svetina 2014). The inclusion of the final weight and the replicate weights in M*plus* is straightforward: In the VARIABLE section, researchers can

Table 8.1 Overview of M*plus* options to address PIAAC data issues

Data issue	M*plus* sample options
Weighting	WEIGHT = SPFWT0; REPWEIGHTS = SPFWT1-SPFWT80; REPSE = JACKKNIFE; REPSE = JACKKNIFE2; REPSE = BOOTSTRAP;
Nested data structure	CLUSTER = CNTRYID; TYPE = COMPLEX; TYPE = TWOLEVEL; TYPE = TWOLEVEL RANDOM;
Plausible values	TYPE = IMPUTATION;
Missing data	MISSING ARE ALL;

specify the final weight using the WEIGHT option and the REPWEIGHTS option for the replicate weights. Replicate weights can be accompanied by several additional specifications, such as the type of standard error adjustment (REPSE). Furthermore, weights can be scaled using the WTSCALE option.
- *Nested data structure.* To account for the clustering of the individual data in, for instance, regions or countries, researchers have at least two options: First, they may account for the nested data structure by adjusting the standard errors of the SEM parameters using the TYPE = COMPLEX option. This option does not call for a multilevel model that models the level of nesting explicitly. It is accompanied by the robust maximum likelihood estimator (MLR) and the specification of the clustering variable (e.g. CLUSTER = CNTRYID). Second, researchers may want to model the nested data structure through multilevel modelling in order to quantify and explain between-country variation in PIAAC variables, or relations among them. The corresponding commands for the two-level models with random intercepts and/or slopes are TYPE = TWOLEVEL and/or TYPE = TWOLEVEL RANDOM.
- *Plausible values.* PIAAC uses plausible values to represent literacy, numeracy, and problem solving in technology-rich environments. In the extant literature, several procedures have been applied to include these sets of performance scores. Among these procedures, the following deals best with the variation within and between the sets of plausible values (Laukaityte and Wiberg 2017; Rutkowski et al. 2010): The SEM analyses are conducted for each of the ten datasets containing the ten plausible values. The resultant model parameters are subsequently pooled as the means across all ten sets of model parameters, and their variances are quantified according to Rubin's combination rules. These rules incorporate the variances within and between plausible values and the number of plausible values (e.g. Laukaityte and Wiberg 2017). M*plus* offers a convenience option (TYPE = IMPUTATION) that performs SEM for each set of plausible values and combines the resultant model parameters. Although combining means, variances, covariances, and path coefficients may be straightforward with this procedure (Enders 2010), the combined fit statistics require further adjustments (Enders and Mansolf 2018; Meng and Rubin 1992). As far as the M*plus* documentation goes, the adjustments of the chi-square statistic and the model deviance are performed by default in the software with (robust) maximum-likelihood estimation (Asparouhov and Muthén 2010).
- *Missing data.* Missing data may occur in the background variables for several reasons. Without reviewing the details behind the mechanisms of missingness, I note that M*plus* has several options to deal with missing data. They include multiple imputation and model-based approaches with or without auxiliary variables (Enders 2010). Researchers also have the opportunity to perform multiple imputation in alternative software packages (e.g. the R package 'mice') and submit the resulting complete datasets to M*plus* for SEM (e.g. Enders et al. 2016; Grund et al. 2018).

8.2 A Brief Review of PIAAC Secondary Data Analyses Using SEM

To review the current status of how SEM is utilised for the analysis of PIAAC data, I performed a search in the databases PsycINFO and ERIC using the search terms *PIAAC AND (structural equation model* OR path model* OR factor analysis OR CFI OR RMSEA OR indirect effect OR mediation)* and retrieved seven publications (as of 25 February 2019). An additional search for the term 'PIAAC' in the Elsevier Scopus database yielded 17 further publications and cross-references to two further publications. Of these 26 publications, 12 presented the application of SEM to PIAAC data. Table 8.2 shows a description of these publications, including the models the authors specified and the extent to which the complexity of the data was addressed.

Most secondary analyses were based on multiple PIAAC samples (75%), comprising 18–29 participating countries. The types of structural equation models covered single-level path models (33.3%); single-level structural equation models (50.0%), including exploratory (8.3%) and confirmatory factor analyses (25.0%); and multilevel SEM (16.7%). The software package *Mplus* dominated the list of analytic tools (80%), next to LISREL (10%) and the R package lavaan (10%). Only 1 of the 12 publications did not make explicit whether and how the complexity of the PIAAC data was considered during SEM. With some exceptions (25%), the authors included sampling weights in their analyses. In the analyses involving plausible values, Rubin's combination rules were mainly applied; however, one study averaged the ten plausible values provided by the PIAAC database, and one study used these values as manifest indicators of a latent variable to represent participants' skills. Finally, the procedures for handling missing data varied considerably and included multiple imputation, full information maximum-likelihood estimation, and listwise deletion procedures.

Overall, this brief, and by no means complete, review suggested that SEM is making its way into the secondary analysis of PIAAC data. At the same time, the procedures for handling the data complexities varied between studies and call for a framework that may guide researchers in their SEM analysis.

8.3 PIAAC Data and Measures Used in the Illustrative Examples

The following illustrative examples of classes of structural equation models are based on two datasets: the first contains the Norwegian ($N = 5128$) and German ($N = 5465$) PIAAC data; the second contains the data from 27 countries participating in PIAAC ($N = 181,236$), excluding the data from Austria, Cyprus, Russia, and Turkey (the reasoning for this exclusion can be found in Borgonovi and Pokropek 2017b). These data have been made publicly available by the OECD

Table 8.2 Sample papers using SEM to analyse PIAAC data

References	Description	Data	Model	Complexity	Software
Borgonovi and Pokropek (2017a)	Relations among education, generalised trust, mediated by literacy skills, income, and occupational prestige; country differences due to birthplace diversity, and income inequality	PIAAC background questionnaire and skills data from 29 participating countries	Multilevel SEM (within-level, individuals; between-level, countries)	C, M, P, W	M*plus*
Borgonovi and Pokropek (2017b)	Country differences and disparities in external political efficacy, mediated by parental socio-economic status and cognitive abilities	PIAAC background questionnaire and skills data from 28 participating countries	Multilevel SEM (within-level, individuals; between-level, countries)	C, M, P, W	M*plus*
Cincinnato et al. (2016)	Relations among parents' education, educational attainment, readiness to learn, and participation in adult education	PIAAC background questionnaire data from 23 participating countries	Path model	C, M, W	M*plus*
Duchhardt et al. (2017)	Relations among the use of mathematics and numeracy skills, controlled for background characteristics, mathematical requirements on the job, and education	PIAAC background questionnaire and skills data from Germany	Path model	P, W	M*plus*
Ganzach and Patel (2018)	Role of general mental ability (g) and specific abilities in predicting wages, controlled for gender and age	PIAAC background questionnaire and skills data from 19 participating countries	Path model	M	NA
Gorges et al. (2016)	Invariance testing of the motivation-to-learn scale across countries and relations to learning engagement, controlled for literacy	PIAAC background questionnaire data from 18 participating countries	Multi-group CFA	C, M, W	M*plus*

Gorges et al. (2017)	Invariance testing of the motivation-to-learn scale across gender, age groups, and migration background within countries	PIAAC background questionnaire data from 21 participating countries	Multi-group CFA (graded response model)	C, W	*Mplus*
Hahs-Vaughn (2017)	Factor structure of the cognitive skills and work abilities indices	PIAAC background questionnaire data from the United States, participants who were 25–29 years of age, employed or participated in education or training during the last 12 months, and reported their education as 'above high school'	CFA	None	LISREL, *Mplus*
Heisig (2018)	Factor structure of the measures of the signalling value of education	PIAAC background questionnaire and skills data from 21 participating countries	EFA	C, M, P, W	NA
Scandurra and Calero (2017)	Relations among literacy, skills exposure at home and in the workplace, education, family background, controlled for gender, age, and language/migration status	PIAAC background questionnaire and skills data from 21 participating countries, participants who were 16–25 years of age	SEM	M, P, W	*Mplus*
Sikora et al. (2019)	Impact of adolescent home library size on adult education, occupation, frequency of reading outside of work, and literacy skills	PIAAC background questionnaire and skills data from 28 societies, participants who were 16–25 years of age	Multilevel SEM (within-level, individuals; between-level, countries)	C, M, P, W	*Mplus*
Trapp et al. (2019)	Testing the openness-fluid-crystallised-intelligence model and the environment enhancement hypothesis	PIAAC background questionnaire and skills data from Germany	SEM	M	R (lavaan)

Note. NA information not available, C clustering of data in countries modelled (either as fixed or random effects), M missing data handling (e.g. multiple imputation, listwise deletion, maximum-likelihood-based procedures), P plausible values handling through Rubin's combination rules (other procedures excluded), W weighting (e.g. replicate weights, case weights)

(2016) and contain the full study samples in these countries covering a broad age range (16–65 years). For details of the descriptive sample statistics, readers are referred to the public use files provided by the OECD. The illustrative examples in this chapter explore the relations among several cognitive skills measures in PIAAC and measures from the PIAAC background questionnaire (Table 8.3).

Table 8.3 Overview of the variables included in the illustrative examples

Variable	Description
CNTRYID	Country ID (ISO 3166, numeric code)
GERMAN	Dummy-coded variable ($1 = Germany$, $0 = Norway$)
FEMALE	Participant's gender ($1 = Female$, $0 = Male$)
HOMLANG	Test language same as language spoken most often at home (*derived;* $1 = $ *Test language same as home language*, $0 = $ *Test language not the same as home language*)
Curiosity	PIAAC scale 'Learning strategies' ($0 = $ *Not at all*, $1 = $ *Very little*, $2 = $ *To some extent*, $3 = $ *To a high extent*, $4 = $ *To a very high extent*)
I_Q04b	Relate new ideas into real life
I_Q04d	Like learning new things
I_Q04h	Attribute something new
I_Q04j	Get to the bottom of difficult things
I_Q04l	Figure out how different ideas fit together
I_Q04m	Looking for additional info
Skills use at work	PIAAC scale 'Skill use work – ICT – Internet' ($0 = $ *Never*, $1 = $ *Once a month*, $2 = $ *Less than once a week but at least once a month*, $3 = $ *At least once a week but not every day*, $4 = $ *Every day*)
G_Q05a	How often—for mail
G_Q05c	How often—work-related info
G_Q05e	How often—spreadsheets
G_Q05f	How often—word
Skills use everyday	PIAAC scale 'Skill use everyday life – ICT – Internet' ($0 = $ *Never*, $1 = $ *Once a month*, $2 = $ *Less than once a week but at least once a month*, $3 = $ *At least once a week but not every day*, $4 = $ *Every day*)
H_Q05a	How often—for mail
H_Q05c	How often—in order to better understand various issues
H_Q05e	How often—spreadsheets
H_Q05f	How often—word
PVLIT1–PVLIT10	Literacy (LIT) scale scores—plausible values 1–10
PVPSL1–PVPSL10	Problem solving in technology-rich environments (PS-TRE) scale scores—plausible values 1–10
SPFWT0	Final full sample weight
SPFWT1–SPFWT80	Final replicate weights (1–80)

8.4 Measurement Models

8.4.1 Confirmatory Factor Analysis with Categorical or Continuous Indicators

To establish a measurement model of a construct, researchers may choose among several procedures. These include, but are not limited to, confirmatory factor analysis (CFA), exploratory factor analysis (EFA), and exploratory structural equation modelling (ESEM)—the latter bringing together the features of CFA and EFA (Brown 2015; Marsh et al. 2014). In this section, I will focus on CFA as a means to develop a suitable measurement model that represents the latent (unobserved) variable of interest.

A CFA model comprises one or more latent variables that are measured by a set of categorical or continuous indicators, such as item responses, subscale scores, or item parcels. For the ith indicator and the jth person in the dataset, y_{ij}, a one-factor model with only one latent variable η is specified as $y_{ij} = v_i + \lambda_i \eta_j + \varepsilon_{ij}$, where λ_i denotes the factor loading of this indicator, v_i the item intercept, and ε_{ij} the residual. Using matrix notation, the resultant model can be described as $y = v + \lambda \eta + \varepsilon$ with $y \sim N(\mathbf{0}, \mathbf{\Sigma})$, $\eta \sim N(\mathbf{0}, \mathbf{\Psi})$, and $\varepsilon \sim N(\mathbf{0}, \mathbf{\Theta})$. The underlying covariance structure of this model is $\mathbf{\Sigma} = \mathbf{\Lambda \Psi \Lambda}' + \mathbf{\Theta}$, where $\mathbf{\Lambda}$ represents the matrix of factor loadings, $\mathbf{\Psi}$ the matrix of factor variances and covariances, and $\mathbf{\Theta}$ the matrix of residual variances and covariances (for more details, please refer to Brown 2015).

When performing CFA, researchers are faced with several decisions, such as the treatment of the indicators as categorical or continuous variables. Despite the option of robust maximum likelihood estimation (M*plus*: ESTIMATOR = MLR) to account for possible deviations from a normal distribution of the continuous indicators, the choice of an appropriate estimator is especially relevant for indicators that are semi-continuous. More specifically, when researchers intend to use item responses that are based on frequency, agreement, or rating scales with a categorical set of response options (e.g. ranging from *0 = not at all* to *5 = always*), they have to decide whether to treat these responses categorically or continuously. Without reviewing the extant literature on this topic to the full extent, the existing body of research suggests that five or more response options and tolerable deviations of the item response distributions from normality may justify the treatment of item responses as continuous variables (e.g. Finney and DiStefano 2013). In such a situation, the CFA model becomes more parsimonious because only one item intercept is estimated in the model instead of several thresholds between the response categories (Kline 2016). In M*plus*, maximum-likelihood-based estimators (e.g. Robust ML [MLR]) and the weighted least square mean and variance adjusted (WLSMV) estimator are available to treat item responses categorically (Brown 2015). However, these two estimators may not perform equally well in CFA with ordinal data. Li (2016), for instance, found that the WLSMV estimator was less biased in estimating factor loadings yet overestimated the correlations between factors (see also Beauducel and Herzberg 2006). The following example illustrates the specification and performance of these two estimation approaches.

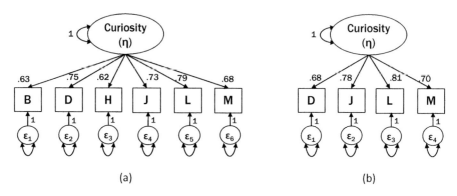

Fig. 8.1 Measurement models of curiosity with categorically treated item indicators (WLSMV estimator) based on (**a**) six and (**b**) four items

The PIAAC participants were asked to indicate on a five-point rating scale the degree to which they agreed with six statements concerning their curiosity (see Table 8.3). A CFA model assuming a single latent variable measured by the six item responses and treating these responses continuously resulted in a marginal fit to the data, $\chi^2(9) = 516.4$, $p < 0.001$, RMSEA $= 0.074$, CFI $= 0.926$, SRMR $= 0.043$. Gorges et al. (2017) reviewed the theoretical anchoring of the six items in existing curiosity frameworks and argued that four items (I_Q04D, J, L, M) represented the construct. Moreover, evaluating the factor loadings revealed that items I_Q04B and I_Q04H showed lower values in comparison to the remaining items—this observation indicates that they represent what is shared among all items to a smaller extent. As a consequence, the initial measurement model was refined by deleting these two items, $\chi^2(2) = 90.9$, $p < 0.001$, RMSEA $= 0.066$, CFI $= 0.979$, SRMR $= 0.022$ (Syntax 8.1).

The same model exhibited an acceptable fit to the data when treating the four-item responses categorically through WLSMV estimation, $\chi^2(2) = 151.7$, $p < 0.001$, RMSEA $= 0.085$, CFI $= 0.988$, SRMR $= 0.0170$. To specify this model in M*plus*, the item responses have to be defined as categorical using the CATEGORICAL ARE I_Q04d-I_Q04m command. Moreover, the WLSMV is called by ESTIMATOR = WLSMV, and the theta parameterisation is selected by the PARAMETERIZATION = THETA command (for more details about this parameterisation, please refer to Kline 2016). The factor loadings of the models based on six and four items are shown in Fig. 8.1.

Syntax 8.1: CFA Model Describing the Factor Structure of Curiosity
```
VARIABLE: [...]
    USEVARIABLES ARE I_Q04d I_Q04j I_Q04l I_Q04m;
```

(continued)

```
    ! Missing data coding
    MISSING ARE ALL(-99);

    ! Final participant weight
    WEIGHT = SPFWT0;
ANALYSIS:

    ESTIMATOR = MLR;
    H1ITERATIONS = 10000;
    PROCESSORS = 4;
MODEL:

    ! Measurement model
    CURIOUS BY I_Q04d I_Q04j I_Q04l I_Q04m;
OUTPUT:

    SAMPSTAT; ! Sample statistics
    STDYX;    ! Fully standardized parameters
    MOD(ALL); ! Modification indices
```

The second example illustrating the specification and estimation of CFA models in M*plus* concerns PIAAC participants' exposure to certain skills (see Table 8.2). Differentiating between skills needed at work and in everyday life, researchers may specify a factor model with two correlated factors (Fig. 8.2). Given that items are formulated similarly for work and everyday life situations, a covariance structure is

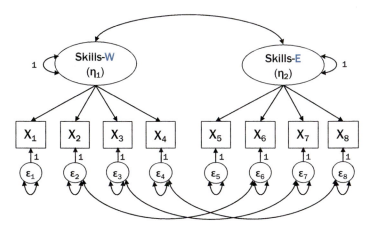

Fig. 8.2 Measurement model of participants' skills use at work (Skills-W) and in everyday life (Skills-E)

added to the residuals to account for any relations among items after controlling for the two latent variables. These residual covariances are specified in the two-factor model as shown in Syntax 8.2.

> **Syntax 8.2: Model Syntax of the Skills Use Measurement Model**
> ```
> MODEL:
>     ! Measurement model
>     ! Two-factor model with correlated residuals
>     WORK BY G_Q05a G_Q05c G_Q05e G_Q05f;
>     LIFE BY H_Q05a H_Q05c H_Q05e H_Q05f;
>
>     ! Modifications
>     ! Residual covariances
>     G_Q05C WITH H_Q05C;
>     G_Q05E WITH H_Q05E;
>     G_Q05F WITH H_Q05F;
> ```

Treating item responses continuously, this model exhibited a substantial fit to the data, $\chi^2(16) = 429.6$, $p < 0.001$, RMSEA $= 0.052$, CFI $= 0.936$, SRMR $= 0.038$. Treating item responses categorically, and using the WLSMV estimator, the model showed an acceptable fit, $\chi^2(16) = 422.9$, $p < 0.001$, RMSEA $= 0.052$, CFI $= 0.975$, SRMR $= 0.034$. In the first model, the correlation between the two factors was positive and significant ($\rho = 0.501$); in the second model, this correlation was only marginally smaller ($\rho = 0.479$). Given the existence of residual covariances in the model, the latent variables η_1 and η_2 can no longer be considered unidimensional constructs—alternative model specifications with nested factors can facilitate a clearer interpretation of these constructs (Koch et al. 2018).

Overall, the specification of measurement models in M*plus* allows researchers to treat indicators categorically or continuously. Deviations from the multivariate normality assumption can be compensated (at least partly) by the robust ML estimation. Deviations from a simple structure—that is, a factor structure without any residual covariances and possible cross-loadings—can also be implemented in the software package.

8.4.2 Measurement Invariance Testing with Few Groups

In many scenarios, group comparisons are of major interest to researchers. Such comparisons may refer to the differences in means of variables or differences in the relations among constructs. In both cases, researchers have to establish that the variables used in group comparisons are comparable to a sufficient degree. More specifically, mean differences or differences in structural relations across

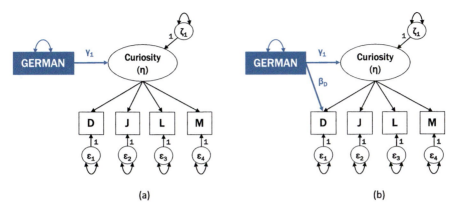

Fig. 8.3 (a) MIMIC and (b) MIMIC-DIF model of curiosity with GERMAN as covariate

groups can have several causes, including actual mean differences and differences in structural relations, but also possible differences in the functioning of items, scales, or entire tests (Meredith 1993). To examine the extent to which possible differential item functioning may affect the group differences found by researchers, several procedures have been developed under the umbrellas of 'measurement invariance' and 'differential item functioning' (Millsap 2011). In the following, I will illustrate how to implement these procedures in M*plus*, focusing on scenarios with few groups. The full input and output files can be accessed through the Supplementary Material.

MIMIC Models and Differential Item Functioning
Multiple causes multiple indicator (MIMIC) models are usually comprised of a latent variable (measured by multiple indicators) and one or more covariates (multiple causes; Brown 2015). These models represent probably the simplest of structural equation models and allow researchers to examine the effects of covariates on the latent trait—for example, to identify possible group differences. The latter, however, is based on the assumption that the measurement model holds for the different groups—in other words, the model is based on measurement invariance assumptions that can facilitate the meaningful interpretation of factor means (Kim et al. 2012b).

In the following data example, differences in participants' curiosity between the Norwegian and the German PIAAC samples are examined. The binary variable GERMAN (*1 = Germany, 0 = Norway*) serves as the covariate of the latent variable 'Curiosity' (Fig. 8.3 (a)). Using the regression command in M*plus*, curiosity is simply regressed on the covariate (Syntax 8.3). Given that GERMAN is binary, the regression coefficient γ_1 is partially standardised (STDY standardisation; Muthén et al. 2017).

Syntax 8.3: Model Syntax of the MIMIC Model of Curiosity with GERMAN as Covariate
```
MODEL:
    ! Measurement model
    CURIOUS BY I_Q04d I_Q04j I_Q04l I_Q04m;

    ! Structural part
    CURIOUS ON GERMAN;

OUTPUT:

    TECH1;
    TECH8;
    STDY;  ! Due to the binary predictor GERMAN
```

The MIMIC model exhibited an acceptable fit to the data, $\chi^2(5) = 386.6$, $p < 0.001$, RMSEA $= 0.086$, CFI $= 0.942$, SRMR $= 0.032$. The relation between the binary country variable GERMAN and curiosity was statistically significant ($\gamma_1 = -0.315$, $SE = 0.024$, 95% CI [-0.361, -0.268], $p < 0.001$) and suggested that the Norwegian sample showed higher curiosity than the German sample. However, this interpretation does not consider the possibility of differential item functioning across the two countries.

To identify whether specific manifest indicator variables (i.e. items) exhibit differential item functioning between the German and the Norwegian samples—that is, a situation in which the probability of responding to an item differs between groups although they have the same level on the latent variable (Millsap 2011)—the MIMIC model can be extended to a MIMIC-DIF model by adding structural paths to the specific variables (see Fig. 8.3 (b)). This model provides information not only about possible factor mean differences but also about differences in the item intercepts (Kim et al. 2012b). Hence, the MIMIC-DIF model allows researchers to test for the DIF of specific items and extract factor mean differences controlling for item DIF. In M*plus*, the item intercepts are regressed on the covariate, in this case by adding the command line I_Q04d ON GERMAN to obtain the parameter β_D. (Note: for categorical indicators, the item thresholds are regressed on the covariate.) In this example, the DIF parameter of item D was $\beta_D = -0.140$, $SE = 0.018$, 95% CI [-0.176, -0.105], $p < 0.001$. The corresponding differences in the factor mean of curiosity were $\gamma_1 = -0.276$, $SE = 0.025$, 95% CI [-0.325, -0.227], $p < 0.001$. The MIMIC-DIF model outperformed the MIMIC model in terms of model fit, $\Delta\chi^2(1) = 54.4$, $p < 0.001$. Hence, there is evidence for cross-country differences in curiosity favouring the Norwegian sample and the differential functioning of item D.

The MIMIC-DIF approach has been further developed to test not only so-called uniform DIF effects but also non-uniform DIF effects by including an interaction term between the latent variable and the covariate (Woods and Grimm 2011). Bauer (2017) proposed the more general framework of moderated factor analysis to examine uniform and non-uniform DIF effects of categorical, continuous, or both types of covariates.

Multi-group Confirmatory Factor Analysis
Besides the testing of differential item functioning with the help of MIMIC- and MIMIC-DIF models, there is multi-group CFA, a procedure that allows researchers to specify and estimate a set of models for which the parameters in the CFA model can be constrained to equality across groups. Multi-group CFA has become the standard approach to measurement invariance testing in education and psychology (Putnick and Bornstein 2016; Scherer and Greiff 2018) and forms the basis for several extensions, such as multi-group ESEM, the alignment optimisation method, and Bayesian measurement invariance testing (Marsh et al. 2013, 2018; Muthén and Asparouhov 2012).

Typically, three multi-group CFA models are specified to test for measurement invariance based on continuously treated item indicators of a latent variable η (Van de Schoot et al. 2012): (1) The *configural invariance model* assumes the same factor structure (i.e. number of factors and the pattern of the links between the latent variable and the manifest indicators) across groups. This model is often used as the baseline model against which all other models with additional parameter constraints are compared. All model parameters are freely estimated across groups. Specifically, for the ith item indicator and the jth person in the kth group, a configural one-factor model is specified for the manifest indicator variable y_{ijk}, the latent variable η_{jk}, the group-specific intercept ν_{ij}, and the residual term ε_{ijk} as $y_{ijk} = \nu_{ik} + \lambda_{ik}\eta_{jk} + \varepsilon_{ijk}$, where λ_{ik} denotes the factor loading of the ith item for the kth group. The factor means are fixed to zero, and the factor variance are fixed to 1 for all groups. (2) The *metric invariance model* constrains the factor loadings λ_{ik} to equality across groups based on the configural model, $y_{ijk} = \nu_{ik} + \lambda_i\eta_{jk} + \varepsilon_{ijk}$. Again, the factor means are constrained to zero, yet the factor variance is freely estimated to identify the model. If metric invariance holds, factor variances and covariances can be compared across groups. (3) The *scalar invariance model* further constrains the item intercepts ν_j to equality across groups, $y_{ijk} = \nu_i + \lambda_i\eta_{jk} + \varepsilon_{ijk}$. To identify the mean structure in the model, factor means are freely estimated; factor variances are also freely estimated. If scalar invariance holds, factor means can be compared across groups. In all models, residuals are assumed to be uncorrelated to the latent variable and to have a mean zero (Muthén and Asparouhov 2018). Marsh et al. (2009) proposed extending this measurement invariance framework by systematically testing additional parameter constraints—these constraints involve the factor means, variances, covariances, and item residuals. Apart from these extensions, the measurement literature often includes the invariance of item residual (co-)variances θ in addition to the scalar invariance constraints to test whether the measurement models indicate the same reliabilities (Raykov and Marcoulides 2006). The resulting model is referred to as the *strict invariance model*. If strict invariance holds, (manifest) scale means can be compared across groups.

To determine which level of measurement invariance holds for a given dataset, several indicators are available, including the results of chi-square difference testing and the differences in fit indices between models with different parameter constraints (Brown 2015). For instance, if comparing the configural and metric invariance models results in an insignificant chi-square difference test, this can be interpreted as evidence that the constraints on the factor loadings do not deteriorate the overall model fit—hence, metric invariance can be retained. However, in large samples, and for complex datasets, the chi-square difference test may result in a significant test statistic although the constraints on model parameters do not substantially deteriorate the model fit (Yuan and Chan 2016). As a consequence, differences in fit indices provide additional sources of information. For these differences, several cut-off criteria were suggested: (a) ΔCFI less than -0.010 (Cheung and Rensvold 2002); (b) ΔCFI less than -0.010, ΔRMSEA less than 0.015, and ΔSRMR less than 0.030 (Chen 2007); and (c) ΔCFI less than -0.008 (Meade et al. 2008). However, these criteria should not be considered to be 'golden rules', as they depend on several factors, such as the type of the factor model (Khojasteh and Lo 2015), the types of invariance models that are compared (Rutkowski and Svetina 2014), or whether the invariance of mean or covariance structures is examined (Fan and Sivo 2009). Moreover, the application of these guidelines varies in that some researchers compare all models against the configural model, whereas others compare adjacent models to identify the effects of additional parameter constraints given the constraints in the previous model. Note that similar criteria apply to the measurement invariance testing in situations where item indicators are treated categorically. Please review Liu et al. (2017) for more details.

Example 1: Gender as the Grouping Variable The following example uses the variable FEMALE as the grouping variable and focuses on the three standard measurement invariance models (i.e. configural, metric, and scalar invariance) using the M*plus* convenience option MODEL = CONFIGURAL METRIC SCALAR. This option specifies all three models with either continuously treated (MLR estimator) or categorically treated item responses (WLSMV estimator) and compares them with the help of chi-square difference testing. Syntax 8.4 shows the corresponding commands. These models can also be specified by imposing the parameter constraints directly. The corresponding syntax files are part of the Supplementary Material (from file 'MM6c-Curiosity-MG-Gender.inp' to 'MM6f-Curiosity-MG-Gender.inp').

Syntax 8.4: Multi-group CFA Models with FEMALE as the Grouping Variable
```
VARIABLE: [...]
    ! Grouping specification
    GROUPING IS FEMALE (0 = Men 1 = Women);
```

(continued)

```
ANALYSIS:
   ESTIMATOR = MLR;
   H1ITERATIONS = 10000;
   PROCESSORS = 4;
   MODEL = CONFIGURAL METRIC SCALAR;
   ! Invariance models
MODEL:
   ! Measurement model
   CURIOUS BY I_Q04d I_Q04j I_Q04l I_Q04m;
OUTPUT:
   TECH1;
   TECH8;
   SAMPSTAT;
```

To further test whether strict invariance holds, this syntax can be modified so that the equality of residual variances across groups is imposed (Syntax 8.5).

Syntax 8.5: Multi-group CFA Model Assuming Strict Invariance Across Gender

```
VARIABLE: [...]
   ! Grouping specification
   GROUPING IS FEMALE (0 = Men 1 = Women);
ANALYSIS:
   ESTIMATOR = MLR;
   H1ITERATIONS = 10000;
   PROCESSORS = 4;
MODEL:
   ! Measurement model
   ! Factor loadings constrained to equality across
  groups
   ! Factor loadings labelled as L2-L4
   CURIOUS BY
         I_Q04d
         I_Q04j(L2)
         I_Q04l(L3)
         I_Q04m(L4);

   ! Item intercepts constrained to equality across
  groups
```

(continued)

```
      ! labelled as I1-I4
      [I_Q04d-I_Q04m](I1-I4);

      ! To identify the mean structure, the factor
  mean is now
      ! freely estimated.
      [CURIOUS*];

      ! Item residual variances constrained to
  equality
      ! across groups
      ! labelled as R1-R4
      I_Q04d-I_Q04m(R1-R4);

MODEL WOMEN:
      ! Nothing needs to be specified here
OUTPUT:
      TECH1;
      TECH8;
      SAMPSTAT;
      STDYX;
```

The resulting model fit indices and their comparisons between models are shown in Tables 8.4 and 8.5. All models exhibited an acceptable fit to the data. Considering the results of the chi-square difference testing, metric invariance could be assumed. Considering the differences in the CFI, RMSEA, and the SRMR between the configural model and all other models, strict invariance could be assumed. Considering the changes in the CFI, RMSEA, and the SRMR after imposing more constraints on the model parameters (i.e. between adjacent models), strict invariance could be assumed. Overall, the invariance testing suggested that strict measurement invariance holds across gender. In this situation, researchers can interpret possible gender differences in the means of curiosity as actual mean differences.

Example 2: Country as the Grouping Variable Following the same procedure, the testing of measurement invariance across the two PIAAC participating countries Germany and Norway resulted in a good model fit for the configural and metric models, but not for the scalar and strict invariance models (Table 8.4). Moreover, the model comparisons suggest that metric invariance can be retained (Table 8.5). In this case, mean differences in curiosity between the two countries are camouflaged by the differential functioning of the scale or, more precisely, the non-invariance of the measurement model.

8.4.3 Measurement Invariance Testing with Many Groups

With the increasing number of countries, language groups, and educational systems participating in international large-scale assessments comes the challenge of establishing that the measures used for comparisons are sufficiently invariant (Rutkowski et al. 2018). However, the commonly used approach of multi-group CFA to establish measurement invariance across many groups may increase the chances of falsely detecting non-invariance due to the large number of pairwise comparisons of model parameters (Rutkowski and Svetina 2013). Addressing this issue, several alternative approaches to invariance testing with many groups have been developed. These include, but are not limited to, (a) the alignment method (Asparouhov and Muthén 2014), (b) the alignment-within-CFA method (Marsh et al. 2018), (c) multilevel CFA (Kim et al. 2012a), (d) multilevel factor mixture modelling (Kim et al. 2016b), and (e) Bayesian approximate invariance testing (Van de Schoot et al. 2013). These approaches have strengths and weaknesses, a thorough review of which is beyond the scope of this chapter. Readers are referred to the extant literature comparing the performance of measurement invariance testing procedures (e.g. Desa 2014; Kim et al. 2017; Muthén and Asparouhov 2018).

In the following, I will illustrate the application of the alignment optimisation method, the alignment-within-CFA method (AwC), and multilevel CFA to the PIAAC data, focusing on the invariance of the curiosity scale across 27 of the participating countries. (Note: Due to quality issues, the data from Austria, Cyprus, Russia, and Turkey were excluded; Borgonovi and Pokropek 2017b). The M*plus* syntax files can be found in the Supplementary Material.

Alignment Optimisation Method The alignment optimisation method represents an approach to multi-group CFA or item response theory that estimates the factor means and variances for each group, based on the assumption of the configural measurement invariance model (Asparouhov and Muthén 2014). This method is aimed at minimising the departures from the invariance of the model parameters.

Table 8.4 Fit indices of the multi-group CFA models for curiosity

Model	$\chi^2(df)$	CFI	RMSEA	SRMR	AIC	BIC
Grouping is FEMALE						
Configural	95.2 (4)*	0.978	0.066	0.023	96,883	97,057
Metric	103.6 (7)*	0.977	0.052	0.027	96,891	97,043
Scalar	115.5 (10)*	0.975	0.045	0.030	96,904	97,034
Strict	118.1 (14)*	0.975	0.038	0.029	96,914	97,016
Grouping is GERMAN						
Configural	117.1 (4)*	0.983	0.074	0.019	93,906	94,080
Metric	133.8 (7)*	0.981	0.059	0.026	93,918	94,070
Scalar	954.6 (10)*	0.861	0.135	0.086	94,983	95,113
Strict	978.6 (14)*	0.858	0.116	0.102	95,059	95,160

Note. The scaling correction factors and information criteria can be found in the Supplementary Material
*$p < 0.001$

Table 8.5 Comparisons of the multi-group CFA models for curiosity

Model	$\Delta\chi^2(df)$	ΔCFI	$\Delta RMSEA$	$\Delta SRMR$
Grouping is FEMALE				
Configural vs. metric	6.3 (3), $p = 0.10$	−0.001	−0.006	+0.004
Configural vs. scalar	14.8 (6), $p = 0.02$	−0.003	−0.021	+0.007
Configural vs. strict	21.3 (10), $p = 0.02$	−0.003	−0.028	+0.006
Metric vs. scalar	8.6 (3), $p = 0.04$	−0.002	−0.007	+0.003
Metric vs. strict	15.0 (7), $p = 0.04$	−0.002	−0.017	+0.002
Scalar vs. strict	2.7 (4), $p = 0.14$	0.000	−0.007	−0.001
Grouping is GERMAN				
Configural vs. metric	13.4 (3), $p < 0.01$	−0.002	−0.015	+0.007
Configural vs. scalar	876.5 (6)*	−0.122	+0.061	+0.067
Configural vs. strict	871.1 (10)*	−0.125	+0.042	+0.083
Metric vs. scalar	916.0 (3)*	−0.120	+0.076	+0.060
Metric vs. strict	849.8 (7)*	−0.125	+0.057	+0.076
Scalar vs. strict	55.7 (4)*	−0.003	−0.019	+0.016

*$p < 0.001$

It begins with specifying a null model—that is, the configural model with freely estimated factor loadings and item intercepts, the factor means constrained to zero, and the factor variances constrained to 1. Without deteriorating the fit of this model, the alignment method performs a transformation of the factor means so that the non-invariance of the factor loadings and item intercepts is minimised with the help of a simplicity function (Muthén and Asparouhov 2014). Asparouhov and Muthén (2014) explain the details of this transformation and how it reduces non-invariance. Overall, the extant literature on the performance of the alignment optimisation suggests that this method is suitable for estimating group-specific factor means and variances without relying on the often unrealistic assumptions of scalar invariance across countries. It also estimates the model parameters efficiently and is less computationally demanding than alternative methods, such as multilevel CFA. Among alternative methods, it can detect non-invariance reasonably well (Kim et al. 2017).

For the example of measuring curiosity across the 27 PIAAC countries, the M*plus* syntax to specify the alignment method without setting a reference country (i.e. free alignment) is shown in Syntax 8.6. The grouping must be specified in the context of a mixture model using the KNOWNCLASS option. Once this has been set, the alignment method is called (ALIGNMENT = FREE) and the corresponding output requested (ALIGN). In this example, the free alignment method estimates the factor mean of the first group freely; M*plus* also offers a fixed alignment option (ALIGNMENT = FIXED()) that constrains the factor mean of the first group or that of another group to zero.

Syntax 8.6: Alignment Optimisation Method Applied to the Curiosity Measurement Model Across Countries

```
VARIABLE: [...]
   ! Grouping specification
   ! Define the 27 countries by the ISO code
   CLASSES = c(27);
   KNOWNCLASS = c(CNTRYID=56 124 152 203 208 233
   246 250 276 300 372 376
   380 392 410 440 528 554 578 616 702 703 705 724
   752 826 840);

ANALYSIS:
   TYPE = MIXTURE;
   ESTIMATOR = MLR;
   H1ITERATIONS = 10000;
   PROCESSORS = 4;

   ALIGNMENT = FREE;
   ! Call the free alignment method

   ! Alternative specification
   ! ALIGNMENT = FIXED(56);
   ! Call the fixed alignment method with Belgium
   (ISO code 56)
   ! as the reference group
   ! similar to the scalar invariance model
MODEL:
   %OVERALL%
   ! Measurement model
   CURIOUS BY I_Q04d I_Q04j I_Q04l I_Q04m;

OUTPUT:
   TECH1;
   TECH8;
   ALIGN;
   SVALUES;
```

The output file contains information about the degree of non-invariance (Output 8.1) and the estimated factor means (Output 8.2) for the free alignment method. Output 8.1 indicates the (non-)invariance of the factor loadings and item intercepts among the 27 countries. (Note: non-invariance is indicated by the country's ISO code shown in brackets.) Output 8.2 shows the ranking of the countries based on their factor means.

Output 8.1: (Non-)Invariance of Factor Loadings and Item Intercepts

APPROXIMATE MEASUREMENT INVARIANCE (NONINVARIANCE) FOR GROUPS	
Item intercepts	
I_Q04B	(56) 124 (152) 203 (208) (233) (246) 250 276 (300) (372) 376 (380) (392) (410) (440) (528) (554) (578) 616 (702) (703) (705) 724 (752) (826) 840
I_Q04D	(56) 124 (152) (203) (208) (233) 246 250 276 (300) (372) (376) (380) (392) (410) (440) 528 (554) (578) (616) (702) (703) (705) (724) (752) (826) 840
I_Q04H	(56) (124) 152 (203) (208) (233) (246) (250) 276 300 372 (376) (380) 392 (410) (440) (528) 554 (578) 616 702 (703) (705) 724 (752) 826 840
I_Q04J	(56) 124 152 (203) 208 (233) (246) (250) (276) (300) (372) (376) (380) (392) (410) (440) (528) 554 (578) (616) (702) (703) 705 (724) (752) (826) 840
I_Q04L	(56) 124 152 203 208 233 (246) 250 276 (300) (372) 376 380 (392) (410) (440) (528) 554 (578) (616) 702 (703) 705 (724) (752) (826) 840
I_Q04M	56 124 (152) (203) (208) 233 (246) 250 (276) (300) 372 376 (380) (392) 410 (440) 528 (554) (578) (616) (702) (703) (705) (724) (752) 826 840
Factor loadings	
I_Q04B	56 124 152 203 208 233 246 250 (276) 300 372 376 380 392 410 (440) 528 554 578 (616) (702) (703) 705 724 752 826 840
I_Q04D	56 124 152 203 208 (233) 246 250 (276) 300 372 376 380 (392) 410 (440) 528 554 578 616 (702) 703 (705) 724 (752) 826 840
I_Q04H	56 124 152 203 208 233 (246) (250) (276) 300 372 376 380 392 410 (440) 528 554 578 616 702 703 705 724 (752) 826 840
I_Q04J	(56) 124 152 203 208 (233) 246 (250) 276 300 372 (376) (380) 392 410 440 528 554 578 616 (702) 703 705 724 (752) 826 840
I_Q04L	(56) 124 (152) 203 208 233 246 250 276 (300) 372 376 (380) (392) (410) (440) 528 554 578 (616) (702) (703) (705) (724) (752) 826 840
I_Q04M	56 124 152 (203) 208 (233) 246 (250) 276 300 372 376 380 392 (410) 440 528 554 578 (616) 702 (703) 705 724 752 826 840

Alignment-Within-CFA Method Similar to the conceptualisation of exploratory SEM, Marsh et al. (2018) extended the alignment method in order to make accessible analyses that could not be conducted with the original alignment optimisation approach. These analyses include, for instance, testing the invariance of residual or factor variances and covariances, the estimation of covariate effects in MIMIC models, the direct testing of factor mean differences, and the relations to other variables and constructs. Essentially, the extended alignment-within-CFA (AwC) method comprises two analytic steps: In the first step, the alignment optimisation method is performed, and the resulting parameters of the measurement models across countries are saved. These parameters form the starting values for a standard multi-group CFA model in the second step; in this model, some parameters are fixed to identify the model and mimic the exploratory alignment estimates. The starting values from the fixed alignment method with Belgium (i.e. the first group, ISO code 56) are requested using the SVALUES option in the output section of the M*plus*

8 Analysing PIAAC Data with Structural Equation Modelling in Mplus 187

Output 8.2: Ranking of Countries Based on the Curiosity Factor Means

FACTOR MEAN COMPARISON AT THE 5% SIGNIFICANCE LEVEL IN DESCENDING ORDER

Results for factor CURIOUS

Ranking	Latent class	Group value	Factor mean	Groups with significantly smaller factor mean
1	7	246	0.635	840 752 152 208 124 554 724 578 376 250 380 703 300 826 372 705 616 203 276 233 528 440 56 702 392 410
2	27	840	0.580	152 208 124 554 724 578 376 250 380 703 300 826 372 705 616 203 276 233 528 440 56 702 392 410
3	25	752	0.521	124 554 724 578 376 250 380 703 300 826 372 705 616 203 276 233 528 440 56 702 392 410
4	3	152	0.488	724 578 376 250 380 703 300 826 372 705 616 203 276 233 528 440 56 702 392 410
5	5	208	0.469	724 578 376 250 380 703 300 826 372 705 616 203 276 233 528 440 56 702 392 410
6	2	124	0.466	724 578 376 250 380 703 300 826 372 705 616 203 276 233 528 440 56 702 392 410
7	18	554	0.448	724 578 376 250 380 703 300 826 372 705 616 203 276 233 528 440 56 702 392 410
8	24	724	0.379	376 250 380 703 300 826 372 705 616 203 276 233 528 440 56 702 392 410
9	19	578	0.365	250 380 703 300 826 372 705 616 203 276 233 528 440 56 702 392 410
10	12	376	0.322	380 703 300 826 372 705 616 203 276 233 528 440 56 702 392 410
11	8	250	0.284	703 300 826 372 705 616 203 276 233 528 440 56 702 392 410
12	13	380	0.261	703 300 826 372 705 616 203 276 233 528 440 56 702 392 410
13	22	703	0.207	705 616 203 276 233 528 440 56 702 392 410
14	10	300	0.200	616 203 276 233 528 440 56 702 392 410
15	26	826	0.176	616 203 276 233 528 440 56 702 392 410
16	11	372	0.174	616 203 276 233 528 440 56 702 392 410
17	23	705	0.149	203 276 233 528 440 56 702 392 410
18	20	616	0.124	203 276 233 528 440 56 702 392 410
19	4	203	0.058	233 528 440 56 702 392 410
20	9	276	0.056	233 528 440 56 702 392 410
21	6	233	−0.013	56 702 392 410
22	17	528	−0.052	702 392 410
23	16	440	−0.054	702 392 410
24	1	56	−0.092	702 392 410
25	21	702	−0.156	392 410
26	14	392	−0.776	410
27	15	410	−0.931	

syntax. These values are pasted into the syntax of the second AwC step, and some factor loadings and intercepts are fixed to these values for identification (Syntax 8.7).

Syntax 8.7: AwC Method Applied to the Curiosity Measurement Model Across Countries

```
VARIABLE: [...]

    ! Grouping specification
    ! Define the 27 countries by the ISO code
    GROUPING IS
    CNTRYID(56 124 152 203 208 233 246 250 276 300
    372 376 380 392
    410 440 528 554 578 616 702 703 705 724 752 826
    840);

ANALYSIS:

    ESTIMATOR = MLR;
    H1ITERATIONS = 10000;
    PROCESSORS = 4;

MODEL:

    ! Overall measurement model
    CURIOUS BY I_Q04d I_Q04j I_Q04l I_Q04m;

    ! What follows are the measurement models for
    each
    ! country with the starting values from the free
    ! alignment method and the first factor loading
    fixed
    ! its starting value for identification
    purposes.
    ! The same goes for the intercept of the first
    item.

MODEL 56:

    ! Belgium
    curious BY i_q04d@0.58087; !fixed to identify
    the model
    curious BY i_q04j*0.87936;
    curious BY i_q04l*0.77616;
    curious BY i_q04m*0.64888;
```

(continued)

```
    [ i_q04d@2.74282 ];  !fixed to identify the mean
structure
    [ i_q04j*2.10687 ];
    [ i_q04l*2.08939 ];
    [ i_q04m*2.75272 ];
    [ curious*0 ];

    i_q04d*0.47764;
    i_q04j*0.39830;
    i_q04l*0.33275;
    i_q04m*0.38442;
    curious*1;

MODEL 124:

    ! Canada
    curious BY i_q04d@0.60476;
    curious BY i_q04j*0.79433;
    curious BY i_q04l*0.84478;
    curious BY i_q04m*0.61792;

    [ i_q04d@2.74774 ];
    [ i_q04j*2.35664 ];
    [ i_q04l*2.14924 ];
    [ i_q04m*2.69570 ];
    [ curious*0.64712 ];

    i_q04d*0.40232;
    i_q04j*0.36653;
    i_q04l*0.30741;
    i_q04m*0.37838;
    curious*0.79731;
    [...]
```

The overall fit of this model was acceptable, $\chi^2(54) = 1715.1$, $p < 0.001$, RMSEA $= 0.068$, CFI $= 0.985$, SRMR $= 0.019$. In fact, the AwC model fit was identical to the fit of the configural multi-group CFA model; however, the AwC model improved the comparability of factor means across countries based on the initial alignment optimisation (Step 1). This model forms the basis for further country comparisons of, for instance, factor means. Marsh et al. (2018) noted that the factor means differences between countries obtained using the AwC method are similar to those of the scalar invariance model, although the latter may not be accepted due to marginal model fit. For the curiosity scale, the scalar invariance model did indeed show a marginal fit to the data, $\chi^2(210) = 11682.1$, $p < 0.001$,

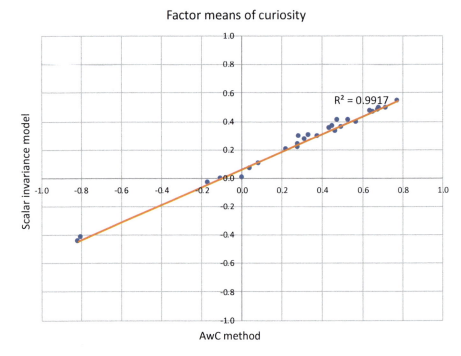

Fig. 8.4 Factor means of the PIAAC countries obtained from the scalar invariance model and the AwC method
Note. each data point represents a country

RMSEA = 0.091, CFI = 0.896, SRMR = 0.088. Figure 8.4 shows that the factor means obtained from this model and the AwC method correlated highly, $r = 0.996$.

As noted earlier, the AwC method can be extended to multi-group structural equation models in order, for example, to examine the effects of covariates (e.g. socio-economic status), additional group differences (e.g. across gender), or relations to outcome variables (e.g. numeracy). This flexibility represents a major strength of the method and allows researchers to approximate scalar invariance without imposing parameter constraints that are often not met in large-scale assessment datasets.

Multilevel Confirmatory Factor Analysis Both multi-group CFA and the alignment methods represent approaches to the invariance across many groups assuming groups as fixed and thereby drawing inferences to the groups in the sample (Muthén and Asparouhov 2018). In contrast to this assumption, multilevel CFA models allow researchers to draw inferences to the population level, assuming that the groups were drawn from a population of groups. Independent of the level of inferences, multilevel models can include random effects of the parameters in the measurement models (i.e. factor loadings and item intercepts or thresholds) to quantify possible between-group variation (Fox and Verhagen 2010). For instance, for a given factor model, loadings may vary between the groups and thus indicate that metric invariance may not hold (Kim et al. 2017). In the psychometric literature, this scenario is often referred to as 'cluster bias' (Jak et al. 2014). Besides the random effects in factor loadings, random effects in the item intercepts can be specified at the between level. In a situation where a random-intercept model fits the data better than a model with fixed intercepts, researchers have gained some evidence for violations of the scalar invariance assumption (Muthén and Asparouhov 2018). Besides these invariance tests of model parameters using random effects, testing whether the measurement model is similar across the levels of analysis represents another critical step. Muthén and Asparouhov (2018) argued that different factor structures may well occur for the within level and the between level in a multilevel model. Kaplan (2009), for instance, observed a two-factor model for students' self-efficacy in mathematics assessed in the PISA 2003 study at the within (i.e. student) level, while a one-factor model held at the between (i.e. school) level. Establishing that the same factor structure holds between levels represents an invariance test that is similar to the configural invariance model. Jak (2018) emphasised the importance of establishing cross-level measurement invariance by constraining the factor loadings of the measurement model to equality across levels. She showed that the lack of this constraint may result in estimation issues, biased parameter estimates, and biased standard errors. Ultimately, the meaning of the latent variables differs between the levels of analysis. To establish whether cross-level invariance holds, researchers can compare a model with the equality constraints to a model without these constraints.

The general form of a multilevel CFA model with random intercepts and fixed factor loadings is as follows (see Fig. 8.5; e.g. Davidov et al. 2012): The ith item indicator y_{ij} of the jth person in the kth group can be decomposed into

$$\text{Level 1 (Within level)}: \quad y_{ijk} = \upsilon_{ik} + \lambda_{W_{ik}} \eta_{W_{jk}} + \varepsilon_{W_{ijk}} \quad (8.1)$$

$$\text{Level 2 (Between level)}: \quad \upsilon_{ik} = \upsilon_i + \lambda_{B_i} \eta_{B_k} + \varepsilon_{B_{ik}} \quad (8.2)$$

where υ_{ik} is the ith item intercept of the kth group, υ_i the ith item intercept across all groups, λ_W and λ_B the within- and between-level factor loadings, $\eta_{W_{jk}}$ and η_{B_k} the within- and between-level scores of the latent variable, and $\varepsilon_{W_{ijk}}$ and $\varepsilon_{B_{ik}}$ the level-specific residuals. Assuming that the within- and between-level item scores are not correlated, the covariance structure of y_{ijk} (Σ_T) can be decomposed into the sum of the within- (Σ_W) and between-level (Σ_B) covariances (e.g. Hox 2013; Muthén and Asparouhov 2018):

$$\Sigma_T = \Sigma_W + \Sigma_B = \Lambda_W \Psi_W \Lambda'_W + \Theta_W + \Lambda_B \Psi_B \Lambda'_B + \Theta_B \quad (8.3)$$

This model forms the basis for testing the invariance of factor loadings, item intercepts, and residual variances across groups, as well as cross-level invariance (Kim et al. 2016a).

Evaluating the fit of multilevel CFA models—with or without random effects in the model parameters—is based on examining fit indices. However, validating

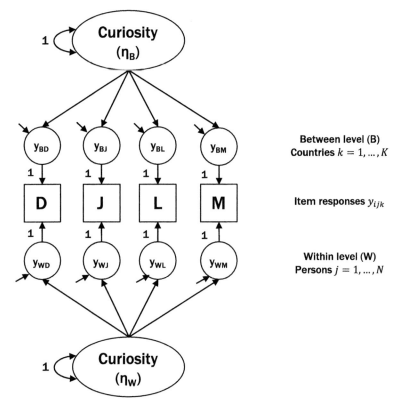

Fig. 8.5 Multilevel CFA with factor structures at both levels

the suggested guidelines for these indices still requires some research. Hsu et al. (2015) found that the common fit indices applied in SEM (i.e. CFI, TLI, RMSEA, SRMR) are not equally sensitive to model misspecifications in multilevel situations. For instance, whereas the CFI, TLI, and RMSEA were especially sensitive to misspecifications in the factor loadings and structural parameters, the SRMR-within flagged misspecifications of the factor covariance at the within level; at the between level, only the SRMR-between indicated model misspecifications. Ryu (2014b) suggested estimating level-specific fit indices and taking several steps to detect possible misfit in multilevel CFA (see also Ryu and West 2009). Her approach involves specifying and comparing at least three multilevel CFA models: (a) a model with the factor structure at the within level and the saturated between level (i.e. only variances and covariance among variables are estimated); (b) a model with the saturated within level and a factor structure at the between level; and (c) a model with the factor structure at both the within and the between levels. Comparing these models, and exploring the factor structure at one level while saturating the other, allows researchers to identify possible sources of misfit. Stapleton (2013) suggested specifying two independent baseline models against which the three models can

Table 8.6 Fit indices of the multilevel CFA models

Model	Description	$\chi^2(df)$	CFI	RMSEA	$SRMR_w$	$SRMR_b$
1	W: Factor structure B: Saturated	252.3 (2)*	0.991	0.026	0.021	0.000
2	W: Saturated B: Factor structure	5.2 (2), $p = 0.07$	1.000	0.000	0.000	0.025
3	W: Factor structure B: Factor structure	469.0 (4)*	0.983	0.025	0.021	0.025
4	M3 with cross-level invariance	753.2 (8)*	0.973	0.023	0.021	2.835

Notes. The scaling correction factors and information criteria can be found in the Supplementary Material. *B* between level, *W* within level
*$p < 0.001$

be compared (see also Finch and Bolin 2017). The multilevel CFA approach can readily be extended to multi-group or MIMIC models by, for instance, introducing a grouping variable at the within or between level (Ryu 2014a) or by adding between-level covariates that may explain possible variation (i.e. random effects) in the model parameters and, ultimately, possible differential item functioning (Davidov et al. 2016).

In the following, I will illustrate the specification of the multilevel CFA models in M*plus*. The PIAAC participating countries are considered to be the groups or, in M*plus* terms, the clusters (CLUSTER = CNTRYID). Table 8.6 shows the resulting fit indices. The first model specifies the factor structure at the within level and saturates the between level (Syntax 8.8). Similarly, the second model saturates the within level and specifies the factor structure at the between level (Model 2). Model 3 assumes the same factor structure at both levels.

Syntax 8.8: Multilevel CFA: Factor Structure at the Within Level, Saturated Between Level
```
VARIABLE: [...]

    ! Countries as clusters
    CLUSTER = CNTRYID;

ANALYSIS:
    TYPE = TWOLEVEL;
    ESTIMATOR = MLR;
    H1ITERATIONS = 10000;
    PROCESSORS = 4;

MODEL:
```
(continued)

```
%WITHIN%
! Individual participant level
! Measurement model
CURIOUSw BY I_Q04d I_Q04j I_Q04l I_Q04m;

%BETWEEN%
! Country level
! Saturated measurement model
I_Q04d-I_Q04m WITH I_Q04d-I_Q04m;
```

Models 1–3 indicate that the factor structure of the curiosity construct is well-described at the within and the between level—neither the model parameters (see Supplementary Material) nor the fit indices indicate severe misfit. At the same time, the number of groups (i.e. countries) in these models is relatively small (i.e. $k = 27$), thus leading to large standard errors in some parameters. The resulting parameters may be biased and must therefore be interpreted with caution (Kim et al. 2016a). To further reduce the number of model parameters, researchers may consider saturating one level of analysis, especially when only country-level inferences are of major interest (Stapleton et al. 2016).

Regarding the cross-level invariance, Model 4 did not fit the data well (Table 8.6, Syntax 8.9), and the comparison between Models 3 and 4 suggested a significant deterioration in model fit after imposing the equality constraints on the factor loadings, $\Delta\chi^2(4) = 26.1$, $p < 0.001$, $\Delta\text{CFI} = -0.010$, $\Delta\text{RMSEA} = -0.002$, $\Delta\text{SRMR}_w = 0.000$, $\Delta\text{SRMR}_b = +2.810$. Hence, cross-level invariance does not hold.

To test further levels of between-country invariance, additional constraints on the between-level intercepts (M*plus* syntax: `[I_Q04d-I_Q04m] (I1-I4);`) and item residuals (M*plus* syntax: `I_Q04d-I_Q04m(R1-R4);`) can be imposed on the multilevel CFA model with factor structures at both levels (Model 3). Finch and Bolin (2017) present and discuss the implementation of these constraints in M*plus*.

Syntax 8.9: Multilevel CFA: Factor Structure at Both Levels with Cross-Level Invariance

```
VARIABLE: [...]

    ! Countries as clusters
    CLUSTER = CNTRYID;

ANALYSIS:
```

(continued)

```
    TYPE = TWOLEVEL;
    ESTIMATOR = MLR;
    H1ITERATIONS = 10000;
    PROCESSORS = 4;
MODEL:
    %WITHIN%
    ! Individual participant level
    ! Measurement model
    CURIOUSw BY
    I_Q04d*(L1)
    I_Q04j(L2)
    I_Q04l(L3)
    I_Q04m(L4);

    ! Fixed factor variance
    CURIOUSw@1;

    %BETWEEN%
    ! Country level
    ! Measurement model
    CURIOUSb BY
    I_Q04d*(L1)
    I_Q04j(L2)
    I_Q04l(L3)
    I_Q04m(L4);

    ! Fixed factor variance
    CURIOUSb@1;
```

8.5 Structural Models

After specifying measurement models, specifying structural models that describe the relations among manifest and/or latent variables represents the second step in SEM (Kline 2016). In the following, several examples of structural equation models and their implementation in M*plus* are presented, including path models, structural models with latent variables, and multi-group structural equation models. As these examples contain the PIAAC cognitive skills measures of problem solving and literacy, all analyses were conducted using the M*plus* option TYPE = IMPUTATION. Hence, the model parameters presented here were combined using Rubin's rules.

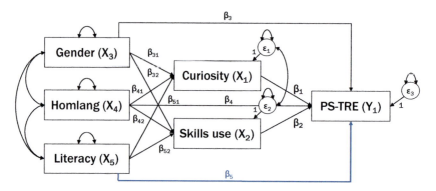

Fig. 8.6 Example of a path model

8.5.1 Path Models

The following model describes the relationships among participants' background variables (i.e. gender, home language, literacy) and their performance on the PIAAC problem-solving test (PS-TRE). Researchers may hypothesise that these relationships follow a certain mechanism with indirect effects via curiosity and the use of skills. Figure 8.6 depicts the corresponding path model containing only manifest variables. Notably, this model serves only illustrative purposes and does not fully represent the theoretical assumptions that researchers may have about the relations among the variables.

Researchers may be interested in the existence of the direct path between literacy and problem solving, testing the null hypothesis that $\beta_5 = 0$. In a sequence of steps, several models may be specified to test this hypothesis:

1. The first model contains all regression paths and freely estimates the parameter β_5 (see Syntax 8.10). This model is just-identified ($df = 0$) and fits the data perfectly. The corresponding, average information criteria were $\overline{AIC} = 70{,}353$ and $\overline{BIC} = 70{,}550$. Across the ten datasets containing one plausible value of the cognitive skills measure each, the direct path between literacy and problem solving was $\overline{\beta}_5 = 0.775$, $SE = 0.010$, 95% CI [0.756, 0.794], $p < 0.001$.
2. The second model restricts the direct path to zero ($\beta_5 = 0$). The resulting average information criteria were considerably higher than those in the first model, $\overline{AIC} = 78{,}149$ and $\overline{BIC} = 78{,}338$. Moreover, this model exhibited a poor fit to the data, $\overline{CFI} = 0.201$, $\overline{RMSEA} = 0.622$, $\overline{SRMR} = 0.130$.
3. The third model uses the Wald test of parameter constraints to test whether $\beta_5 = 0$. This is implemented in M*plus* by adding the following syntax after the model commands: MODEL TEST: b5 = 0; (*Note:* the path coefficient β_5 is named b5 in this example; see Syntax 8.10). The resulting test was statistically significant (Wald-$\chi^2[1] = 2493.2$, $p < 0.001$), indicating that the path between literacy and problem solving significantly deviates from zero. Together with the

superior fit of the model that freely estimates the path coefficient β_5, this provides evidence for the existence of the direct path.

Besides the direct path, researchers may also be interested in the indirect effects of the participants' background variables on problem solving via curiosity and skills use. To estimate these effects, M*plus* offers several approaches, one of which is the MODEL INDIRECT option (Syntax 8.10). This option estimates all indirect, direct, and total effects in the model and can be used in conjunction with the standardisation commands and the call for confidence intervals. At the time of writing, the bootstrapped confidence intervals were not available for multiply imputed datasets. The total indirect effect of literacy on problem solving was $\overline{\beta}_{TInd} = 0.044$, $SE = 0.006$, 95% Wald CI [0.032, 0.056], $p < 0.001$. The specific indirect effect of literacy on problem solving via curiosity was $\overline{\beta}_{SInd} = -0.001$, $SE = 0.004$, 95% Wald CI [−0.010, 0.007], $p = 0.72$. The specific indirect effect of literacy on problem solving via skills use was $\overline{\beta}_{SInd} = 0.045$, $SE = 0.005$, 95% Wald CI [0.035, 0.055], $p < 0.001$.

Syntax 8.10: Model Commands for the Path Model Example

```
MODEL:

    ! Structural model
    ! Note: LIFE represents skills use in everyday
    life (X2).
    PSTRE ON LIFE CURIOUS FEMALE HOMLANG LIT(b5);
    LIFE ON FEMALE HOMLANG LIT;
    CURIOUS ON FEMALE HOMLANG LIT;

    ! Remaining covariances among residuals
    CURIOUS WITH LIFE;

    ! Covariances among predictors
    FEMALE WITH HOMLANG LIT;
    HOMLANG WITH LIT;

MODEL INDIRECT:

    ! Indirect, direct, and total effects
    PSTRE IND FEMALE;
    PSTRE IND HOMLANG;
    PSTRE IND LIT;

MODEL TEST:

    ! Calls the Wald test of parameter constraints
    b5 = 0;
```

(continued)

```
OUTPUT:
    STDY;
    STDYX;
    CINTERVAL;  ! Wald confidence intervals
```

8.5.2 Structural Equation Models

As path models contain manifest variables that are prone to measurement error, substituting them with latent variables can improve the approximation of the true variances and covariances in a structural equation model (Kline 2016; Raykov and Marcoulides 2006). To accomplish this, researchers have several options, such as using the participants' item responses or item parcels as indicators of latent variables or single-indicator variables that are corrected for unreliability (Kline 2016; Little 2013). In the following example, item responses form the indicators of the latent variables (Fig. 8.7). The Supplementary Material contains additional structural equation models using item parcels to represent curiosity.

Except for the inclusion of latent variables, this model's structural part is identical to that of the path model with manifest variables. As a result, the model syntax only has to be modified by adding the measurement models of the latent variables 'Curiosity' and 'Skills use'. The specification of indirect effects and the Wald test remains (Syntax 8.11).

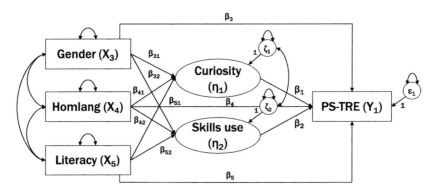

Fig. 8.7 Example of a structural equation model

Syntax 8.11: Model Commands for the Structural Equation Model Example

```
MODEL:

  ! Measurement models
  ! Note: LIFE represents skills use in everyday
  life.
  LIFE BY H_Q05a H_Q05c H_Q05e H_Q05f;

  ! CURIOSITY
  CURIOUS BY I_Q04d I_Q04j I_Q04l I_Q04m;

  ! Structural model
  PSTRE ON LIFE CURIOUS FEMALE HOMLANG LIT;
  LIFE ON FEMALE HOMLANG LIT;
  CURIOUS ON FEMALE HOMLANG LIT;

  ! Remaining covariances among residuals
  CURIOUS WITH LIFE;

  ! Covariances among predictors
  FEMALE WITH HOMLANG LIT;
  HOMLANG WITH LIT;
```

This model exhibited a good fit to the data, as indicated by the following fit indices: $\overline{\chi}^2(43) = 869.5$, $p < 0.001$, $\overline{CFI} = 0.936$, $\overline{RMSEA} = 0.043$, $\overline{SRMR} = 0.040$, $\overline{AIC} = 2{,}313{,}912$, $\overline{BIC} = 231{,}732$. The corresponding indices for each of the ten plausible value datasets varied only marginally between datasets. Across the ten imputed datasets, the factor loadings of the curiosity variable ranged between 0.652 and 0.753 and between 0.571 and 0.678 for skills use. The average direct effect of literacy on problem solving was slightly smaller than that obtained from the path model, $\overline{\beta}_5 = 0.755$, $SE = 0.011$, 95% CI [0.732, 0.777], $p < 0.001$. The total indirect effect of literacy on problem solving via curiosity and skills use was $\overline{\beta}_{TInd} = 0.064$, $SE = 0.008$, 95% CI [0.048, 0.079], $p < 0.001$. Similar to the path model, only the specific indirect effect via skills use was statistically significant, $\overline{\beta}_{SInd} = 0.070$, $SE = 0.008$, 95% CI [0.054, 0.086], $p < 0.001$. This structural equation model may well be compared to alternative models through likelihood-ratio testing (Asparouhov and Muthén 2010; Enders and Mansolf 2018).

8.5.3 Multi-group Structural Equation Models and Structural Invariance Testing

Both path models and structural equation models can be extended to multi-group models in order to test possible differences in structural coefficients across groups. However, if latent variables are part of the model, the comparisons of structural coefficients are meaningful only if at least metric invariance holds (Guenole and Brown 2014; Raykov and Marcoulides 2006; Sass and Schmitt 2013). In the following example, the structural equation model displayed in Fig. 8.7 is specified for the German and the Norwegian sample assuming metric invariance across the two countries (Syntax 8.12). This specification uses the M*plus* option GROUPING IS GERMAN(0 = Norway 1 = Germany).

Syntax 8.12: Model Commands for the Multi-group Structural Equation Model Example

```
MODEL:

  ! Measurement models
  ! Note: LIFE represents skills use in everyday
  life.
  LIFE BY H_Q05a* H_Q05c H_Q05e H_Q05f;

  ! CURIOSITY
  CURIOUS BY I_Q04d* I_Q04j I_Q04l I_Q04m;

  ! Factor variances fixed to 1 to identify the
  model
  LIFE@1;
  CURIOUS@1;

  ! Structural model
  PSTRE ON LIFE CURIOUS FEMALE HOMLANG LIT;
  LIFE ON FEMALE HOMLANG LIT;
  CURIOUS ON FEMALE HOMLANG LIT;

  ! Remaining covariances among residuals
  CURIOUS WITH LIFE;

  ! Covariances among predictors
  FEMALE WITH HOMLANG LIT;
  HOMLANG WITH LIT;

  ! Freely estimated item intercepts
  [H_Q05a-H_Q05f*];
  [I_Q04d-I_Q04m*];
```

(continued)

```
    ! Constrained factor means to identify the mean
    structure
    [LIFE@0];
    [CURIOUS@0];

    ! Freely estimated residual variances
    H_Q05a-H_Q05f*;
    I_Q04d-I_Q04m*;

MODEL NORWAY:

    ! Nothing is specified here.
```

This multi-group model resulted in an acceptable fit, $\overline{\chi}^2(94) = 1715.9, p < 0.001$, $\overline{CFI} = 0.929$, $\overline{RMSEA} = 0.058$, $\overline{SRMR} = 0.053$, $\overline{AIC} = 198,047$, $\overline{BIC} = 198,539$. The direct effect of literacy on problem solving was $\overline{\beta}_5 = 0.763$ ($SE = 0.014$, 95% CI [0.736, 0.790], $p < 0.001$) for the German sample and $\overline{\beta}_5 = 0.753$ ($SE = 0.012$, 95% CI [0.729, 0.777], $p < 0.001$) for the Norwegian sample. Although these two path coefficients are quite similar, researchers may want to test for their invariance across countries. Modifying the structural part under the MODEL command by labelling the structural coefficient between literacy and problem solving (e.g., PSTRE BY ... LIT(P1)) restricts this coefficient to equality across the two countries. The resulting model did not deteriorate the model fit substantially, $\overline{\chi}^2(95) = 1718.6, p < 0.001$, $\overline{CFI} = 0.929$, $\overline{RMSEA} = 0.058$, $\overline{SRMR} = 0.053$, $\overline{AIC} = 198,049$, $\overline{BIC} = 198533.7$. Reviewing the goodness-of-fit indices and the information criteria, there is no convincing evidence suggesting that the effects of literacy on problem solving differ between the German and Norwegian samples. As a consequence, researchers may conclude that the structural parameter β_5 is invariant. To further back up this conclusion, researchers should conduct the model comparison for each of the ten datasets separately to rule out that the variation in the plausible values between these datasets may have affected these tests.

8.6 Some Recommendations for SEM Analyses

Given the aims associated with performing SEM, and considering the complexity of the PIAAC data, researchers are faced with several methodological decisions. The following, by no means exhaustive, recommendations may aid this decision-making process.

- *Treatment of item indicators.* Item indicators that are based on rating scales can be treated categorically or continuously using a range of estimation procedures. If researchers are primarily interested in the psychometric quality of a scale and

its items, the categorical treatment of item indicators provides more information than the continuous treatment (e.g. multiple item thresholds are estimated as opposed to one item intercept per indicator). Moreover, in many situations, the categorical treatment of indicators is preferred over the continuous treatment, especially when the item response distributions are skewed (Li 2016; Suh 2015). Nevertheless, if five or more response categories exist, the response distributions deviate from normality only to some extent, and researchers are primarily interested in controlling for measurement error in a structural equation model with latent variables, treating item indicators continuously is a viable alternative (Rhemtulla et al. 2012).
- *Inclusion of performance scores.* Whenever performance scores are included in any structural equation model, all plausible values should be used, model estimations should be performed for each set of plausible values, and the resulting model parameters should be combined following Rubin's combination rules (Laukaityte and Wiberg 2017; Rutkowski and Rutkowski 2016). Including only one plausible value in a structural equation model may be feasible when researchers want to perform initial checks of their hypotheses. However, it does not provide correct standard errors of the model parameters.
- *Hierarchical data structure.* In situations where multiple countries are included in the analyses, accounting for the hierarchical structural of the data (i.e. participants nested in countries) prevents ecological fallacies. The SEM framework offers several options to achieve this: (a) countries can be treated as groups, and country differences are modelled as fixed effects, for instance, through multiple-group SEM, MIMIC models, or alignment procedures; (b) countries can be treated as groups, and country differences are modelled as random effects through multilevel SEM. If researchers are aiming at comparing only a few countries, the former approaches are suitable. If researchers are aiming at quantifying and explaining the variance of certain SEM parameters (e.g. factor loadings, intercepts) between a large number of countries, the latter approach is suitable (Kim et al. 2017; Muthén and Asparouhov 2018).
- *Effects of using weights.* While the inclusion of weights is recommended for obtaining accurate model parameters and standard errors, the effects of not including any weights in specific analytic situations have not yet been fully understood (Laukaityte and Wiberg 2018; Stapleton 2002). Researchers are therefore encouraged to examine the effects of including weights on the parameters of their structural equation models.

8.7 Summary

Overall, SEM provides a flexible framework in order for researchers to address questions surrounding the psychometric quality of a scale, the structural relations among constructs, and ultimately the testing of specific theories and hypotheses. This framework is well applicable to international large-scale assessment data

(Rutkowski and Zhou 2014)—data sources that contain not only manifest scores and indices representing participants' background characteristics and test performance but also multiple-items scales representing constructs. Besides the great potential of SEM for analysing PIAAC data, several methodological issues must be considered. They include, but are not limited to, (a) handling missing data, (b) weighting individual-level and country-level data, (c) establishing the comparability of scores and/or relations among variables whenever comparisons between countries and subgroups within the PIAAC samples are conducted, (d) modelling the complex structure of the PIAAC data, and (e) handling multiple datasets of plausible values. As far as the range of structural equation models presented in this chapter goes, the software package M*plus* can handle these complexities through a set of ready-made specification options, including the use of weights, imputed data, and convenience functions for investigating measurement invariance across multiple groups. Moreover, the software allows researchers to perform several types of estimation procedures, including maximum-likelihood, weighted least squares, and Bayesian estimation.

As the primary goal of this chapter was to present worked examples, I hope to encourage researchers to consider conducting SEM for testing their substantive theories and hypotheses using the PIAAC data. At the same time, researchers should be aware of the above-mentioned data issues and the current methodological developments to address them. In fact, I believe that using the PIAAC data for SEM requires a continuous review and updating of these developments.

Supplementary Material

The Supplementary Material contains the M*plus* (version 8.2) input and output files for the models presented in this chapter. Readers can access these files through the Open Science Framework at https://doi.org/10.17605/OSF.IO/HGBFK. (ZIP 83340 kb)

References[1]

Asparouhov, T., & Muthén, B. O. (2010). *Chi-square statistics with multiple imputation*. Los Angeles: Muthén & Muthén. Retrieved June 20, 2019, from https://www.statmodel.com/download/MI7.pdf.

Asparouhov, T., & Muthén, B. O. (2014). Multiple-group factor analysis alignment. *Structural Equation Modeling: A Multidisciplinary Journal, 21*(4), 495–508. https://doi.org/10.1080/10705511.2014.919210.

---

[1] References marked with an asterisk indicate examples of PIAAC secondary analyses using SEM.

Bauer, D. J. (2017). A more general model for testing measurement invariance and differential item functioning. *Psychological Methods, 22*, 507–526. https://doi.org/10.1037/met0000077.

Beauducel, A., & Herzberg, P. Y. (2006). On the performance of maximum likelihood versus means and variance adjusted weighted least squares estimation in CFA. *Structural Equation Modeling: A Multidisciplinary Journal, 13*(2), 186–203. https://doi.org/10.1207/s15328007sem1302_2.

*Borgonovi, F., & Pokropek, A. (2017a). Birthplace diversity, income inequality and education gradients in generalised trust. OECD Education Working Papers, 164, 1–40. https://doi.org/10.1787/f16a8bae-en.

*Borgonovi, F., & Pokropek, A. (2017b). Mind that gap: The mediating role of intelligence and individuals' socio-economic status in explaining disparities in external political efficacy in 28 countries. *Intelligence, 62*, 125–137. https://doi.org/10.1016/j.intell.2017.03.006.

Brown, T. A. (2015). *Confirmatory factor analysis for applied research* (2nd ed.). New York: Guilford Press.

Chen, F. F. (2007). Sensitivity of goodness of fit indexes to lack of measurement invariance. *Structural Equation Modeling: A Multidisciplinary Journal, 14*(3), 464–504. https://doi.org/10.1080/10705510701301834.

Cheung, G. W., & Rensvold, R. B. (2002). Evaluating goodness-of-fit indexes for testing measurement invariance. *Structural Equation Modeling: A Multidisciplinary Journal, 9*(2), 233–255. https://doi.org/10.1207/S15328007SEM0902_5.

*Cincinnato, S De Wever, B., Van Keer, H., Valcke, M. (2016). The influence of social background on participation in adult education: Applying the cultural capital framework. *Adult Education Quarterly, 66*(2), 143–168. https://doi.org/10.1177/0741713615626714

Davidov, E., Dülmer, H., Cieciuch, J., Kuntz, A., Seddig, D., & Schmidt, P. (2016). Explaining measurement nonequivalence using multilevel structural equation modeling: The case of attitudes toward citizenship rights. *Sociological Methods & Research, 47*(4), 729–760. https://doi.org/10.1177/0049124116672678.

Davidov, E., Dülmer, H., Schlüter, E., Schmidt, P., & Meuleman, B. (2012). Using a multilevel structural equation modeling approach to explain cross-cultural measurement noninvariance. *Journal of Cross-Cultural Psychology, 43*(4), 558–575. https://doi.org/10.1177/0022022112438397.

Desa, D. (2014). Evaluating measurement invariance of TALIS 2013 complex scales. *OECD Education Working Papers, 103*. https://doi.org/10.1787/5jz2kbbvlb7k-en.

*Duchhardt, C., Jordan, A.-K., Ehmke, T. J. I. J. o. S Education, M. (2017). Adults' use of mathematics and its influence on mathematical competence. *International Journal of Science and Mathematics Education 15*(1), 155–174. https://doi.org/10.1007/s10763-015-9670-1.

Enders, C. K. (2010). *Applied missing data analysis*. New York: The Guilford Press.

Enders, C. K., & Mansolf, M. (2018). Assessing the fit of structural equation models with multiply imputed data. *Psychological Methods, 23*(1), 76–93. https://doi.org/10.1037/met0000102.

Enders, C. K., Mistler, S. A., & Keller, B. T. (2016). Multilevel multiple imputation: A review and evaluation of joint modeling and chained equations imputation. *Psychological Methods, 21*(2), 222–240. https://doi.org/10.1037/met0000063.

Fan, X., & Sivo, S. A. (2009). Using Δgoodness-of-fit indexes in assessing mean structure invariance. *Structural Equation Modeling, 16*(1), 54–69. https://doi.org/10.1080/10705510802561311.

Finch, W. H., & Bolin, J. E. (2017). *Multilevel modeling using Mplus*. Boca Rayon: CRC Press.

Finney, S. J., & DiStefano, C. (2013). Nonnormal and categorical data in structural equation modeling. In G. R. Hancock & R. O. Mueller (Eds.), *Structural equation modeling: A second course* (2nd ed., pp. 439–492). Charlotte: Information Age Publishing.

Fox, J.-P., & Verhagen, A. J. (2010). Random item effects modeling for cross-national survey data. In E. Davidov, P. Schmidt, & J. Billiet (Eds.), *Cross-cultural analysis: Methods and applications* (pp. 467–488). London: Routledge.

*Ganzach, Y., & Patel, P. C. (2018). Wages, mental abilities and assessments in large scale international surveys: Still not much more than g. *Intelligence, 69*, 1–7. https://doi.org/10.1016/j.intell.2018.03.014.

*Gorges, J., Koch, T., Maehler, D. B., & Offerhaus, J. J. (2017). Same but different? Measurement invariance of the PIAAC motivation-to-learn scale across key socio-demographic groups. *Large-scale Assessment in Education, 5*(1). https://doi.org/10.1186/s40536-017-0047-5.

*Gorges, J., Maehler, D. B., Koch, T., & Offerhaus, J. J. (2016). Who likes to learn new things? Measuring adult motivation to learn with PIAAC data from 21 countries. *Large-scale Assessment in Education, 4*(1). https://doi.org/10.1186/s40536-016-0024-4.

Grund, S., Lüdtke, O., & Robitzsch, A. (2018). Multiple imputation of missing data for multilevel models: Simulations and recommendations. *Organizational Research Methods, 21*(1), 111–149. https://doi.org/10.1177/1094428117703686.

Guenole, N., & Brown, A. (2014). The Consequences of ignoring measurement invariance for path coefficients in structural equation models. *Frontiers in Psychology, 5*(980). https://doi.org/10.3389/fpsyg.2014.00980.

*Hahs-Vaughn, D. L. (2017). *Applied multivariate statistical concepts* [chapter 10]. New York: Routledge by Taylor & Francis.

Hancock, G. R., & Mueller, R. O. (2013). *Structural equation modeling: A second course* (2nd ed.). Charlotte, NC: Information Age Publishing.

*Heisig, J. P. J. (2018). Measuring the signaling value of educational degrees: Secondary education systems and the internal homogeneity of educational groups. *Large-scale Assessment in Education, 6*(1). https://doi.org/10.1186/s40536-018-0062-1.

Hox, J. J. (2013). Multilevel regression and multilevel structural equation modeling. In T. D. Little (Ed.), *The Oxford handbook of quantitative methods in psychology (Vol. 2: Statistical analysis)* (pp. 281–294). Oxford: Oxford University Press.

Hoyle, R. H. (2012). *Handbook of structural equation modeling*. New York: The Guilford Press.

Hsu, H.-Y., Kwok, O.-M., Lin, J. H., & Acosta, S. (2015). Detecting misspecified multilevel structural equation models with common fit indices: A Monte Carlo study. *Multivariate Behavioral Research, 50*(2), 197–215. https://doi.org/10.1080/00273171.2014.977429.

Jak, S. (2018). Cross-level invariance in multilevel factor models. *Structural Equation Modeling: A Multidisciplinary Journal*, 1–16. https://doi.org/10.1080/10705511.2018.1534205.

Jak, S., Oort, F. J., & Dolan, C. V. (2014). Measurement bias in multilevel data. *Structural Equation Modeling: A Multidisciplinary Journal, 21*(1), 31–39. https://doi.org/10.1080/10705511.2014.856694.

Kaplan, D. (2009). *Structural equation modeling: Foundations and extensions* (2nd ed.). Thousand Oaks: SAGE Publications.

Khojasteh, J., & Lo, W.-J. (2015). Investigating the sensitivity of goodness-of-fit indices to detect measurement invariance in a bifactor model. *Structural Equation Modeling: A Multidisciplinary Journal, 22*(4), 531–541. https://doi.org/10.1080/10705511.2014.937791.

Kim, E. S., Cao, C., Wang, Y., & Nguyen, D. T. (2017). Measurement invariance testing with many groups: A comparison of five approaches. *Structural Equation Modeling: A Multidisciplinary Journal, 24*(4), 524–544. https://doi.org/10.1080/10705511.2017.1304822.

Kim, E. S., Dedrick, R. F., Cao, C., & Ferron, J. M. (2016a). Multilevel factor analysis: Reporting guidelines and a review of reporting practices. *Multivariate Behavioral Research, 51*(6), 881–898. https://doi.org/10.1080/00273171.2016.1228042.

Kim, E. S., Joo, S.-H., Lee, P., Wang, Y., & Stark, S. (2016b). Measurement invariance testing across between-level latent classes using multilevel factor mixture modeling. *Structural Equation Modeling: A Multidisciplinary Journal, 23*(6), 870–887. https://doi.org/10.1080/10705511.2016.1196108.

Kim, E. S., Kwok, O.-M., & Yoon, M. (2012a). Testing factorial invariance in multilevel data: A Monte Carlo study. *Structural Equation Modeling: A Multidisciplinary Journal, 19*(2), 250–267. https://doi.org/10.1080/10705511.2012.659623.

Kim, E. S., Yoon, M., & Lee, T. (2012b). Testing measurement invariance using MIMIC. *Educational and Psychological Measurement, 72*(3), 469–492. https://doi.org/10.1177/0013164411427395.

Kline, R. B. (2016). *Principles and practice of structural equation modeling* (4th ed.). New York: Guilford Press.

Koch, T., Holtmann, J., Bohn, J., & Eid, M. (2018). Explaining general and specific factors in longitudinal, multimethod, and bifactor models: Some caveats and recommendations. *Psychological Methods, 23*(3), 505–523. https://doi.org/10.1037/met0000146.

Laukaityte, I., & Wiberg, M. (2017). Using plausible values in secondary analysis in large-scale assessments. *Communications in Statistics – Theory and Methods, 46*(22), 11341–11357. https://doi.org/10.1080/03610926.2016.1267764.

Laukaityte, I., & Wiberg, M. (2018). Importance of sampling weights in multilevel modeling of international large-scale assessment data. *Communications in Statistics – Theory and Methods, 47*(20), 4991–5012. https://doi.org/10.1080/03610926.2017.1383429.

Li, C.-H. (2016). Confirmatory factor analysis with ordinal data: Comparing robust maximum likelihood and diagonally weighted least squares. *Behavior Research Methods, 48*(3), 936–949. https://doi.org/10.3758/s13428-015-0619-7.

Little, T. D. (2013). *Longitudinal structural equation modeling*. New York: The Guilford Press.

Liu, Y., Millsap, R. E., West, S. G., Tein, J.-Y., Tanaka, R., & Grimm, K. J. (2017). Testing measurement invariance in longitudinal data with ordered-categorical measures. *Psychological Methods, 22*(3), 486–506. https://doi.org/10.1037/met0000075.

Loehlin, J. C., & Beaujean, A. A. (2017). *Latent variable models: An introduction to factor, path, and structural equation models* (5th ed.). New York: Routledge.

Marsh, H. W., Guo, J., Parker, P. D., Nagengast, B., Asparouhov, T., Muthén, B., & Dicke, T. (2018). What to do when scalar invariance fails: The extended alignment method for multigroup factor analysis comparison of latent means across many groups. *Psychological Methods, 23*(3), 524–545. https://doi.org/10.1037/met0000113.

Marsh, H. W., Morin, A. J. S., Parker, P. D., & Kaur, G. (2014). Exploratory structural equation modeling. *An integration of the best features of exploratory and confirmatory factor analysis., 10*(1), 85–110. https://doi.org/10.1146/annurev-clinpsy-032813-153700.

Marsh, H. W., Muthén, B., Asparouhov, T., Lüdtke, O., Robitzsch, A., Morin, A. J. S., & Trautwein, U. (2009). Exploratory structural equation modeling, integrating CFA and EFA: Application to students' evaluations of university teaching. *Structural Equation Modeling: A Multidisciplinary Journal, 16*(3), 439–476. https://doi.org/10.1080/10705510903008220.

Marsh, H. W., Nagengast, B., & Morin, A. J. S. (2013). Measurement invariance of big-five factors over the life span: ESEM tests of gender, age, plasticity, maturity, and la dolce vita effects. *Developmental Psychology, 49*(6), 1194–1218. https://doi.org/10.1037/a0026913.

Meade, A. W., Johnson, E. C., & Braddy, P. W. (2008). Power and sensitivity of alternative fit indices in tests of measurement invariance. *Journal of Applied Psychology, 93*(3), 568–592. https://doi.org/10.1037/0021-9010.93.3.568.

Meng, X.-L., & Rubin, D. B. (1992). Performing likelihood ratio tests with multiply-imputed data sets. *Biometrika, 79*(1), 103–111. https://doi.org/10.1093/biomet/79.1.103.

Meredith, W. (1993). Measurement invariance, factor analysis and factorial invariance. *Psychometrika, 58*(4), 525–543. https://doi.org/10.1007/BF02294825.

Millsap, R. E. (2011). *Statistical approaches to measurement invariance*. New York: Routledge.

Muthén, B., & Asparouhov, T. (2012). Bayesian structural equation modeling: A more flexible representation of substantive theory. *Psychological Methods, 17*(3), 313–335. https://doi.org/10.1037/a0026802.

Muthén, B., & Asparouhov, T. (2014). IRT studies of many groups: The alignment method. *Frontiers in Psychology, 5*(978). https://doi.org/10.3389/fpsyg.2014.00978.

Muthén, B., & Asparouhov, T. (2018). Recent methods for the study of measurement invariance with many groups: Alignment and random effects. *Sociological Methods & Research, 47*(4), 637–664. https://doi.org/10.1177/0049124117701488.

Muthén, B., Muthén, L. K., & Asparouhov, T. (2017). *Regression and mediation analysis using Mplus*. Los Angeles: Muthén & Muthén.

Muthén, L., & Muthén, B. (1998–2017). *Mplus user's guide* (8th ed.). Los Angeles: Muthén & Muthén.

OECD. (2013). *Technical report of the survey of adult skills (PIAAC)*. Paris: OECD Publishing. Retrieved June 20, 2019, from https://www.oecd.org/skills/piaac/_Technical%20Report_17OCT13.pdf.

OECD. (2016). *Programme for the international assessment of adult competencies (PIAAC): Public use files*. Paris: OECD Publishing. Retrieved from: http://www.oecd.org/skills/piaac/publicdataaandanalysis/.

Putnick, D. L., & Bornstein, M. H. (2016). Measurement invariance conventions and reporting: The state of the art and future directions for psychological research. *Developmental Review, 41*, 71–90. https://doi.org/10.1016/j.dr.2016.06.004.

Raykov, T., & Marcoulides, G. A. (2006). *A first course in structural equation modeling* (2nd ed.). Mahwah: Lawrence Erlbaum Associates Publishers.

Rhemtulla, M., Brosseau-Liard, P. É., & Savalei, V. (2012). When can categorical variables be treated as continuous? A comparison of robust continuous and categorical SEM estimation methods under suboptimal conditions. *Psychological Methods, 17*(3), 354–373. https://doi.org/10.1037/a0029315.

Rutkowski, D., Rutkowski, L., & Liaw, Y.-L. (2018). Measuring widening proficiency differences in international assessments: Are current approaches enough? *Educational Measurement: Issues and Practice, 37*(4), 40–48. https://doi.org/10.1111/emip.12225.

Rutkowski, L., Gonzalez, E., Joncas, M., & von Davier, M. (2010). International large-scale assessment data:Issues in secondary analysis and reporting. *Educational Researcher, 39*(2), 142–151. https://doi.org/10.3102/0013189x10363170.

Rutkowski, L., & Rutkowski, D. (2016). A call for a more measured approach to reporting and interpreting PISA results. *Educational Researcher, 45*(4), 252–257. https://doi.org/10.3102/0013189x16649961.

Rutkowski, L., & Svetina, D. (2013). Assessing the hypothesis of measurement invariance in the context of large-scale international surveys. *Educational and Psychological Measurement, 74*(1), 31–57. https://doi.org/10.1177/0013164413498257.

Rutkowski, L., & Svetina, D. (2014). Assessing the hypothesis of measurement invariance in the context of large-scale international surveys. *Educational and Psychological Measurement, 74*(1), 31–57. https://doi.org/10.1177/0013164413498257.

Rutkowski, L., & Zhou, Y. (2014). Using structural equation models to analyze ILSA data. In L. Rutkowski, M. Von Davier, & D. Rutkowski (Eds.), *Handbook of international large-scale assessment: Background, technical issues, and methods of data analysis* (pp. 425–450). Boca Raton: CRC Press.

Ryu, E. (2014a). Factorial invariance in multilevel confirmatory factor analysis. *British Journal of Mathematical and Statistical Psychology, 67*(1), 172–194. https://doi.org/10.1111/bmsp.12014.

Ryu, E. (2014b). Model fit evaluation in multilevel structural equation models. *Frontiers in Psychology, 5*(81). https://doi.org/10.3389/fpsyg.2014.00081.

Ryu, E., & West, S. G. (2009). Level-specific evaluation of model fit in multilevel structural equation modeling. *Structural Equation Modeling, 16*(4), 583–601. https://doi.org/10.1080/10705510903203466.

Sass, D. A., & Schmitt, T. A. (2013). Testing measurement and structural invariance. In T. Teo (Ed.), *Handbook of quantitative methods for educational research* (pp. 315–345). Rotterdam: SensePublishers.

Scherer, R., & Greiff, S. (2018). Still comparing apples with oranges? Some thoughts on the principles and practices of measurement invariance testing. *European Journal of Psychological Assessment, 34*(3), 141–144. https://doi.org/10.1027/1015-5759/a000487.

*Scandurra, R., & Calero, J. (2017). Modelling adult skills in OECD countries. 43(4), 781–804. https://doi.org/10.1002/berj.3290.

*Sikora, J., Evans, M. D. R., Kelley, J. (2019). Scholarly culture: How books in adolescence enhance adult literacy, numeracy and technology skills in 31 societies. *Social Science Research, 77*, 1–15. https://doi.org/10.1016/j.ssresearch.2018.10.003.

Stapleton, L. M. (2002). The incorporation of sample weights into multilevel structural equation models. *Structural Equation Modeling: A Multidisciplinary Journal, 9*(4), 475–502. https://doi.org/10.1207/S15328007SEM0904_2.

Stapleton, L. M. (2013). Multilevel structural equation modeling with complex sample data. In G. R. Hancock & R. O. Mueller (Eds.), *Structural equation modeling: A second course* (pp. 521–562). Charlotte: Information Age Publishing.

Stapleton, L. M., McNeish, D. M., & Yang, J. S. (2016). Multilevel and single-level models for measured and latent variables when data are clustered. *Educational Psychologist, 51*(3–4), 317–330. https://doi.org/10.1080/00461520.2016.1207178.

Suh, Y. (2015). The performance of maximum likelihood and weighted least square mean and variance adjusted estimators in testing differential item functioning with nonnormal trait distributions. *Structural Equation Modeling: A Multidisciplinary Journal, 22*(4), 568–580. https://doi.org/10.1080/10705511.2014.937669.

*Trapp, S., Blömeke, S., Ziegler, M. (2019). The openness-fluid-crystallized-intelligence (OFCI) model and the environmental enrichment hypothesis. *Intelligence, 73*, 30–40. https://doi.org/10.1016/j.intell.2019.01.009.

Van de Schoot, R., Kluytmans, A., Tummers, L., Lugtig, P., Hox, J., & Muthén, B. (2013). Facing off with Scylla and Charybdis: A comparison of scalar, partial, and the novel possibility of approximate measurement invariance. *Frontiers in Psychology, 4*(770). https://doi.org/10.3389/fpsyg.2013.00770.

Van de Schoot, R., Lugtig, P., & Hox, J. (2012). A checklist for testing measurement invariance. *European Journal of Developmental Psychology, 9*(4), 486–492. https://doi.org/10.1080/17405629.2012.686740.

Woods, C. M., & Grimm, K. J. (2011). Testing for nonuniform differential item functioning with multiple mndicator multiple cause models. *Applied Psychological Measurement, 35*(5), 339–361. https://doi.org/10.1177/0146621611405984.

Yuan, K.-H., & Chan, W. (2016). Measurement invariance via multigroup SEM: Issues and solutions with chi-square-difference tests. *Psychological Methods, 21*(3), 405–426. https://doi.org/10.1037/met0000080.

Open Access This chapter is licensed under the terms of the Creative Commons Attribution 4.0 International License (http://creativecommons.org/licenses/by/4.0/), which permits use, sharing, adaptation, distribution and reproduction in any medium or format, as long as you give appropriate credit to the original author(s) and the source, provide a link to the Creative Commons license and indicate if changes were made.

The images or other third party material in this chapter are included in the chapter's Creative Commons license, unless indicated otherwise in a credit line to the material. If material is not included in the chapter's Creative Commons license and your intended use is not permitted by statutory regulation or exceeds the permitted use, you will need to obtain permission directly from the copyright holder.

Chapter 9
Using EdSurvey to Analyse PIAAC Data

Paul Bailey, Michael Lee, Trang Nguyen, and Ting Zhang

Abstract This chapter describes the use of the R package EdSurvey and its use in analysing PIAAC data. The package allows users to download public use PIAAC data, explore the codebooks, explore data, read in and edit relevant variables, and run analyses such as regression, logistic regression, and gap analysis.

9.1 Introduction

The EdSurvey package is a collection of functions for use in the R programming language R Core Team (2019) to help users easily work with data from the National Center for Education Statistics (NCES) and international large-scale assessments. Developed by the American Institutes for Research and commissioned by the NCES, this package manages the entire process of analyses of Programme for the International Assessment of Adult Competencies (PIAAC) data: downloading, searching the codebook and other metadata, conducting exploratory data analysis, cleaning and manipulating the data, extracting variables of interest, and finally data

---

This publication was prepared for NCES under Contract No. ED-IES-12-D-0002 with the American Institutes for Research. Mention of trade names, commercial products, or organisations does not imply endorsement by the US government.

P. Bailey (✉) · M. Lee · T. Zhang
American Institutes for Research, Washington, DC, USA
e-mail: pbailey@air.org; mlee@air.org; tzhang@air.org

T. Nguyen
Tamr Inc., Cambridge, MA, USA

© The Author(s) 2020
D. B. Maehler, B. Rammstedt (eds.), *Large-Scale Cognitive Assessment*, Methodology of Educational Measurement and Assessment, https://doi.org/10.1007/978-3-030-47515-4_9

analysis. This chapter describes the use of `EdSurvey` for each activity, with a focus on PIAAC data.[1,2]

Because of the scope and complexity of data from large-scale assessment programmes, such as PIAAC, the analysis of their data requires proper statistical methods—namely, the use of weights and plausible values. The `EdSurvey` package gives users intuitive one-line functions to perform analyses that account for these methods.

Given the size of large-scale data and the constraint of limited computer memory, the `EdSurvey` package is designed to minimise memory usage. Users with computers that have insufficient memory to read in entire datasets—the OECD Cycle 1 data are over a gigabyte once read in to R—can still perform analyses without having to write special code to limit the dataset. This is all addressed directly in the `EdSurvey` package—behind the scenes and without any additional intervention by the user—allowing researchers to more efficiently explore and analyse variables of interest.

The results of analyses on this saved data connection can then be stored or further manipulated. Alternatively, the `getData` function reads in selected variables of interest to generate an R `data.frame`. Individuals familiar with R programming might prefer to clean and explore their data using supplementary packages, which `EdSurvey` supports. These `data.frames` can then be used with all `EdSurvey` analytical functions.

The next section shows how to load `EdSurvey` and download and read in PIAAC data. The third section describes how you can see survey attributes in `EdSurvey`. The fourth deals with exploring PIAAC data. The fifth section describes data manipulation. The sixth section describes data analysis. The final section explains how to stay current with new developments in `EdSurvey`.

9.2 Getting Started

R is an open-source software and can be downloaded free of charge from www.r-project.org/ R Core Team (2019). The Comprehensive R Archive Network (CRAN) stores extensions to the base R functionality and can be used to install `EdSurvey` using the command

---

[1] `EdSurvey` 2.4 also can work with public and/or restricted use datasets from ECLS:K, ICCS, ICILS, NAEP, PIRLS, ePIRLS, PISA, TALIS, TIMSS, and TIMSS advanced; more datasets are added with each release.

[2] `EdSurvey` uses a variety of other packages; for a complete list, see https://CRAN.R-project.org/package=EdSurvey.

9 Using EdSurvey to Analyse PIAAC Data

```
> install.packages('EdSurvey')
```

Having downloaded the `EdSurvey` package from CRAN, it must be loaded in every session with the command

```
> library('EdSurvey')
```

Then the user can download the OECD 2012 files with

```
> downloadPIAAC('~/')
```

When `downloadPIAAC` is run, the data are stored in a folder in the directory that the user specifies, here an operating system-defined folder called `'~/'`. On all machines this is the user's home folder. After the download is complete, users can manually change the folder structure. This chapter will assume that the download call used the folder `'~/'`, and the data were not subsequently moved from that folder. Within the target folder, the user specified (here `'~/'`) the data will be stored in a subfolder named 'PIAAC'. All data for participating countries in Cycle 1 will be stored in the subdirectory 'PIAAC/Cycle 1'. At the time of writing, only Cycle 1 is available for download.

One also can manually download desirable PIAAC data from the Organisation for Economic Co-operation and Development (OECD) webpage[3], including the 2012/2014 data, or acquire a data licence and access the restricted-use data files. When downloading manually, note that the PIAAC read-in function, `readPIAAC`, requires both the .csv files with the data and a codebook spreadsheet (.xlsx file) to be in the same folder

The next step in running analysis is reading in the data. For PIAAC data, this is accomplished with the `readPIAAC` function, which creates an `edsurvey.data.frame` that stores information about the specific data files processed. This includes the location on disk, the file format and layout of those files, and the metadata that will allow EdSurvey to analyse the data. A PIAAC `edsurvey.data.frame` includes information for all variables at the individual level and any household-level variables.

Upon the first read-in, the EdSurvey package caches existing data as a flat text file; for all future sessions, this flat file stores the variables needed for any analysis. The PIAAC Cycle 1 data can be read-in by pointing to the pathway in the PIAAC Cycle 1 data folder and defining the country of interest. By setting `countries = c('ITA')` in a call to `readPIAAC`, an `edsurvey.data.frame` containing Cycle 1 data for Italy is created as the object `ita`:

---

[3] https://www.oecd.org/skills/piaac/data/

```
> ita <- readPIAAC('~/PIAAC/Cycle 1/', countries='ITA')
Found cached data for country code "ita".
```

The function uses the three-digit International Organization for Standardization country code to select countries to import (here, 'ITA'). Section 9.6.3 describes how to read in and analyse data from multiple countries at once. For now, other countries can be read in and analysed separately by repeating the above command with the code of another country, such as the Netherlands:

```
> nld <- readPIAAC('~/PIAAC/Cycle 1/', countries='NLD')
Found cached data for country code "nld".
```

9.3 Survey Design Attributes

When analysing data with EdSurvey, the package automatically accounts for the plausible values of scores as well as the sample survey design when conducting data analyses by storing metadata in the edsurvey.data.frame. There are four important survey design attributes that have a great influence on the output of later analysis: plausible values, weights, omitted levels, and achievement levels. This section describes these metadata elements and how users can display them.

PIAAC Cycle 1 data have ten plausible values for each domain (numeracy, literacy, and problem solving), as shown in the output of showPlausibleValues function. The showPlausibleValues function not only tells users about the PIAAC domain of skills this round of survey questionnaires contains but also shows the plausible value domain names representing their corresponding domain/subject scale as used in EdSurvey analytical functions.

```
> showPlausibleValues(ita, verbose=TRUE)
There are 3 subject scale(s) or subscale(s) in this
   edsurvey.data.frame:
'lit' subject scale or subscale with 10 plausible values
(the default).
   The plausible value variables are: 'pvlit1', 'pvlit2',
   'pvlit3', 'pvlit4', 'pvlit5', 'pvlit6', 'pvlit7',
   'pvlit8', 'pvlit9', and 'pvlit10'

'num' subject scale or subscale with 10 plausible values.
```

(continued)

```
      The plausible value variables are: 'pvnum1', 'pvnum2',
      'pvnum3', 'pvnum4', 'pvnum5', 'pvnum6', 'pvnum7',
      'pvnum8', 'pvnum9', and 'pvnum10'

   'ps1' subject scale or subscale with 10 plausible values.
      The plausible value variables are: 'pvps11', 'pvps12',
      'pvps13', 'pvps14', 'pvps15', 'pvps16', 'pvps17',
      'pvps18', 'pvps19', and 'pvps110'
```

For example, the ten variables named pvlit1 to pvlit10 store an individual set of plausible values for the literacy scale score domain. These ten variables can simply be referred to by the name lit, and EdSurvey functions will correctly account for the plausible values in both estimation and variance estimation.

The PIAAC sample is a probability sample that was a single stage sample in some countries but a multistage sample in other countries Mohadjer et al. (2016). In addition, because of oversampling and nonresponse, the weights are informative. Users can print the available weights with the showWeights function

```
> showWeights(ita)

There is 1 full sample weight in this edsurvey.data.
   frame:
   'spfwt0' with 80 JK replicate weights (the default).
```

Similar to other PIAAC Cycle 1 countries, only one full sample weight (spfwt0) is available for Italy data, and the showWeights function displays it along with 80 replicate weights associated with it. Because it is the default and exclusive full sample weight, it is not necessary to specify the weight in EdSurvey analytical functions; spfwt0 will be used by default. In addition, the jackknife replicates associated with spfwt0 will be used by the variance estimation procedures without the user having to further specify anything.

By default, EdSurvey will show results from the analyses after listwise deletion of respondents with any special values, which are referred as 'omitted levels' in EdSurvey. For any data, the omitted levels can be seen with the omittedLevels command

```
> getAttributes(ita, 'omittedLevels')
```

(continued)

```
[1] "(Missing)"                    "DON'T KNOW"
[3] "NOT STATED OR INFERRED"       "VALID SKIP"
[5] "REFUSED"                      "DON'T KNOW/REFUSED"
[7] "NO RESPONSE"                  "NOT REACHED/NOT
                                    ATTEMPTED"
[9] "ALL ZERO RESPONSE"            NA
```

Users wishing to include these levels in their analysis can do so, usually, by recoding them or setting `omittedLevels=TRUE`. More information is available in the help documentation for each respective function.

To see all this information at once, the user can simply 'show' the data by typing the name of the `edsurvey.data.frame` object (i.e. `ita`) in the console

```
> ita
edsurvey.data.frame for Round 1 PIAAC (Numeracy,
Literacy, and Problem Solving) in Italy
Dimensions: 4621 rows and 1328 columns.

There is 1 full sample weight in this edsurvey.data.
frame:
  'spfwt0' with 80 JK replicate weights (the default).

There are 3 subject scale(s) or subscale(s) in this
  edsurvey.data.frame:
'lit' subject scale or subscale with 10 plausible values
 (the default).

'num' subject scale or subscale with 10 plausible values.

'psl' subject scale or subscale with 10 plausible values.


Omitted Levels: '(Missing)','DON'T KNOW','NOT STATED OR
            INFERRED','VALID SKIP','REFUSED','DON'T
            KNOW/REFUSED','NO RESPONSE','NOT REACHED/
            NOT ATTEMPTED','ALL ZERO RESPONSE', and
            'NA'
Achievement Levels:
Numeracy:
Proficiency Level 1: 176.00
Proficiency Level 2: 226.00
```

(continued)

```
Proficiency Level 3: 276.00
Proficiency Level 4: 326.00
Proficiency Level 5: 376.00
Achievement Levels:
Literacy:
Proficiency Level 1: 176.00
Proficiency Level 2: 226.00
Proficiency Level 3: 276.00
Proficiency Level 4: 326.00
Proficiency Level 5: 376.00
Achievement Levels:
Problem Solving:
Proficiency Level 1: 241.00
Proficiency Level 2: 291.00
Proficiency Level 3: 341.00
```

9.4 Exploring PIAAC Data

Once the desired data have been read in, `EdSurvey` provides data exploration functions that users can use in combination with PIAAC codebooks and technical documents in preparation for analysis.

It is worth mentioning that many of the basic functions that work on a `data.frame`, such as `dim`, `nrow`, `ncol`, and `$`, also work on an `edsurvey.data.frame` and can be used for exploration. Editing data is not similar to a `data.frame` and is covered in Sect. 9.5.2.

To view the codebook, the user can use the `showCodebook` function. The output will be long, given the number of columns in the PIAAC data; use the function `View` to display it in spreadsheet format

```
> View(showCodebook(ita))
```

Even with spreadsheet formatting, the codebook can be somewhat daunting to browse. The `searchSDF` function allows the user to search the codebook variable names and labels

```
> searchSDF('income', data=ita)

   variableName
1      d_q18a_t
```

(continued)

```
2  monthlyincpr
3   yearlyincpr
                                                             Labels
1 ANNUAL NET INCOME BEFORE TAXES AND DEDUCTIONS
    (TREND-IALS/ALL)
2                 MONTHLY INCOME PERCENTILE RANK CATEGORY
                     (DERIVED)
3                  YEARLY INCOME PERCENTILE RANK CATEGORY
                     (DERIVED)
```

Notice that the search is not case sensitive and uses regular expressions. The search can be refined by adding additional terms in a vector, using the c function; this refines the search to just those rows where all the strings named are present. This search refines the previous results to a single variable

```
> searchSDF(c('income','annual'), data=ita)

   variableName
1       d_q18a_t
                                                             Labels
1 ANNUAL NET INCOME BEFORE TAXES AND DEDUCTIONS
    (TREND-IALS/ALL)
```

Sometimes knowing the variable name and label is insufficient, and knowing the levels helps. Users can show these levels by setting the levels argument to TRUE

```
> searchSDF(c('income','annual'), data=ita, levels=TRUE)

Variable: d_q18a_t
Label: ANNUAL NET INCOME BEFORE TAXES AND DEDUCTIONS
         (TREND-IALS/ALL)
Levels (Lowest level first):
      0. NO INCOME
      1. LOWEST QUINTILE
      2. NEXT LOWEST QUINTILE
      3. MID-LEVEL QUINTILE
      4. NEXT TO HIGHEST QUINTILE
      5. HIGHEST QUINTILE
      6. VALID SKIP
      7. DON'T KNOW
      8. REFUSED
      9. NOT STATED OR INFERRED
```

9 Using EdSurvey to Analyse PIAAC Data

To get an initial insight into a variable's response frequencies, population estimated response frequencies, and response percentages, use the `summary2` function. The function prints out weighted summary statistics using the default weight variable, which is automatically picked up in `readPIAAC` function. The summary statistics for the variable `'d_q18a_t'` are shown in Table 9.1

```
> summary2(ita, 'd_q18a_t')
```

Note that `EdSurvey` will show variables that OECD includes in the data, some of which will be entirely missing; `summary2` will show this. An example of this is the `d_q18a_t` variable in Canada.

Similarly, `summary2` can show summary statistics for continuous variables. The following example code shows the summary statistics for the set of plausible values for the literature domain (`'lit'`), as shown in Table 9.2

Table 9.1 Results from `summary2(ita, 'd_q18a_t')`

d_q18a_t	N	Weighted N	Weighted percent	Weighted percent SE
(Missing)	2350	21896886.00	55.62	0.82
NO INCOME	43	345319.76	0.88	0.14
LOWEST QUINTILE	418	3428919.30	8.71	0.47
NEXT LOWEST QUINTILE	415	3414626.97	8.67	0.51
MID-LEVEL QUINTILE	423	3457583.24	8.78	0.48
NEXT TO HIGHEST QUINTILE	468	3378711.90	8.58	0.47
HIGHEST QUINTILE	504	3447782.84	8.76	0.39

Note. Estimates are weighted using weight variable `spfwt0`

Table 9.2 Results from `summary2(ita, 'lit')`

d_q18a_t	N	Weighted N	Weighted percent	Weighted percent SE
(Missing)	2350	21896886.00	55.62	0.82
NO INCOME	43	345319.76	0.88	0.14
LOWEST QUINTILE	418	3428919.30	8.71	0.47
NEXT LOWEST QUINTILE	415	3414626.97	8.67	0.51
MID-LEVEL QUINTILE	423	3457583.24	8.78	0.48
NEXT TO HIGHEST QUINTILE	468	3378711.90	8.58	0.47
HIGHEST QUINTILE	504	3447782.84	8.76	0.39

Note. Estimates are weighted using weight variable `spfwt0`

```
> summary2(ita, 'lit')
```

Another powerful exploratory function in the package is edsurveyTable. This function allows users to run weighted cross-tab analyses for any number of categorical variables along with or without an outcome (or continuous) variable.

The following example shows how to create a cross-tab table of employment status (c_d05) by age groups in 10-year intervals (ageg10lfs) on literacy outcome

```
> edsurveyTable(lit ~ ageg10lfs, data = ita)

Formula: lit ~ ageg10lfs

Plausible values: 10
jrrIMax: 1
Weight variable: 'spfwt0'
Variance method: jackknife
JK replicates: 80
full data n: 4621
n used: 4589


Summary Table:
   ageg10lfs    N    WTD_N      PCT   SE(PCT)      MEAN  SE(MEAN)
  24 OR LESS  524  5649536 14.44420 0.1710222  260.8013  2.689490
       25-34  784  7359208 18.81533 0.3123164  260.2447  2.334559
       35-44 1229  9524266 24.35075 0.3821840  252.7739  1.817189
       45-54 1021  8554035 21.87015 0.3640822  248.7787  1.817378
     55 PLUS 1031  8025778 20.51956 0.2523894  233.3650  2.260212
```

Similar to summary2, the edsurveyTable function returns the weighted percentage (PCT) and conditional means (MEAN) of a selected outcome variable—in this case the literacy score.

The results also can be broken down by multiple variables by using a plus (+) between variables. For example, we add c_d05, the current employment status, in the equation.

```
> edsurveyTable(lit ~ ageg10lfs + c_d05, data = ita)
  # output not shown
```

Finally, the correlation function can help users explore associations between variables. The function cor.sdf allows for Pearson (for bivariate normal variables), Spearman (for two continuous variables), polyserial (for one continuous and one discrete variable), and polychoric (for two discrete variables) correlations.[4]

```
> cor.sdf('lit','d_q18a_t',data=ita,method='polyserial')
Method: polyserial
full data n: 4621
n used: 2271

Correlation: 0.1973387

Correlation Levels:
  Levels for Variable 'd_q18a_t' (Lowest level first):
    1. NO INCOME
    2. LOWEST QUINTILE
    3. NEXT LOWEST QUINTILE
    4. MID-LEVEL QUINTILE
    5. NEXT TO HIGHEST QUINTILE
    6. HIGHEST QUINTILE
```

These results show a polyserial correlation between literacy and income quintile as .20 (after rounding), with weight spfwt0 applied by default. Because a correlation analysis assumes that the discrete outcome is ordered, the levels of the discrete variable d_q18a_t are shown to allow users to check that it moves in one direction; here, increasing from 1 to 6.

9.5 Accessing and Manipulating PIAAC Data

Typically, before performing an analysis, users edit data consistent with their research goals. This can happen in one of two ways in the EdSurvey package:

1. Clean and analyse data within the EdSurvey package functions,
2. Use getData to extract a data.frame to clean and edit with any R tool, and then use rebindAttributes to use EdSurvey functions to analyse the data.

This section describes these two ways of preparing data for an analysis for use in the EdSurvey package (see fig. 9.1 for an overview).

---

[4]For more details on the correlations and their computation, see vignette('wCorrFormulas',package='wCorr').

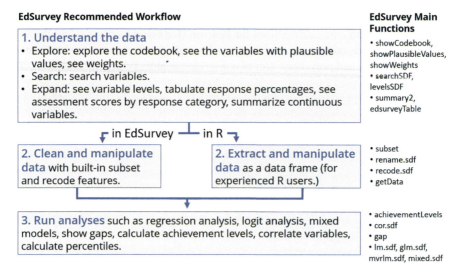

Fig. 9.1 EdSurvey workflow and functions

9.5.1 Cleaning Data in `EdSurvey`

`EdSurvey` provides three data manipulation functions: `subset`, `recode`, and `rename`.

The subset function limits the rows that are used in an analysis to those that meet a condition. For example, to return the summary statistics for the literacy variable, restricting the population of interest to Italian males, one could use `subset`. Note the level label (e.g. the 'MALE' in the following code) needs to be consistent with the label that is in the data, which can be revealed through a call such as `table(ita$gender_r)`.

```
> itaM <- subset(ita, gender_r %in% 'MALE')
> summary2(itaM, 'lit')
Estimates are weighted using weight variable 'spfwt0'
  Variable    N Weighted N    Min.   1st Qu.   Median     Mean
1      lit 2235   19679710 88.20746 219.5522 251.8223 250.3554
    3rd Qu.    Max.         SD   NA's Zero-weights
1 283.9397 399.2344 46.42543    15            0
```

The `recode` function allows us to change the labels or condense on a discrete variable. For example, the user may want to generate conditional means of the employment status variable (c_d05), wherein those individuals who are (a) 'UNEMPLOYED' or (b) 'OUT OF THE LABOUR FORCE' are condensed to one

9 Using EdSurvey to Analyse PIAAC Data

level to compare to the subgroup of individuals employed. This leaves a level ('NOT KNOWN') that is then removed with `subset`.

```
> itaRecode <- recode.sdf(ita, recode=
+                list(c_d05=
+                     list(from=c('OUT OF THE LABOUR FORCE',
+                                 'UNEMPLOYED'),
+                          to=c('NOT EMPLOYED')))) 
> itaRecode <- subset(itaRecode, !c_d05
                %in% c('NOT KNOWN'))
> edsurveyTable(lit ~ c_d05, data=itaRecode)

Formula: lit ~ c_d05

Plausible values: 10
jrrIMax: 1
Weight variable: 'spfwt0'
Variance method: jackknife
JK replicates: 80
full data n: 4621
n used: 4587


Summary Table:
       c_d05    N    WTD_N      PCT    SE(PCT)     MEAN
    EMPLOYED 2869 21957948 56.19657 0.06896769 254.4060
NOT EMPLOYED 1718 17115519 43.80343 0.06896769 245.5068

                                              SE(MEAN)
                                              1.468391
                                              1.521626
```

Finally, `rename` allows the user to adjust a variable's name.

```
> itaRecode <- rename.sdf(itaRecode, oldnames='c_d05',
  newnames='emp')
> edsurveyTable(lit ~ emp, data=itaRecode)

Formula: lit ~ emp

Plausible values: 10
jrrIMax: 1
Weight variable: 'spfwt0'
Variance method: jackknife
JK replicates: 80
```

(continued)

```
full data n: 4621
n used: 4587


Summary Table:
          emp    N     WTD_N      PCT     SE(PCT)      MEAN
     EMPLOYED 2869 21957948 56.19657 0.06896769  254.4060
 NOT EMPLOYED 1718 17115519 43.80343 0.06896769  245.5068

                                                  SE(MEAN)
                                                  1.468391
                                                  1.521626
```

9.5.2 Using `getData`

Users may want to perform extensive recoding of variables but have preferred methods of recoding using specific R packages. The `getData` function allows users to select variables to read into memory, extract, and then edit freely. The `rebindAttributes` function allows the final `data.frame` to be used with EdSurvey analysis functions.

```
> itaRaw <- getData(data=ita,
+                   varnames=c('lit', 'spfwt0',
                               'gender_r', 'c_d05'))
```

In this example, `getData` extracts the following:

- two variables: `gender_r` and `c_d05`
- ten plausible values associated with `lit`
- the weight for this data frame: `spfwt0`

Some important things to note:

1. `addAttributes` is set to the default value of `FALSE`. Setting add Attributes = TRUE is one method in which the resultant data object (`itaRaw`) can be passed to other `EdSurvey` package functions.
2. All the jackknife replicate weights are returned automatically (`spfwt1` to `spfwt80`).
3. `omittedLevels` is set to TRUE, the default, so that variables with special values (such as multiple entries or NAs) are removed by `getData`. This setting removes these values from factors that are not typically included in regression

9 Using EdSurvey to Analyse PIAAC Data

analysis and cross-tabulation. Alternatively, this can be set to FALSE to be manipulated by the user.

The itaRaw data object is a class data.frame, which allows it to be manipulated with any supplementary R function. For instance, the head function shows us a preview of our data, focusing on Columns 1 through 15, revealing the requested variables and the first few rows of the resulting data

```
> head(x = itaRaw[,1:15])
  gender_r                            c_d05    pvlit1   pvlit2   pvlit3
1     MALE                         EMPLOYED  239.8982 258.2188 261.3314
2   FEMALE                         EMPLOYED  261.4386 246.9221 276.6944
3     MALE                         EMPLOYED  310.1177 328.5708 308.8707
4   FEMALE                         EMPLOYED  280.5043 255.7476 261.8692
5     MALE                         EMPLOYED  288.1527 307.2000 298.3016
6   FEMALE OUT OF THE LABOUR FORCE  223.8645 216.0648 243.9239
     pvlit4    pvlit5   pvlit6   pvlit7   pvlit8   pvlit9  pvlit10
1  271.8589  255.7649 243.9113 262.1387 249.3910 276.2055 244.6589
2  258.2071  246.7529 245.5175 257.0885 264.5383 254.7749 252.8056
3  311.5167  296.3410 306.3655 309.7482 308.1918 304.6406 307.8876
4  248.4239  270.5346 279.4498 294.2028 289.6540 259.8313 272.2326
5  338.3870  303.7172 297.3620 300.9883 300.2252 316.3354 328.8312
6  283.3290  167.0126 252.9510 228.5226 280.0687 207.0705 242.5360
       spfwt1      spfwt2    spfwt3
1    2076.916    2151.808  2139.313
2   11421.905   11409.298 11372.425
3   11125.408   11378.000 11020.750
4    2165.858    2177.041  2179.606
5    4415.642    4409.966  4398.984
6    8739.920    8692.451  8708.170
```

To replicate the data manipulation from Sect. 9.5.1, gsub, a base R function that uses pattern matching to replace values in a variable, recodes the values in the variable c_d05. The base function subset then removes the level 'NOT KNOWN'.

```
> itaRaw$c_d05 <- gsub(pattern = 'OUT OF THE LABOUR
                                 FORCE|UNEMPLOYED',
+                      replacement = 'not employed',
+                      x = itaRaw$c_d05)
> itaRaw <- subset(itaRaw, !c_d05 %in% 'NOT KNOWN')
```

The rebindAttributes function allows us to reassign survey attributes so that EdSurvey package functions are accessible. Simply call the manipulated data frame and the edsurvey.data.frame containing the requisite attributes

```
> itaRawRebinded <- rebindAttributes(itaRaw, ita)
```

Now we can apply `EdSurvey` functions, for example,

```
> edsurveyTable(lit ~ c_d05, data=itaRawRebinded)
Formula: lit ~ c_d05

Plausible values: 10
jrrIMax: 1
Weight variable: 'spfwt0'
Variance method: jackknife
JK replicates: 80
full data n: 4621
n used: 4587


Summary Table:
       c_d05    N    WTD_N       PCT    SE(PCT)      MEAN
    EMPLOYED 2869 21957948  56.19657 0.06896769  254.4060
not employed 1718 17115519  43.80343 0.06896769  245.5068

                                                 SE(MEAN)
                                                 1.468391
                                                 1.521626
```

9.6 Data Analysis

9.6.1 Regression

Regression is a well-known and frequently used tool that `EdSurvey` provides in the `lm.sdf` function. Regression equations are typically written as

$$y_i = \alpha + \beta_1 x_{1i} + \beta_2 x_{2i} + \epsilon_i \tag{9.1}$$

where y_i is the outcome for individual i, α is an intercept, x_{ki} is the level of the kth explanatory (exogenous) variable, β_k is the kth regression coefficient, and ϵ_i is the regression residual for individual i.

As an example, the outcome is the literacy score (`lit`), which is described as a function of income quintile (`d_q18a_t`) and age (`age_r`). See results in Table 9.3.

9 Using EdSurvey to Analyse PIAAC Data

Table 9.3 Results from summary(lm1)

	coef	se	t	dof	Pr(> |t|)
(Intercept)	282.65	11.09	25.50	34.86	0.00
d_q18a_tLOWEST QUINTILE	−17.23	10.11	−1.70	20.83	0.10
d_q18a_tNEXT LOWEST QUINTILE	−10.86	10.42	−1.04	28.10	0.31
d_q18a_tMID-LEVEL QUINTILE	1.46	9.79	0.15	24.35	0.88
d_q18a_tNEXT TO HIGHEST QUINTILE	6.16	10.16	0.61	26.19	0.55
d_q18a_tHIGHEST QUINTILE	13.47	9.73	1.38	25.00	0.18
age_r	−0.65	0.13	−5.13	71.39	0.00

```
> lm1 <- lm.sdf(lit ~ d_q18a_t + age_r, data=ita)
> summary(lm1)
```

In R, the formula for this regression equation is written as y ~x1 + x2. Note that there is no need to generate dummy codes for discrete variables like d_q18a_t.

The typical outcome contains a header similar to edsurveyTable, which is not shown for brevity. To explore the unprinted attributes, print summary(lm1) in the console.

EdSurvey calculates the regression coefficients by running one weighted regression per plausible value:

$$\hat{\beta}_k = \frac{1}{P} \sum_{p=1}^{P} \beta_k^{(p)} \qquad (9.2)$$

where there are P plausible values, each indexed with a p, and the superscript (p) indicates the pth plausible value was used.

Variance estimation is complicated because of the presence of the plausible values and because many countries used a multistage, geography-based, sampling technique to form the PIAAC sample. Because of the geographic proximity between respondents, there is a correlation between respondents' scores within a sampled group, relative to two randomly selected individuals. The variance estimator EdSurvey uses accounts for both of these using the variance estimator

$$V = V_I + V_S \qquad (9.3)$$

where V is the total variance of an estimator, V_I is the imputation variance—accounting for the plausible values—and V_S is the sampling variance, accounting for the covariance between geographically clustered individuals. V_I is estimated according to Rubin's rule (Rubin 1987)

$$V_I = \frac{M}{M+1} \sum_{p=1}^{P} \left(\beta_k^{(p)} - \beta_k \right) \tag{9.4}$$

where β_k is averaged across the plausible values (Eq. 9.2). Then the sampling variance frequently uses the jackknife variance estimator and can be estimated with each plausible value as

$$V_S^{(p)} = \sum_{j=1}^{J} \left(\beta_{kj}^{(p)} - \beta_k \right) \tag{9.5}$$

where $\beta_{kj}^{(p)}$ is the estimate of the regressor estimated with the jth replicate weights, with the pth plausible value. In EdSurvey, the jrrIMax argument sets the number of plausible values used; any number is valid, but lower numbers are faster.

$$V_S = \frac{1}{\text{jrrIMax}} \sum_{p=1}^{\text{jrrIMax}} V_S^{(p)} \tag{9.6}$$

As a convenience, EdSurvey sets values larger than the number of plausible values equal to the number of plausible values, so using jrrIMax=Inf uses all plausible values.

The EdSurvey package also can use a Taylor series variance estimator—available by adding the argument varMethod='Taylor' (Binder 1983). More details regarding variance estimation can be found in the EdSurvey Statistics vignette.

Although most of the model details are returned in the regression output, a few additional elements are available to inform interpretation of the results. First, there is a head block that describes the weight used (spfwt0), the variance method (jackknife), the number of jackknife replicates (80), the full data n-size (4,621), and the n-size for this regression (2,271). The latter n-size includes the extent of listwise deletion.

The coefficients block has many typically displayed statistics, including the degrees of freedom (dof) by coefficient. This is calculated using the Welch-Satterthwaite equation (Satterthwaite 1946). For the kth coefficient, the notation of (Wikipedia Contributors 2019), $k_i = 1$ and $s_i = \beta_{kj} - \beta_k$, indicates the difference between the estimated value for the jth jackknife replicate weight and the value estimated with the full sample weights (β_k). Because this statistic varies by coefficient, so do the degrees of freedom. EdSurvey applies the Rust and Johnson modification to the Welch-Satterthwaite equation that multiplies the Welch-Satterthwaite degrees of freedom by a factor of $3.16 - \frac{2.77}{J^{1/2}}$, where J is the number of jackknife replicates (Rust and Johnson 1992).

9.6.2 Binomial Regression

When a regression's dependent variable (outcome) is binary—consisting of 1s and 0s or true and false—the regression is a binomial regression. EdSurvey allows for two such regressions: logistic regression and probit regression. The corresponding functions for these methods are `logit.sdf` and `probit.sdf`. This section focuses on `logit.sdf`, but most components also apply to `probit.sdf`.

An example of a binomial regression is to look at the outcome of income percentile being in the mid-quintile or higher as described by mother's education (`j_q06b`) and own age (`age_r`). The user may first wish to inspect `j_q06b` (results in Table 9.4).[5]

```
> summary2(ita,'j_q06b')
```

When a regression is run, EdSurvey will exclude the values other than 'ISCED 1, 2, AND 3C SHORT', 'ISCED 3 (EXCLUDING 3C SHORT) AND 4', and 'ISCED 5 AND 6'; the first of these levels will be the omitted group and treated as the reference.

For binomial regression, we recommend explicitly dichotomising the dependent variable in the `logit.sdf` call so that the desired level has the 'high state' associated with positive regressors—this is done with the `I(·)` function. Here, the function makes the dependent variable a 1 when the condition is TRUE and a 0 when the condition is FALSE; the results are shown in Table 9.5.

Table 9.4 Results from `summary2(ita,'j_q06b')`

j_q06b	N	Weighted N	Weighted percent	Weighted percent SE
(Missing)	2	16688.34	0.04	0.04
ISCED 1, 2, AND 3C SHORT	3639	31437133.66	79.85	0.66
ISCED 3 (EXCL 3C SHORT) AND 4	758	6057515.46	15.39	0.57
ISCED 5 AND 6	176	1471224.40	3.74	0.32
DON'T KNOW	10	107909.31	0.27	0.09
REFUSED	3	24560.83	0.06	0.03
NOT STATED OR INFERRED	33	254798.01	0.65	0.16

---

[5] In the tables the level 'ISCED 3 (EXCLUDING 3C SHORT) AND 4' is sometimes shortened to 'ISCED 3 (EXCL 3C SHORT) AND 4'.

Table 9.5 Results from summary(logit1)

	coef	se	t	dof	Pr(> |t|)
(Intercept)	−1.25	0.24	−5.20	73.08	0.00
j_q06bISCED 3 (EXCL 3C SHORT) AND 4	0.62	0.14	4.59	77.55	0.00
j_q06bISCED 5 AND 6	0.07	0.25	0.28	67.79	0.78
age_r	0.04	0.01	6.87	87.51	0.00

Table 9.6 Results from oddsRatio(logit1)

	OR	2.5%	97.5%
(Intercept)	0.29	0.15	0.42
j_q06bISCED 3 (EXCLUDING 3C SHORT) AND 4	1.86	1.37	2.35
j_q06bISCED 5 AND 6	1.07	0.54	1.60
age_r	1.04	1.03	1.05

```
> logit1 <- logit.sdf(I(d_q18a_t %in% c
                    ('MID-LEVEL QUINTILE',
+                    'NEXT TO HIGHEST QUINTILE',
+                    'HIGHEST QUINTILE')) ~
+                    j_q06b + age_r, data=ita)
> summary(logit1)
```

This regression shows that there is a larger contrast between individuals with mother's highest education in 'ISCED 3 (EXCLUDING 3C SHORT) AND 4' and the reference group ('ISCED 1, 2, AND 3C SHORT') at 0.62 than there is between 'ISCED 5 and 6') and the reference group at 0.07, with the former coefficient being statistically significant and the latter not. Some researchers appreciate the odds ratios when interpreting regression results. The oddsRatio function can show these, along with their confidence intervals. The results are shown in Table 9.6.

```
> oddsRatio(logit1)
```

The oddsRatio function works only for results from the logit.sdf function—not probit.sdf results—because only logistic regression has invariant odds ratios.

Although the t-test statistic in logistic regression output is a good test for an individual regressor (such as age_r), a Wald test is needed to conduct joint hypothesis testing. Typically, it is possible to use the Akaike information criterion (AIC) (Akaike 1974) or a likelihood-ratio test. However, the likelihood shown in the results is actually a pseudo-likelihood, or a population estimate likelihood for the model. Because the entire population was not sampled, deviance-based tests—such as those shown in McCullagh and Nelder (1989)—cannot be used. Although it would be possible to use Lumley and Scott (2015) to form an AIC comparison, that does not account for plausible values.[6]

For example, it would be reasonable to ask if the j_j06b variable is jointly significant. To test this, we can use a Wald test

```
> waldTest(model=logit1, coef='j_q06b')

Wald test:
----------
H0:
j_q06bISCED 3 (EXCLUDING 3C SHORT) AND 4 = 0
j_q06bISCED 5 AND 6 = 0

Chi-square test:
X2 = 21.1, df = 2, P(> X2) = 2.6e-05

F test:
W = 10.4, df1 = 2, df2 = 79, P(> W) = 9.6e-05
```

This is a test of both coefficients in j_q06b being zero. Two test results are shown: the chi-square test and the F-test. In the case of a well-known sample design, it probably makes more sense to use the F-test (Korn and Graubard 1990).

9.6.3 Gap Analysis

A gap analysis compares the levels of two groups and tests if they are different. The gap function supports testing gaps in mean scores, survey responses, score percentiles, and achievement levels. In this section, we discuss gaps in mean scores.

The simplest gap is within a single survey on a score and requires a selection of two groups. In the following example, we compare literacy scores of the self-employed and those who are employees

---

[6]The use of plausible values is allowed by logit.sdf and probit.sdf. An example of an outcome with plausible values would be a comparison of literature scores above the user-specified cutoff.

```
> gap(variable='lit', data=ita, groupA= d_q04 %in%
                                        'SELF-EMPLOYED',
+                               groupB= d_q04
                                        %in% 'EMPLOYEE')
Call: gap(variable = "lit", data = ita, groupA = d_q04
                                        %in% "SELF-EMPLOYED",
    groupB = d_q04 %in% "EMPLOYEE")
Labels:
 group                  definition nFullData nUsed
     A d_q04 %in% "SELF-EMPLOYED"      4621   637
     B      d_q04 %in% "EMPLOYEE"      4621  2165

Percentage:
     pctA      pctAse     pctB     pctBse     diffAB
 23.05259  0.8760763  76.94741  0.8760763  -53.89482

                                        covAB  diffABse
                                   -0.7675097  1.752153

 diffABpValue     dofAB
            0  87.26671

Results:
   estimateA estimateAse estimateB estimateBse     diffAB
    256.6286    2.483797  253.5839    1.567581   3.044695
                                                    covAB
                                                0.9716681

 diffABse diffABpValue    dofAB
 2.585192     0.243015 67.82052
```

The gap output contains three blocks: labels, percentage, and results.

In the first block, 'labels', the definition of the groups A and B is shown, along with a reminder of the full data *n* count (nFullData) and the *n* count of the number of individuals who are in the two subgroups with valid scores (nUsed).

The second block, 'percentage', shows the percentage of individuals who fall into each category, with omitted levels removed. In the preceding example, the estimated percentage of Italians who are self-employed (in Group A) is shown in the pctA column, and the percentage of employees (in Group B) is shown in the pctB column. In this case, the only nonomitted levels are 'SELF-EMPLOYED' and 'EMPLOYEE', so they add up to 100%. The other columns listed in the 'percentage' block regard uncertainty in those percentages and tests determining whether the two percentages are equal.

The third block, 'results', shows the estimated average literacy score for Italians who are self-employed (Group A) in column `estimateA` and the estimated average literacy score of Italians who are employees in column `estimateB`. The `diffAB` column shows that the estimated difference between these two statistics is 3.04 literacy scale score points, whereas the `diffABse` column shows that the estimate has a standard error of 2.59 scale score points. A *t*-test for the difference being zero has a *p*-value of 0.24 is shown in column `difABpValue`.

Some software does not calculate a covariance between groups when the groups consist of distinct individuals. When survey collection was administered in such a way that respondents have more in common than randomly selected individuals—as in the Italian PIAAC sample—this is not consistent with the survey design. When there is no covariance between two units in the same variance estimation strata—as in the case of countries that use one-stage sampling—there is little harm in estimating the covariance, because it will be close to zero.

The gap output information listed is not exhaustive; similar to other `EdSurvey` functions, the user can see the list of output variables using the ? function and typing the function of interest.

```
> ?gap # output not shown
```

The 'Value' section describes all columns contained in gap outputs.

Another type of gap compares results across samples. For example, the male/female gap in literacy scores can be compared between Italy and the Netherlands by forming an `edsurvey.data.frame.list` and running `gap` with that combined data.

```
> # form the edsurvey.data.frame.list
> ita_nld <- edsurvey.data.frame.list(datalist=list(ita, nld))
> # run the gap
> gap(variable='lit', data=ita_nld, groupA= gender_r %in% 'MALE',
+                                   groupB= gender_r %in% 'FEMALE')
gapList
Call: gap(variable = "lit", data = ita_nld, groupA = gender_r %in%
    "MALE", groupB = gender_r %in% "FEMALE")

Labels:
 group          definition
     A   gender_r %in% "MALE"
     B   gender_r %in% "FEMALE"

Percentage:
       country      pctA      pctAse      pctB      pctBse         diffAB
         Italy  50.00314  0.05349453  49.99686  0.05349453   0.006289097
   Netherlands  50.20262  0.12935306  49.79738  0.12935306   0.405249502
```

(continued)

```
              covAB   diffABse diffABpValue      dofAB      diffAA      covAA
     -0.002861664  0.1069891    0.9536079   24.20301          NA         NA
     -0.016732214  0.2587061    0.1225427   59.55281  -0.1994802          0
        diffAAse diffAApValue       dofAA      diffBB      covBB    diffBBse
              NA           NA          NA          NA         NA          NA
       0.1399781    0.1582179   76.18208   0.1994802          0   0.1399781
    diffBBpValue        dofBB     diffABAB   covABAB  diffABABse diffABABpValue
              NA           NA          NA          NA         NA          NA
       0.1582179     76.18208  -0.3989604           0   0.2799563      0.1582179
         dofABAB
              NA
        76.18208

Results:
       country  estimateA estimateAse  estimateB estimateBse       diffAB
         Italy   250.3554    1.488650   250.6100    1.325433    -0.254644
   Netherlands   287.0560    1.066479   280.9205    1.023297     6.135510
           covAB   diffABse diffABpValue      dofAB     diffAA     covAA    diffAAse
      0.44350144  1.756658  0.8851353824   74.31867         NA        NA          NA
     -0.06822208  1.523469  0.0001594966   60.61344  -36.70064         0    1.831244
    diffAApValue      dofAA       diffBB      covBB   diffBBse diffBBpValue     dofBB
              NA         NA           NA         NA         NA           NA        NA
               0   161.3324   -30.31049           0   1.674488            0  127.6201
        diffABAB   covABAB   diffABABse  diffABABpValue   dofABAB   sameSurvey
              NA        NA           NA              NA        NA           NA
       -6.390154         0     2.325254    0.006814802  134.7154        FALSE
```

This output contains the same three blocks and columns as in the previous gap analysis. Several additional columns have been added, focusing on the contrasts between Italy and the Netherlands. The results block columns labelled with an AA, such as diffAA, compare Italian males to Dutch males. The columns labelled with a BB, such as diffBB, compare Italian females to Dutch females. Here the diffAA column has a value of −36.7, indicating that Italian males have an average scale score 36.7 points less than Dutch males. The column diffAAse has a value of 1.83, indicating that the standard error of that difference is 1.83. The two samples were collected separately, so there is no covariance in these estimates, and the covAA column is zero.

It also is possible to compare the male/female gap in literacy scores within and across countries. Looking at the diffAB column, the gap is −0.25 in Italy and 6.13 in the Netherlands, indicating that females outscore males in Italy, but males outscore females in the Netherlands. The diffABAB column shows that the difference in the gaps is −6.39, with a standard error (taken from diffABABse) of 2.32, and an associated p-value of 0.007, taken from diffABABpValue.

Table 9.7 Results from percentile(variable = 'lit', percentiles = c(10, 25, 50, 75, 90), data = ita)

Percentile	Estimate	se	df	confInt.ci_lower	confInt.ci_upper
10.00	192.37	2.28	22.30	187.22	196.75
25.00	221.86	1.46	11.08	217.99	225.34
50.00	252.44	1.32	16.07	249.82	255.25
75.00	282.17	1.17	14.62	279.63	284.77
90.00	306.16	1.22	22.55	303.28	309.42

9.6.4 Percentile Analysis

Discussions presented so far have focused on the mean and other measures of centrality. This section describes the percentile function, which calculates statistics regarding the distribution of continuous variables—namely, the percentiles of a numeric variable in the range 0 to 100 for a survey dataset. For example, to compare the PIAAC index of reading skills at home ('lit') at the 10th, 25th, 50th, 75th, and 90th percentile, include these as integers in the percentiles argument; the results are shown in Table 9.7.

```
> percentile(variable = 'lit',
+            percentiles = c(10, 25, 50, 75, 90),
+            data = ita)
```

If researchers are interested in a comparison of percentile distributions between males and females, the subset function can be used together with the percentile function. Alternatively, EdSurvey's gap function, covered in Sect. 9.6.3, can calculate distributions in percentiles. The results of the percentile by gender are shown in Table 9.8.

```
> percentile(variable = 'lit',
+            percentiles = c(25, 50, 75),
+            data = subset(ita, gender_r %in% 'MALE'))
> percentile(variable = 'lit',
+            percentiles = c(25, 50, 75),
+            data = subset(ita, gender_r %in% 'FEMALE'))
```

Table 9.8 Results from `percentile` by `gender_r`

gender_r	Percentile	Estimate	se	df	confInt.ci_lower	confInt.ci_upper
MALE	25.00	219.55	2.94	10.90	214.76	224.24
MALE	50.00	251.82	1.85	17.52	247.98	256.11
MALE	75.00	283.94	2.08	18.42	279.94	287.91
FEMALE	25.00	223.70	2.16	22.93	219.49	227.81
FEMALE	50.00	252.90	0.97	15.79	249.85	256.02
FEMALE	75.00	280.59	1.33	12.13	277.46	284.04

9.6.5 Proficiency Level Analysis

Scale score averages and distributions have the advantage of being numeric expressions of respondent ability; they also have the disadvantage of being essentially impossible to interpret or compare to an external benchmark. Proficiency levels, developed by experts to compare scores with performance criteria, provide an external benchmark against which scale scores can be compared (PIAAC Numeracy Expert Group 2009).

In EdSurvey, users can see the proficiency level cutpoints with the showCutPoints function:

```
> showCutPoints(ita)
Achievement Levels:
  Numeracy:   176, 226, 276, 326, 376
  Literacy:   176, 226, 276, 326, 376
  Problem Solving:   241, 291, 341
```

The achievementLevels function applies appropriate weights and the variance estimation method for each edsurvey.data.frame, with several arguments for customising the aggregation and output of the analysis results.[7] Namely, by using these optional arguments, users can

– choose to generate the percentage of individuals performing at each proficiency level (**discrete**) or at or above each proficiency level (**cumulative**),

---

[7]The terms *proficiency levels*, *benchmarks*, or *achievement levels* are all operationalised in the same way: individuals above a cutpoint are regarded as having met that level of proficiency or benchmark or have that achievement. EdSurvey calls all these *achievement levels* in the function names, cutpoints, and documentation. But the difference is entirely semantic and so can be ignored.

Table 9.9 Results from achievementLevels(c('lit', 'gender_r'), data=ita, aggregateBy = 'gender_r', returnDiscrete = FALSE, returnCumulative = TRUE)

Level	gender_r	N	wtdN	Percent	StandardError
Below PL 1	MALE	107.00	1178474.99	6.03	0.86
At or Above PL 1	MALE	2113.00	18379167.00	93.97	0.86
At or Above PL 2	MALE	1651.80	13848243.51	70.81	1.51
At or Above PL 3	MALE	756.00	6060156.78	30.99	1.50
At or Above PL 4	MALE	101.40	796244.02	4.07	0.55
At PL 5	MALE	2.70	14647.88	0.07	0.08
Below PL 1	FEMALE	111.90	995395.47	5.09	0.74
At or Above PL 1	FEMALE	2257.10	18559786.68	94.91	0.74
At or Above PL 2	FEMALE	1794.10	14366053.72	73.46	1.39
At or Above PL 3	FEMALE	761.40	5622973.69	28.75	1.39
At or Above PL 4	FEMALE	76.70	510122.91	2.61	0.45
At PL 5	FEMALE	1.50	7064.90	0.04	0.05

- calculate the percentage distribution of individuals by proficiency level (discrete or cumulative) and selected characteristics (specified in aggregateBy), and
- compute the percentage distribution of individuals by selected characteristics within a specific proficiency level.

The achievementLevels function also can produce statistics by both discrete and cumulative proficiency levels. By default, the achievementLevels function produces the results only for discrete proficiency levels. Setting the returnCumulative argument to TRUE generates results by both discrete and cumulative proficiency levels.

The achievementLevels function can calculate the overall cumulative proficiency level analysis of the literacy. These results are shown in Table 9.9, where the term 'Performance Level' has been replaced by 'PL' for brevity.

```
> achievementLevels(c('lit', 'gender_r'),
+                   data=ita,
+                   aggregateBy='gender_r',
+                   returnDiscrete=FALSE,
+                   returnCumulative=TRUE)
```

This call requests that the Italian literacy proficiency levels can be broken down by the gender_r variable—the aggregateBy argument is set to 'gender_r' and therefore the Percent column sums to 100 within each gender. The results show that 31% of Italian males are at or above Proficiency Level 3, whereas 28.8%

of Italian females are at or above Proficiency Level 3. Note that proficiency levels are useful only if considered in the context of the descriptor, which is available from NCES at https://nces.ed.gov/surveys/piaac/litproficiencylevel.asp.

The advantage of cumulative proficiency levels is that increases are always unambiguously good. Conversely, discrete proficiency levels can change because individuals moved between levels, making their interpretation ambiguous, although increases in the highest and lowest proficiency levels are always unambiguously good (highest) or bad (lowest).

9.7 Expansion

The `EdSurvey` package continues to be developed, and new features are added in each subsequent release. To learn about current features, visit the EdSurvey webpage to see the latest version and most recent documentation.[8] The webpage also has many user guides and a complete explanation of the methodology involved in `EdSurvey`.

References

Akaike, H. (1974). A new look at the statistical model identification. *IEEE Transactions on Automatic Control, 19*(6), 716–723.

Binder, D. A. (1983). On the variances of asymptotically normal estimators from complex surveys. *International Statistical Review, 51*(3), 279–292, doi:10.2307/1402588.

Korn, E. L., & Graubard, B. I. (1990). Simultaneous testing of regression coefficients with complex survey data: Use of Bonferroni t statistics. *The American Statistician, 44*(4):270–276, doi:10.1080/00031305.1990.10475737.

Lumley, T., & Scott, A. (2015). AIC and BIC for modeling with complex survey data. *Journal of Survey Statistics and Methodology, 3*(1), 1–18, doi:10.1093/jssam/smu021.

McCullagh, P., & Nelder, J. (1989). *Generalized linear models* (Chapman and Hall/CRC Monographs on statistics and applied probability series, 2nd ed.) Boca Raton: Chapman & Hall.

Mohadjer, L., Krenzke, T., Van de Kerckhove, W., & Li, L. (2016). Sampling design. In I. Kirsch, & W. Thorn (Eds.), *Survey of adult skills technical report* (2nd ed., chapter 14, pp. 14-1–14-36). Paris: OECD.

PIAAC Numeracy Expert Group. (2009). *PIAAC numeracy: A conceptual framework*. Technical Report 35. Paris: OECD Publishing.

R Core Team. (2019). *R: A language and environment for statistical computing*. Vienna: R Foundation for Statistical Computing.

Rubin, D. B. (1987). *Multiple imputation for nonresponse in surveys*. Hoboken: Wiley.

Rust, K., & Johnson, E. (1992). Sampling and weighting in the national assessment. *Journal of Educational and Behavioral Statistics, 17*(2), 111–129, doi:10.3102/10769986017002111.

---

[8] https://www.air.org/project/nces-data-r-project-edsurvey

Satterthwaite, F. E. (1946). An approximate distribution of estimates of variance components. *Biometrics Bulletin, 2*(6), 110–114.
Wikipedia Contributors. (2019). *Welch-Satterthwaite equation—Wikipedia, the free encyclopedia.* [Online; Accessed 24 Feb 2019]

Open Access This chapter is licensed under the terms of the Creative Commons Attribution 4.0 International License (http://creativecommons.org/licenses/by/4.0/), which permits use, sharing, adaptation, distribution and reproduction in any medium or format, as long as you give appropriate credit to the original author(s) and the source, provide a link to the Creative Commons license and indicate if changes were made.

The images or other third party material in this chapter are included in the chapter's Creative Commons license, unless indicated otherwise in a credit line to the material. If material is not included in the chapter's Creative Commons license and your intended use is not permitted by statutory regulation or exceeds the permitted use, you will need to obtain permission directly from the copyright holder.

Chapter 10
Analysing Log File Data from PIAAC

Frank Goldhammer, Carolin Hahnel, and Ulf Kroehne

Abstract The OECD Programme for the International Assessment of Adult Competencies (PIAAC) was the first computer-based large-scale assessment to provide anonymised log file data from the cognitive assessment together with extensive online documentation and a data analysis support tool. The goal of the chapter is to familiarise researchers with how to access, understand, and analyse PIAAC log file data for their research purposes. After providing some conceptual background on the multiple uses of log file data and how to infer states of information processing from log file data, previous research using PIAAC log file data is reviewed. Then, the accessibility, structure, and documentation of the PIAAC log file data are described in detail, as well as how to use the PIAAC LogDataAnalyzer to extract predefined process indicators and how to create new process indicators based on the raw log data export.

The Programme for the International Assessment of Adult Competencies (PIAAC) is an Organisation for Economic Co-operation and Development (OECD) study that assesses and analyses adult skills in the cognitive domains of literacy, numeracy, and problem solving in technology-rich environments (PS-TRE). The computer-based assessment requires respondents to solve a series of tasks (items). The tasks are related to information presented to the respondent on the screen (e.g. a text from a newspaper, a simulated webpage). When solving a task, the respondent interacts with the assessment system—for example, by entering or highlighting text or clicking graphical elements, buttons, or links. The assessment system logs all these interactions and stores related events (e.g. keypress) and time stamps in log files.

F. Goldhammer (✉) · C. Hahnel · U. Kroehne
DIPF | Leibniz Institute for Research and Information in Education, Centre for International Student Assessment [ZIB], Frankfurt, Germany
e-mail: goldhammer@dipf.de

For the cognitive assessment in Round 1 of PIAAC (2011–2012), the OECD has provided both the log data and a supporting infrastructure (i.e. the extraction tool PIAAC LogDataAnalyzer and online documentations) to make the log data accessible and interpretable (OECD 2019). Overall, 17 of the participating countries (i.e. Austria, Belgium [Flanders], Denmark, Estonia, Finland, France, Germany, Ireland, Italy, Korea, the Netherlands, Norway, Poland, Slovak Republic, Spain, the United Kingdom [England and Northern Ireland], and the United States) agreed to share their log data with the research community. Log file data are available from the computer-based assessment of all three PIAAC cognitive domains—literacy, numeracy, and PS-TRE—but not for the background questionnaire. The log file data extend the PIAAC Public Use File, which mainly includes the result data (i.e. scored item responses) of the individual respondents from the cognitive assessment and the background questionnaire.

The goal of this chapter is to familiarise researchers with how to access, understand, and analyse PIAAC log file data for their research purposes. Therefore, it deals with the following conceptual and practice-oriented topics: In the first part, we will provide some conceptual background on the multiple uses of log file data and how to infer states of information processing by means of log file data. The second part reviews existing research using PIAAC log file data and process indicators included in the PIAAC Public Use File. The third part presents the PIAAC log file data by describing their accessibility, structure, and documentation. The final part addresses the preprocessing, extraction, and analysis of PIAAC log file data using the PIAAC LogDataAnalyzer.

10.1 Log File Data Analysis

10.1.1 Conceptual Remarks: What Can Log File Data from Technology-Based Assessments Be Used For?

The reasons for using log file data in educational assessment can be diverse and driven by substantive research questions and technical measurement issues. To classify the potential uses of log file data from technology-based assessments, we use models of the evidence-centred design (ECD) framework (Mislevy et al. 2003). The original ECD terminology refers to the assessment of students, but the approach is equally applicable to assessments of the general adult population (such as PIAAC). The ECD framework is a flexible approach for designing, producing, and delivering educational assessments in which the assessment cycle is divided into models. The ECD models of interest are (a) the student model, (b) the evidence model, (c) the task model, and (d) the assembly model. Applying the principles of ECD means specifying first what construct should be measured and what claims about the respondent are to be made based on the test score (student model). Then, the type of evidence needed to infer the targeted construct and the way it can be synthesised to a test score across multiple items is explicated (evidence model). Based on that, the items are designed in such a way that they can elicit the empirical evidence needed to measure the construct (task model). Finally, the items are assembled to obtain a measurement that is reliable and that validly represents the construct (assembly model). Although the ECD framework was originally developed for assessments focusing on result or product data (i.e. item scores derived from the respondent's work product), it is suitable for identifying the potential uses of log file data in the fields of educational and psychological assessment, as shown in the following.

The *student model,* (a), addresses the question of what latent constructs we want to measure (knowledge, skills, and attributes) in order to answer, for example, a substantive research question. Thus, one reason to use log file data is to measure constructs representing attributes of the work process—that is, individual differences in how respondents approached or completed the tasks—for instance (domain-specific) speed (Goldhammer and Klein Entink 2011; van der Linden 2007), the propensity to use a certain solution strategy (Greiff et al. 2016), or the use of planning when solving a complex problem (Eichmann et al. 2019).

The *evidence model,* (b), deals with the question of how to estimate the variables defined in the student model (constructs) given the observed performance of the respondent. For this purpose, two components are needed: the evidence rules and the measurement model. The *evidence rules* are used to identify observable evidence for the targeted construct. In this sense, log file data and process indicators calculated from it (see Sect. 10.1.2) provide evidence for assessing the process-related constructs mentioned above. For instance, the public use file of Round 1 of PIAAC (2011–2012) includes process indicators, such as the total time spent on an item, which can be used as an indicator of speed or for deriving indicators of test-taking engagement (Goldhammer et al. 2016). Log file data may also play an important role when identifying evidence for product-related constructs (e.g. ability, competence) measured by traditional product indicators. Here, log file data are a suitable complement to evidence rules in multiple ways. They can be used to obtain a more fine-grained (partial credit) scoring of the work product, depending on whether interactions contributing to the correct outcome were carried out or not (e.g. problem solving in PISA 2012; OECD 2013a), to inform the coding of missing responses (e.g. responses in PIAAC without any interaction and a time on task less than 5 s were coded as 'Not reached/not attempted'; OECD 2013b), and to detect suspicious cases showing aberrant response behaviour (van der Linden and Guo 2008) or data fabrication (Yamamoto and Lennon 2018).

As a second component, the evidence model includes a *statistical (measurement) model* for synthesising evidence across items. Here, multiple process indicators can identify a latent variable representing a process-related construct (e.g. planning, speed, test-taking engagement) and may complement product indicators to improve the construct representation. A more technical reason to identify a process-related construct is to make the estimation of the product-related (ability) construct more precise, which requires joint modelling of both constructs (e.g. two-dimensional ability–speed measurement models; Bolsinova and Tijmstra 2018; Klein Entink et al. 2009). Related to that, timing data can be helpful to model the missing data mechanism (Pohl et al. 2019) and to investigate the comparability between modes (Kroehne et al. 2019). Another interesting application of process indicators within measurement models for ability constructs is to select the item response model that is appropriate for a particular observation, depending on the type of response behaviour (solution behaviour vs. rapid guessing; Wise and DeMars 2006).

The *task model,* (c), is about designing tasks and/or situations (i.e. item stimuli) in a way that the evidence required to infer the targeted student model variable is elicited. Regarding process indicators based on log file data, this means that item stimuli must provide adequate opportunities for interaction with the task environment (Goldhammer and Zehner 2017). In PIAAC, this issue is briefly discussed in the conceptual assessment framework for PS-TRE (PIAAC Expert Group in Problem Solving in Technology-Rich Environments 2009), where tasks require the respondent to operate and interact with (multiple) simulated software applications.

The *assembly model,* (d), refers to the combination of items on a test, determining how accurate the targeted construct is measured and how well the assessment represents the breadth of the construct. In adaptive testing, timing information can be used to improve item selection and thereby obtain a more efficient measurement (van der Linden 2008). Moreover, timing data can be used to optimise test design— in particular, to control the speededness of different test forms in adaptive testing (van der Linden 2005). In this elaborated sense, PIAAC (2011–2012) did not use timing information for its adaptive two-stage testing; however, timing information was used to assemble the cognitive assessment in order to obtain an expected overall test length of about 1 h for most of the respondents. An assessment may be adaptive or responsive not only in terms of item selection but also in a more general sense. Log file data may be used for triggering interventions if the response behaviour is not in line with the instruction—for example, if test-takers omit responses or switch to disengaged responding. This information can be fed back to the individual test-taker via prompts (Buerger et al. 2019), so that he or she can adapt, or to the proctor via a dashboard, so that he or she can intervene if needed (Wise et al. 2019).

10.1.2 *Methodological Remarks: How to Identify States of Information Processing by Log File Data?*

Log file data represent a type of paradata—that is, additional information about assessments generated as a by-product of computer-assisted data collection methods (Couper 1998). Extracting *process indicators* from log file data has not yet attracted much attention from a methodological perspective. The challenge becomes evident when one examines attempts to provide an overview of the heterogeneous types of paradata. The taxonomy of paradata provided by Kroehne and Goldhammer (2018), for example, shows that only a limited set of paradata can be directly linked to the substantive data of the assessment (i.e. answers to questionnaire or test items). Only the response-related paradata—that is, all answer-change log events (e.g. selection of a radio button in a multiple choice item)—are directly related to the final response. However, the relationship of paradata to substantive data is of utmost interest when it comes to describing the test-taking process and explaining performance. Therefore, additional steps to process the information stored in log file data are necessary in order to extract meaningful *process indicators* that are related either at the surface (behavioural) level to the test-taking process or, preferably, to underlying cognitive processes (see Sect. 10.1.1).

Conceptually, the goal of creating process indicators can be described as the integration of three different sources of information: characteristics of the (evidence-centred) task design (see Sect. 10.1.1), expected (and observed) test-taking behaviour given the task design, and available log events specific to the concrete assessment system that may be suitable for inferring or reconstructing the test-taking behaviour. In combination with these sources, the process indicators are created to represent targeted attributes of the work process and to inform about the interaction between the test-taker and the task within an assessment platform (testing situation). At least two approaches can be conceptualised as to how process indicators can be defined: A first approach is to extract the indicators directly from the three aforementioned sources and to define them operationally with the concrete implementation in a particular programming language, such as Java, R, or SPSS syntax. A second more formal and generic approach can be distinguished, in which the algorithmic extraction of the indicators is first described and defined abstractly with respect to so-called states (Kroehne and Goldhammer 2018) before the actual process indicators are computed. In this framework, states are conceptualised as sections of the interaction between respondent and task within the assessment platform. How sections and states, respectively, are defined depends on the theory or model that is used to describe the test-taking and task solution process (e.g. a typical state would be 'reading the task instruction'). Indicators can be derived from properties of the reconstructed sequence of states (e.g. the total time spent on reading the task instruction). Reconstructing the sequence of states for a given test-taker from the log file data of a particular task requires that all transitions between states be identified with log events captured by the platform (e.g. by presenting the task instruction and the stimulus on different pages). Thus, the more formal approach to defining the extraction of process indicators from log file data provides the possibility of describing the relationship of the test-taking process to hypothesised cognitive processes (and their potential relationship to succeeding or failing in a task as represented by the substantive data). For that purpose, the theory-based mapping of states, transition between states, or sequences of state visits to cognitive processes is required.

However, the formal approach is not only relevant in the design phase of an assessment for planning, interpreting, and validating process indicators. It can also be used operationally to formally represent a given stream of events in a log file from the beginning to the end of a task. For that purpose, the log events are provided as input to one or multiple so-called finite state machines (Kroehne and

Goldhammer 2018) that process the events and change their state according to the machine's definition of states and state transitions triggered by certain events. This results in a reconstructed sequence of states for each test-taker who interacted with a particular task. Using properties of this reconstructed sequence of states allows for the extraction of process indicators, such as those programmed in the PIAAC LogDataAnalyzer (see Sect. 10.4.1, Table 10.2).

Given the available log file data, alternative states might be defined, depending on the specific research questions. The only requirement is the availability of log events that can be used to identify the transitions between states. If the log file data contain events that can be used to reconstruct the sequence of states for a particular decomposition of the test-taking process into states, indicators can be derived from properties of this reconstructed sequence.

The formal approach also allows the completeness of log file data to be judged. The general question of whether *all* log events are gathered in a specific assessment (e.g. PIAAC) is difficult or impossible to answer without considering the targeted process indicators. In this sense, log file completeness can be judged with respect to a known set of finite state machines representing all states and transitions of interest (e.g. to address a certain research question). If all transitions between states as defined by the finite state machine can be identified using information from the log file, the log file data are complete with respect to the finite state machines (described as *state completeness* in Kroehne and Goldhammer 2018).

10.2 Review of Research Work Using PIAAC Log File Data

With appropriate treatment, the PIAAC log file data (OECD 2017a, b, c, d, e, f, g, h, j, k, l, m, n, o, p, q, r) allow for the creation of a large number of informative indicators. Three generic process indicators derived from log file data are already included in the PIAAC Public Use File at the level of items—namely, total time on task, time to first action, and the number of interactions. This section provides a brief overview of the various research directions in which PIAAC log file data have been used so far. These studies include research on all three PIAAC domains, selected domains, and even specific items. They refer both to the data collected in the PIAAC main study and to the data collected in the field test, which was used to assemble the final instruments and to refine the operating procedures of the PIAAC main study (Kirsch et al. 2016). So far, PIAAC log files have been used to provide insights into the valid interpretation of test scores (e.g. Engelhardt and Goldhammer 2019; Goldhammer et al. 2014), test-taking engagement (e.g. Goldhammer et al. 2017a), dealing with missing responses (Weeks et al. 2016), and suspected data fabrication (Yamamoto and Lennon 2018). Other studies have concentrated on the highly interactive tasks in the domain of PS-TRE (He et al. 2019; He and von Davier 2015, 2016; Liao et al. 2019; Naumann et al. 2014; Stelter et al. 2015; Tóth et al. 2017; Vörös and Rouet 2016) and contributed to a better understanding of the adult competencies in operation.

The studies reviewed (Table 10.1) demonstrate how PIAAC log file data can contribute to describing the competencies of adults and the quality of test-taking, but as Maddox et al. (2018; see also Goldhammer and Zehner 2017) objected to the capturing of log events, inferences about cognitive processes are limited, and process indicators must be interpreted carefully.

10.2.1 Studies of Time Components Across Competence Domains

Processing times reflect the duration of cognitive processing when performing a task. Provided that information about the time allocation of individuals is available, several time-based indicators can be defined, such as the time until respondents first interact with a task or the time between the respondents' last action and their final response submission (OECD 2019). Previous research has often focused on 'time on task'—that is, the overall time that a respondent spent on the item. For example, analysis of the PIAAC log file data showed considerable variation of time on tasks in literacy and numeracy across countries, age groups, and levels of education, but comparatively less variability between the competence domains and gender (OECD 2019).

The (average) effect of time on task on a respondent's probability of task success is often referred to as 'time on task effect'. Using a mixed effect modelling approach, Goldhammer et al. (2014; see also Goldhammer et al. 2017a) found an overall positive relationship for the domain of problem solving, but a negative overall relationship for the domain of reading literacy. Based on theories of dual processing, this inverse pattern was explained in terms of different cognitive processes required; while problem solving requires a rather controlled processing of information, reading literacy relies on component skills that are highly automatised in skilled readers. The strength and direction of the time on task effect still varied according to individual skill level and task characteristics, such as the task difficulty and the type of tasks considered. Following this line of reasoning, Engelhardt and Goldhammer (2019) used a latent variable modelling approach to provide validity evidence for the construct interpretation of PIAAC literacy scores. They identified a latent speed factor based on the log-transformed time on task and demonstrated that the effect of reading speed on reading literacy becomes more positive for readers with highly automated word meaning activation skills, while—as hypothesised—no such positive interaction was revealed for perceptual speed.

Timing data are commonly used to derive indicators of disengagement (e.g. rapid guessing, rapid omissions) reflecting whether or not respondents have devoted sufficient effort to completing assigned tasks (Wise and Gao 2017). Several methods have been proposed that rely on response time thresholds, such as fixed thresholds (e.g. 3000 or 5000 ms) and visual inspection of the item-level response time distribution (for a brief description, see Goldhammer et al. 2016). The methods

Table 10.1 Overview of studies analysing log files from the PIAAC data base

Study	Data	Domain	Items(s)	Process representation
Engelhardt and Goldhammer (2019)	PIAAC-L (DE)	Literacy	49 items	Time on task
Goldhammer et al. (2014)	PIAAC field test (DE)	Literacy PS-TRE	49 literacy items 13 PS-TRE items	Time on task
Goldhammer et al. (2016)	PIAAC main study 22 countries	All	49 literacy items 49 numeracy items 14 PS-TRE items	Time on task
Goldhammer et al. (2017a)	PIAAC main study (CA)	All	49 literacy items 49 numeracy items 14 PS-TRE items	Time on task
He et al. (2019)	PIAAC main study (GB, IE, JP, NL, US)	PS-TRE	7 items (module PS2)	Longest common subsequences
He and von Davier (2015)	PIAAC main study (JP, NL, US)	PS-TRE	Club Membership Member ID	n-grams (unigrams, bigrams, trigrams)
He and von Davier (2016)	PIAAC main study (JP, NL, US)	PS-TRE	Club Membership Member ID	n-grams (unigrams, bigrams, trigrams)
Liao et al. (2019)	PIAAC main study (US)	PS-TRE	Meeting rooms	Time on task n-grams (unigrams, bigrams, trigrams)
Naumann et al. (2014)	PIAAC field test (CA, DE)	PS-TRE	20 items	No. of interactions
OECD (2019)	PIAAC main study 16 countries	All	49 literacy items 49 numeracy items 14 PS-TRE items	Time on task Time since last action Time to first interaction
Stelter et al. (2015)	PIAAC field test (DE)	PS-TRE	6 items	Time on task Time on routine steps
Tóth et al. (2017)	PIAAC field test (DE)	PS-TRE	*job search (released item)	No. of website visits No. of visits to different websites No. of visits to relevant websites Ratio of time spent on the relevant websites No. of bookmarked websites

(continued)

Table 10.1 (continued)

Vörös and Rouet (2016)	PIAAC main study 16 countries	PS-TRE	Club membership member ID, digital photography book purchase, meeting rooms	No. of interactions (recoded in categorical groups of low, medium, and high) Time on task (recoded in categorical groups of low, medium, and high)
Weeks et al. (2016)	PIAAC main study 22 countries	Literacy Numeracy	49 literacy items 49 numeracy items	Time on task
Yamamoto and Lennon (2018)	PIAAC main study 2 countries	All	BQ and cognitive assessment	Various aspects of time information, including time on task, time to first interaction, and timing associated with keystroke sequences

Note. *https://piaac-logdata.tbahosting.de/public/problemsolving/JobSearchPart1/pages/jsp1-home.html

of P+ > 0% (Goldhammer et al. 2016, 2017a) and T-disengagement (OECD 2019) determine item-specific thresholds below which it is not assumed that respondents have made serious attempts to solve an item. P+ > 0% combines the response times with a probability level higher than that of a randomly correct response (in case of the PIAAC items, the chance level was assumed to be zero since most of the response formats allowed for a variety of different responses). The T-disengagement indicator further restricts this definition by implementing an additional 5-second boundary that treats all responses below this boundary as disengaged. Main results of these studies (Goldhammer et al. 2016, 2017a; OECD 2019) revealed that, although PIAAC is a low-stakes assessment, the proportions of disengagement across countries were comparatively low and consistent across domains. Nevertheless, disengagement rates differed significantly across countries, and the absolute level of disengagement was highest for the domain of problem solving. Other factors that promote disengagement included the respondents' level of education, the language in which the test was taken, respondents' level of proficiency, and their familiarity with ICT, as well as task characteristics, such as the difficulty and position of a task, which indicated a reduction in test-taking effort on more difficult tasks and tasks administered later in the assessment.

Similar to the issue of respondents' test engagement, time on task can be used to determine how to treat missing responses that may occur for various reasons, such as low ability, low motivation, or lack of time. In particular, omitted responses are an issue of the appropriate scaling of a test, because improperly treating omits as accidentally missing or incorrect could result in imprecise or biased estimates (Weeks et al. 2016). In the PIAAC main study (OECD 2013b), a missing response with no interaction and a response time under 5 s is treated as if the respondent did not see the item ('not reached/not attempted'). Timing information can help to determine if this cut-off criterion is suitable and reflective of respondents having had enough time to respond to the item. Weeks et al. (2016) investigated the time on task associated with PIAAC respondents' assessment in literacy and numeracy to determine whether or not omitted responses should be treated as not administered or as incorrect. Based on descriptive results and model-based analyses comparing response times of incorrect and omitted responses, they concluded that the commonly used 5-second rule is suitable for the identification of rapidly given responses, whereas it would be too strict for assigning incorrect responses.

The consideration of time information was also used to detect data falsifications that can massively affect the comparability of results. Taking into account various aspects of time information, ranging from time on task to timing related to keystrokes, Yamamoto and Lennon (2018) argued that obtaining an identical series of responses is highly unlikely, especially considering PIAAC's adaptive multistage design. They described the cases of two countries that had attracted attention because a large number of respondents were interviewed by only a few interviewers. In these countries, the authors identified cases in which the processing of single cognitive modules was identical down to the time information; even entire cases were duplicated. Other results showed systematic omissions of cognitive modules with short response times. Consequently, suspicious cases (or parts of them) were dropped or treated as not administered in the corresponding countries.

10.2.2 Studies of the Domain of PS-TRE

The PIAAC domain of PS-TRE measures adult proficiency in dealing with problems related to the use of information and communication technologies (OECD 2012). Such problems can range from searching the web for suitable information to organising folder structures in digital environments. Accordingly, the PS-TRE tasks portray nonroutine settings requiring effective use of digital resources and the identification of necessary steps to access and process information. Within the PS-TRE tasks, cognitive processes of individuals and related sequences of states can be mapped onto explicit behavioural actions recorded during the problem-solving process. Clicks showing, for example, that a particular link or email has been accessed provide an indication of how and what information a person has collected. By contrast, other cognitive processes, such as evaluating the content of information, are more difficult to clearly associate with recorded events in log files.

Previous research in the domain of PS-TRE has analysed the relationship between problem-solving success and the way in which individuals interacted with the digital environment. They have drawn on a large number of methods and indicators for process analysis, which include the investigation of single indicators (e.g. Tóth et al. 2017) and entire action sequences (e.g. He and von Davier 2015, 2016).

A comparatively simple indicator that has a high predictive value for PS-TRE is the number of interactions with a digital environment during the problem-solving process. Supporting the assumption that skilled problem solvers will engage in trial-and-error and exploration strategies, this action count positively predicted success in the PS-TRE tasks for the German and Canadian PIAAC field test data (Naumann et al. 2014; see also Goldhammer et al. 2017b) and for the 16 countries in the PIAAC main study (Vörös and Rouet 2016). Naumann et al. (2014) even found that the association was reversely U-shaped and moderated by the number of required steps in a task. Taking into account the time spent on PS-TRE tasks, Vörös and Rouet (2016) further showed that the overall positive relationship between the number of interactions and success on the PS-TRE tasks was constant across tasks, while the effect of time on task increased as a function of task difficulty. They also revealed different time–action patterns depending on task difficulty. Respondents who successfully completed an easy task were more likely to show either a low action count with a high time on task or a high action count with a low time on task. In contrast, the more time respondents spent on the task, and the more they interacted with it, the more likely they were to solve a medium and a hard task. Although both Naumann et al. (2014) and Vörös and Rouet (2016) investigated the respondents' interactions within the technology-rich environments, they used different operationalisations—namely, a log-transformed interaction count and a percentile grouping variable of low, medium, and high interaction counts, respectively. However, they obtained similar and even complementary results, indicating that the interpretation of interactions during the process of problem solving might be more complex than a more-is-better explanation, providing valuable information on solution behaviours and strategies.

Process indicators can also combine different process information. Stelter et al. (2015; see also Goldhammer et al. 2017b) investigated a log file indicator that combined the execution of particular steps in the PS-TRE tasks with time information. Assuming that a release of cognitive resources benefits the problem-solving process, they identified routine steps in six PS-TRE tasks (using a bookmark tool, moving an email, and closing a dialog box) and measured the time respondents needed to perform these steps by determining the time interval between events that started and ended sequences of interest (e.g. opening and closing the bookmark tool; see Sect. 10.4.2). By means of logistic regressions at the task level, they showed that the probability of success on the PS-TRE tasks tended to increase inversely with the time spent on routine steps, indicating that highly automated, routine processing supports the problem-solving process.

While the number of interactions and the time spent on routine steps are generic indicators applicable to several different tasks, indicators can also be highly task-specific. Tóth et al. (2017) classified the problem-solving behaviour of respondents of the German PIAAC field test using the data mining technique of decision trees. In the 'Job Search' item[1], which was included in the PIAAC field test and now serves as a released sample task of the PS-TRE domain, respondents were asked to

---

[1] https://piaac-logdata.tba-hosting.de/public/problemsolving/JobSearchPart1/pages/jsp1-home.html

bookmark websites of job search portals in a search engine environment that did not have a registration or fee requirement. The best predictors included as decision nodes were the number of different website visits (top node of the tree) and the number of bookmarked websites. Respondents who visited eight or more different websites and bookmarked exactly two websites had the highest chance of giving a correct response. Using this simple model, 96.7% of the respondents were correctly classified.

Other important contributions in analysing response behaviour in the domain of PS-TRE were made by adopting exploratory approaches from the field of text mining (He and von Davier 2015, 2016; Liao et al. 2019). He and von Davier (2015, 2016) detected and analysed robust n-grams—that is, sequences of n adjacent actions that were performed during the problem-solving process and have a high information value (e.g. the sequence [viewed_email_1, viewed_email_2, viewed_email_1] may represent a trigram of states suggesting that a respondent revisited the first email displayed after having seen the second email displayed). He and von Davier (2015, 2016) compared the frequencies of certain n-grams between persons who could solve a particular PS-TRE task and those who could not, as well as across three countries to determine which sequences were most common in these subgroups. The results were quite consistent across countries and showed that the high-performing group more often utilised search and sort tools and showed a clearer understanding of sub-goals compared to the low-performing group.

Similarly, Liao et al. (2019) detected typical action sequences for subgroups that were determined based on background variables, such as the monthly earnings (first vs. fourth quartile), level of educational attainment, age, test language, and skill use at work. They examined the action sequences generated within a task in which respondents were required to organise several meeting room requests using different digital environments including the web, a word processor, and an email interface. Findings by Liao et al. show not only which particular action sequences were most prominent in groups with different levels of background variables but also that the same log event might suggest different psychological interpretations depending on the subgroup. Transitions between the different digital environments, for example, may be an indication of undirected behaviour if they are the predominant feature; but they may also reflect steps necessary to accomplish the task if accompanied by a variety of other features. However, although such in-detail item analyses can provide deep insights into the respondents' processing, their results can hardly be generalised to other problem-solving tasks, as they are highly dependent on the analysed context.

Extending this research direction to a general perspective across multiple items, He et al. (2019) applied another method rooted in natural language processing and biostatistics by comparing entire action sequences of respondents with the optimal (partly multiple) solution paths of items. By doing so, they determined the longest common subsequence that the respondents' action sequences had in common with the optimal paths. He et al. were thus able to derive measurements on how similar the paths of the respondents were to the optimal sequence and how consistent they were between the items. They found that most respondents in the countries investigated showed overall consistent behaviour patterns. More consistent patterns were observed in particularly good- and particularly poor-performing groups. A comparison of similarity across countries by items also showed the potential of the method for explaining why items might function differently between countries (differential item functioning, DIF; Holland and Wainer 1993), for instance, when an item is more difficult in one country than in the others.

10.3 The Released PIAAC Log File Data

With the aim of making the PIAAC log file data available to the research community and the public, the OECD provided funding for the development of infrastructure and software tools to disseminate and facilitate the use of the log file data. Carried out by the GESIS – Leibniz Institute for the Social Sciences and the DIPF | Leibniz Institute for Research and Information in Education, the PIAAC log file data were anonymised and archived; the log file data and the corresponding PIAAC tasks were described in interactive online documentation; and a software tool, the PIAAC LogDataAnalyzer (LDA), enables researchers to preprocess and analyse PIAAC log file data. In the following, the PIAAC test design is outlined (Sect. 10.3.1). With this background, the structure of the PIAAC log file data (Sect. 10.3.2) is presented, and we explain how the available documentation of items (see also Chap. 4 in this volume) and related log events can be used to make sense of the log file data (Sect. 10.3.3).

10.3.1 Overview of PIAAC Test Design

PIAAC (2011–2012) included several assessment parts and adaptive routing to ensure an efficient estimation of adult proficiencies in the target population (Fig. 10.1; for details, see Kirsch et al. 2016; OECD 2019; Chap. 2 in this volume). After a computer-assisted personal interview (CAPI), in which the background of respondents was surveyed (background questionnaire, BQ), the respondents started either with the computer-based assessment (CBA) by default or—if they did not report any experience with information and communication technologies (ICT)—with the paper-based assessment (PBA). When routed to the CBA, respondents were first asked to complete a core assessment in which their basic ICT skills and cognitive skills were assessed (CBA Core Stages 1 and 2). If they passed, they were led to the direct assessment of literacy, numeracy, or—in countries taking this option—problem solving in technology-rich environments (PS-TRE). On average, about 77% of the respondents in all the participating countries completed the direct assessment on the computer—for example, 82% in Germany and 84% in the United States (Mamedova and Pawlowski 2018).

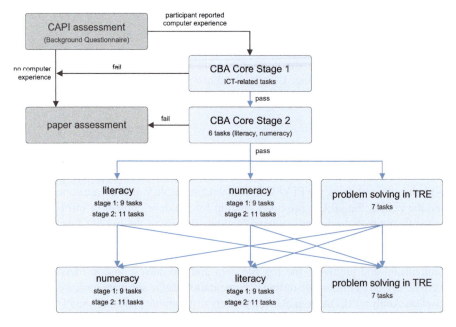

Fig. 10.1 Illustration of the CBA parts of the PIAAC assessment
Note. For the complete design, see OECD 2013b, p. 10

Terminologically, a set of cognitive items is called a *module*. Each respondent received two *modules* during the regular cognitive assessment. For the domains of literacy and numeracy, a module consists of two *testlets,* as literacy and numeracy were assessed adaptively. Specifically, both the literacy and the numeracy modules comprised two stages, each of which consisted of alternative testlets differing in difficulty (three testlets at Stage 1, four testlets at Stage 2). Note that within a stage, items could be included in more than one testlet. Due to the unique nature of PS-TRE, this domain was organised into two fixed modules of seven tasks each.

According to the conception and the design of the PIAAC study, the entire computer-based cognitive assessment was expected to take about 60 min. However, since PIAAC was not a timed assessment (OECD 2013b, p. 8), some respondents may have spent more time on the completion of the cognitive assessment. Log file data are available only for the CBA parts of the PIAAC study (coloured boxes in Fig. 10.1).

10.3.2 File Structure and Accessibility

The raw PIAAC log files are XML files that contain records of the respondents' interactions with the computer test application used for PIAAC (TAO: Jadoul et al.

10 Analysing Log File Data from PIAAC 253

Fig. 10.2 Example of the appearance of a raw XML file

2016; CBA ItemBuilder: Rölke 2012). Specifically, the logged actions of respondents (e.g. starting a task, opening a website, selecting or typing an answer) were recorded and stored with time stamps. Figure 10.2 shows an example screenshot of the content of an XML file. However, users interested in working with the PIAAC log file data for literacy, numeracy, and PS-TRE items are not required to further process the raw XML files. Instead, they can use the PIAAC LogDataAnalyzer (LDA) as a tool for preprocessing and analysing the log file data (see Sect. 10.4; this does not apply to the log file data of the core assessment parts UIC and Core2).

There is a log file for each assessment component that a respondent took during the test. In total, 18 different components were administered, depending on the tested domain and the stage:

- CBA Core Stage 1 (UIC)
- CBA Core Stage 2 (Core2)
- Literacy at Stage 1 (three testlets, L11–L13) and Stage 2 (four testlets, L21–L24)
- Numeracy at Stage 1 (three testlets, N11–N13) and Stage 2 (four testlets, N21–N24)
- Problem solving in technology-rich environments (modules PS1 and PS2)

Figure 10.3 shows the log files of the respondent with the code 4747 as an example. This respondent completed the CBA Core assessments (UIC and Core2), two testlets of the literacy assessment (L12, L24), and two testlets of the numeracy assessment (N12, N24). Note that PS-TRE was an optional part of the cognitive assessment. For this reason, the data files of France, Italy, and Spain do not include any files with regard to PS-TRE.

As stated before, the log file data contain data only on the CBA parts of the PIAAC study. The responses to the background questionnaire (BQ) and the scored responses of the cognitive assessment are part of the PIAAC Public Use Files, which also include additional information, such as sampling weights, the results of the PBA, and observations of the interviewer. The public use files also include a limited set of process indicators (i.e. total time on task, time to first action, and the number

Name	Typ	Komprimie...	Kenn...	Größe	Verh...	Änderungsdatum
4747-Core2-Log	XML-Doku...	6 KB	Nein	73 KB	93%	25.10.2017 12:45
4747-L12-Log	XML-Doku...	10 KB	Nein	177 KB	95%	25.10.2017 12:45
4747-L24-Log	XML-Doku...	8 KB	Nein	108 KB	94%	25.10.2017 12:45
4747-N12-Log	XML-Doku...	6 KB	Nein	73 KB	93%	25.10.2017 12:45
4747-N24-Log	XML-Doku...	6 KB	Nein	83 KB	93%	25.10.2017 12:45
4747-UIC-Log	XML-Doku...	2 KB	Nein	16 KB	89%	25.10.2017 12:45

Fig. 10.3 Available XML raw files of the respondent with the code 4747

of interactions) for cognitive items of the CBA. The international PIAAC Public Use Files are available on the OECD website[2]. For academic research, the German Scientific Use File[3], including additional and more detailed variables than the international public use file, can be combined with the PIAAC log file data as well. The data can be merged using the variables CNTRYID, which is an identification key for each country, and SEQID, which is a unique identifier for individuals within each country.[4] By merging these data, detailed analyses can be carried out on, for example, how the behaviour of the respondents during the cognitive assessment relates to their task success or their background (see Sect. 10.2 for examples).

Researchers and academic teachers who wish to work with the PIAAC log file data (OECD 2017a – OECD 2017r) must register with the GESIS Data Archive[5] and the data repository service datorium (see also Chap. 4 in this volume). Accepting the terms of use will provide access to the PIAAC log file data[6] under the study code 'ZA6712, Programme for the International Assessment of Adult Competencies (PIAAC), log files', which then allows access to the raw PIAAC log files, compressed in ZIP files per country. All downloadable files have been anonymised—that is, all information that potentially identifies individual respondents has been removed or replaced with neutral character strings. Otherwise, the log file data are as complete as they were when logged for individual respondents. In addition to data access, the GESIS Data Archive provides users of PIAAC log file data with further information—for example, on the bibliographic citation and descriptions of content and methodological aspects of the PIAAC log file data.[7]

---

[2] http://www.oecd.org/skills/piaac/publicdataandanalysis/

[3] https://www.gesis.org/en/piaac/rdc/data/national-scientific-use-files

[4] Note that SEQID is not unique across countries and therefore has to be combined with CNTRYID to create unique individual identifiers across countries.

[5] https://search.gesis.org/research_data/ZA6712

[6] https://doi.org/10.4232/1.12955

[7] see also: https://www.gesis.org/en/piaac/rdc/data/international-piaac-log-files

10 Analysing Log File Data from PIAAC

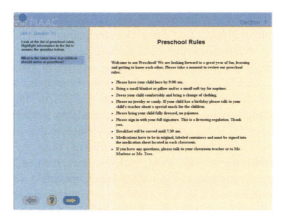

Fig. 10.4 Top: A PIAAC item consists of a question part including general instructions (blue-shaded) and a stimulus part (orange-shaded). Bottom: Example of recorded events in a data frame format for a respondent working on the first item of the testlet L13
Notes. See also Sect. 10.4.2; Log events that reflect interactions with the question part are blue-shaded (event_name: *taoPIAAC*); log events that reflect interactions with the stimulus are orange-shaded (event_name: *stimulus*)

10.3.3 Documentation of Items and Log Events

Before using the PIAAC log file data, users should be aware that PIAAC items consist of two general parts—the question part including general instructions on the blue background (*taoPIAAC*) and the stimulus next to it (*stimulus*; Fig. 10.4, top). The elements in the PIAAC log file data are assigned to these parts (Fig. 10.4, bottom). Depending on the item response format, respondents were required to give a response using elements of the question part (e.g. entering input in a text field on the left panel) or the stimulus (e.g. highlighting text in the stimulus). An overview of the specific response formats of the literacy and numeracy items can be retrieved from the online PIAAC Log Data Documentation.[8]

---

[8] https://piaac-logdata.tba-hosting.de/itemid.html

The PIAAC items are documented in the PIAAC Reader's Companion[9] as well as in the online PIAAC Log Data Documentation.[10] While the Reader's Companion briefly summarises the assessed competence domains and gives a general description of the items in the cognitive assessment and the background questionnaire, the online documentation displays the exact items and interactively provides details of the mapping with events in the PIAAC log file data (Fig. 10.5). The documentation of released items is available for all users (e.g. Job Search,[11] MP3 Player[12]). Although they were not administered as part of the PIAAC main study, the released items demonstrate how PIAAC items are documented. If researchers wish to access the full PIAAC item documentation and the items of the main study, they must complete an application form[13] including a short description of their research interest and a signed confidentiality agreement and send it to the contact officer at the OECD.[14] In case of a successful application, researchers will receive a username and password for the online platform with which they can access all documentation.

In the online documentation, possible event types are displayed in the form of pop-up dialogs where they occur within the items. The pop-up dialogs are activated when the mouse cursor moves over a sensitive item element. The documentation includes all items of the PS-TRE domain and a subset of the literacy and numeracy items that demonstrate the implemented response formats and therefore represent the range of possible log events in literacy and numeracy items. The logged events in the generated XML files follow a particular structure:

```
<taoEvent Name ="origin" Type ="Event Type" Time ="ms">
                                               </taoEvent>
```

An event tag bracketed by <taoEvent> and </taoEvent> denotes that one interaction of the respondent with the item environment was recorded. An interaction with one item element might trigger the logging of multiple event tags. The attributes within the tags specify the interaction in detail. The attribute Name states the environment of the element with which a respondent interacted (e.g. *taoPIAAC* or *stimulus*). The attribute Type classifies the recorded event (e.g. TOOLBAR, MENU, or BUTTON), while the attribute Time provides a time stamp in milliseconds, which is reset to zero at the start of each unit. A list[15] of all possible

---

[9]https://www.oecd.org/skills/piaac/Skills%20(vol%202)-Reader%20companion%2D%2Dv7%20eBook%20(Press%20quality)-29%20oct%200213.pdf

[10]https://piaac-logdata.tba-hosting.de/

[11]https://piaac-logdata.tba-hosting.de/public/problemsolving/JobSearchPart1/pages/jsp1-home.html

[12]https://piaac-logdata.tba-hosting.de/public/problemsolving/MP3/pages/mp3-start.html

[13]http://www.oecd.org/skills/piaac/log-file/Application.pdf

[14]edu.piaac@oecd.org

[15]https://piaac-logdata.tba-hosting.de/additionalinformation.html

10 Analysing Log File Data from PIAAC

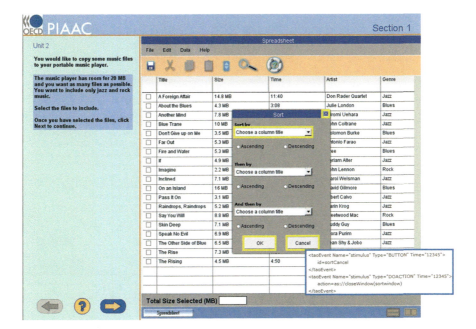

Fig. 10.5 Example item
Notes. MP3 Player (see also OECD 2012, *Literacy, Numeracy and Problem Solving in Technology-Rich Environments*, p. 55.). Moving the mouse cursor over sensitive areas (here the Cancel button) displays blue-framed pop-up dialogs containing details about the structure of the recorded events. Yellow-framed areas are clickable parts of the item documentation and open new screens. Available at: https://piaac-logdata.tba-hosting.de/public/problemsolving/MP3/pages/mp3-start.html

log events is provided in the online PIAAC Log Data Documentation for the items assessing literacy and numeracy (tab *Events-Literacy, Numeracy*) and PS-TRE (tab *Events-Problem Solving in Technology-Rich Environments*)[16].

10.4 Preprocessing and Analysing PIAAC Log File Data

The software PIAAC LogDataAnalyzer (LDA) was developed for the OECD by the TBA Centre at the DIPF in cooperation with TBA21 Hungary Limited to facilitate the analysis of log file data—that is, to handle the huge amount of XML files (e.g. the log file data from Germany comprises 24.320 XML files of 1.9 gigabytes) and to preprocess the log file data for further analyses in statistical software packages, such as R (R Core Team 2016).

---

[16] https://piaac-logdata.tba-hosting.de/

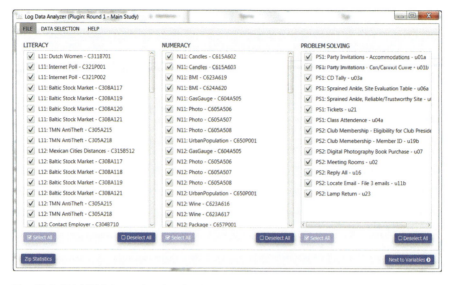

Fig. 10.6 PIAAC LDA user interface for the selection of items by domain

Essentially, the PIAAC LDA fulfils two main purposes: the extraction of predefined aggregated variables from XML files (Sect. 10.4.1) and the extraction of raw log file data from XML files for creating user-defined aggregated variables (Sect. 10.4.2). Note that all the XML files from the literacy, numeracy, and problem-solving modules are included in the preprocessing, but the XML files from CBA Core Stage 1 (UIC) and CBA Core Stage 2 (Core2) are not.

The LDA software was developed for MS Windows (e.g. 7, 10; both 32 bit and 64 bit) and can be accessed and downloaded via the OECD's PIAAC Log File Website[17]. The help area of the LDA does include detailed information about the LDA software itself. It describes how to import a ZIP file that includes a country's log file data; how to select items within domains; how to select aggregated variables (including visual screening); and how to export aggregated variables and raw log file data. Furthermore, there is extensive information about how the LDA software handles errors or unexpected issues (e.g. the handling of negative time stamps).

The typical workflow for using the PIAAC LDA starts with importing a country's ZIP file, including all the XML files. For demonstration purposes, the LDA also provides a small ZIP file (sample_round1_main.ZIP). The import ends with a brief report presenting details about the ZIP file and the included data.[18] Next, the user can select the domains and items by selecting those of interest and deselecting those to be excluded (see Fig. 10.6).

---

[17] http://piaac-logdata.tba-hosting.de/download/

[18] If the verification of the ZIP file failed, for instance, because a corrupt or wrong ZIP file was selected, an error message is presented that the data is invalid.

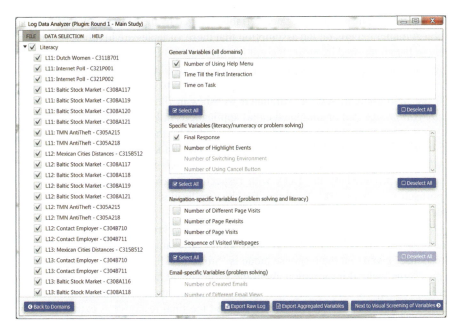

Fig. 10.7 PIAAC LDA user interface for exporting aggregated variables and raw log file data

This selection should be used if only a subset of data is needed for a particular research question. All subsequent data processing steps include only this subset, which helps to reduce data processing time. Note that due to the PIAAC test design (see Sect. 10.3.1), a particular item may be included in more than one testlet (e.g. Photo—C605A506 is part of testlet N11 and testlet N12; see Fig. 10.6). To gather the complete data for an item, all occurrences in testlets have to be selected. An overview of the booklet structure, including testlets, can be found in the online PIAAC Log Data Documentation (tab *Booklet Order*).[19]

Clicking the button 'Next to Variables' (Fig. 10.6) opens the view for exporting data for the selected items (Fig. 10.7). If needed, the item selection can be modified in the left panel.

10.4.1 Aggregated Variables Provided by the PIAAC Log Data Analyzer

The selection of aggregated variables offered in the right panel depends on the selection of items, because some of the aggregated variables are available only for

---
[19]https://piaac-logdata.tba-hosting.de/additionalinformation.html

specific items. The set of aggregated variables offered by the LDA was predefined by subject matter experts on the assumption that these variables are highly relevant for researchers interested in the analysis of log file data. Table 10.2 gives an overview of the available aggregated variables that apply either to all items (*general*), to selected items depending on the domain (*item-specific*), or to selected items depending on the item content, such as simulated websites in literacy and problem solving (*navigation-specific*) or simulated email applications in PS-TRE (*email-specific*).

Following Sect. 10.1.2, the indicators provided by the LDA can be represented in terms of properties of the reconstructed sequence of states (Table 10.2, columns *Defined State(s)* and *Property of the reconstructed sequence*). Describing the indicators provided by the LDA with respect to states used in the more formal approach (see Sect. 10.1.2) allows for the similarities between the indicators to become apparent.

A detailed description of all the aggregated variables can be found in the help menu of the PIAAC LDA. Figure 10.8 shows an example for the variable 'Final Response' given that the response mode is 'Stimulus Clicking'. The help page provides some general information about the variable and how it is extracted from log events (e.g. event 'itemScoreResult' including the attribute 'selectedImageAreas'). This is complemented by an example log and the final response as extracted from the log (e.g. final response: I3|I4, indicating that the image areas I3 and I4 were selected by the respondent).

By pressing 'Next to Visual Screening of Variables' (Fig. 10.7), the PIAAC LDA offers a screening for aggregated variables. The user can quickly examine the selected variables by generating simple descriptive statistics (minimum, maximum, average, and standard deviation) and charts (pie chart or histogram). Based on the screening, for instance, variables showing no variance could be deselected.

The export of selected aggregated variables is done by pressing the button 'Export Aggregated Variables'. The output file is a CSV file using tabulators as separators. The traditional wide format shows cases in rows and variables in columns. The first two columns show the CNTRYID and SEQID, which are needed to merge aggregated variables with variables from the PIAAC Public Use File. The CSV file can be imported by statistical analysis software, such as R, for further investigation.

10.4.2 User-Defined Aggregated Variables

Researchers who cannot find what they are looking for in the set of predefined variables can export the raw log file data of selected items by pressing the 'Export Raw Log' button. Based on this exported data, they can create their own aggregated variables using statistical software. The output file is a text file that includes all the log events stored in the XML files. The output file has a long format—that is, the log events of a person extend over multiple rows as indicated by identical CNTRYID and SEQID (Fig. 10.9). Each line in the file contains information that

10 Analysing Log File Data from PIAAC 261

Table 10.2 Aggregated variables provided by the PIAAC LDA

Indicator created by the PIAAC LogDataAnalyzer (LDA)	Type	Domain L	Domain N	Domain PS	Defined state(s)	Property of the reconstructed sequence
Time on task	G	x	x	x	One single state corresponding to the complete task	Total time on the state
Number of using cancel button	S	–	–	x		Count of a dedicated event
Number of using help	G	x	x	x		Count of a dedicated event
Number of highlight events	S	x	–	–		Count of a dedicated event
Time till the first interaction	G	x	x	x	Three states for each task (one prior to the first interaction, one after the last answer selection, one in between)	Total time on the first state
Time since last answer interaction	S	x	x	–		Total time on the third state
Number of switching environment	S	–	–	x^1	State for each environment (in relevant tasks)	Number of transitions
Sequence of switching environment	S	–	–	x^1		Sequence of states (n-grams)
Number of created email	E	–	–	x^2	State for the email environment (in relevant tasks)	Count of dedicated events
Sequence of viewed email	E	–	–	x^2	State for each email (in relevant tasks)	Sequence of states (n-grams)
Number of email views	E	–	–	x^2		Number of state visits
Number of different email views	E	–	–	x^2		Number of unique state visits
Number of revisited emails	E	–	–	x^2		Number of state revisits
Sequence of visited webpages	N	x^3	–	x^3	States for each page (in relevant tasks)	Sequence of states (n-grams)
Time sequence of spent time on webpages	N	x^3	–	x^3		Sequence of time on state for a state sequence (n-grams)
Number of different page visits	N	x^3	–	x^3		Number of unique state visits
Number of page visits	N	x^3	–	x^3		Number of state visits
Number of page revisits	N	x^3	–	x^3		Number of state revisits

Notes. [1] Available for items including multiple software applications; [2] Available for items including a simulated email application; [3] Available for items including a simulated web browser; Domain: *L* literacy, *N* numeracy, *PS* problem solving; Type: *G* general variables, *S* specific variables, *E* email-specific variables, *N* navigation-specific variables

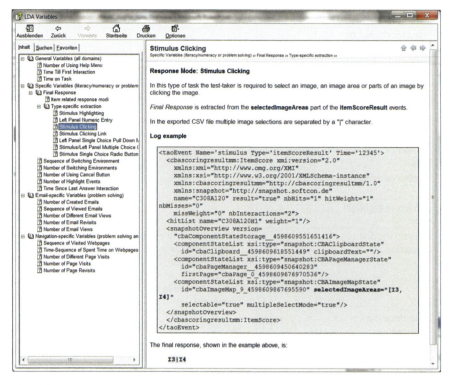

Fig. 10.8 Example help page from the PIAAC LogDataAnalyzer (LDA) providing information about the aggregated variable 'Final response' for the response mode 'Stimulus Clicking'

was extracted from the attributes of the event tags in the XML log files (see Sect. 10.3.3). This information is converted into a data table format separated by tabs with the following columns: CNTRYID, SEQID, booklet_id, item_id, event_name, event_type, time_stamp, and event_description.

The booklet_id indicates the testlet for literacy and numeracy and the module for PS-TRE. The item_id gives the position of the item in the respective testlet or module. The corresponding PIAAC item identifier can be obtained from the booklet documentation (see the online PIAAC Log Data Documentation[20], tab *Booklet Order*). The event_name represents the environment from which the event is logged. Values can be *stimulus* for events traced within the stimulus, *taoPIAAC* for events from outside the stimulus, and *service* for other parts of a unit. The event_type represents the event category. The time_stamp provides a time stamp in milliseconds with the beginning of each unit as reference point (time_stamp: 0). Finally, the event_description provides the values that characterise a certain event

---

[20]https://piaac-logdata.tba-hosting.de/additionalinformation.html

10 Analysing Log File Data from PIAAC

	CNTRYID	SEQID	booklet_id	item_id	event_name	event_type	timestamp	event_description
	...	...	...	...	...	...	...	...
1	sample_round1_main	295	PS1	5	taoPIAAC	START	0	TEST_TIME=327
2	sample_round1_main	295	PS1	5	stimulus	MENU	4050	id=file-menu
3	sample_round1_main	295	PS1	5	stimulus	MENUITEM	7315	key=cut
4	sample_round1_main	295	PS1	5	stimulus	COPY	7315	content=undefined
5	sample_round1_main	295	PS1	5	stimulus	TOOLBAR	17184	id=toolbar_back_btn
6	sample_round1_main	295	PS1	5	stimulus	HISTORY_BACK	17184	pageid=unit06bdefault|*$title=Websearch\|*$url=www.websearch.com/treatmentspraindedankle
7	sample_round1_main	295	PS1	5	stimulus	DOACTION	17187	action=as://historyBack(toolbar_back_btn)
8	sample_round1_main	295	PS1	5	stimulus	TOOLBAR	19222	id=toolbar_forward_btn
9	sample_round1_main	295	PS1	5	stimulus	HISTORY_NEXT	19222	pageid=unit06bdefault|*$title=Websearch\|*$url=www.websearch.com/treatmentspraindedankle
10	sample_round1_main	295	PS1	5	stimulus	DOACTION	19224	action=as://historyForward(toolbar_forward_btn)
11	sample_round1_main	295	PS1	5	stimulus	TOOLBAR	21906	id=toolbar_home_btn
12	sample_round1_main	295	PS1	5	stimulus	HISTORY_ADD	21909	pageid=unit06bdefault|*$title=Websearch\|*$url=www.websearch.com/treatmentspraindedankle
13	sample_round1_main	295	PS1	5	stimulus	DOACTION	21909	action=as://gotoURL(unit06bdefault,_self,unknown)
14	sample_round1_main	295	PS1	5	stimulus	MENU	24954	id=wb-bookmarks-menu
15	sample_round1_main	295	PS1	5	stimulus	MENUITEM	26987	key=bookmark-add
16	sample_round1_main	295	PS1	5	stimulus	BOOKMARK_ADD	30772	pageid=unit06bdefault|*$title=Websearch\|*$url=www.websearch.com/treatmentspraindedankle
17	sample_round1_main	295	PS1	5	stimulus	BUTTON	30977	id=add_bookmark_validation
18	sample_round1_main	295	PS1	5	stimulus	DOACTION	30977	action=as://hide(addbookmark_window)
19	sample_round1_main	295	PS1	5	stimulus	MENU	33677	id=wb-bookmarks-menu
20	sample_round1_main	295	PS1	5	stimulus	MENUITEM	34842	key=bookmark-manage
21	sample_round1_main	295	PS1	5	stimulus	BUTTON	40915	id=manage_bookmark_window_validation
22	sample_round1_main	295	PS1	5	stimulus	DOACTION	40916	action=as://hide(managebookmark_window)
23	sample_round1_main	295	PS1	5	stimulus	TEXTBOX_ONFO	45326	id=u06b_default_txt2|*$value=Treatment sprained ankle
	...	...	...	...	...	...	...	...

Fig. 10.9 Example raw log file data extracted from XML files

type. A detailed overview of possible event types and related values can be found in the online PIAAC Log Data Documentation.[21]

Figure 10.9 shows an example of raw log file data extracted from XML files and transformed to a long format. The test-taker is identified by CNTRYID (CNTRYID=sample_round1_main) and SEQID (SEQID: 295). He or she completed the fifth item (item_id: 5, which is "U06b - Sprained Ankle") in the PS-TRE module PS1 (booklet_id: PS1). Line 14 in Fig. 10.9 shows that the test-taker needed 24,954 milliseconds after starting the unit (time_stamp: 24954) to click on the menu bar of a simulated web browser (event_type: MENU) within the stimulus (event_name: stimulus); more specifically, it was the menu for bookmarking (event_description: id=wb-bookmarks-menu).

New aggregated variables can be extracted from this exported raw log file data. For example, a researcher might be interested in the time a test-taker needs to bookmark the current webpage (Stelter et al. 2015). Such an indicator can be described as the time in a particular state and understood as a specific part of the interaction between the test-taker and assessment platform (i.e. item), which, here, would be the of bookmarking. Traces of the test-taking process in the log file data can be used to reconstruct the occurrence of this state by using the menu events 'clicking the bookmarking menu', which describes the beginning of the state (event_description: id = wb-bookmarks-menu; line 14 in Fig. 10.9) and 'confirm the intended bookmark', which describes the end of the state and the transition to any subsequent state (event_description: id=add_bookmark_validation; line 17 in Fig. 10.9). When the two identifying events can be determined without considering previous or subsequent events, as in this example, indicators can be extracted directly from the log file data without specific tools. Instead, it is sufficient to filter the raw log events in such a way that only the two events of interest remain in chronological order in a dataset. The value for the indicator per person and for each

---
[21] https://piaac-logdata.tba-hosting.de/additionalinformation.html

state occurrence is the difference of the time stamps of successive events. Using the example provided in Fig. 10.9, the value of the indicator for that particular respondent is the difference of the two time stamps in lines 17 and 14 (i.e. 30,977– 24,954 = 6023 milliseconds). If the meaning of events requires the context of the previous and subsequent events to be taken into account, algorithms to extract process indicators from log files can be formulated—for example, using finite state machines as described by Kroehne and Goldhammer (2018).

10.5 Conclusions

A major goal of this chapter was to make the PIAAC log file data accessible to researchers. As demonstrated for the case of PIAAC, providing this kind of data has some implications and challenges. It requires dealing with data formats and data structures other than usual assessment data while no established standards are yet available. As a consequence, there is also a lack of general tools that facilitate the preprocessing and transformation of raw log events. Another major issue is the documentation of items and log events triggered by the respondent's interaction with the assessment system. Without proper documentation, researchers who were not involved in the item development process can hardly make sense of the raw log data and therefore will not use it.

Assuming that a supporting infrastructure is available in the future, the use of log file data will likely no longer be an exception; rather, their use will grow in popularity. However, as indicated above, the creation of meaningful process indicators is limited in that they can be inferred only from states for which a beginning and an end are identified in the log data. This depends conceptually on the careful design of the task and its interactivity and technically on the design of the assessment system. Another issue to be considered is the interpretation of process indicators, which needs to be challenged by appropriate validation strategies (as it is usually required for the interpretation of test scores). Moreover, opening the stage for process indicators also requires statistical models to appropriately capture the more complex structure of dependencies between process and product indicators within items (e.g. Goldhammer et al. 2014; Klotzke and Fox 2019). Overall, users of log file data will have to face a series of conceptual and methodological tasks and challenges, but they will also be able to gain deeper insights into the behaviour and information processing of respondents.

References

Bolsinova, M., & Tijmstra, J. (2018). Improving precision of ability estimation: Getting more from response times. *British Journal of Mathematical and Statistical Psychology, 71*, 13–38. https://doi.org/10.1111/bmsp.12104.

Buerger, S., Kroehne, U., Koehler, C., & Goldhammer, F. (2019). What makes the difference? The impact of item properties on mode effects in reading assessments. *Studies in Educational Evaluation, 62*, 1–9. https://doi.org/10.1016/j.stueduc.2019.04.005.

Couper, M. (1998). Measuring survey quality in a CASIC environment. In: *Proceedings of the section on survey research methods of the American Statistical Association*, (pp. 41–49).

Eichmann, B., Goldhammer, F., Greiff, S., Pucite, L., & Naumann, J. (2019). The role of planning in complex problem solving. *Computers & Education, 128*, 1–12. https://doi.org/10.1016/j.compedu.2018.08.004.

Engelhardt, L., & Goldhammer, F. (2019). Validating test score interpretations using time information. *Frontiers in Psychology, 10*, 1–30.

Goldhammer, F., & Klein Entink, R. H. (2011). Speed of reasoning and its relation to reasoning ability. *Intelligence, 39*, 108–119. https://doi.org/10.1016/j.intell.2011.02.001.

Goldhammer, F., & Zehner, F. (2017). What to make of and how to interpret process data. *Measurement: Interdisciplinary Research and Perspectives, 15*, 128–132. https://doi.org/10.1080/15366367.2017.1411651.

Goldhammer, F., Naumann, J., Stelter, A., Tóth, K., Rölke, H., & Klieme, E. (2014). The time on task effect in reading and problem solving is moderated by task difficulty and skill: Insights from a computer-based large-scale assessment. *Journal of Educational Psychology, 106*, 608–626.

Goldhammer, F., Martens, T., Christoph, G., & Lüdtke, O. (2016). *Test-taking engagement in PIAAC* (no. 133). Paris: OECD Publishing. https://doi.org/10.1787/5jlzfl6fhxs2-en.

Goldhammer, F., Martens, T., & Lüdtke, O. (2017a). Conditioning factors of test-taking engagement in PIAAC: An exploratory IRT modelling approach considering person and item characteristics. *Large-Scale Assessments in Education, 5*, 1–25. https://doi.org/10.1186/s40536-017-0051-9.

Goldhammer, F., Naumann, J., Rölke, H., Stelter, A., & Tóth, K. (2017b). Relating product data to process data from computer-based competency assessment. In D. Leutner, J. Fleischer, J. Grünkorn, & E. Klieme (Eds.), *Competence assessment in education* (pp. 407–425). Cham: Springer. https://doi.org/10.1007/978-3-319-50030-0_24.

Greiff, S., Niepel, C., Scherer, R., & Martin, R. (2016). Understanding students' performance in a computer-based assessment of complex problem solving: An analysis of behavioral data from computer-generated log files. *Computers in Human Behavior, 61*, 36–46. https://doi.org/10.1016/j.chb.2016.02.095.

He, Q., & von Davier, M. (2015). Identifying feature sequences from process data in problem-solving items with n-grams. In L. A. van der Ark, D. M. Bolt, W.-C. Wang, J. A. Douglas, & S.-M. Chow (Eds.), *Quantitative psychology research* (Vol. 140, pp. 173–190). Cham: Springer. https://doi.org/10.1007/978-3-319-19977-1_13.

He, Q., & von Davier, M. (2016). Analyzing process data from problem-solving items with n-grams: Insights from a computer-based large-scale assessment. In Y. Rosen, S. Ferrara, & M. Mosharraf (Eds.), *Handbook of research on technology tools for real-world skill development* (pp. 749–776). Hershey: IGI Global. https://doi.org/10.4018/978-1-4666-9441-5.

He, Q., Borgonovi, F., & Paccagnella, M. (2019). *Using process data to identify generalized patterns across problem-solving items*. Paper presented at the Annual Meeting of National Council on Measurement in Education, Toronto, CA.

Holland, P., & Wainer, H. (Eds.). (1993). *Differential item functioning*. New York: Routledge. https://doi.org/10.4324/9780203357811.

Jadoul, R., Plichart, P., Bogaerts, J., Henry, C., & Latour, T. (2016). The TAO platform. In OECD (Ed.), *Technical report of the Survey of Adult Skills (PIAAC) (2nd edition)*. Paris: OECD Publishing. Retrieved from https://www.oecd.org/skills/piaac/PIAAC_Technical_Report_2nd_Edition_Full_Report.pdf

Kirsch, I., Yamamoto, K., & Garber, D. (2016). Assessment design. In OECD (Ed.), *Technical report of the Survey of Adult Skills (PIAAC) (2nd edition)*. Paris: OECD Publishing. Retrieved from https://www.oecd.org/skills/piaac/PIAAC_Technical_Report_2nd_Edition_Full_Report.pdf

Klein Entink, R. H., Fox, J.-P., & van der Linden, W. J. (2009). A multivariate multilevel approach to the modeling of accuracy and speed of test takers. *Psychometrika, 74*, 21–48. https://doi.org/10.1007/s11336-008-9075-y.

Klotzke, K., & Fox, J.-P. (2019). Bayesian covariance structure modeling of responses and process data. *Frontiers in Psychology, 10*. https://doi.org/10.3389/fpsyg.2019.01675.

Kroehne, U., & Goldhammer, F. (2018). How to conceptualize, represent, and analyze log data from technology-based assessments? A generic framework and an application to questionnaire items. *Behaviormetrika, 45*, 527–563. https://doi.org/10.1007/s41237-018-0063-y.

Kroehne, U., Hahnel, C., & Goldhammer, F. (2019). Invariance of the response processes between gender and modes in an assessment of reading. *Frontiers in Applied Mathematics and Statistics, 5*, 1–16. https://doi.org/10.3389/fams.2019.00002.

Liao, D., He, Q., & Jiao, H. (2019). Mapping background variables with sequential patterns in problem-solving environments: An investigation of United States adults' employment status in PIAAC. *Frontiers in Psychology, 10*, 1–32. https://doi.org/10.3389/fpsyg.2019.00646.

Maddox, B., Bayliss, A. P., Fleming, P., Engelhardt, P. E., Edwards, S. G., & Borgonovi, F. (2018). Observing response processes with eye tracking in international large-scale assessments: Evidence from the OECD PIAAC assessment. *European Journal of Psychology of Education, 33*, 543–558. https://doi.org/10.1007/s10212-018-0380-2.

Mamedova, S., & Pawlowski, E. (2018). *Statistics in brief: A description of U.S. adults who are not digitally literate*. National Center for Education Statistics (NCES). Retrieved from https://nces.ed.gov/pubsearch/pubsinfo.asp?pubid=2018161

Mislevy, R. J., Almond, R. G., & Lukas, J. F. (2003). A brief introduction to evidence-centered design (ETS research report series, 1–29). https://doi.org/10.1002/j.2333-8504.2003.tb01908.x.

Naumann, J., Goldhammer, F., Rölke, H., & Stelter, A. (2014). Erfolgreiches Problemlösen in technologiebasierten Umgebungen: Wechselwirkungen zwischen Interaktionsschritten und Aufgabenanforderungen [Successful Problem Solving in Technology Rich Environments: Interactions Between Number of Actions and Task Demands]. *Zeitschrift für Pädagogische Psychologie, 28*, 193–203. https://doi.org/10.1024/1010-0652/a000134.

Organisation for Economic Co-operation and Development (OECD). (2019). *Beyond proficiency: Using log files to understand respondent behaviour in the survey of adult skills*. Paris: OECD Publishing. https://doi.org/10.1787/0b1414ed-en.

Organisation for Economic Co-operation and Development (OECD). (2012). *Literacy, numeracy and problem solving in technology-rich environments: Framework for the OECD survey of adult skills*. Paris: OECD Publishing. https://doi.org/10.1787/9789264128859-en.

Organisation for Economic Co-operation and Development (OECD). (2013a). *PISA 2012 Assessment and Analytical Framework: Mathematics, Reading, Science, Problem Solving and Financial Literacy*. Paris: OECD Publishing.

Organisation for Economic Co-operation and Development (OECD). (2013b). *Technical report of the survey of adult skills (PIAAC)*. Paris: OECD Publishing.

Organisation for Economic Co-operation and Development (OECD). (2017a). *Programme for the International Assessment of Adult Competencies (PIAAC), Austria log file*. Data file version 2.0.0 [ZA6712_AT.data.zip]. Cologne: GESIS Data Archive. doi:https://doi.org/10.4232/1.12955

Organisation for Economic Co-operation and Development (OECD). (2017b). *Programme for the International Assessment of Adult Competencies (PIAAC), Belgium log file*. Data file version 2.0.0 [ZA6712_BE.data.zip]. Cologne: GESIS Data Archive. doi:https://doi.org/10.4232/1.12955

Organisation for Economic Co-operation and Development (OECD). (2017c). *Programme for the International Assessment of Adult Competencies (PIAAC), Germany log file*. Data file version 2.0.0 [ZA6712_DE.data.zip]. Cologne: GESIS Data Archive. doi:https://doi.org/10.4232/1.12955

Organisation for Economic Co-operation and Development (OECD). (2017d). *Programme for the International Assessment of Adult Competencies (PIAAC), Denmark log file*. Data file version 2.0.0 [ZA6712_DK.data.zip]. Cologne: GESIS Data Archive. doi:https://doi.org/10.4232/1.12955

Organisation for Economic Co-operation and Development (OECD). (2017e). *Programme for the International Assessment of Adult Competencies (PIAAC), Estonia log file*. Data file version 2.0.0 [ZA6712_EE.data.zip]. Cologne: GESIS Data Archive. doi:https://doi.org/10.4232/1.12955

Organisation for Economic Co-operation and Development (OECD). (2017f). *Programme for the International Assessment of Adult Competencies (PIAAC), Spain log file*. Data file version 2.0.0 [ZA6712_ES.data.zip]. Cologne: GESIS Data Archive. doi:https://doi.org/10.4232/1.12955

Organisation for Economic Co-operation and Development (OECD). (2017g). *Programme for the International Assessment of Adult Competencies (PIAAC), Finland log file*. Data file version 2.0.0 [ZA6712_FI.data.zip]. Cologne: GESIS Data Archive. doi:https://doi.org/10.4232/1.12955

Organisation for Economic Co-operation and Development (OECD). (2017h). *Programme for the International Assessment of Adult Competencies (PIAAC), France log file*. Data file version 2.0.0 [ZA6712_FR.data.zip]. Cologne: GESIS Data Archive. doi:https://doi.org/10.4232/1.12955

Organisation for Economic Co-operation and Development (OECD). (2017j). *Programme for the International Assessment of Adult Competencies (PIAAC), United Kingdom log file*. Data file version 2.0.0 [ZA6712_GB.data.zip]. Cologne: GESIS Data Archive. doi:https://doi.org/10.4232/1.12955

Organisation for Economic Co-operation and Development (OECD). (2017k). *Programme for the International Assessment of Adult Competencies (PIAAC), Ireland log file*. Data file version 2.0.0 [ZA6712_IE.data.zip]. Cologne: GESIS Data Archive. doi:https://doi.org/10.4232/1.12955

Organisation for Economic Co-operation and Development (OECD)). (2017l). *Programme for the International Assessment of Adult Competencies (PIAAC), Italy log file*. Data file version 2.0.0 [ZA6712_IT.data.zip]. Cologne: GESIS Data Archive. doi:https://doi.org/10.4232/1.12955

Organisation for Economic Co-operation and Development (OECD). (2017m). *Programme for the International Assessment of Adult Competencies (PIAAC), South Korea log file*. Data file version 2.0.0 [ZA6712_KR.data.zip]. Cologne: GESIS Data Archive. doi:https://doi.org/10.4232/1.12955

Organisation for Economic Co-operation and Development (OECD)). (2017n). *Programme for the International Assessment of Adult Competencies (PIAAC), Netherlands log file*. Data file version 2.0.0 [ZA6712_NL.data.zip]. Cologne: GESIS Data Archive. doi:https://doi.org/10.4232/1.12955

Organisation for Economic Co-operation and Development (OECD). (2017o). *Programme for the International Assessment of Adult Competencies (PIAAC), Norway log file*. Data file version 2.0.0 [ZA6712_NO.data.zip]. Cologne: GESIS Data Archive. doi:https://doi.org/10.4232/1.12955

Organisation for Economic Co-operation and Development (OECD). (2017p). *Programme for the International Assessment of Adult Competencies (PIAAC), Poland log file*. Data file version 2.0.0 [ZA6712_PL.data.zip]. Cologne: GESIS Data Archive. doi:https://doi.org/10.4232/1.12955

Organisation for Economic Co-operation and Development (OECD). (2017q). *Programme for the International Assessment of Adult Competencies (PIAAC), Slovakia log file*. Data file version 2.0.0 [ZA6712_SK.data.zip]. Cologne: GESIS Data Archive. doi:https://doi.org/10.4232/1.12955

Organisation for Economic Co-operation and Development (OECD). (2017r). *Programme for the International Assessment of Adult Competencies (PIAAC), United States log file*. Data file version 2.0.0 [ZA6712_US.data.zip]. Cologne: GESIS Data Archive. doi:https://doi.org/10.4232/1.12955

PIAAC Expert Group in Problem Solving in Technology-Rich Environments. (2009). *PIAAC problem solving in technology-rich environments: A conceptual framework*. Paris: OECD Publishing.

Pohl, S., Ulitzsch, E., & von Davier, M. (2019). Using response times to model not-reached items due to time limits. *Psychometrika*, 1–29. https://doi.org/10.1007/s11336-019-09669-2.

R Core Team. (2016). *R: A language and environment for statistical computing*. Vienna: R Foundation for Statistical Computing.

Rölke, H. (2012). *The ItemBuilder: A graphical authoring system for complex item development*. Paper presented at the World Conference on E-Learning in Corporate, Government, Healthcare, and Higher Education, Montréal, Quebec, Canada.

Stelter, A., Goldhammer, F., Naumann, J., & Rölke, H. (2015). Die Automatisierung prozeduralen Wissens: Eine Analyse basierend auf Prozessdaten [The automation of procedural knowledge: An analysis based on process data]. In J. Stiller & C. Laschke (Eds.), *Berlin-Brandenburger Beitrage zur Bildungsforschung 2015: Herausforderungen, Befunde und Perspektiven Interdisziplinärer Bildungsforschung* (pp. 111–131). https://doi.org/10.3726/978-3-653-04961-9.

Tóth, K., Rölke, H., Goldhammer, F., & Barkow, I. (2017). Educational process mining: New possibilities for understanding students' problem-solving skills. In B. Csapó & J. Funke (Eds.), *The nature of problem solving: Using research to inspire 21st century learning* (pp. 193–209). Frankfurt am Main: Peter Lang. https://doi.org/10.1787/9789264273955-14-en.

Van der Linden, W. J. (2005). *Linear models for optimal test design*. New York: Springer.

Van der Linden, W. J. (2007). A hierarchical framework for modeling speed and accuracy on test items. *Psychometrika, 72*, 287–308. https://doi.org/10.1007/s11336-006-1478-z.

Van der Linden, W. J. (2008). Using response times for item selection in adaptive testing. *Journal of Educational and Behavioral Statistics, 33*, 5–20. https://doi.org/10.3102/1076998607302626.

Van der Linden, W. J., & Guo, F. (2008). Bayesian procedures for identifying aberrant response-time patterns in adaptive testing. *Psychometrika, 73*, 365–384. https://doi.org/10.1007/s11336-007-9046-8.

Vörös, Z., & Rouet, J.-F. (2016). Laypersons' digital problem solving: Relationships between strategy and performance in a large-scale international survey. *Computers in Human Behavior, 64*, 108–116. https://doi.org/10.1016/j.chb.2016.06.018.

Weeks, J. P., von Davier, M., & Yamamoto, K. (2016). Using response time data to inform the coding of omitted responses. *Psychological Test and Assessment Modeling, 58*, 671–701.

Wise, S. L., & DeMars, C. E. (2006). An application of item response time: The effort-moderated IRT model. *Journal of Educational Measurement, 43*, 19–38. https://doi.org/10.1111/j.1745-3984.2006.00002.x

Wise, S. L., & Gao, L. (2017). A general approach to measuring test-taking effort on computer-based tests. *Applied Measurement in Education, 30*, 343–354. https://doi.org/10.1080/08957347.2017.1353992.

Wise, S. L., Kuhfeld, M. R., & Soland, J. (2019). The effects of effort monitoring with proctor notification on test-taking engagement, test performance, and validity. *Applied Measurement in Education, 32*, 183–192. https://doi.org/10.1080/08957347.2019.1577248.

Yamamoto, K., & Lennon, M. L. (2018). Understanding and detecting data fabrication in large-scale assessments. *Quality Assurance in Education, 26*, 196–212. https://doi.org/10.1108/QAE-07-2017-0038.

Open Access This chapter is licensed under the terms of the Creative Commons Attribution 4.0 International License (http://creativecommons.org/licenses/by/4.0/), which permits use, sharing, adaptation, distribution and reproduction in any medium or format, as long as you give appropriate credit to the original author(s) and the source, provide a link to the Creative Commons license and indicate if changes were made.

The images or other third party material in this chapter are included in the chapter's Creative Commons license, unless indicated otherwise in a credit line to the material. If material is not included in the chapter's Creative Commons license and your intended use is not permitted by statutory regulation or exceeds the permitted use, you will need to obtain permission directly from the copyright holder.

Chapter 11
Linking PIAAC Data to Individual Administrative Data: Insights from a German Pilot Project

Jessica Daikeler, Britta Gauly, and Matthias Rosenthal

Abstract Linking survey data to administrative data offers researchers many opportunities. In particular, it enables them to enrich survey data with additional information without increasing the burden on respondents. German PIAAC data on individual skills, for example, can be combined with administrative data on individual employment histories. However, as the linkage of survey data with administrative data records requires the consent of respondents, there may be bias in the linked dataset if only a subsample of respondents—for example, high-educated individuals—give their consent. The present chapter provides an overview of the pilot project about linking the German PIAAC data with individual administrative data. In a first step, we illustrate characteristics of the linkable datasets and describe the linkage process and its methodological challenges. In a second step, we provide an illustrative example of the use of the linked data and investigate how the skills assessed in PIAAC are associated with the linkage decision.

11.1 The Importance of Enriching Survey Data with Administrative Data

Linking survey data to other data sources offers many opportunities, such as enriching survey data with additional information without increasing the burden on respondents (Calderwood and Lessof 2009; Sakshaug 2018; Sakshaug and Kreuter 2012). Thus, from a researcher's perspective, data linkage is a respondent-friendly, cost-effective, and quick way of generating data.

J. Daikeler (✉) · B. Gauly
GESIS – Leibniz Institute for the Social Sciences, Mannheim, Germany
e-mail: jessica.daikeler@gesis.org

M. Rosenthal
University of Stuttgart, Stuttgart, Germany

© The Author(s) 2020
D. B. Maehler, B. Rammstedt (eds.), *Large-Scale Cognitive Assessment*, Methodology of Educational Measurement and Assessment,
https://doi.org/10.1007/978-3-030-47515-4_11

In this context, linking survey data with administrative data is probably the most established method of data enrichment. Administrative data are typically provided by administrative sources, for example, notifications by employers to social security institutions or data from operational processes of employment agencies. This linkage has several benefits. For example, it provides a possibility of creating longitudinal data by linking cross-sectional survey data to administrative longitudinal data, or by linking different administrative datasets to each other. Administrative data may also contain historical records and accurate retrospective information that would be difficult or impossible to collect using traditional survey methods. And, at least in theory, administrative data contain information that provides full coverage of the population of interest (Calderwood and Lessof 2009). The data are neither affected by recall error, nor can they suffer from other deficiencies of survey data, such as social desirability bias, systematic drop-outs and item nonresponse, or panel mortality. Furthermore, the linkage of survey data with administrative data allows for a validation of survey data, for example, on earnings (Gauly et al. 2019; Sakshaug and Antoni 2017).

Despite its potential benefits, data linkage has methodological and practical challenges. The validity and usability of the linked data depend on respondents' consent to data linkage. Refusal to give this consent can result in a biased sample, especially if those who consent to the linkage differ significantly in their characteristics from those who refuse (Al Baghal et al. 2014). Moreover, these differences can create biased estimates obtained from linked data (Sakshaug and Kreuter 2012). However, the explicit consent to linkage by the respondents is necessary in order to comply with privacy rights and data protection policies.

The present chapter provides an overview on how to work with the data of the German sample of the Programme for the International Assessment of Adult Competencies (PIAAC), which was linked to administrative data held by the Institute for Employment Research (IAB), the research institute of the German Federal Employment Agency (BA). The resulting linked dataset, PIAAC-L-ADIAB, is part of a pilot project. The next section describes the linkage process and the challenges that it involves. Section 11.3 provides an illustrative example of data linkage, with a focus on the role of cognitive skills in the respondent's decision to consent to linkage. Section 11.4 concludes with practical recommendations for the linkage of PIAAC data to administrative records.

11.2 Linking PIAAC Data to IEB Data

The administrative data that are linked to the data of the German PIAAC 2012 sample are the data from the Integrated Employment Biographies (IEB) of the IAB. The IEB contain information on every individual in western Germany since 1975 and in eastern Germany since 1992 who has one of the following statuses: in employment subject to social security (recorded from 1975 onwards); in marginal part-time

11 Linking PIAAC Data to Individual Administrative Data: Insights...

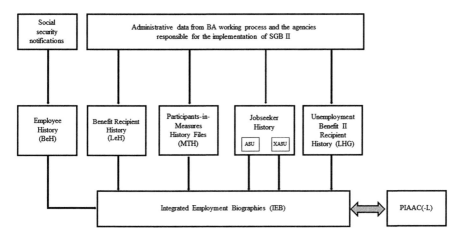

Fig. 11.1 Data sources of the Integrated Employment Biographies (Source: adapted from Antoni et al. 2017)

employment (recorded from 1999 onwards)[1]; in receipt of benefits in accordance with German Social Code[2]; registered as a jobseeker (recorded from 1997 onwards); or participating in an active labour market policy programme (recorded since 2000; for more details see Antoni et al. 2019a). The data originate from different sources within the German social security system: data on employment spells stem from compulsory notifications by employers to social security agencies; data on benefit receipt, job search spells, and participation in labour market programmes are entered mainly by caseworkers at the local employment agencies (see Fig. 11.1).

The consent question on linking survey data with administrative data was not part of the original PIAAC 2012 survey, but of the German follow-up panel study PIAAC-Longitudinal (PIAAC-L). This study followed up the German PIAAC respondents and comprised three additional waves conducted in 2014, 2015, and 2016 (for detailed information on PIAAC-L, see Rammstedt et al. 2017).

---

[1]Marginal part-time employment: (1) short-term employment with a maximum duration of 3 months or a maximum of 70 working days per calendar year; (2) employment with a monthly salary of no more than 450 euros; (3) employment in private households as a special type of marginal part-time employment.

[2]This comprises benefits according to Social Code Book III—namely, unemployment benefit, unemployment assistance and maintenance allowance (since 1975), as well as benefits in accordance with Social Code Book II, which covers both basic social security benefits (e.g. Unemployment Benefit II) and supplements to unemployment benefit or additional benefits (since 2005; Antoni et al. 2019a).

> Preliminary remarks:
> In the interview, various topics were discussed, including work and occupation. In order to be able to carry out detailed statistical analyses in the field of employment, we would like to include data from another database in the analysis. As already explained in our data protection sheet, these data (see below) are available from the Institute for Employment Research (IAB) of the Federal Employment Agency (BA) in Nuremberg. Further information on these BA/IAB data can be found at http://fdz.iab.de/de/FDZ_Overview_of_Data.aspx.
>
> For data protection reasons, the IAB requires the following consent in order to merge the data, which we would like to ask you to give below. Your consent is of course voluntary. Participation in PIAAC-L is possible independently of this consent.
>
> **Consent to record linkage of selected register data with your data from the PIAAC-L/PIAAC surveys**
>
> **I consent to a query being sent to the Institute for Employment Research (IAB) of the Federal Employment Agency (BA) in Nuremberg regarding data that are available about me. These data are information about my working life, employment relationships and spells of unemployment. My contact details may be sent to the IAB to request this information. The IAB data may then be merged with my data from the PIAAC-L/PIAAC surveys in order to include them anonymously in the analyses. My contact data shall be deleted after the query has been carried out. I have been informed that all data protection regulations will be complied with. I reserve the right to withdraw my consent at any time.**

Fig. 11.2 English translation of consent to linkage question
(Source: see Steinacker and Wolfert 2017, for the original German-language version)

All PIAAC 2012 anchor persons[3] who participated in the second wave (2015) of the German PIAAC-L study were asked at the end of the interview to consent to the linking of their survey data to administrative data from the IAB (see Fig. 11.2 for the English translation of the linkage question). The linkage required written consent, and respondents could give this consent in two different ways—directly at the interview, or afterwards by sending the consent form to the survey institute at their discretion (Zabal et al. 2017).

In total, 2363 (72.4%) of the 3263 anchor persons in PIAAC-L 2015 gave their consent to the linkage of their survey data to administrative data. For these respondents, personal information (including name, name at birth, date of birth, gender, and place of residence) were transmitted to the IAB.[4] This information was

---

[3] The PIAAC anchor persons are those respondents who already participated in the original PIAAC 2012 survey. In addition, PIAAC-L also surveyed partners and household members of the PIAAC 2012 anchor persons.

[4] Linkage was performed by the staff of the German Record Linkage Center (GRLC; see Antoni and Schnell 2019).

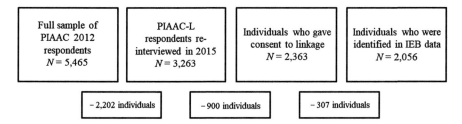

Fig. 11.3 Drop-out of respondents from PIAAC 2012 to PIAAC-L 2015 and PIAAC-L-ADIAB

subsequently used to identify the respondents in the IEB data (for more detailed information on the linkage procedure, see Braun 2016; GESIS – Leibniz Institute for the Social Sciences and Institute for Employment Research (IAB) 2017).

11.2.1 Sample Differences

Of the PIAAC-L 2015, participants who gave their consent to data linkage, 2056 (87%) could be identified in the IEB data.[5] Thus, the sample of individuals that can be used for joint analyses with PIAAC and IEB data (referred to in what follows as 'PIAAC-L-ADIAB') is significantly smaller than the full sample of individuals participating in PIAAC-L 2015 ($N = 3263$) as well as the original and representative PIAAC 2012 sample ($N = 5465$) due to sample attrition, missing consent, and missing IEB data (see Fig. 11.3).

Table 11.1 presents the (unweighted) distributions of sociodemographic characteristics in the various samples. It is clear from the table that the samples differ with regard to the distribution of these characteristics. For example, individuals in the PIAAC-L-ADIAB sample are on average older compared with all individuals who participated in PIAAC-L 2015 or compared with those who gave their consent to data linkage. In addition, the share of women and the share of individuals with a primary or lower secondary qualification (ISCED 1 and 2) are lower in PIAAC-L-ADIAB. Thus, researchers working with the linked PIAAC-L-ADIAB data have to be aware of sample selection bias. For example, if only high-educated individuals consent to linkage (as the unconditional distribution in Table 11.1 suggests), the average educational level is higher in the linked sample, and the estimated relationships between education and any other variable might be biased. Following this, results obtained from the linked sample cannot be generalised to the population at large.

---

[5]Civil servants, self-employed persons, and individuals doing only unpaid domestic work are not included in the IAB data unless they have previously or incidentally been in dependent employment, registered as unemployed, registered as jobseekers, or had one of the other statuses mentioned in Sect. 11.2. Thus, these respondents could not be identified and linked in the IAB data.

Table 11.1 Sample statistics for PIAAC 2012, PIAAC-L 2015, the 'linkage consent sample', and PIAAC-L-ADIAB

	PIAAC 2012 $N = 5465$	PIAAC-L 2015 $N = 3263$	Linkage Consent $N = 2363$	PIAAC-L-ADIAB $N = 2056$
Age (mean)	39.8	44.4	44.2	50.9
Female (%)	51.0	51.3	48.9	43.9
Education (%)	$(m = 90)$			
ISCED 1/2	17.0	8.9	8.2	8.6
ISCED 3/4	51.5	55.2	54.8	57.1
ISCED 5B	12.0	11.9	12.3	12.1
ISCED 5A/6	19.5	24.1	24.7	22.2
Native speaker (%)	89.0 $(m = 90)$	91.8	93.4	93.4
Employed (%)	75.7 $(m = 88)$	77.1	77.5	78.2
Eastern Germany (%)	20.5	21.6 $(m = 1)$	22.4 $(m = 1)$	23.1 $(m = 1)$

Notes. The percentages refer to the persons for whom valid values are available. The numbers in parentheses $(m = \ldots)$ indicate the number of missing values for each variable. No weighting included. There are no significant differences in any of the variables listed here between the PIAAC-L 2015 and the linkage consent sample (indicated by t-test)

11.2.2 Working with the Linked Data

In order to be able to access and use the linked data, a number of steps were required within the pilot project.[6] First, a data usage agreement with the PIAAC Research Data Center (RDC) at GESIS – Leibniz Institute for the Social Sciences for using PIAAC and PIAAC-L data is mandatory. Second, a data usage application must be submitted to the IAB's RDC. Once the application is confirmed, an agreement must be concluded between the researcher and the IAB. The IAB then issues the researcher with a user ID and a password for data access.

As the use of administrative data is subject to restrictions under data protection legislation, the data must be analysed either on-site or via remote access. The advantage of on-site use is the opportunity to view the results directly. Remote data access means that researchers submit scripts (e.g. Stata do-files) to the RDC and, after verification of compliance with data protection legislation, access the approved results.[7]

If data access is granted and the technical requirements are fulfilled, the next step is the data merging. The personal identifier (*SEQID*) from PIAAC is added to the IEB data, thereby rendering it possible to merge the two data sources via the identifier.

---

[6] All the following administrative steps and the list of available variables (Table 11.2) refer to data access within the pilot project. When accessing PIAAC-L linked data in the future, these steps and the variables available may be different.

[7] For more information, see https://fdz.iab.de/en/FDZ_Data_Access/FDZ_Remote_Data_Access.aspx.

```
. clear all
. version 14

. * --------- ( merge PIAAC 2012 and IEB data ) --------- *

. global data_path "..."

. *** load PIAAC data ***

. use "$data_path\ZA5845_v2-2-0.dta"

. sort SEQID

. *** merge with IEB data ***

. merge 1:m SEQID using "$data_path/PIAAC-L-ADIAB_7514_v1_SUF-ID.dta"
```

Fig. 11.4 Example of syntax to merge PIAAC 2012 and IEB data

Figure 11.4 provides a simple example of the 'merge' syntax for linking the PIAAC and IEB data in Stata.[8] As is apparent from the figure, the data are not linked 'one to one' (1:1) but rather 'one to many' (1:m). This means that one row (respondent) in PIAAC is merged with multiple rows in the IEB data. This is due to the 'spell format' of the IEB data, which means that there are several observations per person, each covering a period of time (spell) during which the person had a given employment status—for example, employed or unemployed. A new spell is created whenever an employer reports new information (e.g. change in employment status, change in establishment, or change in daily wage).

Figure 11.5 provides a fictional example of the spell structure: like any other person in PIAAC, Respondent no. 1111 has exactly one row in the PIAAC data (left side of the graph). However, as Respondent no. 1111 has three different entries in the IEB data (e.g. due to a period of unemployment between January and June 2011), he or she has three rows (spells) in the IEB data (right side of the graph). By linking the PIAAC data with the IEB data, the information from PIAAC is replicated and passed to each of the respondent's three rows in the IEB data ranges.

Unfortunately, it also happens that some of the spells in the IEB data overlap, which means that different information may be available for an individual for the same period of time (see, e.g. Figs. 11.5 and 11.6, Respondent no. 1113 in the period between December 1, 2005, and December 31, 2005). To create completely nonoverlapping periods, so-called episode splitting is performed as shown in Fig.

---

[8]This example refers only to the linkage of the administrative data with the data from PIAAC 2012. The additional waves of PIAAC-L have to be merged separately (via the personal identifier *SEQID*).

SEQID	piaac_var1	piaac_var2
1111	1	20
1112	1	30
1113	0	20
1114	1	50
1115	0	40

SEQID	spell	startdate	enddate	iab_var1
1111	1	01-01-2001	31-12-2010	1
1111	2	01-01-2011	30-06-2011	1
1111	3	01-07-2011	31-12-2012	1
1112	1	01-01-1990	31-12-2011	0
1113	1	01-01-2005	31-12-2005	1
1113	2	01-12-2005	31-12-2010	0

Fig. 11.5 Individual data given in PIAAC and IEB
Notes. The left-hand side shows an example of data provided in the PIAAC survey. The right-hand side shows an example of the PIAAC-L-ADIAB data, which contains information from both PIAAC and IEB data

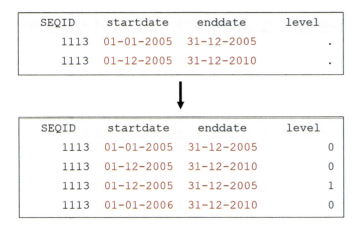

Fig. 11.6 Example of episode splitting

11.6.[9] In this way, the episodes (period between December 1, 2005, and December 31, 2005) are replaced by artificial episodes with new start and end dates.[10]

Once the two datasets have been linked, users can access a wide range of additional labour market-related information. Table 11.2 provides a list of the variables that were available in the IEB data during the pilot project (for an overview, also see Antoni et al. 2019a). In addition to these variables, further sensitive characteristics, such as nationality and occupational subgroup, can be requested from the RDC. However, as these variables would enable the identification of particular individuals or establishments, they are disclosed in their original form only if it is necessary for the study objective and explicitly justified in the application for data access. The specific variables that are classified as sensitive are documented in Antoni et al. (2019a).

---

[9]The *level* variable counts how often information is repeated for the same time period. The value '0' indicates that the information is available for the first time; '1' indicates the first repetition.

[10]'Episode splitting' is part of the preparation of the IEB data and is not specifically related to PIAAC. For more details, see Antoni et al. (2019a).

11 Linking PIAAC Data to Individual Administrative Data: Insights...

Table 11.2 Variables available in IEB data

Variable name	Variable label
Persnr	Individual ID
Betrnr	Establishment ID
spell	Observation counter per person
quelle	Source of spell
begorig	Original start date of observation
endorig	Original end date of observation
begepi	Start date of split episode
endepi	End date of split episode
frau	Gender
gebjahr	Year of birth
nation_gr	Nationality, aggregated
famst	Marital status
kind	Number of children
ausbildung	Vocational training
schule	School leaving qualification
tentgelt	Daily wage, daily benefit rate
beruf	Occupation—current/most recent (KldB 1988)[a]
beruf2010_3	Occupation—current/most recent (KldB 1988)[a]
niveau	Level of requirement—current/most recent (KldB 2010)[a]
teilzeit	Part-time status
erwstat	Employment status
gleitz	Transition zone
leih	Temporary agency work
befrist	Fixed-term contract
grund	Reason of cancellation/notification/termination
estatvor	Employment status prior to job search
estatnach	Employment status after job search
profil	Client profile
art_kuend	Type of termination of last job
arbzeit	Desired working hours of the job sought
restanspruch	Residual claim/planned duration
treager	Type of institution
alo_beg	Start of date of unemployment
alo_dau	Duration of unemployment
wo_bula	Place of residence: federal state (*Bundesland*)
wo_rd	Place of residence: regional directorate

Notes.[a] KldB = Klassifikation der Berufe (German Classification of Occupations)

The linked data can then be used for various substantive and methodological research questions. Substantive research questions may focus, for example, on the relationship between earnings development (IEB data) and skill level (survey data). Methodological questions that exploit the potential of these two data sources may deal, for example, with the evaluation of the measurement error in the survey data by assessing it against (less error-prone) administrative data (see also Antoni et al. 2019b; Gauly et al. 2019).

In the next section, we examine the role of cognitive skills in the respondent's decision to consent to data linkage.

11.3 Illustrative Example: Is Consent to Linkage Less Likely Among Low-Skilled Individuals?

In the present example, we extend existing research on the determinants of consent to linkage. In particular, we explore the role of cognitive skills. The sociodemographic correlates of linkage consent have been well researched. For example, previous research has shown that education, and thus human capital, has a strong and positive association with consent to linkage (see Table 11.3). However, education, which has been tested in a large number of studies, is only a proxy for a person's concrete ability and skills (see, e.g. Hanushek et al. 2015) and might not give sufficient insight into how abilities and skills are related to the decision to consent, or withhold consent, to data linkage. So far, comprehensive evidence on the role of skills in the respondent's decision to consent to data linkage is missing, as survey data containing objective skill measures are in short supply.

For researchers who work with the linked PIAAC(-L) data, it is important to know whether the linked sample differs significantly from the initial sample and to be aware of the mechanisms involved in the linkage consent process. As the majority of analyses with PIAAC data involve the skills assessed, our analysis focuses on the relationship between skills and consent to linkage.

As an example for such possible mechanisms, low-skilled individuals who receive public benefits are highly dependent on the decision of the institutions that allocate the benefits. Thus, these individuals may be more sceptical when asked for additional information, anticipating a potential change in their benefits compared to medium-skilled individuals who have less contact with institutions. High-skilled individuals are less dependent on the institutions' decisions, but may follow public debate on data security more closely. This may lead to a higher sensitivity for the transfer of sensitive data and a higher rate of linkage refusals compared with low- or medium-skilled persons who follow public debate less closely.

The next section provides an overview of existing literature on the determinants of consent to data linkage before we present our own analysis strategy and results.

11 Linking PIAAC Data to Individual Administrative Data: Insights...

Table 11.3 Overview of relationship between sociodemographic variables and consent to linkage

	Antoni (2013)	Baker et al. (2000)	Bates and Pascale (2005)	Beste (2011)	Dahlhamer and Cox (2007)	Finkelstein (2001)	Haider and Solon (2000)	Hartmann and Krug (2009)	Jenkins et al. (2006)	Knies et al. (2012)	Knies and Burton (2014)	Korbmacher and Schroeder (2013)	vPascale (2011)	Sakshaug et al. (2012)	Sala et al. (2010)	Warnke (2017)
Age	−	ns	−	ns	−	ns	ns	ns	+	−	ns	+	−	ns	−	+
Female	ns	ns	−	ns	−	ns	+	−	ns	−	−	ns	+	ns	−/ns	ns
Education	ns		+	ns	−/ns	ns	ns	ns	ns	+	+/−	ns	+	+	+	−
Literacy	ns															
Numeracy	ns															
Native speaker	ns			+										ns		
Foreign citizen	ns			−	−		ns	−						ns		ns
Employed	+						+	ns						ns		
Health status		ns	ns		+		+	ns	ns	+/ns	ns	ns	ns	ns	ns	
Interview duration								ns	+			ns				
Occupation	s			ns				ns			s/ns					s/ns
Income	ns		+	+	ns	ns	+	+	−	ns	+/ns	+	ns	ns	ns	
Eastern Germany	+							+				+				+
Country	GER	UK	USA	GER	US	USA	USA	GER	UK	UK	UK	GER	USA	USA	UK	GER

Notes. The overview primarily includes studies that simultaneously tested multiple correlations of demographic variables and other predictors with consent to linkage. We report the results of the full models. Cells containing multiple entries represent different results for different samples within the same publication. *s* significant; ns = not significant; + positive significant, − negative significant, *GER*: Germany, *USA*: United States of America, *UK*: United Kingdom

11.3.1 Previous Evidence on Consent to Linkage

As mentioned above, the linkage of survey data to administrative data offers many possibilities and advantages, not only for researchers (e.g. enhanced data variety or the creation longitudinal datasets) but also for respondents (shortening the survey). However, the rates of consent to linkage vary depending on the cultural context, survey content, and sample. For example, linking survey data from the National Educational Panel Study to administrative data, Antoni et al. (2018) obtained a consent rate of over 90%; Sakshaug and Kreuter (2014) were able to achieve consent rates of 60% in a stratified random sample in Germany, whereas in the British Household Panel Survey, Sala et al. (2010) achieved only 32% consent to linkage with administrative data.

When explaining these variations in the rate of consent to linkage, most of the literature has focused on respondents' characteristics (Sakshaug et al. 2012). Common determinants of consent include age, gender, income, foreign citizenship, health/disability status, and benefit receipt (Knies and Burton 2014; Sakshaug and Kreuter 2012; Sala et al. 2010).

Table 11.3 summarises studies that have examined the association between sociodemographic variables and the decision to consent to the linkage of survey data to other data sources. Surprisingly, the findings of previous studies vary considerably in almost all sociodemographics, and it is hard to identify specific variables that consistently influenced the decision to consent to linkage across all studies.

Age, for example, was found in seven studies to have no correlation with linkage consent (e.g. Knies and Burton 2014; Sakshaug et al. 2012) and in six studies to have a negative correlation (e.g. Antoni 2013; Sala et al. 2010). Three studies found that age had a positive correlation, suggesting that consent to linkage becomes more likely with increasing age (e.g. Jenkins et al. 2006; Warnke 2017).

Education is the only variable that was found by almost all the studies considered to have a significant association with linkage consent (e.g. Knies and Burton 2014; Sala et al. 2010). With three exceptions (Dahlhamer and Cox 2007; Knies et al. 2012; Warnke 2017), higher-educated respondents were found to be more likely than lower-educated respondents to consent to linkage.

The two studies that directly investigated the association between skills, in terms of literacy and numeracy, and linkage consent (Antoni 2013; Sakshaug et al. 2012) found no correlation between the two variables. However, both of these studies exhibit shortcomings: Antoni (2013) used only self-reported (and, thus, subjective) skills measures, and Sakshaug et al. (2012) focused only on a restricted sample (adults aged 50 years or older). Therefore, Antoni's (2013) results cannot be generalised to objective skill measures, and Sakshaug et al.'s (2012) results cannot be generalised to the population at large.

In the present study, we contribute to closing this research gap by investigating whether objective measures of individual skills are associated with respondents' willingness to consent to linkage with administrative data.

11.3.2 Estimation Strategy and Measures

Our main goal in this research was to estimate the relationship between the skills assessed in PIAAC and individuals' consent to the linkage of their survey data to administrative data. To that end, we applied logistic regression models and calculated average marginal effects (AMEs):

$$\Pr(consent_i = 1|X) = G(\beta X) \tag{11.1}$$

where i indicates the individual and $G(\bullet)$ is a standard logistic cumulative distribution function yielding a logit model. *Consent* is a dummy variable that equals *1* if an individual gave consent to linkage and *0* otherwise, X is a vector of covariates, and the coefficient vector β contains parameters to be estimated.

We conducted several different regression analyses. As our key explanatory variables, we analysed the cognitive skills assessed in PIAAC. Thus, our first three models included either a standardised (mean, 0; standard deviation, 1) measure of numeracy, literacy, or problem solving in technology-rich environments (PS-TRE) skills.[11]

In our second set of models, we focused only on numeracy skills, 'the ability to access, use, interpret, and communicate mathematical information and ideas in order to engage in and manage the mathematical demands of a range of situations in adult life' (OECD 2013). As there is a strong correlation between all three skill domains, ranging from 0.753 to 0.872, we decided to report results for numeracy skills in the main model only.[12]

Additionally, we included control variables that previous studies have identified as common predictors of consent to linkage, in order to control for spurious correlations between skills and consent to linkage: age (continuous, in years); gender (1 = *female*, 0 = *male*); education (four categories; 1 = *ISCED 1/2*; 2 = *ISCED 3/4*; 3 = *ISCED 5B*; 4 = *ISCED 5A/6*); native language (1 = *non-German*, 0 = *German*); region (1 = *eastern Germany*, 0 = *western Germany*); and employment status (three categories; 1 = *employed*; 2 = *unemployed*; 3 = *non-employed*). Furthermore, we added the total duration in minutes of the survey interview in 2015 as a proxy for respondent burden. For individuals who were employed at the time of the survey, we additionally included their occupational group (four categories: 1 = *elementary*; 2 = *semi-skilled blue-collar*; 3 = *semi-skilled white-collar*; 4 = *skilled*) as well as the quartile of their monthly net income (four categories).

We present our results in Table 11.4.

---

[11] Plausible values were taken into account in all models. For detailed information on the definition and assessment of skills in PIAAC, see Chap. 3 in the present volume.

[12] Sensitivity analyses showed the results for the other skills to be very similar. Results are available from the authors on request.

Table 11.4 Probability of giving consent to linkage (average marginal effects and standard errors obtained from logistic regression models)

	(1)	(2)	(3)	(4)	(5)
Numeracy (std.)	0.042***(0.010)			0.014(0.012)	0.006(0.015)
Literacy (std.)		0.041***(0.010)			
PS-TRE (std.)			0.031***(0.010)		
Education (ref: ISCED 3/4)					
ISCED 1/2				0.047(0.038)	0.078(0.055)
ISCED 5B				0.076#(0.045)	0.122#(0.063)
ISCED 5A/6				0.090*(0.043)	0.141*(0.061)
Age				−0.001#(0.001)	−0.001(0.001)
Female				−0.018(0.019)	−0.022(0.025)
Non-native speaker				−0.151***(0.040)	−0.137**(0.048)
LF status (ref: employed)					
Unemployed				0.079#(0.046)	
Not employed				0.007(0.025)	
Eastern Germany				0.024(0.023)	0.043(0.027)
Interview duration				0.002***(0.001)	0.001(0.001)
Occupation (ref: elementary)					
Semi-skilled white-collar					0.014(0.030)
Semi-skilled blue-collar					−0.037(0.037)
Elementary					−0.008(0.052)
Monthly net income (ref:Q1)					
Q2					0.040(0.033)
Q3					0.031(0.035)
Q4					0.021(0.036)
R^2	0.010	0.010	0.004	0.026	0.026
N[a]	3256	3256	2804[b]	3256	2232

Notes: [a] Our sample size of 3256 in these analyses is based on all respondents for whom there were no missing values on any of our explanatory variables. When we focused only on employed individuals, our sample size dropped to 2232 (Column 5). [b] We had less observations in the model with PS-TRE skills, as only those persons who had computer experience and were willing to participate in the computer assessment can have values for these skills

LF status = labour force status

$p \leq 0.1$; * $p \leq 0.05$; ** $p \leq 0.01$; *** $p \leq 0.001$

11.3.3 Results: Do Cognitive Skills Influence the Linkage-Consent Decision?

Our results show that, in the baseline models (that included only literacy or numeracy or PS-TRE skills), skills had a positive association with the decision to consent to data linkage (Table 11.4, Columns 1–3). All three measures were positive and highly significant (numeracy: 0.042***; literacy: 0.041***; PS-TRE: 0.031***), which means that the higher the skills, the higher is the likelihood to consent to linkage.

Adding control variables to the model including numeracy skills, we observed that educational level had a positive association with the linkage-consent decision (Columns 4 and 5 in Table 11.4). The higher a respondent's level of education was, the more likely he or she was to agree to data linkage. Furthermore, we found a lower probability of consenting to linkage in PIAAC if German was not the respondent's first language. We also found a small significant positive correlation for the duration of the interview, which was probably due to reverse causality, whereby consenting to linkage resulted in a longer interview. After controlling for the sociodemographic variables and interview duration, the significant association with skills disappeared. Age, gender, and income did not influence the linkage decision in any of the models.

11.3.4 The Role of Cognitive Skills in Consent to Data Linkage

In the present example, we hypothesised that numeracy, literacy, and PS-TRE skills measured in PIAAC were related to respondents' decision to consent, or refuse consent, to the linkage of their PIAAC(−L) data to administrative employment history data of the IAB. Our results show that, in models without control variables, all three skill measures correlated positively with consent to linkage. This means that the higher a person's skills were, the more likely he or she was to consent to the linkage of his or her survey data to the administrative employment history records. In other words, in our baseline models, individuals with low skills were less likely to consent to data linkage.

With this knowledge, questionnaire designers could use responsive design to adapt their linkage question to low-skilled respondents. This means that, depending on the skill level achieved in the PIAAC survey, the question of consent to data linkage would be individually adjusted. However, this presupposes that the skill value of the respondent is known before the linkage question is asked. Responsive design would allow the targeted addressing of respondents' concerns. For example, for individuals with low skills, the question could be formulated in more simple language. Of course, data protection provisions would still have to be adhered to and privacy concerns addressed. It could also be emphasised that, during the linkage process, researchers are independent of institutions such as the employment agency.

We found that the decision of PIAAC(-L) respondents to consent to linkage was not affected by the sociodemographic variables gender, age, income, or employment status. However, respondents' education and native language (German/non-German) did play a particularly important role in the consent decision. These results are largely consistent with previous literature, which has identified mixed findings for sociodemographic variables and their connection with the linkage decision. However, especially the significant correlations revealed for education and native language suggest that respondents may not be able to properly understand the linkage question and its implications and that further effort should be invested in the framing of this question (e.g. Sakshaug et al. 2013).

11.4 Conclusion

The focus of this chapter was on describing the process of linking data from the German PIAAC(-L) sample to administrative data of the IAB. We focused on the technical side of data linkage and the methodological challenges involved. In addition, we provided a summary of recent findings on selective consent to data linkage and illustrated how the cognitive skills assessed in PIAAC affect the decision to consent—or withhold consent—to data linkage.

The use of linked datasets has a number of advantages: survey data can be enriched with additional information without increasing respondent burden, cross-sectional surveys can be extended with longitudinal information from other data sources, and the quality of the survey information can be evaluated against an additional (more objective) data source. Thus, linked data samples allow researchers to explore completely new fields of research.

By using the linked PIAAC-L-ADIAB sample, for instance, researchers can address questions concerning the relationship between the individual labour market history and cognitive skills. From a survey methodology perspective, the linked dataset provides many opportunities, such as research on consent to data linkage, as well as possibilities for the evaluation of survey and administrative data (Gauly et al. 2019; Sakshaug and Antoni 2017).

However, the use of linked data also involves challenges. First, when combining PIAAC and IEB data, researchers have to be aware that the latter are available in so-called spell format. This means that not only one but rather several pieces of information from the administrative data will be linked to each respondent in the survey data and that a number of steps are required before the researcher can access and use the linked data.

Second, researchers face challenges in the use of the linked PIAAC-L-ADIAB data due to the small sample size. The linkage question was included only in PIAAC-L 2015, so only those individuals who participated in both PIAAC 2012 and PIAAC-L were asked for their consent to the linkage of their survey data with administrative data. Of those respondents who were asked for their consent, only a subsample agreed to the linkage; and of those who agreed, only a subsample could be identified within the administrative data. Thus, we were left with a total sample of only 2056 individuals in the linked PIAAC-L-ADIAB dataset, which reduces statistical power and makes subsample analyses difficult.

And finally, there is a risk of selection bias in the linked PIAAC-L-ADIAB dataset. This arose for two reasons. The first selection occurred at the transition from PIAAC 2012 to PIAAC-L 2015. Research shows that PIAAC respondents who were willing to participate in the first wave of the longitudinal PIAAC survey differed significantly in terms of educational attainment, literacy skills, and native language from the initial PIAAC 2012 sample (Martin et al. 2019). The second selection resulted from the consent to data linkage, as the distribution of the sociodemographic characteristics in the linked dataset differs from that in the PIAAC-L 2015 sample (see Table 11.1). Numerous studies have shown that individual characteristics influence the consent to link survey with administrative data (see Table 11.3). As a result, not all sociodemographic groups are adequately represented in the linked dataset, and analyses will not obtain representative results. For instance, in the PIAAC-L-ADIAB sample, higher-educated individuals are overrepresented, which can lead to bias in the estimation of the relationship between education and any other variable.

In the example of the use of the PIAAC-L-ADIAB data presented here, we showed a positive and statistically significant association of the skills assessed in PIAAC and respondents' willingness to consent to data linkage. Our results indicate that individuals with low skills are less likely to consent to linkage than their high-skilled peers. However, this finding holds only for the zero-order correlations (models without control variables), as the coefficients became statistically insignificant when we controlled for individual characteristics. Moreover, our results show no statistically significant relationship between the decision to consent to linkage and sociodemographic variables, such as gender, age, income, or employment status. These results are largely consistent with previous literature, which has shown mixed findings for sociodemographic variables and their connection with the linkage decision. In contrast, respondents' education and native language (German/non-German) seem to be associated with the consent decision, which suggests that consent is related to the comprehension of the linkage question. In the light of these findings, further research should be conducted on how linkage questions should be framed and how responsive design could be used to achieve a higher linkage rate and low linkage bias (e.g. Sakshaug et al. 2013).

However, our findings do not imply that all individual characteristics play a negligible role in the linkage decision and that all individuals have the same probability of being represented in a linked dataset. This would suggest that there were no differences between the PIAAC-L 2015 sample, the original PIAAC 2012 sample, and the subsample of individuals who consented to linkage with administrative information. Instead, as can be seen from Table 11.1, the linked dataset (PIAAC-L-ADIAB) and the PIAAC-L 2015 and PIAAC 2012 datasets differ in terms of the sociodemographic characteristics of the respective samples. The decision to participate in PIAAC-L seems to have been affected by certain characteristics (see, e.g. Martin et al. 2019), and this sample selection bias translated also into the PIAAC-L-ADIAB sample. This suggests that future surveys would benefit from including the linkage question in the first wave of a (longitudinal) survey. In that way, panel mortality would not have a distorting effect on the sample that is asked the consent question and that could potentially be part of a linked dataset. However, we also found noticeable differences in the share of females and the average age between PIAAC-L 2015 and PIAAC-L-ADIAB when we considered unconditional sample differences. This can probably be explained by the fact that (especially older) women are less likely to be employed. Similarly, younger people are often not yet employed, which contributes to the age bias. Summing up, we want to emphasise that researchers working with the linked data need to be aware of these biases, which preclude the drawing of conclusions for the general population. These sample selection biases may lead to over- or underestimation of true effects, depending on whether the panel attrition is systematic, which would mean, for example, that lower-educated individuals who consent to data linkage are significantly different in unobserved characteristics than low-educated individuals who withhold consent to linkage.

References

Al Baghal, T., Knies, G., & Burton, J. (2014). *Linking administrative records to surveys: Differences in the correlates to consent decisions* (Understanding Society Working Paper Series No. 9). Colchester: Institute for Social and Economic Research University of Essex.

Antoni, M. (2013). *Essays on the measurement and analysis of educational and skill inequalities.* Nuremberg: Institute for Employment Research.

Antoni, M., & Schnell, R. (2019). The past, present and future of the German Record Linkage Center (GRLC). *Jahrbücher für Nationalökonomie und Statistik, 239*(2), 1–13. https://doi.org/10.1515/jbnst-2017-1004

Antoni, M., Dummert, S., & Trenkle, S. (2017). *PASS-Befragungsdaten verknüpft mit administrativen Daten des IAB (PASS-ADIAB) 1975–2015* (FDZ Datenreport, 06/2017). Nuremberg: Institute for Employment Research.

Antoni, M., Bachbauer, N., Eberle, J., & Vicari, B. (2018). *NEPS-SC6 survey data linked to administrative data of the IAB (NEPS-SC6-ADIAB 7515).* (FDZ-Datenreport, 02/2018). Nuremberg: Institute for Employment Research.

Antoni, M., Schmucker, A., Seth, S., & vom Berge, P. (2019a). *Sample of Integrated Labour Market Biographies (SIAB) 1975–2017* (FDZ Datenreport, 02/2019). Nuremberg: Institute for Employment Research.

Antoni, M., Bela, D., & Vicari, B. (2019b). Validating earnings in the German National Educational Panel Study: Determinants of measurement accuracy of survey questions on earnings. *Methods, Data, Analyses, 13*(1), 59–90. https://di.org/10.12758/mda.2018.08

Baker, R., Shiels, C., Stevenson, K., Fraser, R., & Stone, M. (2000). What proportion of patients refuse consent to data collection from their records for research purposes? *British Journal of General Practice, 50*(457), 655–656. Avaibable at http://www.amstat.org/committees/ethics/linksdir/Jsm2005Bates.pdf

Bates, N., & Pascale, J. (2005). Development and testing of informed consent questions to link survey data with administrative records. In: *Proceedings of the Survey Research Methods Section*, American Statistical Association, pp. 3786–3793.

Beste, J. (2011). *Selektivitätsprozesse bei der Verknüpfung von Befragungs- mit Prozessdaten: Record Linkage mit Daten des Panels „Arbeitsmarkt und soziale Sicherung" und adminis-*

trativen Daten der Bundesagentur für Arbeit (FDZ Methodenreport 09/2011). Nuremberg: Institute for Employment Research.

Braun, D. (2016). *Dokumentation zur Erstellung einer Verlinkungsdatei von PIAAC/PIAAC-L Befragungsdaten mit administrativen Daten der Bundesagentur für Arbeit*. Nuremberg: Institute for Employment Research. Unpublished manuscript.

Calderwood, L., & Lessof, C. (2009). *Enhancing longitudinal surveys by linking to administrative data*. University of Essex, Methodology of Longitudinal Surveys. Available at https://www.iser.essex.ac.uk/files/survey/ulsc/methodological-research/mols-2006/scientific-social-programme/papers/Calderwood.pdf

Dahlhamer, J. M., & Cox, C. S. (2007, November). *Respondent consent to link survey data with administrative records: Results from a split-ballot field test with the 2007 National Health Interview Survey*. Paper presented at the Federal Committee on Statistical Methodology Research Conference, Arlington, VA.

Finkelstein, M. M. (2001). Do factors other than need determine utilization of physicians' services in Ontario? *CMAJ, 165*(5), 565–570.

Gauly, B., Daikeler, J., Gummer, T., & Rammstedt, B. (2019). What's my wage again? Comparing survey and administrative data to validate earnings measures. *International Journal of Social Research Methodology, 23*(2), 125–228. https://doi.org/10.1080/13645579.2019.1657691

GESIS – Leibniz Institute for the Social Sciences & Institute for Employment Research (IAB). (2017). *PIAAC-L-ADIAB* [Data file; Version 2]. Unpublished data. Nuremberg: Institute for Employment Research.

Haider, S., & Solon, G. (2000). *Nonrandom selection in the HRS social security earnings sample* (Working Paper No. 00-01). RAND Labor and Population Program.

Hanushek, E., Schwerdt, G., Woessmann, L., & Wiederhold, S. (2015). Returns to skills around the world: Evidence from PIAAC. *European Economic Review, 73*, 103–130. https://doi.org/10.1016/j.euroecorev.2014.10.006

Hartmann, J., & Krug, G. (2009). Verknüpfung von personenbezogenen Prozess-und Befragungsdaten–Selektivität durch fehlende Zustimmung der Befragten? *Zeitschrift für ArbeitsmarktForschung, 42*(2), 121–139. https://doi.org/10.1007/s12651-009-0013-y

Jenkins, S. P., Cappellari, L., Lynn, P., Jäckle, A., & Sala, E. (2006). Patterns of consent: Evidence from a general household survey. *Journal of the Royal Statistical Society: Series A, 169*(4), 701–722. https://doi.org/10.1111/j.1467-985X.2006.00417.x

Knies, G., & Burton, J. (2014) Analysis of four studies in a comparative framework reveals: health linkage consent rates on British cohort studies higher than on UK household panel surveys. *BMC Medical Research Methodology, 14*(1), 125–136. https://doi.org/10.1186/1471-2288-14-125

Knies, G., Burton, J., & Sala, E. (2012). Consenting to health record linkage: Evidence from a multi-purpose longitudinal survey of a general population. *BMC Health Services Research, 12*(1), 52–57. https://doi.org/10.1186/1472-6963-12-52

Korbmacher, J. M., & Schroeder, M. (2013). Consent when linking survey data with administrative records: The role of the interviewer. *Survey Research Methods, 7*(2), 115–131. https://doi.org/10.18148/srm/2013.v7i2.5067

Martin, S., Lechner, C., Kleinert, C., & Rammstedt, B. (2020). Literacy skills predict probability of refusal in follow-up wave: Evidence from two longitudinal assessment surveys. *International Journal of Social Research Methodology*. Advance online publication.

OECD. (2013). *OECD skills outlook 2013: First results from the Survey of Adult Skills*. Paris: OECD Publishing.

Pascale, J. (2011). Requesting consent to link survey data to administrative records: Results from a split-ballot experiment in the Survey of Health Insurance and Program Participation (SHIPP). *Survey Methodology, 03*.

Rammstedt, B., Martin, S., Zabal, A., Carstensen, C., & Schupp, J. (2017). The PIAAC longitudinal study in Germany: Rationale and design. *Large-Scale Assessments in Education, 5*(1), 4. https://doi.org/10.1186/s40536-017-0040-z

Sakshaug, J. W. (2018). Methods of linking survey data to official records. In D. L. Vannette & J. A. Krosnik (Eds.), *The Palgrave handbook of survey research* (pp. 257–261). Cham: Palgrave Macmillan.

Sakshaug, J. W., & Antoni, M. (2017). Errors in linking survey and administrative data. In: P. P. Biemer et al. (Eds.), *Total Survey Error in Practice* (pp. 557–573), Hoboken: John Wiley & Sons.

Sakshaug, J. W., & Kreuter, F. (2012). Assessing the magnitude of non-consent biases in linked survey and administrative data. *Survey Research Methods, 6*(2), 113–122. https://doi.org/10.18148/srm/2012.v6i2.509

Sakshaug, J. W., & Kreuter, F. (2014). The effect of benefit wording on consent to link survey and administrative records in a web survey. *Public Opinion Quarterly, 78*(1), 166–176. https://doi.org/10.1093/poq/nfu001

Sakshaug, J. W., Couper, M. P., Ofstedal, M. B., & Weir, D. R. (2012). Linking survey and administrative records: Mechanisms of consent. *Sociological Methods & Research, 41*(4), 535–569. https://doi.org/10.1177/0049124112460381

Sakshaug, J. W., Tutz, V., & Kreuter, F. (2013). Placement, wording, and interviewers: Identifying correlates of consent to link survey and administrative data. *Survey Research Methods, 7*(2), 133–144. https://doi.org/10.18148/srm/2013.v7i2.5395

Sala, E., Burton, J., & Knies, G. (2010). Correlates of obtaining informed consent to data linkage: Respondent, interview, and interviewer characteristics. *Sociological Methods & Research, 41*(3), 414–439. https://doi.org/10.1177/0049124112457330

Steinacker, G., & Wolfert, S. (2017). *Durchführung der 2. Erhebungswelle von PIAAC-L (Kooperative längsschnittliche Weiterverfolgung der PIAAC-Studie in Deutschland): Feldbericht zur Erhebung 2015* (GESIS Papers 2017|04). Mannheim: GESIS – Leibniz Institute for the Social Sciences. https://doi.org/10.21241/ssoar.50488

Warnke, A. J. (2017). *An investigation of record linkage refusal and its implications for empirical research* (ZEW Discussion Paper 17-031). Mannheim: ZEW - Leibniz Centre for European Economic Research.

Zabal, A., Martin, S., & Rammstedt, B. (2017). *PIAAC-L data collection 2015: Technical report* (GESIS Papers 2017|29). Mannheim: GESIS – Leibniz-Institute for the Social Sciences. https://doi.org/10.21241/ssoar.55155

Open Access This chapter is licensed under the terms of the Creative Commons Attribution 4.0 International License (http://creativecommons.org/licenses/by/4.0/), which permits use, sharing, adaptation, distribution and reproduction in any medium or format, as long as you give appropriate credit to the original author(s) and the source, provide a link to the Creative Commons license and indicate if changes were made.

The images or other third party material in this chapter are included in the chapter's Creative Commons license, unless indicated otherwise in a credit line to the material. If material is not included in the chapter's Creative Commons license and your intended use is not permitted by statutory regulation or exceeds the permitted use, you will need to obtain permission directly from the copyright holder.

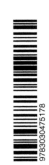